CONTESTING CYBERSPACE
IN CHINA

CONTESTING CYBERSPACE IN CHINA

ONLINE EXPRESSION AND AUTHORITARIAN RESILIENCE

RONGBIN HAN

COLUMBIA UNIVERSITY PRESS
New York

Columbia University Press
Publishers Since 1893
New York Chichester, West Sussex
cup.columbia.edu

Library of Congress Cataloging-in-Publication Data
Names: Han, Rongbin, 1980– author.
Title: Contesting cyberspace in China : online expression and
authoritarian resilience / Rongbin Han.
Description: New York : Columbia University Press, [2018] |
Includes bibliographical references and index.
Identifiers: LCCN 2017038716| ISBN 9780231184748 (cloth : alk. paper) |
ISBN 9780231184755 (pbk.) | ISBN 9780231545655 (ebook) Subjects: LCSH:
Internet—Government policy—China. | Internet—Political aspects—China.
| Freedom of speech—China. | Censorship—China. | Authoritarianism—
China.
Classification: LCC HN740.Z9 I567434 2018 | DDC 302.23/10951—dc23
LC record available at https://lccn.loc.gov/2017038716

Cover design: Noah Arlow

To my daughter, Audrey Zhiyan Han,
and my wife, Yi Fu

CONTENTS

PREFACE

In 1999, as a freshman at Peking University, I lived on the Changping campus together with about eight hundred other social sciences and humanities majors. The campus, located on the outskirts of Beijing, was at least an hour away from the main campus (and from Beijing) by bus. It was rural and isolated, surrounded by wild woods, apple and peach orchards, and cornfields. The isolation was not just geographical. There were no telephones in our dorms, and Internet access in our dorms was an even more remote possibility.[1] The entire men's dorm building shared one phone at the doorkeeper's office, which only received calls from outside. To dial out, we had to use one of the three phones on the first floor of the women's dorm building. I cannot remember a single time when I waited for less than an hour to make a call. It was tough: We had high expectations for college life after entering the nation's most prestigious university after succeeding on the brutal college entrance exam—but virtually none of our expectations was met. In fact, many of us still call that year in Changping our fourth year of high school.

As young adults, we detested our geographical and informational isolation, taking every opportunity to visit the main campus. It was during one of those first visits that I got hooked on the Internet. I still remember that day vividly. I was visiting a high school friend. Majoring in biology, he was lucky enough to live in one of the two newest buildings, which had Internet access. I arrived after dinner, and he and his roommates were playing computer games. I watched, somewhat bored as I was not a fan. Around ten o'clock in the evening, my friend took a break and asked, "Anyone want a Coke?" Everyone replied with a yes. He opened a new browser window, typed something, and then returned to his game. Ten minutes later, someone knocked at the door, handed us five cans of Coke, took the money my friend offered, and left. Seeing my confused face, my friend explained, "Oh, I just went online and ordered the Coke. We're lucky to be within their free delivery zone." Apparently, what I had witnessed was one of the earliest business-to-consumer (B2C) e-commerce transactions in China. I was truly amazed.

I have not become another Jack Ma, though this first Internet encounter was about doing business. Rather, my experience with the Internet was soon politicized. In May 2000, a fellow Changping student named Qiu Qingfeng was murdered on her way back from an exam on the main campus. Angered by Peking University's slow and inappropriate reaction, students marched in protest. Our outcry was fruitless and soon died out, as we were disconnected from the outside world. Later, we learned that mobilization had also taken place on the main campus, and this action had been far more influential, longer lasting, and more effective. We also learned that the Internet, especially the campus bulletin board system (BBS), had played a significant role. Regarding this incident, Guobin Yang said, "Although demonstrations and candle vigils [*sic*] took place on campus, it was in cyberspace that the protest first started; it then escalated into radical calls for 1989-style demonstrations, and was sustained for about 10 days amid fiery online exchanges."[2] Apparently, had we been connected to the Internet, the protest on Changping campus could have been more successful. After all, we were the closest to Ms. Qiu. Thus, though I did not personally participate in the online mobilization, I was truly inspired by the Internet's potential for civic engagement and popular protest.

In September 2000, I moved to the main campus and soon became a BBS addict. I spent hours discussing, deliberating, and debating with other users on sites such as Bdwm (Peking University's then semi-official BBS), Ytht (Peking University's student-run BBS), and Smth (then Tsinghua University's official BBS). I was particularly active on Bdwm.

I was active on apolitical boards such as "Feeling" and "Yueju"—the former for users to share their emotions, and the latter for a local opera that I enjoyed—for which I even served as a manager. As someone interested in rural development, I also frequently visited the "RuralChina" board, on which I made friends with like-minded people, including Dr. Xu Zhiyong, the founder of the Open Constitution Initiative and the New Citizen Movement, who was also a regular BBS user at the time.[3] After several long online conversations in late 2001, we decided to go offline, and we founded the Rural China Association at Peking University. I was so into this endeavor that I served both as an administrator of the discussion board and as an executive committee member of the association. To me, the Internet was empowering. In particular, the combination of online forum and offline civic organization gave us special strengths in connecting, mobilizing, and reaching out. We organized and participated in a number of activities on and beyond the campus.

Thanks to my active involvement in board managing, I was appointed one of the first few Three-Star board administrators of Bdwm in 2002. The recognition made me happy. But I did not know then that I was experiencing what was to be the very short heyday of campus forums and my personal BBS life. On January 1, 2003, Peking University staged an official takeover of Bdwm, primarily by moving its server from the computer center to an office under the Communist Youth League. The purpose of the coup, as we called it, was to allow the authorities to unplug the server whenever they felt it was necessary. Though some administrators cooperated, many remonstrated. I, together with hundreds of fellow board administrators, resigned in protest. Soon after, I graduated and left for Singapore to purse my first graduate degree. During this period, China tightened its control over the Internet, particularly over campus forums: In September 2014, Ytht was forced down; in March 2005, Smth was taken over by Tsinghua University;[4] and Bdwm, which had already been taken over by the authorities in 2003, started to restrict off-campus access. In short, the state flexed its muscle, putting online expression under much tighter constraints. This was difficult for me, as I was gradually being deprived of an important part of my life. The pain accompanied me to the University of

California, Berkeley, where I finally decided to examine and reflect on my Internet experience not only from an academic perspective but also as an effort of self-redemption.

Why am I telling you, dear readers, the personal story of my online experience in such detail? Because my story explains the origin of my academic interest in the topic. Indeed, it was my deep involvement in BBS life that led me to question how online expression has, or has not, changed political life in China and its likelihood of bringing about democracy. But my primary purpose is to convey the idea that the Internet, and online expression more specifically, are living experiences to me and to many other Chinese citizens. Such experiences, though sometimes seemingly trivial, are highly complicated, interactive, nuanced, and most importantly alive, as they have undeniably transformed our lives as individuals and as a citizenry collective. I feel lucky as a researcher to be part of this great transformation. We experienced good times when relatively free expression was first made possible by the Internet, when the state still learning how to deal with it. We also experienced bad times when the state attempted to tighten its control and manipulate the Internet to its advantage. As individuals, we are both political and apolitical online. On one hand, we, at least some of us, are political in that we deliberate, debate, and mobilize online, with the hope of having an impact on political processes in China and throughout the world. We demonstrate diverse values, beliefs, and identities in our online interactions. Specifically, in terms of political orientation, some of us have constantly resisted authoritarian rule and contested state control over the Internet, whereas others support the Party-state as true believers or nationalists, or because they disagree with those criticizing the regime. Some of us are indifferent, neutral, or fluctuate among different stances at different times on different issues. On the other hand, many Chinese are online primarily for apolitical purposes. The majority of Chinese netizens surf the Internet to conduct business, search for information, communicate with friends and relatives, play games, watch videos, share life experiences, discuss lifestyle or entertainment topics, and so forth. But these activities are by no means without political implications, as they are deeply embedded in the sociopolitical context of authoritarian rule. Moreover, these apolitical citizens can quickly become politicized, even if just temporarily, when drawn into cyber-events with political significance, such as popular protests against the government, nationalist mobilization, or simply a debate with other netizens on political topics. In this sense, cyberpolitics is highly fluid in both its content and format.

This book was informed by my personal experiences and observations. I sincerely believe that a holistic and balanced view is critical to explain the coexistence of the liberalizing Internet and authoritarianism in China. This is why I have examined not only the struggle over censorship in which the state, service providers, and netizens together negotiate the limits of online expression, but also the discourse competition that demonstrates a pluralization of online norms, identities, and discourses. My analysis shows that there is not a simple answer to why China has not succumbed to the power of the Internet. Yes, the state, with its formidable capacity, has made serious efforts to tame the Internet. But its control is far from perfect. The Internet has proved empowering in many aspects. But its impact has been controlled, mediated, and neutralized by the state, and through daily online interactions. Thus, the Internet has proved far less threatening than many had anticipated. In other words, the Chinese Party-state is not as strong as it seems, and the regime challengers are not as threatening as may have been expected with the advance of freer online expression; thus, the digital era in China has resulted in the maintenance of the status quo. It appears that the empowering effects of the Internet are much more complicated than many would originally have thought.

This project has been an intellectual "long march" of sorts and could not have been accomplished without the immense intellectual, financial, and emotional support of many individuals and institutions.

My academic career can be traced back to Peking University and the National University of Singapore where professors provided me with solid disciplinary training while allowing me to freely develop my interests. I am especially grateful to Dr. Ran Mei, Dr. An Chen, Dr. Yongshun Cai, and Dr. Yusaku Horiuchi for their very helpful courses and mentoring. I am also thankful to these two institutions for the lasting friends who have supported my research continuously.

At the University of California, Berkeley, I was lucky enough to have Professors Tom Gold, Chris Ansell, David Collier, Rachel Stern, and Kevin O'Brien as my mentors. It was under their supervision that I started this project. Tom helped me tremendously by referring me to sources and connections in the field. Chris provided intellectual guidance when I needed it and showed extreme patience when I was working slowly. David, a crystal-sharp thinker, shaped the project in critical ways from beginning to end. Rachel read and commented on all chapters. Her critical comments and suggestions are now indispensable parts of this book. Kevin has been an all-time and all-weather mentor from the very beginning of the project. He saw me through the whole process from picking up the idea, through drafting the dissertation, to finishing the book. He has offered me encouragement, advice, and guidance in his office, via email, over the phone, and out the hiking trails of Mount Diablo. I also received invaluable input and support from many other Berkeley faculty members, particularly Professors You-Tien Hsing, Qiang Xiao, Peter Lorentzen, Steve Weber, and Lowell Dittmer. I cannot fully express my gratitude to them.

Many friends and colleagues at Berkeley also helped me with the project in various ways. I benefited from intellectually rich conversations on the project with Nicholas Bartlett, Margaret Boittin, Alexsia Chan, Crystal Chang, Zongshi Chen, Jennifer Choo, Emily Chua, Julia Chuang, John Givens, Kristi Govella, Paulina Hartono, Jonathan Hassid, Lina Hu, Shih-Yang Kao, Xiaohui Lin, Xiao Liu, Sara Newland, Seung-Youn Oh, Ivo Plsek, Suzanne Scoggins, Li Shao, Chris Sullivan, Chungmin Tsai, Carsten Vala, Gang Wang, Albert Wu, Suowei Xiao, John Yasuda, and many others. I am especially grateful to Alexsia, Julia, Paulina, Sara, and Suzanne, who helped edit and polish my chapters.

I am fortunate to have the privilege to work as a faculty member in the Department of International Affairs at the University of Georgia, where I receive tremendous support from the department, all my colleagues, and the students. My gratitude goes to all of them. In particular, I thank Cas Mudde, Lihi Ben Shitrit, Markus Crepaz, Bob Grafstein, Loch Johnson, and Han Park. Cas, as my faculty mentor, helped edit the book proposal, referred me to new sources, and suggested many improvements. He is also the one who constantly pushed me to think beyond China. Lihi not only generously shared with me her experience of publishing a book, but also helped polish the ideas in this book. Markus, Bob, Loch, and Han have all spent quite some time with me on the project and offered critical comments and suggestions. I am also grateful to Austin Doctor, Juan Du, Linan Jia, Paul Oshinski, and Yuan Wang for their enthusiastic and diligent research assistance.

I have presented my research at various conferences and workshops at which I have been able to interact with and be inspired by many excellent scholars in the field. I am grateful to the organizers as well as the participants, especially Jason Abbott, Bilal Baloch, David Bandurski, Elizabeth Brunner, Christopher Cairns, Chujie Chen, Kevin Deluca, Ashley Esarey, Kecheng Fang, Hualing Fu, Jason Gainous, Mary Gallagher, John Givens, Shaohua Guo, Navid Hassanpour, Yong Hu, Calvin Hui, Min Jiang, Jackie Kerr, Hongmei Li, Jinying Li, Tony Zhiyang Lin, Yawei Liu, Gabriella Lukacs, Andrew MacDonald, Melanie Manion, Bingchun Meng, Penny Prime, Chris Primiano, Xiaoyu Pu, Jack Qiu, Christopher Rea, Maria Repnikova, Elina Rodina, Lotus Ruan, Kris Ruijgrok, Jan Rydzak, Ping Shum, Christoph Steinhardt, Daniela Stockmann, Jonathan Sullivan, Marcella Szablewicz, Yunchao Wen, Fan Yang, Guobin Yang, Hong Zhang, Weiyu Zhang, and Jing Zhao.

I had the privilege to work with two editors, Anne Routon and Caelyn Cobb, at Columbia University Press. I wish to sincerely thank them for their encouragement and kind support. They are absolutely charming, wonderful, and helpful. I am also deeply indebted to Miriam Grossman for her assistance in preparing the book.

This project received financial support from the Graduate School, Department of Political Science, Institute of East Asian Studies, and Center for Chinese Studies at the University of California, Berkeley, as well as the Elvera Kwang Siam Lim Fellowship in Chinese Studies.

Chapter 7 incorporates my article "Defending the Authoritarian Regime Online: China's 'Voluntary Fifty-Cent Army,' " which was published in *The China Quarterly* in 2015. I thank Cambridge University Press for permission to use it.

I am most grateful to many Chinese friends and netizens who have helped me with data collection. I must preserve their anonymity to avoid causing them any trouble, but I cannot stress their contributions enough. They are the heroes, and I owe them my deepest gratitude.

I owe a huge apology to my family members—my parents, parents-in-law, my wife, Yi Fu, and my daughter, Zhiyan, for their huge sacrifices in the process of my academic pursuits and book writing. I am truly blessed to have their full-hearted support. Without their care, understanding, and encouragement, finishing this book would have been mission impossible. Therefore, I dedicate this book to all of you.

CONTESTING CYBERSPACE
IN CHINA

1

INTRODUCTION

Pluralism and Cyberpolitics in China

In 2010, the Middle East was in turmoil. The Tunisian Revolution successfully overthrew President Zine al-Abidine Ben Ali, triggering the start of the Arab Spring. The power of the Internet, particularly social media, garnered global attention.[1] On the other side of the world, critics of the Chinese regime, inspired by the Arab Spring, called for their own Jasmine Revolution, with the hope of disrupting the regime through online and offline mobilization.[2] But these calls had little visible or lasting impact. One demonstration on Wangfujing Street in central Beijing, which had been widely advertised online by democratic activists, turned out to be a micro–street spectacle: Literally a handful of protesters showed up, surrounded by thousands of onlookers and hundreds of policemen and foreign journalists.[3] Before the protesters were finally taken away, they received little support or even sympathy from the bystanders.

As the political scientist Lisa Anderson has perceptively pointed out, the importance of the Arab Spring lies neither in how protesters were inspired by globalized norms of civic engagement nor how they used new technology, but in "how and why these ambitions and techniques resonated in their various local contexts."[4] Compared with regimes that were toppled in the Arab Spring, China has a stronger authoritarian state, which can more effectively control its population, and a robust economy providing more job opportunities.[5] Moreover, the Chinese Party-state has a proven record of adapting to challenges.[6] However, state capacity and adaptability can hardly explain the minuscule scale of mobilization in China considering the pervasiveness of social unrest[7] and Internet-enabled mobilization.[8] In particular, unlike offline mobilization, which tends to center on narrowly defined concrete demands,[9] online activism in China often targets the authoritarian regime in general and poses demands for more freedom and democracy. In effect, Internet users are popularly known as "netizens" in China precisely because the term carries a sense of entitlement and citizenship that is generally absent in authoritarian regimes.

The contrast between the countries involved in the Arab Spring and a more resilient authoritarian regime like China suggests an intriguing relationship among technological development, social empowerment, and authoritarianism. Why has the Internet helped scuttle authoritarian rule in some cases, but failed to do so in others? More specifically, why has online activism not translated into an offline movement in China akin to the Arab Spring? What explains the paradoxical coexistence of an empowering Internet and resilient authoritarianism in China? By investigating the struggles over online expression—both as a cat-and-mouse censorship game and from the perspective of discourse competition—this book makes a counterintuitive twofold claim: (1) The Chinese Party-state can almost *indefinitely* coexist with the expansion of the emancipating Internet; but (2) the key explanation for this coexistence does not lie in the state's capacity to control and adapt, as many have argued, but more in the pluralization of online expression, which empowers not only regime critics, but also pro-regime voices, particularly those representing pro-state nationalism.

The book questions the assumed relationship between state adaptation and authoritarian resilience. Though regimes such as China are highly adaptive to challenges—as witnessed in the highly sophisticated censorship system and various innovative propaganda tactics the state has employed—it is naïve to assume the effectiveness of state adaptation or to assume adaptability is the sole reason for its resilience. As the research in this book shows, the Chinese Party-state has encountered tremendous difficulty in translating its formidable despotic and infrastructural power into effective control over the Internet. The book also interrogates the liberalizing and democratizing power of the Internet from a new angle. Sheri Berman finds that a vigorous civil society may, under certain circumstances, scuttle democracy.[10] Likewise, pluralized online expression may ironically help sustain authoritarian rule by activating and empowering regime defenders. In China, through neutralizing regime-challenging discourses and denigrating regime critics, spontaneous pro-regime groups have rendered online expression less threatening to the Party-state.

Instead of seeing the state and the Internet as single monolithic entities, the book highlights the fragmentation of both. It reveals the complex internal dynamics of Internet control by differentiating the roles of the central state, local authorities, and intermediary actors. It also captures the pluralist nature of online expression by exploring the interactions among the state, its critics, and various netizen groups. In doing so, my argument maintains that the Chinese Party-state is not as strong as it appears but also that the Internet's threat to the regime may have been overestimated. Such findings suggest that neither the regime's resilience nor the Internet's power can be assumed but must be carefully analyzed, assessed, and contextualized.

WHEN THE EMPOWERING INTERNET MEETS THE AUTHORITARIAN REGIME

With its inherent "control-frustrating characteristics,"[11] the Internet has become the locus of debates over political liberalization and democratization in authoritarian regimes. Arguably, it provides "new tools of connectivity, information diffusion, and attention,"[12] which help citizens better connect, express ideas, organize, and mobilize.[13] For instance, in the Arab Spring, social media platforms such as Facebook, Twitter, and YouTube played a critical role in shaping political debates, mobilizing protests on the ground, and promulgating democratic ideas.[14] According to the political scientists Philip Howard and Muzammil Hussain, digital media diffusion rates and the capacity of state censorship are crucial to explain success or failure in achieving regime change.[15]

Though highly censored, China's Internet has created a relatively free discursive space, which some see as an emerging public sphere.[16] Chinese netizens have not only managed to circumvent and challenge state censorship in creative and artful ways, but also transformed the Internet into a platform for online activism.[17] The freer flow of information in cyberspace—as compared to traditional media—has also promoted civil society by enhancing both internal communications and the interconnectedness of civil organizations,[18] and it has facilitated citizen activism by enabling both domestic and overseas Chinese to mobilize against the regime.[19]

There is no question that the Internet has challenged the Party-state. But the state has also adapted itself to control the Internet's disruptive effects. According to Lawrence Lessig, Internet control may operate via four mechanisms: the law, technical architecture (code), social norms, and the market.[20] In China, all four are subject to heavy influence from or direct control of the state. To tame the Internet, the Party-state has undergone a process of policy learning and capacity building and has constructed a complicated and subtle censorship regime over time to control both the network infrastructure and online content.[21] Today, the censorship system allows the state to filter taboo words, block or shut down websites, suppress dissent groups and active netizens, and deter deviant expression.[22] For instance, the state has not only established a nationwide "Great Firewall" to filter and track online information,[23] but it has also attempted to have all personal computer (PC) manufacturers preinstall Green Dam software, meant to filter out pornography and other undesired information from the users' end.[24]

To what extent, then, has the Internet empowered citizens or challenged authoritarian rule in China? To answer the question properly, it is crucial to depart from a perspective that focuses mainly on the dyad of state control versus social resistance in cyberspace.[25] Though the perspective is helpful, it does not account for the diverse activities that occur in Chinese cyberspace and exposes only a limited slice of the politics and role of the Internet in political communication.[26] In particular, it tends "to see politics only in the higher echelons of power or as its outright subversion,"[27] thus preventing effective examination and evaluation of the less confrontational, more creative aspects of online struggles. In effect, the state has gone beyond simple censorship and shifted toward a more subtle management of popular opinion[28] by employing innovative propaganda tactics such as deploying paid Internet commentators, a.k.a. the "fifty-cent army" (*wumao dang*, 五毛党), to fake pro-regime voices[29]and embracing popular cyber culture to make state propaganda appealing.[30] Similarly, social actors have not only fought with the repressive state in artful and creative ways,[31] but have also engaged in practices of online activism that hardly fit neatly into the liberalization-control framework.[32]

This book introduces two specific analytical concerns not fully addressed in the current literature. First, it shows that the impact of the Internet on Chinese politics is much more mixed and complicated than a dyadic model in which either the society or the state dominates. Indeed, it may have contributed more to liberalization than democratization in that it is enabling greater political involvement of Chinese citizens but failing to move China toward a democratic transition;[33] it can function as a safety valve or a vehicle for political activism, depending on whether netizens plunge in ahead of mainstream media.[34] Moreover, this research brings attention to understudied critical actors in Chinese cyberpolitics, including intermediary actors such as forum administrators who directly mediate censorship enforcement[35] and regime defenders such as the "voluntary fifty-cent army" (*zidai ganliang de wumao*, 自带干粮的五毛; literally "the fifty-cent army that brings its own rations").

Second, the book highlights the necessity to disaggregate both the state and cyberspace to better understand cyberpolitics in China. Though scholars have long recognized the internal fragmentation of the Chinese Party-state and its implications for both policy making and implementation,[36] few have explored the horizontal and vertical cleavages within China's Internet governance structure. Evidently, multiple state agencies are involved in content control and discourse competition. Their diverse interests and motivations have together shaped the landscape of online politics in China. Likewise, it is improper to assume a monolithic Chinese cyberspace that is inherently liberalizing and democratizing. While many observers have hailed this new technology for emancipating the society from authoritarian rule, others have emphasized its detrimental, disintegrating effects and suggest that online expression may lead to the polarization or even Balkanization of the public.[37] The research in this book supports such a "fragmentation thesis" through an investigation of the dynamic process of online discourse production, circulation, and interpretation in China.

PUBLIC EXPRESSION ON CHINESE INTERNET FORUMS

As the sociologist Guobin Yang has insightfully pointed out, "The Chinese Internet should not be viewed in isolation from its social, political, and cultural contents and contexts."[38] Interestingly enough, though the struggle over online expression constitutes the core of many studies of cyberpolitics in China, few authors have traced the process of information production, spread, acquisition, and containment in the context of an online environment such as that of Internet forums. This book, through exploring how the state, its critics, and netizens struggle over political expression on Internet forums, addresses precisely this issue.

As platforms for public expression, Internet forums were first introduced to China in the form of the bulletin board system (BBS) by research and educational institutions in the mid-1990s. While early BBS sites provided only telnet access, web platforms were developed later and became mainstream. Besides discussion boards where thematic conversations take place, most forums today also provide within-site mailing and messaging systems, chat rooms, blogging services, and even games to facilitate interaction among users.

Most Internet forums are accessible to both registered and unregistered users. But to engage in discussion, that is, to post or reply to threads, one often must register an account. Though initially a valid email account is sufficient for registration, increasingly more forums are asking for additional identification information such as phone numbers and student or even official identity numbers, partially driven by the state's real-name registration policy push. In some cases, registration is by invitation only. Many forums do not restrict the number of accounts one can register. Even forums that attempt to impose such a limit often fail to do so without actually enforcing real-name registration. Postings are often in textual format, though multimedia postings (i.e., pictures, videos, and audio material) are increasingly common, thanks to improved hardware, bandwidth, and software platforms.

Besides state surveillance, forum management expends significant effort to monitor online expression. Internet content service providers such as forums, blogs, and microblogs have installed keyword-filtering software to prevent postings with taboo words from being published. Manual scrutiny is also important, even for forums with pre-filtering measures, as many netizens are creative enough to circumvent the automatic filtering. Board managers and editors—either selected from users or appointed by forums—are responsible for stamping out noncompliance by deleting posts, suspending or permanently eradicating user accounts, or even banning Internet Protocol (IP) addresses. To guide discussion, forum management can also promote certain posts by highlighting them, recommending them for the front page, or placing them at the top of the board. On large public forums, special content monitoring personnel are often installed in addition to or in place of board managers to ensure more effective surveillance. Apart from private forums set up and run by individuals, most medium-size and large forums are affiliated with larger entities such as academic institutions or companies and managed by them. In some cases, these institutions reserve the power to directly intervene in forum management when they deem necessary.

Internet forums offer a first-rate window onto Internet politics in China. First, they remain popular and together attract around 120 million users despite the rapid expansion of newer social media platforms such as microblog services (e.g., Weibo) and instant messengers such as WeChat (figure 1.1 and table 1.1). As of January 2017, one of the largest forums, Tianya.cn, claims almost 120 million registered users with over one million of them simultaneously online during active periods through the day. Even some campus-based forums, which usually have highly restricted user bases, boast simultaneous user populations of more than one thousand.[39] Admittedly, applications such as the Twitter-like Weibo and the instant messenger WeChat have surpassed forums in terms of popularity and influence in recent years.

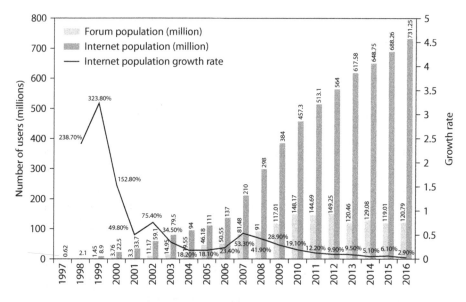

FIGURE 1.1 China's Internet and online forum population (1997–2016)

Notes: Data from CNNIC Statistical Reports on the Internet Development in China. All figures are year-end data of the particular year. The 2007 forum population was not reported.

But studying forums still allows certain advantages, namely, a better "historical sensibility."[40] In fact, the evolution of Internet forums probably captures the history of Chinese Internet politics more completely than other applications.

Second, compared with user-centered social media platforms such as social network services, blogs, and instant messengers (e.g., QQ and WeChat) where the host often has discretion over the topic and audience, online forums are topic centered and essentially more "public." Discussions on forums usually feature common-interest topics and are conducted in a many-to-many communication manner. Such "publicness" makes Internet forums important platforms for political expression and online activism. Though political content may comprise "only an extremely tiny portion of China's cyber-cacophony,"[41] this is not true on popular online forums. In fact, thematic discussion boards devoted to social and political affairs are often among the most popular ones.[42]

TABLE 1.1 Selected Most Frequently Used Online Services (2009–2016)

Year	2009	2010	2011	2012	2013	2014	2015	2016
Service	Year-end user population in millions (Penetration rate)							
News	307.69	353.04	366.87	392.32	491.32	518.94	564.40	613.90
	(80.1%)	(77.2%)	(71.5%)	(73%)	(79.6%)	(80.0%)	(82.0%)	(84%)
Search engine	281.34	374.53	407.40	451.1	489.66	522.23	566.23	602.38
	(73.3%)	(81.9%)	(79.4%)	(80%)	(79.3%)	(80.5%)	(82.3%)	(82.4%)
Instant messaging	272.33	352.58	415.10	467.75	532.15	587.76	624.08	666.28
	(70.9%)	(77.1%)	(80.9%)	(82.9%)	(86.2%)	(90.6%)	(90.7%)	(91.1%)
Online gaming	264.54	304.10	324.28	335.69	338.03	365.85	391.48	417.04
	(68.9%)	(66.5%)	(63.2%)	(59.5%)	(54.7%)	(56.4%)	(56.9%)	(57.0%)
Online video	240.44	283.98	325.31	371.83	428.2	432.98	503.91	544.55
	(62.6%)	(62.1%)	(63.4%)	(65.9%)	(69.3%)	(66.7%)	(73.2%)	(74.5%)
Blog	221.40	294.50	318.64	372.99	436.58	108.96	—	—
	(57.7%)	(64.4%)	(62.1%)	(66.1%)	(70.7%)	(16.8%)		
Email	217.97	249.69	245.77	250.8	259.21	251.78	258.47	248.15
	(56.8%)	(54.6%)	(47.9%)	(44.5%)	(42%)	(38.8%)	(37.6%)	(33.9%)
SNS	175.87	235.05	244.24	275.05	277.69	—	—	—
	(45.8%)	(51.4%)	(47.6%)	(48.8%)	(45%)			
Forum and BBS	117.01	148.17	144.69	149.25	120.46	129.08	119.01	120.79
	(30.5%)	(32.4%)	(28.2%)	(26.5%)	(19.5%)	(19.9%)	(17.3%)	(16.5%)
Microblog	—	63.11	248.88	308.61	280.78	248.84	230.45	271.43
	—	(13.8%)	(48.7%)	(54.7%)	(45.5%)	(38.4%)	(33.5%)	(37.1%)

Abbreviations: BBS, bulletin board system; SNS, social network service.

Note: The blog penetration rate dropped dramatically because the China Internet Network Information Center changed the category in 2014, excluding personal spaces from blogging services.

Source: China Internet Network Information Center Statistical Reports on Internet Development in China; see www.cnnic.net.cn.

Finally, the types of user interaction on popular online services often strongly resemble a forum. In fact, many popular platforms also incorporate the forum function. For instance, on China's social network sites, such as kaixin001.com and renren.com, BBS participation occurs at extremely high rates: More than 80 percent of social media content is in the form of a BBS.[43] In addition, blogs and microblogs become hot spots for online traffic when their hosts gear the discussion toward public affairs. Chinese online news portals have also introduced interactive features so that readers can respond to news reports by clicking expressive icons or adding comments, just like they do on forums.

Though this research has chosen to focus on Internet forums, it is important to note that digital platforms for public expression and social participation in China have evolved over the past two decades. In particular, social media services such as Weibo and WeChat have become the new frontiers of citizen activism and Internet governance. For this reason, the analysis in the book incorporates observations from platforms such as blogs and Weibo whenever relevant.

TWO STRUGGLES OF ONLINE EXPRESSION

Exploring state–society interaction in Chinese cyberspace reveals two different struggles: the struggle over censorship and the struggle over discourse competition. If online expression is a virtual territory, the struggle over censorship centers on the definition of its boundaries, whereas discourse competition emphasizes the landscape within those boundaries (table 1.2). Close examination of both struggles provides an opportunity not only to map the power relations between state and societal actors more accurately, but also to evaluate the political impact of online expression in a more nuanced and balanced way.

The Cat-and-Mouse Censorship Game

Censorship is a boundary-spanning struggle[44] over the limits of what can and cannot be discussed online. Though the struggle over censorship seems to be a story of state censorship versus netizen resistance,

TABLE 1.2 Two Perspectives on Online Expression

	Censorship and Counter-Censorship	Discourse Competition
Main actors	State, intermediary actors, and various netizens groups	State agents, regime critics, and various netizens groups
Battlefield	Boundary spanning: what can and cannot be expressed	Within boundaries: how to express ideas
Framing	Three-actor confrontation (state–intermediary actors–users)	Discourse competition (e.g., struggle for freedom against repressive regime versus defense of nation against sabotage)
Power exercised	State: coercive and technological Forum managers/ netizens: technological and expressive	Expressive and identity

this book suggests a multi-actor perspective that highlights the fragmentation of the authoritarian state, the role of intermediary actors, and the diversity among netizens. This three-actor cat-and-mouse censorship game is vividly illustrated in figure 1.2, with netizens surrounded by various state agencies that attempt to control expression and the intermediary actors being trapped in between.

The Chinese state has demonstrated formidable despotic and infrastructural power both before and in the digital age. To harmonize the Internet, the Party-state, like many other authoritarian states,[45] has undergone a process of policy learning and capacity building through technical, institutional, and administrative means. However, external challenges and internal fragmentation within the regime limit the state's ability to control the flow of online information.

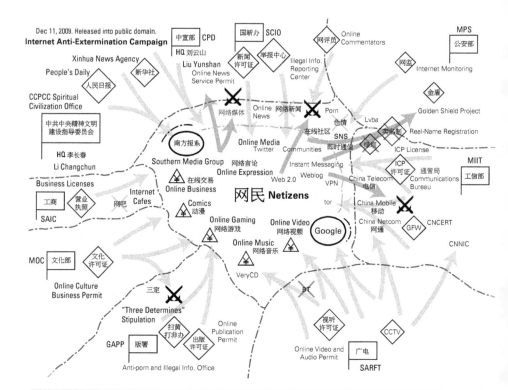

FIGURE 1.2 Anti-extermination campaign online

Notes: The figure has been widely spread online and the original source cannot be identified. This version is adapted (by adding English translation) from: "Tianchao Wangmin de Xiongqi, Fan Weijiao Xingshitu" (Uprising of Chinese Netizens: The Map of Anti-Extermination Campaign), http://itbbs.pconline.com.cn/diy/10854454.html, retrieved August 20, 2012.

In particular, the volume and creativity of online expression have forced the state to rely on rigid techniques such as keyword filtering and, more importantly, the delegation of censorship to intermediary actors such as Internet service providers. Yet, intermediary actors are neither loyal accomplices of the state nor wholehearted allies of netizens. Instead, they take a position of "discontented compliance," complying with state censorship mostly in order to survive, while also occasionally tolerating or encouraging boundary-spanning expression. For netizens, online expression is not merely a realm of digital contention. State censorship, discourse competition, and the pursuit of fun have together driven the fusion of politics and popular expression tactics, contributing to the rise of "pop activism" in which entertainment serves both as a means of spreading political messages and as an end in itself.

The struggle over censorship suggests that state control over online expression is at best quasi-successful. Though successful in keeping politically indifferent netizens away from taboo zones,[46] the state censorship system is regularly circumvented and challenged by savvy netizens using creative counterstrategies. As a result, undesired content has never been eliminated from the web, and censorship alters only the processes of its production, circulation, and consumption. Moreover, censorship is often counterproductive because it undermines regime legitimacy, politicizes otherwise neutral forum managers and netizens, and nurtures the development of rights consciousness, including calls for more than freedom of expression.[47] On one hand, netizens' experiences of being censored are hard lessons through which they learn about the regime's repressive nature; on the other hand, the state's efforts to disguise taboo topics also signal the regime's fears, fuel netizens' curiosity, and drive netizens to seek information on sensitive topics from unapproved, informal sources.

Neither, however, should we overestimate the power of netizen activism. Echoing the argument of "slacktivism," online expression in China mostly remains a low-risk, low-cost form of political engagement, frequently more generative of private amusement than of collective action.[48] This, of course, can be partially attributed to selective state censorship.[49] But state control is not a sufficient explanation, considering netizens' creative and artful contention. In this sense, one needs to go beyond the cat-and-mouse struggle over censorship, which captures only a small part of online politics, and examine what is actually going on within state-imposed boundaries.

Discourse Competition

As the sociologist and communications scholar Manuel Castells puts it, "Violence and the threat of violence always combine with the construction of meaning in the production and reproduction of power relationships in all domains of social life."[50] If the struggle over censorship embodies violence and the threat of violence, discourse competition is one in which state and nonstate actors attempt to engineer popular opinion and construct beliefs, values, and identities online. Figure 1.3 shows the discourse competition scenario in which netizen groups championing different ideologies—liberalism versus patriotism—are fighting fiercely against each other, with onlookers watching what is going on.

Both the regime and its critics have taken advantage of the Internet to spread their preferred discourses. Among other more innovative propaganda strategies, political "astroturfing"—deploying the fifty-cent

FIGURE 1.3 Largest riot ever in history

Notes: The graph has many versions in which the banners are altered to refer to struggles among different camps. This version is from Qianliexian, "Shishang Zuida Baoluan Jishi" (The Largest Riot Ever in History), http://www.bullogger.com/blogs/qianliexian/archives /125944.aspx, retrieved August 20, 2012.

army to covertly manufacture seemingly spontaneous pro-regime content—represents an adaptation of the state to decentralized, fluid, and anonymous online expression. This would seem to be a smart move considering that overt state propaganda is increasingly ineffective. But deeper investigation shows that the persistence of old-fashioned propaganda work has rendered this seemingly shrewd strategy fruitless through the exposure of the existence of the fifty-cent army.

The state is not alone in the game. Many social actors have employed, anonymously, public relations (PR) strategies to advance their agenda online. In effect, tactics such as astroturfing and rumor spreading are natural weapons for regime critics and dissident groups who are constantly suppressed. However, though they might be effective in defaming the regime, such tactics can backfire by leading many netizens to imagine a group of national enemies conducting sabotage and espionage missions in Chinese cyberspace. As a result, rather than viewing the struggle over online expression as a story of social actors allying against the authoritarian state, many netizens develop an alternative framing in which regime challengers are depicted as betrayers or trouble makers. Thus, the struggle over online expression is framed as a counter-espionage story of Chinese patriots defending the nation against betrayers and their foreign sponsors. This framing not only demobilizes many netizens, but also contributes to the rise of a pro-regime discourse.

In fact, some netizens have developed a group identity as the voluntary fifty-cent army and have constructed online communities that sustain a regime-defending discourse.[51] This identity is both passively imposed and actively constructed. It is passively imposed in that the netizens involved are labeled the fifty-cent army by other netizens furious at pro-regime expression owing to the state's censorship and opinion-manipulation efforts. But as victims of labeling wars, they have glorified the disgraceful "fifty-cent army" label by depicting themselves as more patriotic and rational than most netizens—they believe they are defending the nation against online sabotage and emphasize facts and logic in debates. Through repeated interactions among themselves and with regime critics, members of the voluntary fifty-cent army reinforce their identity and sustain a robust pro-regime discourse.

The discourse competition reveals a divided Chinese cyberspace. Coherent and relatively independent communities either sustain a certain dominant discourse or become battlefields of multiple discourses as netizens with distinct political orientations coexist or compete. Interactions among both like-minded and rival netizens socialize Internet users in ways that reinforce their beliefs, which in turn consolidate their group identity.

In discourse competition, state and nonstate actors compete to manipulate popular opinion to their advantage. Unlike the censorship game in which coercive power plays a significant role, players in discourse competition mobilize through identity and expressive strategies. Aware of opinion engineering efforts by both the state and regime challengers, netizens engaging in public discussions are extremely anxious about each other's true identity. This explains why both the state and regime challengers tend to engage in the game anonymously so as to avoid having their strategy backfire, while labeling becomes an effective way of defaming others.

It is worth noting that defamation and attack are the dominant modes of discourse competition on Chinese forums.[52] Among the state and its supporters, efforts to construct and defend a positive image of the regime often prove fruitless, whereas denouncing regime critics as trouble makers and saboteurs is more effective. Among regime challengers who have been defamed and censored by the state, spreading negative news about the regime also works more effectively than posing as a viable alternative to the Party-state, particularly considering that ideological and financial links to Western powers are considered liabilities by nationalistic Chinese netizens.

ONLINE POLITICS, DIGITAL EMPOWERMENT, AND AUTHORITARIAN RESILIENCE

The struggle over online expression reveals that neither the state nor the Internet is monolithic and that the dynamics of state adaptation and popular activism go far beyond a state–society confrontation. Thus, examining interactions among multiple state and social actors in censorship and discourse competition not only provides a more balanced view of Internet politics in China, but also contributes to theoretical enterprises such as state–society relations, authoritarian resilience, and democratization theories.

A Fragmented State and Fragmented Cyberspace

According to Manuel Castells, "the relevance of a given technology, and its acceptance by people at large, do not result from the technology itself, but from appropriation of the technology by individuals and collectives to fit their needs and their culture."[53] An analysis of the struggles over censorship and discourse competition reveals fine-tuned and complex state–society relations in China, in which the state and social actors have both demonstrated great adaptability to new sociopolitical terrain. In the struggle over censorship, though the state enjoys the advantage of coercive power over intermediary actors and netizens, the latter group have evaded state censorship through technological know-how and creativity. In discourse competition, the actors involved, including the state and its critics, resort to grassroots PR strategies to engineer popular opinion. This mode of interaction has created an atmosphere of subterfuge and uncertainty in which participants' beliefs, values, and identities are constantly contested. Such an atmosphere conditions netizens' perceptions of various discourses, as well as their reactions and choices of strategies for online expression.

Both the struggle over censorship and the discourse competition demonstrate the need to disaggregate both the state and the Internet. The understudied role of local and departmental state agencies is particularly worth noting because their interests and motives have also incentivized control initiatives. For instance, while the central state is primarily concerned with the regime's overall stability and legitimacy, local authorities take actions to maintain their own public image, demonstrate their competence to upper levels, or avoid political risks.[54] As a result, they tend to boast about their propaganda achievements while endeavoring to stifle disclosure of local problems. Such actions do severe harm to the regime's legitimacy because they not only disable the safety-valve function of online expression, but also intensify netizens' enmity toward the regime.[55] After all, suppressing tangible grievances is often more effective in provoking the wrath of Chinese citizens than abstract causes. Moreover, local cover-ups indicate the central government's failure, or even worse, its lack of desire, to discipline local agents, which may erode trust in the central government and the regime.[56]

Likewise, recognizing the fragmentation of cyberspace is crucial to understanding Internet politics in China. Chinese netizens have approached the Internet with diverse and mixed purposes. For instance, chapter 4, on pop activism, discusses that online activism is more than a form of digital contention. It can be driven by both netizens' contentious motivations and their pursuit of both fun and recognition. Moreover, as a strategy to promulgate information, pop activism is equally useful for both regime critics and regime supporters. In this regard, understanding online activism merely as a strike against state censorship or the regime has the danger of downplaying the richness of cyberpolitics and overestimating the Internet's potential for civic activism and political change.

In addition, even politically motivated netizens demonstrate distinctive beliefs, values, and ideological inclinations. Given the pervasiveness of opinion-manipulation efforts by the state and its critics, Chinese netizens often are extremely anxious about each other's identity and intention, which in turn facilitates the formation of coherent, relatively isolated online communities. Through repeated amicable interactions among community members and confrontations with rivals, netizens' propositions and group identities are reinforced while the discourses they champion are produced and reproduced. Such a tendency in online expression only fortifies the fragmentation of Chinese cyberspace, preventing these "public sphericules" from evolving into the public sphere, as Johan Lagerkvist predicted.[57]

China's Democratization Prospectus: Revisiting Authoritarian Resilience

What is the impact of online expression on authoritarian rule? Critics have warned against evaluating the impact of online politics merely in terms of whether online activism will lead to regime change.[58] Yet focusing exclusively on online politics as a "gradual revolution" likewise risks reducing online activism to a "weapon of the weak"[59] and shies away from the legitimate questions of whether and how online activism will contribute to possible regime change. Analyzing both the struggle over censorship and the discourse competition offers a testing ground for assessing authoritarian resilience.

Findings presented in this book suggest that it is necessary to rethink the basis for resilient authoritarianism. Struggles over online expression reveal the agility of the Chinese state in adapting and refining its capacity to deal with new challenges. Yet the regime's adaptability cannot fully explain its "resilience" because the state's censorship and opinion-manipulation efforts have often proved fruitless and counterproductive.[60] Rather, the apparent resilience of Chinese authoritarianism in the face of the Internet's liberalizing and democratizing impact is primarily a result of the fragmentation of cyberspace, the pluralization of online expression, and ultimately the lack of consensus on a viable alternative to the current system.

Chinese cyberspace is fragmented in a number of ways, particularly in that netizens have formed a wide range of groups, the majority along apolitically motivated lines.[61] Failing to recognize this point leads to an overestimation of the Internet's impact. In particular, netizen groups are organized around framings not limited to a binary struggle pitting freedom of expression against state repression. Despite the ineffectiveness of the state's own efforts at popular-opinion manipulation, many are mobilized around an alternative frame depicting regime critics as saboteurs of national interests and call on netizens to defend the regime against the nation's enemies.

Moreover, online discourse competition has helped discredit any alternative to the Party-state. In particular, the findings presented in chapters 6 and 7 suggest that nationalism is at odds with China's nascent democratic movement, not because nationalistic citizens are disinclined toward democracy or swayed by state ideology, but because they are highly distrustful of democratic activists. An analysis of nationalistic discourses shows that regime critics are often depicted as voluntary or involuntary foreign agents who lack the capacity or will to represent and defend China's interests. Take the 1989 student leaders as examples: Chai Ling was blamed online for risking other students' lives for her personal ambitions,[62] and Wang Dan has been accused of betraying China's national interests by receiving funds from the United States and Taiwan's pro-independent Democratic Progressive Party.[63] Such distrust weakens regime-challenging voices online, forcing many regime challengers to deny their political ambitions in order to retain public sympathy.[64]

Evidently, to assess authoritarian resilience, one ought not examine only state capacity and adaptability, but also pay close attention to the strategies employed by regime challengers. This perspective helps explain why online expression is not as threatening to authoritarian rule as many have expected. Though freer online expression has empowered regime critics and eroded state legitimacy despite state control, such impact is partially neutralized by the pluralization of online discourses. Among others, pro-regime netizen groups such as the voluntary fifty-cent army have actively denigrated regime challengers and sustained a pro-regime discourse.

A Democratizing Internet or a Democratic Illusion?

The new source of authoritarian resilience that the book brings to light—namely, the weak base of support for challengers—has further implications for China's potential for regime change and democratization. Though political scientists cannot study events that have not yet occurred, it is possible to examine whether and how online expression may contribute to democratic transition, since the process does not take place overnight. Indeed, regime transition does not start at the moment when the authoritarian regime collapses and/or a new regime arises. Long before the shift, society undergoes gradual, preliminary processes in which the regime's authority is delegitimized and the values and ideas of an alternative regime are diffused. Since the Internet is a particularly vulnerable area of China's authoritarian rule, it is an ideal place to observe this process. According to the China expert Johan Lagerkvist, online negotiations between conflicting Party-state, youth/subaltern, and transnational business norms will foster normative change and the erosion of state norms, moving the nation toward inclusive democracy.[65] This book supports Lagerkvists's argument for the erosion of state norms by emphasizing how online expression has helped delegitimize the regime, and how the state's censorship and opinion-manipulation efforts have been largely fruitless and counterproductive. However, the optimistic expectation of a transformation toward inclusive democracy is not supported because the erosion of Party-state norms does not necessarily imply the emergence of liberal and democratic norms.

If understood as a process in which democratic rules and procedures are applied to previously undemocratic political institutions,[66] democratization implies two phases: the collapse of the old regime and the establishment of a democratic one. Though online expression may be contributing to delegitimizing the current regime, it has done little to cultivate a pro-democracy discourse that spreads democratic values and ideas or even to mobilize netizens to struggle for a democratic regime. This echoes the political scientist and commentator Yongnian Zheng's earlier observation that the Internet in China has contributed more to political liberalization than democratization.[67] The ubiquity of defamation in discourse competition vividly demonstrates that both the authoritarian regime and its potential alternatives have been discredited, leading to the erosion of political authority in general. As Samuel Huntington pointed out, "The most important political distinction among countries concerns not their form of government but their degree of government."[68] Failing to indoctrinate netizens with democratic values and ideas or to convince them to support a democratic political order, the "liberalizing" effects of online expression may result in little more than the erosion of the authoritarian regime. For instance, after a series of brutal attacks on schoolchildren across China in early 2010,[69] one picture started to circulate online with the slogan "Every injustice has its perpetrator, and every debt has its debtor. If you go out the door and turn left, you will find the government" (*yuan you tou, zhai you zhu, chumen zuozhuan shi zhengfu*, 冤有头债有主, 出门左转是政府). Clearly, netizens spreading the slogan had little respect for political authority, but saw the regime as the source of all social ills.

In fact, the Chinese Internet shows signs of excessive liberalization rather than democratization: The decay of authority is apparent in online expression of all types. Interpreting this purely as a sign of authoritarian pullback is misleading because it overlooks the erosion of social capital, which many social scientists consider crucial for a democracy to function.[70] The Party-state's authority is of course challenged in online expression, but so is trust in regime challengers and other social actors such intellectuals, journalists, lawyers, and even some nongovernmental organizations.[71] In this regard, a closer examination of such detrimental effects, currently unaddressed in the field, improves on the democratization literature by arguing that certain governance problems that plague new democracies may be the legacy of the liberalization process, rather than legacies of the authoritarian regime per se.[72]

DATA

The book draws on data collected through online and offline research that includes interviews, offline participant observation, online ethnography, and sources such as media reports, official documents, and scholarly studies.

First, I conducted more than sixty online and offline interviews with forum managers, forum users, scholars, and media professionals between 2008 and 2011. The majority of interviewees were recruited through a snowball approach. As a veteran user of Internet forums, my personal connections proved crucial during the initial phases of data collection. In particular, such connections helped recruit several key interviewees who not only provided their inside stories, but offered connections to other sources. Most interviews with forum managers and veteran users were semi-structured, focusing on their experiences with and perceptions of online expression, state control, and forum governance. Some interviewees, particularly those from state media outlets, were reluctant to talk about their jobs in detail. But even their reluctance revealed a great deal about the sensitive relationship between the state and the online public.

During my fieldwork in China, I also participated in two state-sponsored conferences of university Internet forum managers in 2009 and 2010. At these meetings, I not only met with forum managers from across the country, but also observed how they exchanged ideas with each other and interacted with state and market forces, represented by sponsoring state agencies and companies, respectively.

Second, this book relies on data collected through in-depth online ethnographic work, which involved the long-term observation of selected websites with restricted engagement to avoid any problems of reactivity. The approach resembles what Guobin Yang advocates as online "guerrilla ethnography," which emphasizes limited involvement, fluid movement in networks, and exploration of links,[73] but underlines the value of long term immersion in specific online communities. Based on a vision of the Internet featuring openness, fluidity, and connections, Yang argues that long-term ethnographic work on a few sites fails to capture the Internet's real strengths and leads to tunnel vision. However, the very fluidity of online expression requires an approach that allows for the timely compilation of discussion threads (which can be removed at any time because of moderation or censorship) and accumulation of the fluid *metis* (i.e., practical experience and know-how)[74] to read between the lines and accurately interpret the meanings and meta-meanings behind the texts. After all, the Janus-faced Internet features not only openness, fluidity, and connections, but also fragmentation, closure, and border restrictions. A concentrated focus on a few platforms helps bring into focus such underappreciated mechanisms that shape discourse competition, group identity, and community building.

The primary sites included in this research are Bdwm (bdwm.net), Ccthere (ccthere.com), Kdnet (kdnet.net), Mitbbs (mitbbs.com), NewSmth (www.newsmth.net), Qiangguo Luntan (bbs1.people.com.cn), and Tianya (tianya.cn). These forums are relatively large ones that attract more netizens and cover broader issue areas and thus are more influential and representative than smaller ones.[75] To increase representativeness, this book covers both domestic (Bdwm, Kdnet, NewSmth, Qiangguo Luntan, and Tianya) and overseas Chinese forums (Ccthere and Mitbbs). These forums can also be categorized into campus (Bdwm), commercial (Kdnet and Tianya), individual (Ccthere), and state-sponsored (Qiangguo Luntan) ones. Mitbbs and NewSmth, though commercialized, bear characteristics of campus forums because they both originated at universities and attract large numbers of students.[76] The research in this book is not restricted to these forums, however. Instead, they serve as focal points from which my study gradually expanded to other online territories. For instance, I first encountered the voluntary fifty-cent army on NewSmth and then followed their steps to other military forums such as Cjdby (lt.cjdby.net), Fyjs (fyjs.cn), and Sbanzu (sbanzu.com; the forum was closed permanently in 2016).

Additional sites for my online ethnography include platforms where forum managers exchange ideas and information on forum governance such as forum administrators' forums,[77] discussion boards,[78] and instant messenger QQ groups.[79] Both during and after the fieldwork period, I anonymously observed a few such platforms regularly. Ongoing conversations on such platforms provide a unique opportunity to learn about managers of various types of forums, as well as their concerns, practices, and strategies.

In-depth online ethnographic work also provides another important source of data aside from direct observations of netizen and managerial activities. Some forums, particularly campus BBSs, maintain historical data in their archival sections. Such data include forum and board histories, archives of online events and discussion threads, and texts of forum and board regulations. Online archives not only constitute an important and systematic source of how forum and board managers have governed their sites, but also provide an important source of information to check and confirm data collected through interviews and online observation.

Finally, sources such as media reports, official documents, and scholarly studies have also been crucial to my research. For instance, my analysis of online commentators, or the fifty-cent army, draws primarily on leaked official documents and media reports. Given the sensitivity of online opinion engineering, it might be surprising to find that official reports on the topic are sometimes made available. Yet, the state sometimes does not try to conceal information about the fifty-cent army because the online commentator system is regarded as part of its routine propaganda work. Indeed, local governments and propaganda branches often regard their success in this area as an achievement to boast about to higher levels. This explains why a local media report on the training of online commentators in Shanxi Province not only reported on the event, but also provided links to reports by other more influential news portals (e.g., 163.com and qq.com) and mouthpiece outlets (e.g., people.com.cn).[80]

There are potential ethical concerns with this research, especially in terms of the method of data collection for the online ethnography, as it involved observing human subjects without their explicit consent. Such concerns are legitimate, and it is essential to respond to these concerns here. First, the project's study design went through the internal review board review process at the University of California, Berkeley, before it was implemented. Second, my online ethnographic work was done almost exclusively on platforms with free anonymous access, meaning that all user activities are essentially in the public domain. Only a few platforms included in this study require a membership to view their posts. But even these sites are public in nature as they impose no registration restrictions and allow anyone with a valid email address to sign up for an account. In short, all the information I obtained in my online ethnography is publicly accessible and thus does not constitute a violation of netizens' privacy or a risk to them personally. To my knowledge, this is the standard, or at least an accepted, practice in the field. But to further protect the netizens, this book anonymizes them whenever possible. Third, my research has also used leaked documents from state agencies to analyze state intent and behavior online. This is not considered to present an ethnical problem either. Leading scholars such as Gary King and his colleagues at Harvard University have used similar sources in their research.

A PREVIEW OF WHAT FOLLOWS

Aside from this introductory chapter and the concluding chapter, the empirical chapters of the book fall into two major parts. The first part focuses on the cat-and-mouse censorship game, which highlights not only state–society confrontation, but also the intermediary actors at the crux of control implementation. Chapter 2 takes a state-centric perspective and analyzes how the Chinese Party-state has gradually adapted to the digital era by establishing the "world's most sophisticated"[81] censorship system. By discussing the institutional, organizational, technical, and administrative tools employed by the state, the chapter highlights the multi-agency, multi-level, and multi-means features of state censorship. The chapter also reveals how external challenges and internal fragmentation have contributed to the system's rigidity and arbitrariness, which provide maneuvering room for both intermediary actors and netizens, but also occasionally incurs harsher censorship.

Chapter 3 discusses how intermediary actors such as forum managers have balanced state control from above and netizens' challenges from below through "discontented compliance." Though pervasively dissatisfied with censorship, most forum managers nonetheless help preserve state-imposed limitations on online expression, largely because they cannot afford open disagreement. Yet they also engage in everyday forms of low-profile resistance and occasionally turn a blind eye to or even encourage boundary-spanning expressions. The chapter also explores how the affiliation, scale, and primary purposes of Internet forums affect their choice of strategy and thus their position along the discontent–compliance spectrum.

Chapter 4 focuses on netizen activism and explores not only how netizens evade and challenge censorship in innovative ways, but also how they have gone beyond activism against censorship. It argues that Chinese netizens are far from apolitical and have actively engaged in anti-censorship resistance, but many also participate in online activism for entertainment and may target dissident groups, political activities, and foreign actors. In other words, netizen activism has gone beyond "digital contention." Thus, an analysis of netizen activism must accommodate a much broader spectrum of actors and strategies in order to accurately assess the impact of online expression.

Chapters 5, 6, and 7 examine discourse competition and popular-opinion engineering. Chapter 5 explores the state's adaptation beyond censorship. It focuses on the Internet commentator system and details the recruitment, training, functions, and remuneration of the fifty-cent army. The analysis in this chapter shows that Internet commentators are often not properly trained or incentivized and are motivated more to demonstrate their competence to upper levels than to persuade netizens. As a result, the seemingly smart move often causes more trouble than it resolves, as it frequently backfires and chips away at the legitimacy of the Party-state.

Chapter 6 explores how regime challengers take advantage of the Internet to spread regime-challenging voices and how their efforts ironically feed into the state propaganda of a "handful of subversive forces." Echoing state propaganda, nationalistic netizens have developed a pro-regime discourse that defines dissidents, political activists, and foreign forces as national enemies, with the authoritarian state represented as a "necessary evil" to defend national interests. In this way, the struggle over online expression is completely reinterpreted: It is no longer a struggle by concerned citizens against the repressive state for freedom and democracy; it is a national defense war in which patriotic netizens side with the regime to defend China against online saboteurs.

Chapter 7 furthers the argument of a fragmented cyberspace by studying a particular netizen group who call themselves the voluntary fifty-cent army. By examining their repeated interactions with both opposing netizens and fellow community members, the chapter explains how the group has constructed a group identity and sustained a regime-defending discourse. This chapter takes the understanding of online expression in China beyond the empowered-society-versus-repressive-state framework to one that embraces conflicts among social actors themselves. It also shows how freer online expression may unexpectedly work to the advantage of the authoritarian regime.

The concluding chapter discusses the implications of my research findings. It emphasizes that the struggle over online expression is a process shaped by the internal interests and ideological fragmentation of the state, the diverse capacities and agency of intermediary actors, and the heterogeneous identity, values, and beliefs of netizen groups. In particular, it highlights the mismatch between the Party-state's capacity and the challenges presented by the digital age, which explains why the state has had tremendous difficulty translating its power into effective online control. But since regime critics have yet to win netizens' hearts and minds, any expectation of imminent democratization is likely built upon a miscalculation of the Internet's threat to authoritarian rule.

2

HARMONIZING THE INTERNET

State Control Over Online Expression

O n September 20, 1987, a Chinese computer expert sent China's first email from Beijing with the message, "Across the Great Wall we can reach every corner in the world."[1] This email hailed the arrival of China's Internet era with its statement that territorial obstacles between China and the world, as symbolized by the Great Wall, could be overcome by this new technology: the Internet. This message seems somewhat ironic in retrospect, because the Chinese state has since managed to construct the world's most sophisticated virtual "Great Wall" to filter content exchange between the country and the outside world, a system nicknamed the "Great Firewall." Why and how has the Party-state aimed to establish and enhance its control over the Internet? How has state control evolved over time? What are the dynamics shaping its evolution, particularly with regard to the state's institutional adaptation?

This chapter takes a state-centric perspective to explore China's Internet content control regime, defined as the complete set of organizational, institutional, administrative, and technical tools used by the state to limit the boundaries of online expression. The analysis shows that the Chinese state has developed a multi-agency, multi-level, multi-faceted approach to systematically and comprehensively censoring online content. However, this censorship system is plagued by both the Internet's hard-to-control nature and the regime's internal fragmentation, which together have rendered state censorship in China overly rigid but also arbitrary, and thus ineffective and even counterproductive to the state's goals in some cases.

Admittedly, the Chinese state has attempted to shape online expression in more subtle and complicated ways than censorship, often using a combination of control, propaganda, and accommodation approaches.[2] For instance, the state sometimes accommodates citizen participation online through channels such as e-government platforms or official accounts on popular social media platforms. To more directly shape online opinion, the state has adopted more innovative propaganda tactics, such as engaging the public via social media,[3] embracing popular cyber culture,[4] and fabricating pro-regime voices. These manipulative tactics are qualitatively different from censorship, as they ultimately do not depend on the state's coercive capacity. Chapter 5 will explore how the state manipulates rather than censors online expression, with a special focus on the Internet commentator system.

INTERNET GOVERNANCE AND INTERNET CONTENT GOVERNANCE

Internet governance in China is driven by a complicated set of dynamics. In particular, the Chinese state faces a dictator's dilemma. On one hand, it is highly concerned with the economic, technological, and industrial potential of the Internet and related information and communication technologies.[5] On the other hand, it has to deal with the sociopolitical challenges brought about by these new technologies, particularly the freer flow of information. As the political scientist Yongnian Zheng argues, these contradictory tasks have pushed the Party-state to establish a regulatory regime that promotes the development of the Internet as an industry while at the same time attempting to establish a control regime to tame what it considers to be the Internet's disturbing implications.[6] Similarly, Min Jiang argues that China's Internet policies "reflect an Internet development and regulatory model—authoritarian informationalism—that combines elements of capitalism, authoritarianism, and Confucianism."[7]

As the Internet empowers social actors by promoting civil society, facilitating collective mobilization, and encouraging public expression and online activism,[8] authoritarian states are increasingly recognizing a necessity to control it. According to Lawrence Lessig, controlling the Internet involves four mechanisms: the law, technical architecture (i.e., code), social norms, and the market.[9] In China, all of these mechanisms are subject to the heavy influence of or direct intervention by the Party-state. Indeed, studies have found that the Chinese Party-state not only firmly controls the physical network infrastructure, but also makes serious efforts to censor the flow of online information.[10] Scholars and human rights advocates have documented many censorship techniques employed by the state, ranging from automatic taboo word filtering to manual surveillance, and from limiting access to undesired websites using the Great Firewall to shutting down deviant websites and jailing dissenters.[11] The state even completely shut down Internet and mobile services in Xinjiang after ethnic rioting in 2009.[12] Moreover, the state has also attempted to take preemptive measures, such as promoting real-name registration, requiring the pre-installation of filtering software on all personal computers,[13] and encouraging service providers to conduct self-censorship.[14]

These studies reveal how the state controls or attempts to control the Internet, but are insufficient in providing a historical and systematic understanding of Internet governance beyond specific control measures. In addition, they often treat the control regime as a single, undifferentiated entity, which makes it difficult to discern variations in state control over different targets or to recognize the dynamics involved in the state's strategies and techniques. The following sections historicize and contextualize the evolution of China's Internet control, especially the state's institutional, organizational, technical, and administrative adaptations to the ever-increasing challenges of online expression over time.

The Evolution of China's Internet Control Regime

Since the early 1990s, China's Internet control regime has undergone a process of enhancement, expansion, and fine-tuning, with different focuses, characteristics, and implications involved at different stages. Taking a historical approach, Yongnian Zheng has argued that the Chinese state focused on constructing a regulatory regime in the late 1990s, before shifting emphasis to a control regime.[15] Guobin Yang has divided regulatory evolution into three stages, with the first (from 1994 to 1999) focusing on network security, service provision, and institutional restructuring. The second stage (from 2000 to 2002) was characterized by the expansion and refinement of control with stronger content regulation, and the third stage (from 2003 onward) has centered on the further expansion of Internet regulation.[16] Yonggang Li has also argued that Internet control has evolved through three periods. Adopting a policy-learning perspective, Li's analysis provides a better understanding of the development of China's Internet control regime, as it correctly emphasizes the agency of the state.[17]

Like Zheng's, Yang's, and Li's work, my study also considers the state's Internet control regime to have evolved through three phases (table 2.1). I examine the escalation and expansion of state control over time, as well as its shifting emphases at different stages: from regulation to control, and from network security to content control. But my periodization also highlights that the evolution of state control has in fact corresponded to the expansion of the Internet and its ever-increasing sociopolitical impact. After all, as Yongnian Zheng aptly puts it, "The state and social forces are mutually transformative via their interactions."[18]

To highlight both the process and the nuances of state adaptation, the chapter groups the state's Internet control efforts into three major categories: policy enactment (table 2.2), organizational adaptation (table 2.3), and administrative and technical enforcement (table 2.4). Consciously or unconsciously, the state has employed an uneven development strategy in building its control capacities. Its initial responses to online expression came out of its governance inertia and were mostly administrative and technical in nature, thus appearing to be sporadic and unsystematic. Institutional adaptation followed, with the creation of formal rules and norms, as well as organizational capacity building. At this stage, the state did not strictly enforce control regulations. The third stage has been one of capacity use, adjustment, and refinement. During this stage, the state has been trying out its control mechanisms more boldly and adjusting in response to social reaction.

TABLE 2.1 The Evolution of Internet Content Control by the State

	Phase 1: Before 1999	Phase 2: 1999–2003	Phase 3: 2004–Present
Growth of Internet Use	The Internet, with people having limited access, is viewed more as an economic and technological opportunity than a political challenge.	Online expression becomes politically challenging; for example, the case of Sun Zhigang.[a] State adaptation lags behind the expansion of the Internet and online expression.	The Internet becomes increasingly powerful and has more constraints imposed on it by the state. Online expression continues to boom, with new applications such as blogs, WeChat, and Weibo.
Features of State Control	The focus is on network security and promoting the technology.[b] Control is unsystematic and reactive, often via technical and administrative means.	Rapid institutional and organizational adaptation occurs, with a more specific and heavier focus on content control, but overall, state control remains in a trial-and-error process. There are frequent changes in control agencies and conflicts over jurisdiction.[c]	Policy learning has come to a tentative conclusion. Control continues to expand and adjust, becoming increasingly assertive and adopt, with bolder administrative and technical practices in use than ever before.
Policy Enactment (Table 2.2)	Regulations focus on physical network security. Prescriptions regarding content control are often ambiguous and boilerplate.	Content control regulations become more specific, and a systematic framework emerges for licensing, registration, and the monitoring and punishment of online activities.	Regulations are enacted or redrafted to regulate new online applications, fine-tune content control, clarify division of labor, and promote coordination among state agencies.

(continued)

TABLE 2.1 The Evolution of Internet Content Control by the State (*continued*)

	Phase 1: Before 1999	Phase 2: 1999–2003	Phase 3: 2004–Present
Organizational Adaptation (Table 2.3)	The state tries to accommodate Internet governance with its existing apparatus.	The jurisdiction of existing state agencies expands, with specialized content control agencies established and the promotion of self-disciplining organizations.	There is further organizational restructuring, an enhancement of division of labor and coordination, and the promotion of self-disciplining service providers.
Administrative and Technical Control (Table 2.4)	Administrative and technical control are sporadic, but constant attention is paid to campus forums.	Content control practices are intensified to promote official discourses and suppress unwanted information.	Efforts to enforce control are made more rigid and bolder, notably via campaigns with multi-agency cooperation and coordination.

[a] See Zixue Tai, *The Internet in China: Cyberspace and Civil Society* (London: Routledge, 2006), 259–68.
[b] Yongnian Zheng, *Technological Empowerment: The Internet, State, and Society in China* (Stanford, CA: Stanford University Press, 2008), 50–23; Guobin Yang, *The Power of the Internet in China: Citizen Activism Online* (New York: Columbia University Press, 2009), 48.
[c] Yonggang Li, *Women de Fanghuoqiang: Wangluo Shidai de Biaoda Yu Jianguan (Our Great Firewall: Expression and Governance in the Era of the Internet)* (Nanning: Guangxi Normal University Press, 2009), 75.

TABLE 2.2 Policy Enactment

Phase	Major Regulations
Before 1999	■ In 1994, the State Council Information Office issues the *Regulations on the Safety and Protection of Computer Systems of the People's Republic of China*, prohibiting the use of "computer information systems to conduct activities against national interests, public interests, or legitimate interests of citizens."[a]
	■ In 1997, the Ministry of Public Security releases the *Computer Information Network and Internet Security Protection Management Regulations*, prohibiting nine types of information.[b]
1999–2003	■ In 2000, the State Council Information Office publishes the *Telecommunications Regulations of the People's Republic of China* and the *Administrative Measures on Internet Information Services*, which both reiterate the nine prohibitions of the 1997 Ministry of Public Security regulations. The *Administrative Measures on Internet Information Services* also require the registration and licensing of Internet content providers.[c]
	■ In 2000, the Ministry of Information Industry issues the *Regulation on Internet News and Bulletin Boards*, requiring the registration of forums.[d]
	■ In 2000, the State Council Information Office and the Ministry of Information Industry issue the *Interim Provisions for the Administration of News Publication by Internet Sites*, prescribing qualifications for online news service providers.[e]
2004–present	■ In 2005, the State Council Information Office and the Ministry of Information Industry jointly issue the *Administrative Provisions of Internet News Information Services*, adding two more types of prohibited information: information that incites illegal gathering, association, demonstration, or disruption of social order, and information on the activities of illegal nongovernment organizations.[f]
	■ In 2005, the Ministry of Information Industry issues the *Administrative Measures of the Registration of Noncommercial Internet Information Services* to enhance control over noncommercial content providers.[g]
	■ In 2006, sixteen central party and state departments jointly issue the *Work Program for the Coordination of Internet Website Management*, dividing control responsibilities across departments.[h]

(continued)

TABLE 2.2 Policy Enactment (*continued*)

Phase	Major Regulations

- In 2007, the State Administration of Radio, Film, and Television and the Ministry of Information Industry jointly issue the *Administrative Provisions on Internet Audiovisual Program Services*, extending control to multimedia content.[i]

- In 2012, the Cyberspace Administration of China and the Ministry of Industry and Information Technology jointly issue a revised draft of the *Administrative Measures on Internet Information Services* for public comment. These regulations explicitly tie online information control to national security, fine-tune the licensing and registration requirements of service providers, promote real-name registration, and further describe the responsibilities of service providers.[j]

[a] State Council Information Office, *Zhonghua Renmin Gongheguo Jisuanji Xinxi Xitong Anquan Baohu Tiaoli (Regulations on the Safety and Protection of Computer Systems of the People's Republic of China)*, February 18, 1994.
[b] These nine types of information include information that (1) incites people to resist or obstructs the implementation of the constitution, laws, or administrative regulations; (2) incites people to subvert the government or the socialist system; (3) incites separatism or harms national unification; (4) incites ethnic hatred or discrimination or undermines ethnic solidarity; (5) forges or distorts facts or spreads rumors that disturb social stability; (6) spreads superstition, obscenity, pornography, gambling, violence, homicide, terrorism, or instigates crime; (7) openly insults or slanders people with fabricated information; (8) damages the credibility of state apparatus; and (9) any other type of information that violates the constitution, laws, or administrative regulations.
[c] State Council Information Office, *Zhonghua Renmin Gongheguo Dianxin Tiaoli (Telecommunications Regulations of the People's Republic of China)*, September 20, 2000; State Council Information Office, *Hulianwang Xinxi Fuwu Guanli Banfa (Administrative Measures on Internet Information Services)*, September 25, 2000.
[d] Ministry of Information Industry, *Hulianwang Dianzi Gonggao Fuwu Guanli Guiding (Regulation on Internet News and Bulletin Boards)*, October 27, 2000.
[e] State Council Information Office and Ministry of Information Industry, *Hulian Wangzhan Congshi Dengzai Xinwen Yewu Guanli Zanxing Guiding (Interim Provisions for the Administration of News Publication by Internet Sites)*, November 6, 2000.
[f] State Council Information Office and Ministry of Information Industry, *Hulianwang Xinwen Xinxi Fuwu Guanli Guiding (Administrative Provisions of Internet News Information Services)*, September 25, 2005.
[g] Ministry of Information Industry, *Fei Jingyingxing Hulianwang Xinxi Fuwu Beian Guanli Banfa (Administrative Measures of the Registration of Noncommercial Internet Information Services)*, January 28, 2005.
[h] Chinese Communist Party Central Propaganda Department, Ministry of Information Industry, State Council Information Office, Ministry of Education, Ministry of Culture, Ministry of Health, et al., *Hulian Wangzhan Guanli Xietiao Gongzuo Fangan (Work Program for the Coordination of Internet Website Management)*, February 17, 2006.
[i] State Administration of Radio, Film, and Television and Ministry of Information Industry, *Hulianwang Shiting Jiemu Fuwu Guanli Guiding (Administrative Provisions on Internet Audiovisual Program Services)*, December 29, 2007.
[j] Cyberspace Administration of China and Ministry of Industry and Information Technology, *Hulianwang Xinxi Fuwu Guanli Banfa: Xiuding Caoan Zhengqiu Yijian Gao (Administrative Measures on Internet Information Services: Revised Version for Public Comment)*, June 7, 2012.

TABLE 2.3 Organizational Adaptation

Phase	Evolution of the State's Internet Control Apparatus
Before 1999	■ The Ministry of Information Industry is established to better regulate and promote the development of information technologies. ■ The Ministry of Public Security is delegated the power of content control.
1999–2003	■ Extended power is granted to the State Administration of Radio, Film, and Television over online video and audio programs, to the General Administration of Press and Publication over online publications, and to the Ministry of Culture over online cultural and artistic activities, online gaming, and Internet cafés.[a] ■ In April 2000, the State Council Information Office establishes the Internet News and Propaganda Administration Bureau. Local authorities quickly follow suit and establish related offices.[b] ■ Self-disciplining organizations, such as the Internet Society of China, the China Youth Internet Association, and the Wireless Internet Trust and Self-Discipline Alliance are established.
2004–present	■ In 2006, sixteen central party and state departments jointly issue the *Coordination Plan of Internet Website Management*, dividing control responsibilities across departments.[c] Local authorities also establish a joint-leadership mechanism to coordinate Internet control.[d] ■ In 2008, the Ministry of Industry and Information Technology is established, inheriting Internet regulatory and control powers from the Ministry of Information Industry and the State Council Informatization Work Office.[e] ■ In April 2010, the State Council Information Office establishes a Ninth Bureau to guide, coordinate, and supervise Internet cultural development and management.[f] ■ The state continues to promote self-discipline among service providers through efforts such as the establishment of an illegal information reporting center.[g] ■ In 2011, the State Council Information Office establishes the Cyberspace Administration of China as a parallel apparatus to the State Council to enhance control over online content.[h]

(*continued*)

TABLE 2.3 Organizational Adaptation (*continued*)

Phase	Evolution of the State's Internet Control Apparatus
	■ In 2014, the Cyberspace Administration of China is reorganized into the top Internet censorship, oversight, and control agency, which answers directly to Xi Jinping and the Central Leading Group for Internet Security and Informatization.
	■ In November 2016, the National People's Congress passes the Cybersecurity Law. As the latest effort to tighten jurisdictional control over online content, the law reaffirms the state's sovereignty over the Internet. In particular, the law requires network operators to cooperate with the authorities in crime or security investigations, to store within China data gathered or produced in the country, and to verify users' identities before providing services to them.

[a] State Administration of Radio, Film, and Television, "Guanyu Jiaqiang Tongguo Xinxi Wangluo Xiang Gongzhong Chuanbo Guangbo Dianying Dianshi Jiemu Guanli de Tonggao" ("Circular on Strengthening the Management of Broadcasting Radio, Film and TV Programs via the Internet"), October 1999; State Administration of Radio, Film, and Television, *Hulianwang Deng Xinxi Chuanbo Shiting Jiemu Guanli Banfa (Regulations on Broadcasting Video and Audio Programs Through the Internet)*, January 7, 2003; General Administration of Press and Publication and Ministry of Information Industry, *Hulianwang Chuban Guanli Zanxing Guiding (Provisional Regulations on the Administration of Internet Publications)*, June 27, 2002; Ministry of Culture, *Hulianwang Wenhua Guanli Zanxing Guiding (Provisional Regulations on Internet Culture Management)*, May 10, 2003.

[b] In June 2000, the Beijing Municipal Government Information Office established its Internet Propaganda Administration Office to supervise online information services. See the Beijing Association of Online Media website, www.baom.org.cn/biannian/bn2000.html.

[c] See Chinese Communist Party Central Propaganda Department, et al., *Hulian Wangzhan Guanli Xietiao Gongzuo Fangan*. The sixteen agencies include the Central Propaganda Department; the China Food and Drug Administration; the Chinese Academy of Sciences; the General Staff Department Communication Department; the General Administration of Press and Publication; the Ministry of Commerce; the Ministry of Culture; the Ministry of Education; the Ministry of Health; the Ministry of Information Industry; the Ministry of Public Security; the Ministry of State Security; the State Administration for Industry and Commerce; the State Administration of Radio, Film, and Television; the State Council Information Office; and the State Secrets Bureau.

[d] The Beijing Municipal Government formed the Internet Propaganda Administration Leadership Group. See Wang Hao, "Beijingshi Hulianwang Xuanchuan Guanli Lingdao Xiaozu Huiyi Zhaokai" ("Beijing Municipal Internet Propaganda Administration Leadership Group Conference Convened"), *Beijing Ribao (Beijing Daily)*, July 13, 2007.

[e] Though primarily a regulatory agency, the Ministry of Industry and Information Technology plays an indispensable role in censorship because all Internet data centres (IDCs), Internet service providers (ISPs), and Internet content providers (ICPs) must register with it before entering the market.

[f] Su Yongtong, "Guoxinban 'Kuobian,' Wangluo Guanli Jusi Yi Bian Er" ("State Council Information Office Expansion: One Internet Administration Bureau Becomes Two"), *Nanfang Zhoumo (Southern Weekend)*, May 20, 2010.

[g] For instance, see the website of the China Internet Illegal Information Reporting Center, http://ciirc.china.cn/ or www.12377.cn.

[h] "Guojia Hulianwang Xinxi Bangongshi Sheli" ("The Cyberspace Administration of China Is Established"), *Xinhua Net*, May 5, 2011, http://news.xinhuanet.com/it/2011-05/04/c_121376056.htm.

TABLE 2.4 Technical and Administrative Control

Phase	Selected Technical and Administrative Control Efforts
Before 1999	■ Overseas websites considered hostile undergo an ad hoc blockade, and violators are jailed.[a] ■ Service providers are encouraged to conduct self-censorship.[b] ■ The state is highly attentive to campus forums: All major campus forums are carefully monitored and strictly controlled, with sites shut down owing to worries about collective mobilization or during sensitive periods, such as the event of Deng Xiaoping's death.
1999–2003	■ State media are encouraged to conquer "commanding heights of thought and public opinion" online.[c] ■ The Great Firewall starts to function, monitoring information flow online and blocking "hostile" sites through techniques such as IP and URL filtering.[d] ■ There is a crackdown on unregistered Internet cafés; those that remain open are required to record their customers' identification information.[e] ■ More severe measures are taken to punish deviants, including shutting down websites and jailing more citizens for "subverting the state" or "leaking state secrets."[f]
2004–present	■ Enforced registration and licensing are taken more seriously with the establishment of a database of Internet content providers, IP addresses, and domain names.[g] ■ Real-name registration is required for terminal devices (e.g., mobile phones and computers used in Internet cafés) and applications (e.g., blogs, microblogs, and forums).[h] ■ Control is tightened over campus forums: The Ytht BBS is shut down in 2004, and the Ministry of Education mandates campus forums to restrict off-campus access in the spring of 2005. ■ Internet commentators, a.k.a. the fifty-cent army, are introduced to guide public opinion anonymously (see chapter 5).

(continued)

TABLE 2.4 Technical and Administrative Control (*continued*)

Phase	Selected Technical and Administrative Control Efforts
	▪ More efforts are made and state campaigns run to control pornographic, political, and other illegal information. For instance, the Ministry of Industry and Information Technology introduces the filtering Green Dam software (which is revoked following criticism in 2009).[i] In 2013, the state launches a massive anti-rumor-mongering campaign primarily targeting Weibo and other social media platforms.[j]

[a] See Seth Faison, "E-Mail to U.S. Lands Chinese Internet Entrepreneur in Jail," *New York Times*, January 21, 1999.

[b] Jack Linchuan Qiu, "Virtual Censorship in China: Keeping the Gate Between the Cyberspaces," *International Journal of Communications Law and Policy*, no. 4 (2000): 12.

[c] CCTV Online, China.com.cn, China Daily Online, China-Youth Online, CRI Online, People's Daily Online, and Xinhua Net are among the first designated as key Internet news service providers by the State Council Information Office.

[d] Greg Walton, "China's Golden Shield: Corporations and the Development of Surveillance Technology in the People's Republic of China" (Montreal: International Centre for Human Rights and Democratic Development, 2001), www.dd-rd.ca/site/_PDF/publications/globalization/CGS_ENG.PDF.

[e] Li, *Women de Fanghuoqiang*, 90–93. As Li points out, such campaigns have regulatory purposes.

[f] For a detailed list, see Zheng, *Technological Empowerment*, 70–78.

[g] Enacted as early as 2000, the regulation was not seriously enforced until 2004, when fourteen ministries jointly launched a campaign to enforce it. The pressure intensified in the later anti-pornography and illegal information campaigns.

[h] See Jiao Likun, "Shouji Shimingzhi Zuiwan Xiayue Tuichu, Zhongguo Yi Fengsha Wanbu Shouji" ("Real-Name Registration of Cellphones Will Be Implemented Next Month Onward; China Has Banned More Than Ten Thousand Cellphones), *China News*, December 22, 2005, www.chinanews.com/news/2005/2005-12-22/8/668715.shtml; Ying Ni, " 'Wangyou Shimingzhi' Jin Qi Shixing, Xinzheng Zaoyu Zhixingnan" ("Real-Name Registration of Online Gaming Effective Today; the New Policy Encounters Difficulty in Enforcement"), *China News*, August 1, 2010, www.chinanews.com/it/2010/08-01/2438659.shtml; "Tencent QQ Jiang Shixing Wangluo Shimingzhi, QQ Qun Chuangjianzhe Xu Shiming Dengji" ("Tecent QQ Intends to Introduce Real-Name Registration; QQ Group Owners Must Register with Real Names"), *Sohu*, July 21, 2005, http://it.sohu.com/20050721/n240175776.shtml; "Boke Shimingzhi Anran Tuichang, Wangluo Guanzhi Yiyou Fansi" ("Real-Name Registration of Blog Services Abandoned; We Need Reflections on Internet Control), *Nanfang Dushibao (Southern Metropolis Daily)*, May 25, 2007.

[i] Wang Qihua, " 'Lüba' Huangong" ("Green Dam Implementation Postponed), *Caijing Magazine*, no. 14 (July 6, 2009).

[j] For instance, see Chris Buckley, "Crackdown on Bloggers Is Mounted by China," *New York Times*, September 11, 2013.

UNDERSTANDING INTERNET CONTROL IN CHINA

According to the Internet researcher Yonggang Li, state governance of the Internet in China has proceeded through the "garbage can model," which features problematic preferences, unclear technology, and fluid participation[19] in a "categorized governance" model that applies different governing strategies in different realms.[20] By now, the state has established a comprehensive content control regime endowed with a full set of organizational, institutional, technical, and administrative tools.

Organizationally, before the Cyberspace Administration of China (also known as the Office of the Central Leading Group for Cyberspace Affairs) was founded in 2011, the two most important sets of state apparatus responsible for Internet control were the party propaganda system and the government's information office system, headed by the Central Propaganda Department and the State Council Information Office, respectively.[21] The propaganda system, nicknamed the "Department of Truth,"[22] is in charge of ideological work and has ultimate control over the media. The State Council Information Office is in charge of the development and control of online news services and is the de facto top government agency for Internet control. Both the Central Propaganda Department and the State Council Information Office have specific sub-offices for Internet control. The Internet Division of the Bureau of Information and Public Opinion, the Internet News Office under the News Bureau, and the Internet Commentary and Criticism Group are sub-offices of the Central Propaganda Department, and the Fifth and Ninth Bureaus fall under the State Council Information Office.[23] In May 2011, the State Council set up the Cyberspace Administration of China as a parallel agency to take on its Internet regulation and control functions.[24] In 2014, the Cyberspace Administration of China became the central Internet censorship, oversight, and control agency, reporting directly to President Xi Jinping and the then newly formed Central Leading Group for Internet Security and Informatization. With the state's constant organizational adaptation, a redivision of labor and redistribution of power have occurred from time to time among state agencies. For example, since the 1990s, the propaganda system has gradually increased its influence on Internet censorship.[25] The role of the Ministry of Public Security in content control has become relatively less significant as the propaganda and state information systems have gradually built up their organizational capacities.[26]

Institutionally, the two most important regulations that serve as the major legal basis for online content censorship are the *Administrative Measures on Internet Information Services*, issued by the State Council in 2000, and the *Administrative Provisions of Internet News Information Services*, issued by the State Council and the Ministry of Information Industry in 2005. The former set out conditions for websites to operate legally, including registration and licensing. The latter established the online news publication qualification system, dividing online news service providers into three categories: those run by news entities, those run by non-news entities, and those established by news entities to carry already-published content. Only websites in the first category are allowed to report on news events. Those in the second and third categories may only reprint news from news sources approved by the state.

For both netizens and service providers, censorship rules become tangible only when they are enforced, because state regulations and laws are often ambiguous in terms of implementation. For instance, individuals were not allowed to register ".cn" domain names according to both the 2002 and the 2009 versions of the *China Internet Network Information Center Implementation Rules for Domain Name Registration*. But the China Internet Network Information Center did not enforce the regulation until 2009, when China Central Television criticized its loose supervision of domain names in an anti-pornography campaign.[27] Apparently, state regulation in this case served more as a disclaimer to avoid imputation than actually as a means of controlling online content.

According to the former State Council director Wang Chen, state control can be implemented through various means, including the following:

1. Regulating domain names, IP addresses, registration and licensing, and service access.
2. Establishing an entry-and-exit mechanism for online information services; i.e., lawfully implementing registration and licensing of

information services related to ideological security and public interests; establishing and improving management such as routine
supervision, annual review, and administrative penalty; and form-
ing a coordination mechanism among relevant agencies to dispose
harmful information and prevent its infiltration from abroad.
3. Actively exploring real-name registration.[28]

Such control measures are implemented at multiple levels and target individual users and all levels of service providers. According to
their functions, these measures can be categorized into four groups
serving preventive, surveillance, crisis management, and public opinion manipulation goals. Preventive measures are designed to filter the
flow of online information and prevent unwanted information from
being accessed or published. Filtering can be done at various levels.
At the national level, the Great Firewall employs a collection of filtering technologies to disrupt connections that the state deems harmful.
Local authorities often then add taboo terms to filter content specific to
their areas. Most content providers, such as blogs, Internet forums, and
microblogs, also automatically and/or manually screen posts before
letting them through.[29] Measures such as the registration and licensing
of Internet service providers and the real-name registration of users are
also preventive measures in that they enable the state to easily identify
violators and promote self-censorship. Similarly, in some cases, official
takeovers of campus forums by universities could be considered a preemptive action to avoid trouble for university authorities.

Online surveillance is carried out through automatic and manual
screening of the web to check for violators who have managed to elude
preventive measures. Most observers suspect that the state uses search
engine technologies to oversee online expression. Moreover, Internet
police forces, the propaganda system, and many other control agencies
employ inspectors to manually watch the web. Service providers and
universities also keep close watch on online expression and are ready
to remove any "inappropriate" content from sites under their supervision upon state notification or to preempt state intervention. State
surveillance is also supplemented by the illegal information reporting
system, which encourages peer monitoring.

Online crisis management has become routine for both central and local authorities.[30] Online crises are defined broadly here and include the discussion of any topics considered taboo, official scandals, mobilization for online or offline collective action, and any viral cyber-events that the state deems to be going out of control. To defuse crises, monitoring agencies send out directives via phone, email, or instant messenger to service providers, instructing them to take specific actions, such as deleting messages within a time limit, banning users, warning or fining violating websites, and shutting down parts of or entire websites either temporarily or permanently. Individual violators may be "invited to tea" (*bei hecha*, 被喝茶, which refers to the situations where netizens are informally detained and questioned by authorities as if it is a causal meeting for a cup of tea) or even jailed. Sometimes, massive campaigns are launched as part of the state's crisis management effort. For instance, after the Chongqing party chief, Bo Xilai, was removed from his post in early 2012, the Party-state shut down forty-two websites and detained six citizens for "fabricating and disseminating rumors" about Bo's allies in Beijing staging a coup.[31] Moreover, the two Chinese IT giants Sina and Tencent were punished by the state and forced to suspend the comment function of their microblog services for three days, from March 31 to April 3, to get rid of "harmful information."[32] In 2013, the state launched another massive anti-rumor campaign, primarily targeting social media platforms, including Sina Weibo. Many Internet opinion leaders were silenced or even jailed, including Charles Xue, an outspoken American-Chinese venture capitalist who had over twelve million Weibo followers. The campaign reportedly reduced the activity of Weibo opinion leaders by 40 percent compared to the previous year.[33]

Public opinion manipulation represents the state's more aggressive and smarter adaptation to the challenges of online expression. Instead of trying to prevent or remove undesired information, such measures allow the state to engage citizens, promulgate its preferred voices, and directly shape online discourse. For instance, the state regularly issues decrees to content providers such as news portals and forums about its propaganda initiatives.[34] It has also urged government agencies to set up e-government platforms,[35] promoted state media outlets online,[36] set up official accounts on popular social media sites,[37] and embraced creative propaganda tactics such as "ideotainment" (by juxtaposing official ideological constructs and popular cyber culture) and "astro-turfing" (by using the fifty-cent army to produce pro-government content under the guise of ordinary netizens).[38] Through these measures, the state turns online expression into a new frontline for state propaganda and actively promotes its preferred content in cyberspace.

CHALLENGES FROM OUTSIDE AND FROM WITHIN

The Chinese Party-state, as a powerful, well-structured, and quick-learning machine, has adapted its control regime to "harmonize" the Internet.[39] Some argue that it has thus far only reaped economic benefits without having a major political impact on authoritarian rule.[40] However, the difficulty of controlling online expression and the state's internal fragmentation have undermined the state censorship, making it at best quasi-successful. This section situates the Party-state as an internally divided organization within a complicated environment of high-volume anonymous online information exchange and explains how both external and internal challenges have resulted in the rigidity and arbitrariness of state censorship.

External Challenges to the Censorship Regime

The capacity of the state to calibrate "acceptable" expression is out of the question. Online expression challenges the Party-state in several additional ways. For example, the state must reduce an overwhelming amount of information to a manageable level, address the anonymity of online expression to track and punish violators, and operationalize its propaganda initiatives. These external challenges have conditioned the strategies of the state, forcing it to (1) "solidify" virtual space by embedding the Internet in existing institutions to make it less fluid and more accountable;[41] and (2) rely on automated tactics, blacklisting, and, more recently, whitelisting to reduce the volume of information it has to deal with.

The regime has attempted to embed virtual space into the physical world by making the web less anonymous and more accountable. It has pursued the real-name registration of Internet users while establishing a complex system of registration and licensing of service providers. Real-name registration directly targets anonymity. The state has more or less succeeded in controlling Internet cafés insofar as most now require customers to show their identification cards.[42] The real-name registration of cellphones has been partially successful, though SIM cards can be purchased from vendors who seldom check their customers' identities. The state's attempts to force netizens to register on forums, blogs, and microblogs have been met with greater resistance. Except for some campus forums in which student email addresses or identification numbers are required, most forums ask only for a valid email address to register an account. Given that campus forums have become a much smaller force in online expression since the Ministry of Education mandated them to re-form into campus-bound platforms in 2005, the impact of real-name registration has been more symbolic than significant.[43]

The state has also contracted censorship responsibilities to intermediary actors, including Internet service providers, Internet content providers, and research and educational institutions. Through measures such as registration and licensing, service providers and other relevant intermediary actors are held responsible for preventing unwanted information from appearing online. Large service providers, such as Sina and Sohu, have special offices for monitoring content.[44] For smaller websites, webmasters are directly held responsible, with local Internet monitoring agencies often requiring them to be accessible via cellphone around the clock.[45] Most campus forums are now under the direct supervision of university student affairs offices, Communist Youth League committees, or Party committees. Generally, these intermediary actors have considerable discretion to monitor routine online activities, but the state will occasionally intervene to patrol, issue directives, or punish offenders.

As intermediary actors usually have higher stakes than individual netizens, outsourcing censorship responsibilities to them helps reduce the state's workload and encourages self-censorship. For most netizens, the risk of engaging in taboo topics is having their posts deleted or accounts suspended. Such punishments are inconsequential. But for intermediary actors, allowing politically sensitive expression may result in large fines, administrative punishments, or even the loss of their businesses. However, the system that delegates responsibility is often ineffective or even counterproductive. It is ineffective largely because intermediary actors can often evade state control measures. Many small and medium-size forums have managed to bypass licensing and registration by moving overseas or by going through agents who do not authenticate information.[46] The system is also counterproductive at times because it introduces uncertainty and arbitrariness into the censorship system: Though intermediary actors may strictly follow state restrictions, they may also choose not to enforce them faithfully, either for commercial considerations or owing to personal inclinations. In particular, measures to hold intermediary actors accountable sometimes politicize them. This is the main reason that many small-scale website owners sided with Google when the company decided to withdraw from China in early 2010.

In addition to embedding cyberspace in existing institutions, China's Internet control also relies on blacklisting taboo topics and actors. The cybernetic model of organizational choice suggests that when facing great uncertainty, large-scale organizations tend to engage in a servo-mechanistic pattern of decision making; that is, they base their decisions on key indicators and react only when these indicators reach certain thresholds.[47] The high volume and extreme creativity of online expression have made the Internet an uncertain and complex environment for the Party-state. By monitoring a list of taboo words (*mingan ci*, 敏感词) and groups or individuals considered dangerous, the state simplifies its censorship task: It must react only when a taboo topic is detected or when a discussion of a dangerous topic reaches a certain level of intensity. This explains why state censorship often follows a significant burst of participation in a discussion of certain topics.[48]

The blacklisting strategy not only circumscribes the number of indicators the state must watch, but also facilitates automatic filtering. In addition to pornography, most taboos are political; that is, anything the regime deems threatening to its stability or damaging to its image, particularly events such as the 1989 Tiananmen Square democratic movement[49] and any online expression deemed to have the potential for collective mobilization.[50] For instance, the primary function of the Great Firewall is to prevent netizens from accessing blacklisted hostile websites or any webpages that contain forbidden keywords. If any of these sensitive words is detected, the system will not only interrupt the connection, but also reject any sequential attempts to access the server for at least a few minutes. Similarly, the Green Dam software, which the Ministry of Industry and Information Technology attempted, but failed, to have pre-installed on all personal computers in 2009, works by blacklisting keywords and web addresses, as netizens who hacked the software discovered.[51] Internet content providers use the same method to detect politically sensitive expression. Major forums, blog services, and microblog platforms all automatically filter postings that their users try to post. When sensitive words are found, the filtering system either directly rejects the posting, asks the user to modify it, or sends the post to a nonpublic board for manual review by moderators.

The blacklisting mechanism also applies to "dangerous groups or individuals," such as dissidents and online opinion leaders. State agents watch these groups and individuals closely to prevent them from publishing disturbing information online. For instance, Liu Xiaobo, a democratic activist and the 2010 Nobel Peace Prize laureate, was regularly put under house arrest and allowed only restricted telephone and Internet access during politically sensitive periods before he was jailed again in 2009 (after having been jailed several times from the late 1980s through the 1990s).[52] However, actions against high-profile dissidents often prove counterproductive by turning these individuals into iconic heroes internationally, as was the case with Ai Weiwei, the artist who was jailed in 2011 for his dissenting activities, including the investigation of school building collapses in the 2008 Sichuan earthquake (see chapter 4 for more discussion). The state's image is harmed even more among average netizens when the target is not quite political, as was the case when Gao Yaojie, a renowned and respected physician and AIDS activist, was placed under house arrest for weeks to prevent her from receiving an international award for her work in the United States.[53]

Blacklisting may effectively reduce the workload of state censorship but lacks the intelligence required to make contextualized judgments. At times, blacklisting also reveals the hand of the state and even backfires. The blacklisting system is triggered when and only when keywords are detected, which means any variants of the keyword can potentially circumvent the system. For instance, instead of typing "89" (referring to the 1989 Tiananmen Square democratic movement), netizens can insert an asterisk between the two characters ("8*9") to circumvent automatic filtering. (Similarly creative tactics employed by netizens to explore loopholes of state censorship will be discussed more systematically in chapter 4.) Worse than being ineffective, indiscriminate filtering often enrages and politicizes otherwise indifferent netizens. When text such as "in eight or nine cases out of ten" is denied because it contains "eight" and "nine," netizens previously unaware of or indifferent to censorship may start to complain or become curious about the blacklisted topic. Additionally, indiscriminate filtering also stifles pro-regime voices, as netizens supporting the regime also get censored. As a result, they may feel frustrated and start to see the irony of defending a regime that inhibits them from promoting their support.

The Party-state continually updates and refines its blacklist. But its adaptation often comes too late and fails to take into account nuanced and specific situations. For example, new taboo words are often added only once a threshold is reached, by which time the topic may have already been disseminated across the web, potentially reaching the mainstream media. The state's "harmonizing" efforts often only invite criticism and, in some cases, energize the topic by reframing it as an anti-repression story. More than that, state censorship directives typically disregard specific situations, often asking service providers to delete all postings on certain topics regardless of whether they are for the regime or not, or to post a unified official statement (*tonggao*, 通稿) from Xinhua News Agency, the official press agency of the People's Republic of China.[54] Such "one-size-fits-all" approaches have also been used in a series of regulation campaigns since 2005. In such campaigns, many small-scale websites were shut down as collateral casualties because the entire Internet data center that hosts their servers was taken offline due to improper content found on only a few websites.[55]

Internal Challenges to the Censorship Regime

As China scholars have long recognized, the Chinese authoritarian regime is not monolithic, but rather fragmented both vertically and horizontally.[56] If the uncertain and complex environment of the Internet poses external crises for the Party-state, fragmentation within the state constitutes internal challenges to the censorship system. Conflicting functions and interests, along with ideological discrepancies within the state, provide opportunities for online expression, and fragmentation allows for arbitrary censorship actions.

Above all, discrepancies of function and interest between state Internet governing bodies have led to competition and differing agendas. Aside from attempting to contain the Internet's disturbing effects, the Party-state has also been promoting information technology as an industry. Pursuing these sometimes-incompatible goals requires not only a control regime, but also a regulatory regime that regulates the IT industry according to market principles.[57] Compared to the ideology-driven propaganda system, the Ministry of Industry and Information Technology (formerly the Ministry of Information Industry) emphasizes the development of the sector and often does not favor restrictive policies. For instance, the China Internet Network Information Center, taking orders from the Ministry of Industry and Information Technology, was relatively unconcerned with domain name registration until China Central Television criticized it for "passively providing convenience for porn websites" during the 2009 anti-pornography campaign:[58]

> Prior to 2007, nobody cared about domain name or website registration. But now without registration, government agencies will shut down the website. It is undoubtedly a severe consequence. Since the online rectification campaign started, China Telecom[59] has shut down over one hundred thirty thousand unregistered websites, and there might be tens of thousands more accidental injuries.[60]

The pressure not only intensified the Ministry of Industry and Information Technology's efforts, but also forced it to adopt ham-fisted tactics: All small websites were temporarily shut down for close scrutiny, which the Ministry of Industry and Information Technology Minister Li Yizhong claimed was a necessary overcorrection.[61]

State censorship also provides rent-seeking opportunities for involved state agencies and officials. That is, censorship can be used for business purposes. For instance, a PR manager for a multinational corporation boasted the corporation's good relationship with the propaganda system, which he claimed was a more effective PR strategy than any other typical PR technique. Amidst a PR crisis following the voiding of promotional coupons, the company did not care what netizens said, because "whatever they complain about will be eliminated."[62] It is unclear *how* the propaganda system benefited from this process, but it is unlikely that it did everything for free. In fact, official reports have exposed several corruption cases associated with censorship. At the local level, an Internet police officer in Hainan Province allegedly took bribes from counterparts from other localities for removing negative publicity about them.[63] At a higher level, the former deputy director of the Fifth Bureau of the Cyberspace Administration of China and the International Communication Office, Gao Jianyun, was charged for deleting online postings in exchange for bribes.[64]

The political and economic benefits involved in censorship may drive state agencies to compete for regulatory and control power over the Internet.[65] For instance, the Ministry of Culture and the General Administration of Press and Publication have openly fought for the authority to pre-approve online games.[66] Similarly, some observers suspect that the onset of the anti-pornography campaign in 2009 was a result of the long rivalry between the Ministry of Industry and Information Technology and the State Administration of Radio, Film, and Television.[67] Such competition takes place not only among governmental agencies, but also between party and government bodies. Sources claim that the real-name registration of blogs was an effort by the Central Propaganda Department to wrest control over online information services from the State Council Information Office.[68]

State agencies may have different perceptions of risks and benefits. For instance, the Ministry of Education pushed for the real-name registration of campus forums and attempted to turn them into intra-university platforms in 2005. By isolating campus forums and making them less likely to take up hot social topics, the Ministry of Education attempted to limit its own responsibility in this area. But the Chinese Communist Youth League Central Committee showed interest in campus forums because it saw opportunities to expanding its regulatory reach. At the National Campus Bulletin Board System Managers Conference, the sponsoring Chinese Communist Youth League Central Committee subsidiary showed particular interest in establishing a self-disciplinary association and in promoting online ideological indoctrination, job searches, and entrepreneurship through campus forums. These goals are clearly safe for the Chinese Communist Youth League Central Committee since none threatens control over online expression—and achieving these goals would improve the performance evaluations of its officials, as doing so would demonstrate their competence.[69]

Ideological conflicts within the Party-state constitute an even more fundamental and deep-rooted threat to the coherence of the censorship system. Constant struggles, occurring most prominently among different factions during the 1989 democratic movement, illuminate the ideological divisions within the Chinese Communist Party. Many former Party-state officials have defected overseas[70] or departed greatly from Party discipline. They have started to call for constitutional rights, such as freedom of speech, the press, assembly, association, and demonstration.[71] Such ideological and factional struggles have now spilled over into cyberspace. For instance, when former Party chief of Chongqing Bo Xilai was removed in 2012, online debates erupted, with many netizens and several left-wing sites, such as Utopia (www.wyzxsx.com), boldly supporting Bo against the central leadership.[72] To quell such voices, the propaganda machine took a number of measures, including shutting down those online platforms. Such "targeted censorship" (*dingxiang shencha*, 定向审查) reveals that online expression and the censorship regime have become emblematic of political struggle within the Party-state.

Increasing ideological pluralization and increasing media commercialization have started to shake the base of the propaganda state. As Johan Lagerkvist has rightly noted, state agents and political leaders may "slowly begin to doubt the legitimacy and sustainability of the control and censorship regime,"[73] and media elites, reformist officials, and propaganda cadres may influence each other in ways that allow for a freer discursive space.[74] Some mainstream media outlets, such as *Southern Weekend* (*Nanfang Zhoumo*, 南方周末), are known as liberal strongholds, despite heavy-handed state control.[75] When supposed ideological strongholds of the propaganda system and mouthpieces of the Party-state are flawed, the control regime can hardly be as effective as the regime might hope.

Fragmentation exists not only across sectors but also across levels of the Party-state. As power to control the Internet is delegated, principal-agent problems emerge.[76] Being faithful in implementing censorship policies may not be a sensible choice for subordinates when it conflicts with other priorities. For instance, local legislators in Guangzhou worried about the impact of the excessively harsh registration of Internet cafés on public and small businesses.[77] This example helps explain the variation in content control across regions and even across websites.[78] Such a vertical divide provides opportunities for online expression but sometimes also induces more rigid and arbitrary censorship measures, as local agencies tend to showcase their competence or cover up negative publicity under the pressure of the cadre responsibility system.[79] This explains why local authorities have aggressively sought to eliminate "harmful" online information and suppress netizens daring to disclose local scandals heavy-handedly. For instance, a young man named Wang Shuai was detained in Shanghai simply for posting an online complaint about improper land grabs in his hometown of Lingbao County, Henan Province.[80] Such interprovincial pursuits of netizens (*kuasheng zhuibu*, 跨省追捕) demonstrate how far local governments can go.[81] The paramount concern of "stability maintenance" (*weiwen*, 维稳) efforts by local authorities is clearly not just to preserve the legitimacy of the regime, but to reduce trouble for local governments.[82]

CONCLUSION

According to the Chinese media expert David Bandurski, the state's primary means of control is the "fuzzy line" that does not clearly define acceptable and unacceptable content, and its control apparatus is built on "uncertainty and self-censorship, on creating this atmosphere of fear."[83] The analysis in this chapter suggests that the fuzziness of state censorship can be both intentional and unintentional. It can be intentional in that the strategy is indeed cost-effective and thus an optimal option for the state, and it can be unintentional because "fuzziness" can result from structural factors and the state's limited capacity to control. Indeed, China's Internet control regime has undergone a process of policy learning through which the state has gradually built up its institutional, organizational, administrative, and technical capacities to tame the Internet. However, the seemingly formidable content control regime still faces severe external and internal challenges, which create tensions in Internet censorship. On one hand, anonymous and creative online expression has forced the state to rely on servo-mechanistic surveillance techniques and to delegate censorship power to intermediary actors. Though these strategies may help reduce the workload of censoring agencies, they have also made the censorship regime overly rigid, arbitrary, and fuzzy, thus providing room for both intermediary actors and netizens to maneuver. On the other hand, internal fragmentation of the authoritarian state, particularly in terms of interest and value conflicts among state agencies, has introduced heterogeneity into the state censorship apparatus, producing opportunities for online expression in some cases and inducing harsher censorship in others.[84]

Internet content control is not only a process of state adaptation to digital challenges, but also a process of nonstate actors exploring the opportunities and limits of online expression. In particular, nonstate actors, such as various service providers and netizen groups, are continually reacting to the Party-state's censorship efforts. In this chapter, the role of these nonstate actors has been acknowledged, but not detailed. The following two chapters will examine how the governed, particularly forum managers and users, respond to state censorship.

3

TO COMPLY OR TO RESIST?

The Intermediaries' Dilemma

Despite the Party-state's increasing ability to control the flow of information in cyberspace, the high volume of online expression and the creativity of Internet users continue to overwhelm the state's capacity to do so effectively. One strategy to cope with the challenge has been to contract out censorship to intermediary actors. Besides state-sponsored campaigns and a few nationwide control measures such as the Great Firewall, it is intermediary actors, particularly Internet service providers and higher education institutions, who are responsible for enforcing routine surveillance and censorship in Chinese cyberspace. This chapter examines the crucial role of intermediary actors in censorship by focusing on how Internet content providers such as forums balance the demands of state control from above and netizens' challenges from below. It argues that many intermediary actors demonstrate a pattern of "discontented compliance": Although they are pervasively unhappy with state censorship, they comply with the regime because overt resistance is too costly. However, since compliance is often involuntary, intermediary actors have more than enough incentive to tolerate or even encourage boundary-spanning expression when it appears.[1] After all, state censorship is not only incompatible with the pro-liberal political values that many individual intermediary actors embrace, but it also increases the operational costs of service providers and places them in an environment of policy and market uncertainty. Moreover, from the perspective of service providers, boundary-spanning expression may be beneficial, because it often helps boost debates and attract online traffic, which in turn leads to greater profit.

INTERMEDIARY ACTORS IN CENSORSHIP

The role of intermediary actors in Chinese politics has long been recognized in the literature of Chinese politics. Scholars have critiqued the statist model that takes local cadres as the transmission belt of state policies,[2] and the Chinese Party-state has been depicted as "fragmented" by studies that have found increasingly pluralized policy implementation in the realms of both the political economy and contentious politics.[3] In his conceptualization of "fragmented authoritarianism 2.0," the political scientist Andrew Mertha further highlights how new policy entrepreneurs, such as marginalized officials, nongovernmental organizations, and policy activists, have started to influence the policy-making and policy-implementation process.[4] Despite their diverse topics, these studies all emphasize the agency of intermediary actors in the exercise of state power.

Intermediary actors such as Internet service and content providers are indispensable in China's Internet control system, as they are not only the primary information aggregators and distributors,[5] but they have also been formally delegated the responsibility of censoring online expression. As scholars and human rights observers have documented, Internet service and content providers have facilitated censorship by accommodating state censorship actions. In fact, all major Internet content provider firms in China, such as Baidu, Sina, and Tencent, have a track record of complying or even collaborating with the Party-state. Even multinational IT giants have chosen "just doing business"—which means cooperating with the Party-state—over "doing just business" in China.[6] For instance, Cisco Systems equipped China's Golden Shield Project, which later became the backbone of the Great Firewall.[7] Yahoo was heavily criticized for being complicit in the conviction of several Chinese dissidents by providing the state with account information.[8] Skype has allowed its modified Chinese version, TOM-Skype, to censor users' conversations with keywords.[9] Similarly, Microsoft has been known to censor its blog services in China.[10] Google, viewed by many as a positive example in the fight against censorship because of its withdrawal from China in 2010, has also cooperated with the regime, though perhaps unwillingly, by censoring search results before withdrawing from the country.[11]

Indeed, work done by intermediary actors is an increasingly important component of censorship.[12] As the Chinese political scientist Yonggang Li puts it,

> If the "core" of the "national firewall" is under the direct control of the state, its "periphery buffer zone" is then constructed by service providers and individual netizens. The self-censorship of these organizations and the self-discipline of netizens fence in or suppress information and opinion unapproved by the regime, thus constituting the first layer of preemption and filtering.[13]

Evidently, Li sees intermediary actors as the first "layer" of the Chinese censorship regime. However, the core-versus-periphery metaphor underemphasizes the role of intermediary actors who are pivotal to the censorship system in that, in most cases, they are the ones implementing state censorship directives, and their self-censorship efforts are much more pervasive than state censorship.[14] Put simply, the state controls the Internet through intermediary actors. Much of state censorship is not directly carried out by the state apparatus, but by various actors who provide online platforms for public expression, mostly just before or shortly after "offensive" content is detected by the state.

However, depicting intermediary actors as loyal accomplices of the state is misleading, especially considering that both market incentives and the individual motivations of many intermediary actors often counsel against censorship. For instance, Rebecca MacKinnon, an advocate for Internet freedom and the director of the Ranking

Digital Rights project at the New America Foundation, finds that Internet service providers enforce censorship differently owing to a number of factors such as a company's features, a company's owners, and the individual editors managing the portal.[15] But MacKinnon does not elaborate on *how* these factors have affected the implementation of censorship by those service providers. Similarly, the China scholar Johan Lagerkvist argues that IT businesses only conditionally comply with the Party-state's control policies owing to the principal–agent dilemma embedded in state regulation and social control.[16] Lagerkvist argues that Chinese information communication technology entrepreneurs are pulled "in different directions by consumerism, social interest, and state control" and that the Party-state has managed to control them only through the threat of sanctions and policy rewards.[17] Lagerkvist's analysis is of theoretical significance because it highlights the principal–agent problem in censorship enforcement, particularly in terms of the emerging cracks in state–capitalist cooperation—such cooperation has been depicted in the literature as an explanatory factor of authoritarian resilience.[18] However, his empirical evidence is somewhat limited because it relies primarily on one case, that of the Twitter-like microblog service Sina Weibo. Though the platform has served as a critical and popular arena for online expression since its introduction in 2009, it captures only one specific type of mechanism through which the state, intermediary actors, and netizens engage each other.

How do intermediary actors of various natures, purposes, and scales situate themselves within the censorship regime, and how do they perceive their own situation? How do market considerations and individual attitudes toward censorship affect intermediary actors' strategies when balancing the demands of the state and their users? This chapter explores these questions by examining the role of forum administrators in censorship, how faithfully they carry out censorship, and the considerations involved and tactics used to survive and develop their boards or forums. While my analysis generally aligns with the principal-agent model,[19] it further contextualizes interactions between the principal (i.e., the state) and specific agents (i.e., service providers of different scales, affiliations, and purposes).

SITUATING INTERNET FORUMS BETWEEN THE STATE AND NETIZENS

Intermediary actors such as service providers are "sandwiched" between the state and netizens. On one hand, they have been delegated censorship responsibilities by the state. For the authoritarian state, holding service providers and their administrators accountable is a much more cost-effective approach to controlling the Internet and online expression than directly monitoring legions of largely anonymous netizens. Intermediary actors are smaller in number, easier to track through registration and licensing, and have more at stake than anonymous netizens if they deviate from state directives. In addition, they often can respond to user deviance more quickly and effectively than the state, because they possess first hand user data (e.g., account information or IP address) and have tools to silence deviants (e.g., deleting posts, suspending user accounts, or banning IP addresses). Furthermore, forcing intermediary actors to carry out most censorship tasks establishes a scapegoat that diverts the blame for censorship away from the state itself.

On the other hand, from the users' perspective, intermediary actors such as Internet forums are both platform providers and either willing or unwilling accomplices of the state. As far as censorship is concerned, the Party-state is invisible to most users most of the time; forum administrators are the primary censors directly moderating online discussions, removing sensitive threads, and punishing deviants. However, though many netizens dislike censorship and complain about it, they also acknowledge that it is the service providers who make online expression and virtual life possible. As a result, many do not want to risk an entire platform's existence for the sake of a politically sensitive discussion. For instance, after the forced closure of the Ytht BBS, a campus forum established and run primarily by Beijing University students, some of its users blamed politically provocative users, complaining that not only were the political boards gone, but so too were apolitical ones, such as joke, picture, and sex boards, which were more popular among average netizens. Many users also feel obligated to censor themselves, especially when they are institutionally or emotionally tied to a platform, as is the case with most campus forums. For instance, the takeover of Bdwm by Peking University in early 2003 was justified by many users with the rhetoric of "true love for the BBS and the university."[20]

However, for intermediary actors, factors such as market incentives and administrators' personal motivations often run against state censorship.[21] Leading Internet entrepreneurs, including Tencent (QQ.com, QQ, and WeChat) founder and board chair, Ma Huateng, and the former CEO of Sina (Sina.com and Sina Weibo), Wang Zhidong, for example, have openly complained about excessive censorship.[22] Even when personal political orientations are put aside, these commercial service providers compete for users' attention in order to survive and prosper. However, the risk of state repression is real, with anecdotes of websites being shut down and daring forum managers being "invited to tea" serving as control parables to warn intermediary actors not to cross the red line (the boundary that separates the permissible and taboo zones).[23] Constant state pressure makes it sensible to comply, even for those who with liberal political orientations. As the founder of Kdnet Xiao Zengjian (alias Mu Mu) has explained,

> It is unrealistic not to go against our will. Compromise is necessary so far as we can push forward the construction of a political civilization. Even one millimeter forward is progress. If we do not compromise, even that one millimeter is not possible.[24]

Feeling trapped, most intermediary actors demonstrate a pattern of behavior that can be described as "discontented compliance." On one hand, they have chosen to cooperate with the state because they can hardly afford open revolts. On the other hand, since compliance is involuntary, they often engage in low-profile and, at times, more radical resistance. The analysis that follows focuses on forum managers' discontented compliance and explains why forums vary along the discontent–compliance spectrum.

Survival First: The Induced Compliance of Forum Administrators

Most forums have a realistic strategy that prioritizes survival. For example, the user agreement of NewSmth states that "the forum will take any conceivable means to prevent user activities that may threaten the survival of the forum."[25] Evidently, for most Internet forums, the "conceivable means" to ensure survival include implementing state censorship initiatives, enforcing self-censorship, and trying to win the trust of supervisory bodies.

The most basic acts of compliance include following censorship decrees and obeying laws and regulations that govern Internet services and online expression; adherence is especially strong when the state takes transgressions seriously. For instance, largely owing to the anti-pornography campaign of 2009, Internet content provider registration and licensing has become a big issue for small and medium-size forums, many of which simply ignored the state's registration and licensing requirement before the campaign.[26] As a result of the campaign, they had three options: register, shut down, or move abroad.[27] Similarly, the Ministry of Education's 2005 campaign to turn campus forums into internal communication platforms only forced many campus forums to limit registration to their students and to restrict off-campus access. Bdwm, the official BBS of Peking University, has since frequently restricted overseas or off-campus access. Even when the restriction is lifted occasionally, the popular and politically sensitive "Triangle" board has denied access to anonymous off-campus users and limited registered off-campus users (mostly alumni) to reading only, not allowing them to post. In response to the same campaign, the administrators of Tsinghua University's official BBS, Smth, had no choice but to move off campus to flee the jurisdiction of the Ministry of Education, becoming more commercialized and renaming the forum NewSmth. Moreover, the forum had to prohibit anonymous access to its most popular public discussion board, "NewExpress," in 2005, subsequently introducing a scoring system that would allow only veteran users to post beginning February 2006.[28]

Internet forums and other service providers are responsible for implementing state censorship directives. Large commercial portals, such as Sina.com, Sohu.com, and Tianya.cn, often have special divisions that connect with state agencies that communicate censorship requests to on-duty editors or board managers. Since the introduction of the Internet content provider registration and licensing system, the managers of small forums must provide their contact information to authorities so that they can respond to state requests at all hours. For campus forums, censorship orders are often routed through their home universities. For politically sensitive campus forums such as Bdwm and Smth, managers are often scheduled around the clock. To ensure a prompt response to censorship requests, university authorities sometimes demand administrative rights so that they can directly step in when managers are unavailable.

Beyond responding to censorship directives, service providers such as forums are expected to provide user data to the authorities upon request.[29] User agreements often explicitly stipulate that forum administrators may be required to release user data to state agencies. For instance, Tianya's user agreement states that the forum will release users' account information under any of the following conditions: (1) with prior authorization from the user; (2) according to relevant laws and regulations; (3) at the request of relevant government agencies; and (4) for the public interest.[30] If the second condition reflects the forum's legal obligation, the third demonstrates that it has no intention of protecting its users' privacy against any state agencies or agents. Similarly, NewSmth claims that it will deny any requests to check users' data except those from the government.[31]

As well as cooperating with state censorship, forums are delegated the responsibility of monitoring online expression on a routine basis to prevent "deviant" expression.[32] For most forums, this means strict self-censorship to avoid trouble with the state. This goal is achieved through a series of measures that deter, detect, and punish users who violate the rules.

Most forums have enacted specific regulations reiterating state prohibitions. Some forums have also drafted board-specific user guidelines that specify taboo topics and the subsequent punishments if users fail to follow the regulations. Such regulations often disclaim responsibility for user behavior and grant forum administrators the power to monitor user activity and take action they deem proper. Moreover, regulations encourage self-censorship among users by serving as constant reminders of what can and cannot be discussed.

Many forums pre-screen postings through an automatic system that identifies and denies any posts containing taboo words.[33] All large commercial forums have such a filtering system in place, though it is not clear whether they receive a keyword list from the state—existing evidence suggests they do not.[34] Campus forums and small individual forums have also gone to significant effort to establish their own automatic filtering systems. Indeed, at the 2010 Beijing National Campus Bulletin Board System Managers Conference, sponsored by the Chinese Communist Youth League Central Committee, campus BBS managers asked for a keyword list from the state so that they would not have to devise their own, but Committee officials shied away from the request. I have also witnessed administrators of small-scale forums exchanging keyword lists on forums and QQ groups. The very fact that service providers have to devise their own keyword lists not only confirms their indispensable role in the censorship system, but also provides a technical explanation for the variation in censorship enforcement.[35]

Forum managers also surveil published expression closely. Large commercial sites often hire special board or channel editors to weed out posts that are potentially in violation of state censorship regulations.[36] On campus forums, where board managers are usually selected from among a forum's users, popular political boards are frequently directly staffed by administrators close to supervisory bodies, such as university Communist Party committees or Chinese Communist Youth League branches. Small-scale, particularly individual-run, forums often lack sufficient technical and human resources to maintain constant surveillance on their users, and thus they sometimes simply avoid political topics altogether. Many small forums have decided to host only apolitical discussion boards to avoid potential trouble. This appears to be a rational choice because even for forums willing to take risks to attract traffic, which in turn generates revenue, political topics are much less cost-effective than other content such as soft porn, violence, and popular entertainment.

In addition to implementing state censorship initiatives and conducting self-censorship, intermediary actors sometimes seek to lower the risk of state sanctions by cultivating good relations with state agencies. Netizens believe that forums such as Kdnet and Tianya dare to exploit politically sensitive topics from time to time because of their close relationship with local propaganda departments. NewSmth provides another telling example. In early 2012, the forum featured notices and news from the local police branch on its welcome page, which were clearly posted in an effort to please the government and signal its connections with the state.[37] These examples echo what Lagerkvist has found with Century China—one of the most influential websites on which intellectuals congregate—which cooperated closely with the Party-state for financial resources and political connections.[38]

It is essential for every campus BBS to maintain good relations with its home university, not only to obtain financial and technical resources,[39] but also to earn some protection from state intervention, which is often routed through the university.[40] However, to gain trust, a campus BBS often must enforce strict self-censorship to assure the university that it will not cause trouble. Moreover, its managers often try to convince the university that a campus BBS will bring benefits such as enriching campus culture, facilitating dialogue with students, and enhancing the image of the institution.[41]

To demonstrate compliance and win trust from the state, forums sometimes even attempt to embed themselves further in the censorship regime. At both National Campus Bulletin Board System Managers Conferences I attended, a group of forum managers sought incorporation into the Communist Youth League system. They even circulated a proposal asking for specific censorship guidelines. They also promised strict self-regulation. Apparently, these forum managers were attempting to exchange autonomy for safety. Their hope, as one interviewee explained, was to "get some guidance from the state agency to avoid unintentional trespassing."[42]

Restrained Discontent: Management Resistance to Censorship

Though most intermediary actors have chosen to comply with state censorship in most cases, many of them do not genuinely support censorship. Admittedly, they cannot afford open revolt either because they need the service or support from the government or due to the threat of state sanctions.[43] However, they have expressed their discontent through a number of low-profile tactics, particularly grumbling, slacking, technical boycotting, managerial activism, and exit and resurrection.[44]

Almost all forum administrators I met expressed discontent toward the censorship system. Some criticized state censorship because of their pro-liberal stance. For instance, a Qiangguo Luntan editor I interviewed expressed his dissatisfaction toward censorship in a subtle way. Though he refused to talk about his work, he started criticizing Peking University for failing its motto of "freedom of thought, all-embracing attitude" (*jianrong bingbao* 兼容并包) once he learned that I had graduated from the institution. He argued that China's best time was between 1976 (the year of Mao's death) and 1989 (the year of the Tiananmen Square democratic movement) when "ideas interacted with the reality naturally and with passion," and today Chinese intellectuals lack independent personality, and thus are "either parasites or servants."[45]

Many forum managers have complained about being trapped between the state and netizens and blamed by both sides for things beyond their control: the state holds them responsible for netizens' deviance, while netizens blame them for censoring their expression. Even those who deem regulation somewhat necessary grumble about the arbitrariness, rigidity, and ambiguity of censorship measures. "We have to be extremely careful, or someday we will lose the platform."[46] Grumbling alone can hardly undermine the censorship regime. But it helps build solidarity among forum administrators and serves as a signal to both the state and netizens about the discontent of intermediary actors. Indeed, some forum administrators have even complained semi-openly online or to the state. For instance, at the 2009 National Campus Bulletin Board System Managers Conference in Suzhou, a forum manager complained that real-name registration was unnecessary because "truth is never afraid of debate," and "censorship leads only to distrust and facilitates the spread of rumors."[47]

Beyond grumbling, forum administrators have also demonstrated their discontent by enforcing censorship haphazardly; for example, by allowing boundary-spanning expression and delaying the implementation of censorship directives. Daring forum managers may turn a blind eye to boundary-spanning expression when the forum is not closely watched by the state. For example, when Xu Zhiyong, a civil rights activist and law professor at the Beijing University of Posts and Telecommunications, was jailed in July 2009, the topic was prohibited on Xu's home BBS and boards such as NewSmth's "NewExpress," which were supervised closely by the state. Yet, NewSmth's "Beijing University of Posts and Telecommunications" board allowed such discussion, largely because the apolitical alumni board was not a major surveillance target. Similarly, a few discussion threads on the 1989 Tiananmen Square democratic movement, a highly censored topic, appeared on NewSmth's "NetNovel" board in April 2016, and board managers simply ignored them for weeks.[48]

Lax forum administrators sometimes also delay the implementation of state censorship regulations. Many small forums and websites had ignored the Internet content provider registration and licensing policy until the state became serious about it. The policy was stipulated as early as 2000 in the State Council Information Office's *Administrative Measures on Internet Information Services*, but was only gradually implemented through a series of state campaigns. Its enforcement was first emphasized in 2004 when fourteen ministries and commissions launched a joint anti-pornography campaign.[49] Then, in 2007, another anti-pornography campaign forced the Ministry of Information Industry to enforce the policy more seriously.[50] The pressure was further intensified in the 2009 anti-pornography and anti–illegal information campaign.[51] Similarly, for a time, forum administrators pursued real-name registration only half-heartedly. The policy was dutifully implemented by some universities after the Ministry of Education's 2005 mandate to transform campus forums into internal communication platforms, but a manager of an unofficial campus BBS told me that some forum administrators never took the mandate seriously. Here is his clever justification: "We ask for a valid email address to register. That should be considered real-name registration since people are supposed to register their real names when signing up for an email account."[52]

Forum administrators sometimes even dare to delay enforcing specific censorship directives that come with deadlines. According to a large-scale commercial forum editor, upon receiving state directives to delete postings, her colleagues often would not act immediately but instead hold off until the last second. "For every additional second [the post exists], thousands more netizens can read it," she explained.[53]

Sometimes forums establish technical barriers to make state censorship less efficient or effective. As they have been delegated responsibility for routine surveillance, forums are under constant state attention to ensure their compliance: State monitoring agencies screen forum activities manually and use keyword filtering technology similar to that of search engines. Manual monitoring is hard to avoid, but forums can fool scanning software with simple technical barriers. For instance, one reason NewSmth prevents anonymous access to its "NewExpress" may be to prevent censoring software from scanning posts. Some forums recruit new users on an invitation-only basis, thus fending off state monitoring more effectively. A good example is 1984BBS (1984bbs.com). Known for its pro-liberal and anti-censorship stance, this BBS recruited new users only through invitations distributed by existing users and had more than ten thousand registered users before its forced closure in 2010.[54]

Forum administrators may even promote discussion on boundary-spanning topics such as local scandals. For instance, on June 11, 2012, a netizen started a thread on Huashang Forum accusing local family planning officials in Ankang, Shanxi Province, of coercing a woman into an abortion in her seventh month of pregnancy.[55] The topic soon gained momentum online, leading to an investigation and punishment of the involved cadres. Forum administrators played an important yet under-recognized role: Instead of deleting the thread, they highlighted it nine minutes after its appearance and pinned it to the top of the forum webpage five days later (figure 3.1). Surely not all forum managers would be willing to take such risks, nor is the strategy feasible for all topics. But this case shows how forum managers can facilitate boundary-spanning protest by Chinese netizens.

In addition to tolerating or promoting boundary-spanning online activism, intermediary actors may themselves stage protests against state censorship and authoritarian rule in general. For instance, though forum administrators generally avoid open confrontation with

FIGURE 3.1 Forum management promoting disclosure of a scandal

Notes: "Canjue Renhuan! 7 Ge Yue de Taier bei Qiangzhi Yinchan, Haizi Shiti jiu Fangzai Mama Shenbian" (Such a Tragedy! A 7-Month Baby Aborted by Force and the Dead Body Placed Right Next to Her Mom) http://bbs.hsw.cn/read-htm-tid-3697258.html, retrieved Sept, 25, 2012. The text box above the post content shows the operations of forum administrators. One administrator highlighted the posting on June 11, 2012, and another administrator pinned the thread to the top of the forum on June 16, 2012.

the state, they may choose to engage in online activism when state repression jeopardizes the survival of the platform. For instance, many forum and board managers of Bdwm resigned when Peking University officially took over the forum in early 2003. Many board managers also protested by banning the president's official account, PKU, on their boards.[56] The struggle between administrators of Smth BBS (which later moved off campus and became NewSmth) and Tsinghua University authorities during the 2005 Ministry of Education campaign to constrain campus forums was no less dramatic. Many managers resigned, and hundreds of them posted protest messages or sabotaged the forum by deleting all threads on their boards or posting random content such as lists of prime numbers. More importantly, a few top administrators fought hard to "steal" user data, which were stored on university-owned servers, and they succeeded, allowing them to establish NewSmth.[57]

Exit and resurrection can also be viewed as a way to counter state censorship and demonstrate discontent. Forums may take the exit option for business purposes. Many small apolitical forums exit to avoid arbitrary censorship, which can disrupt their services and destroy their hard-earned user bases, as users tend never to return if a forum goes offline, even for just a few days. Outbursts of such exodus occurred when the state tightened up licensing and registration, as well as following Google's withdrawal. This is similar to Albert Hirschman's conception of exit; that is, withdrawal from a relationship.[58] Forums may also exit involuntarily when forced to shut down by the state. In these cases, their user data and reputation may sometimes be carried forward by former administrators and loyal users. For instance, during the 2005 Ministry of Education campaign, a few administrators of the Nanjing University BBS, Lily, the second-largest campus BBS at the time, refused to cooperate with the university, instead re-establishing itself under the name "Wild Lily."[59] In fact, the largest overseas Chinese forum, Mitbbs, is a successor of earlier Peking University and Chinese Academy of Sciences BBS sites that were shut down by the state. Ytht, then the largest campus BBS provides an even better example. After it was shut down in 2004, at least three forums claimed to be its successors.[60] A Peking University graduate inspired by Ytht's free spirit also attempted to re-create a new Ytht from scratch. His insistence on including "ytht" in the domain name and forum name caused him a lot of trouble, as it was considered a challenge to the regime. He was frequently "invited to tea" and forced to shut down the site during sensitive periods even though it had attracted only a few dozen users.

UNDERSTANDING VARIATION ALONG THE DISCONTENT–COMPLIANCE SPECTRUM

If intermediary actors such as forums demonstrate both compliance and discontent, then what accounts for their variation along the discontent–compliance spectrum? How do forum administrators "gauge the limit" (*bawo chidu*, 把握尺度) of expression they will allow and balance the requirements of the state with the desires of netizens? Close

TABLE 3.1 Categorization of Forums and Their Bargaining Options

	State-Run	Commercial/ For-Profit		Campus Forum	
		Large	Small	Official	Unofficial
Examples	Qiangguo Luntan	Kdnet, Sina, Sohu, Tianya	Many	Bdwm, Lily, Smth	NewSmth, Ytht
Affiliations	State media	Large businesses	None	Colleges and universities	None
Primary Purpose	Political	Profit	Profit	Non-profit	Non-profit or Profit
Risk of Shutdown	Low	Low	High	Medium	High
Bargaining Power	Strong	Strong	Weak	Strong	Weak
Options and Strategies	Avoid taboos	Boundary-spanning	Avoid politics	Boundary-spanning	Avoid politics or boundary-spanning

examination suggests that in addition to individual factors, the primary purpose, affiliation, and scale of a site often influence the ability and will of forum administrators to bargain with the state and with users. Table 3.1 categorizes forums sampled in this study into five groups based on their purpose, affiliation, and scale and assesses their bargaining power and options in content control.

For forums run by state media outlets, the primary concern is political correctness, which results in strict monitoring measures. Take Qiangguo Luntan as an example. The forum attracts thousands of users, and its topics are mostly political. Postings go through software filtering and manual scrutiny by editors before being published. And, unlike most forums that run twenty-four hours a day, the forum used to close down between 10:00 PM and 10:00 AM before its upgrade in July 2012.[61] When it is open, there is at least one editor on duty (*zhiban*, 值班) monitoring the discussions. My interaction with one of Qiangguo Luntan's editors demonstrated that the editors are politically alert. Once I had briefed him about the purpose of my research project, he refused to talk about his job, even though his opinions on other topics betrayed a pro-liberal stance.[62]

Though strictly monitored, Qiangguo Luntan still allows various and sometimes critical voices. There are two possible reasons. On one hand, the forum's affiliation with the state might have provided its managers knowledge about where boundaries lie, thus reducing the uncertainty of state censorship faced by other types of forums. On the other hand, as Gary King, Jennifer Pan, and Molly Roberts have suggested, the censorship regime may aim more at curtailing collective action than silencing general criticism of state leaders or policies.[63] Discussion on Qiangguo Luntan is indeed more in line with abstract ideological debate than conversations that might spur collective mobilization.

Large commercial sites rely on users to generate profit. Though the stakes may seem to be higher than for smaller forums if they are forced to shut down, the risk is actually smaller because large commercial websites also have stronger bargaining power vis-à-vis the state: They represent the high-tech industry, which the state supports, and often enjoy better connections with the state.[64] Moreover, the popularity of these sites also forces the Party-state to think twice when considering whether to shut them down, because doing so would affect millions of apolitical users who access the platforms for mundane purposes.[65] As a result, for the largest platforms, such as Sina (Sina.com and Weibo), Tencent (QQ.com and WeChat), and Tianya, the possibility of being shut down is hardly imaginable; fines, reprimands, and punishments for responsible personnel are more likely repercussions. For instance, according to an internal official propaganda circulation, Tencent's QQ.com, one of the largest portals, was severely reprimanded in early 2009 because it produced several critical reports under its own brand and allowed some harsh news comments to be posted.[66] Yet, nothing more serious happened to the online portal. In short, though large commercial sites still keep away from forbidden zones, their business interests—and the pro-liberal values of their leaders and administrators—have often incentivized them to tolerate, or even encourage boundary-spanning expression. According to Yawei Liu of the Carter Center, Tencent deployed a "promotion-and-protection strategy" toward politically sensitive celebrities like himself on its microblog platform. Though he is a verified user, Tencent would temporarily remove his verification whenever he had posted something sensitive. This is an indirect way of protecting Liu because Tencent can plausibly claim to have no knowledge of his identity if the state were to attempt to trace him.[67]

Small for-profit forums, many of which are run by individuals, not only lack scale or strong affiliations with institutions or big businesses to bargain with the state, but also have smaller and weaker user bases than large forums or even campus forums. As a result, they are much more vulnerable to both policy and market turbulence. To avoid risk, small forums discourage political discussion and sometimes host only apolitical boards. They also tend to impose stricter self-censorship to play it safe. For instance, when the state attempted to crack down on rumors centering on the ousted Chongqing Party secretary, Bo Xilai, in early 2012, small forums increased their self-censorship. Consenz, the company that developed the popular platform software Discuz! used by many small-scale forums, added a special search function allowing administrators to more effectively target sensitive information and monitor user activities, which managers welcomed. The following comment reveals the rationale of such small-forum managers: "It is an unusual time, and we need to take it seriously! Where there is life, there is hope!" (*Liude qingshan zai, bupa meichai shao;* 留得青山在, 不怕没柴烧).[68]

Nonetheless, administrators of small-scale forums are not always apolitical. An online survey conducted by a forum popular among forum administrators found that the overwhelming majority of them sympathized with Google when the company chose to withdraw from China.[69] Further, many small forums moved their sites abroad to avoid state intervention, which can easily ruin a fragile business. After all, small-scale forums have little bargaining power with the state and can hardly afford more radical or open actions. In fact, even when they take risks to attract an audience, they often do so with violent or sexual content rather than political topics. The state shows more tolerance toward violent and soft erotic content as long as administrators keep a low profile and clean up their sites when campaigns come along.

Unlike early BBSs run by students, most official campus forums today are supported and controlled by their home universities. The official status has a twofold implication: On one hand, official status means that the forums will receive technical, financial, and even administrative support from their universities;[70] on the other hand, official status also comes with the cost of bringing the forums under the close supervision of university Party committees, Communist Youth League branches, and student affairs offices. Moreover, students serving as administrators of the forum and sensitive discussion boards are often co-opted by university authorities with stipends, promotion opportunities as student cadres, or even scholarships.[71] As a result, the degree of freedom campus forums enjoy hinges on their relationship with the university and the tacit understanding that it is best to avoid political risk, especially following the 2005 Ministry of Education campaign to restrict off-campus access. This struggle against the Ministry of Education was the last major wave of activism against censorship among most campus forums.

Unofficial campus forums often serve mixed purposes. Many such forums are established by interested students to serve their class-mates, and profit is not their priority. Yet, these forums still have to raise funds to sustain themselves and expand.[72] Many unofficial forums have become increasingly similar to small for-profit forums, as their founders treat their projects as a business endeavor. Without official affiliation, these forums enjoy no protection from universities. Their small user bases and limited resources also mean that they have little bargaining power vis-à-vis the state. As a result, these forums cannot afford politically sensitive discussion that may lead to repercussions. However, since their users are mostly students, unofficial campus forums sometimes allow freer and more daring expression when idealistic students dominate. This was especially the case in the earlier years of the BBS era when it was not a business model, as the cases of Ytht and NewYtht demonstrate.[73]

Evidently, affiliation, scale, and the primary purpose of an online platform influence its will and capacity to negotiate with the state, which in turn shape its strategies. Affiliating with the state, large businesses and universities often impose constraints on forums, but also provide advantages such as protection from state censorship or market turbulence.[74] Forums attached to state media outlets are monitored most closely and do not have to appeal to users as much as commercial forums do. They are unlikely to push the boundaries of online expression. However, since they have better ideas about where the red line lies, they are also likely to tolerate certain types of political expression. Large commercial forums are subject to market incentives, rendering them naturally averse to state control that hinders them to meet the market demand for timely and interesting information.[75] Their strong user bases—particularly compared to those of small-scale forums—and links to big businesses also add to their leverage when bargaining with the state. All these factors make them more likely to tolerate boundary-spanning activities even though they are closely watched by the state. The state uses both "carrots" and "sticks" to ensure their compliance.[76] Official campus forums are often controlled by a university supervisory apparatus, but enjoy stable user bases as well as financial, technical, and administrative support from their home institutions. As a result, they can allow boundary-spanning expression as long as it does not upset their supervisors.

The size of an online platform affects its bargaining power with both the state and users in a more straightforward way than affiliations. In general, larger online platforms are better able to bargain with the state, because (1) there will be a bigger impact if the state attempts to shut them down, and (2) they have more financial and social resources that can be mobilized either to cultivate stronger ties with the state or to stage protests. For instance, the state is unlikely to completely shut down giant commercial sites such as Sina Weibo and Tianya.[77] But it can be bold enough to terminate popular forums such as Ytht, which has a smaller user base compared to the commercial sites mentioned earlier but is quite political. Further, for all the criticism that followed the closure of Ytht, tens of thousands of smaller forums have died almost silently. For instance, in the 2009 anti-pornography campaign alone, more than one hundred thirty thousand small-scale websites were shut down, many of which were simply "collateral casualties." In the eyes of the Ministry of Industry and Information Technology minister, Li Yizhong, the loss of these websites was merely a result of a "necessary over-correction."[78]

If scale and affiliation are the primary factors affecting an online platform's capacity to bargain with the state, an online platform's mission shapes the strategies available to administrators. Forums run by state mouthpieces care less about profit than political risk, which explains why Qiangguo Luntan used to close down between 10:00 PM and 10:00 AM. Campus forums, both official and unofficial, are often geared toward serving the students; thus, their purposes are shaped by their users as well as by university authorities. Large commercial forums are in a market that competes for user traffic and user attention; therefore, they are willing to allow limited boundary-spanning expression. Small for-profit forums that are vulnerable to state and market turbulence try hard to attract audiences while avoiding political expression. Even overseas forums, which have not yet been discussed, may choose to compromise with the state if they attempt to attract an audience in China. For instance, Mitbbs established a "cleaner" mirror site—mitbbs.cn—hoping to gain access to the domestic Chinese market. Even the pro-regime Ccthere, a United States–based forum, worked to depoliticize itself by directing political topics, particularly ones related to domestic Chinese politics, to a new site to avoid being blocked by the Great Firewall.[79]

CONCLUSION

This chapter examines how online information service providers, particularly Internet forums, have tried to situate themselves between state censorship and popular demand for free expression. Under the constant threat of state repression, Internet forums and their operators often choose to comply with the state. But many also demonstrate a degree of discontent. After all, state censorship is not only at odds with the political orientations of pro-liberal forum administrators, but also disturbs the operation of forums by imposing on them the cost of enforcing censorship and by increasing the policy and market uncertainty forums face. Owing to the diversity and large number of Internet forums, this chapter's analysis does not address the full spectrum of online platforms.[80] Nor does it examine every aspect of forum governance or disaggregate the individuals who make up the management group. But it is evident that affiliation, scale, and the purpose of a forum all affect a forum's mode of interaction with the authoritarian state, netizens, and the market.

As Daniela Stockmann has argued, the Party-state's control over traditional media is built on an institutional framework through which the state exerts "control over the organization, personnel decisions, and the editorial process."[81] By delegating censorship responsibility to intermediary actors, the Party-state has established an institutional framework that is similar to but also distinct from that governing the traditional media, one that enhances its control over the Internet. In this way, the Party-state attempts to bring Internet control back into a realm in which it has rich experience, strong capacity, and abundant resources. However, as this chapter has shown, state control over intermediary actors has been implemented inconsistently, because the intermediary actors situate themselves differently vis-à-vis the Party-state. These intermediary actors thus have opted for a variety of strategies to balance the need for state censorship with the demands of netizens.

The Party-state and intermediary actors are not the only players in the struggle over control of online expression, however. After all, netizens are the ultimate targets of state censorship, both as consumers and producers. With the stage set by the state and forum management, how do Chinese netizens pursue their virtual experience? In particular, how do they react to the censorship regime, given their pluralized interests and motivations? Chapter 4 completes the picture of the censorship game in China by focusing on popular activism by Chinese netizens.

4

POP ACTIVISM

Playful Netizens in Cyberpolitics

Weapons are an important factor in war, but not the decisive factor; it is people, not things, that are decisive. The contest of strength is not only a contest of military and economic power, but also a contest of human power and morale. Military and economic power is necessarily wielded by people.[1]

—MAO TSE TUNG, IN "ON PROTRACTED WAR"

C hinese cyberspace is highly contested given the Internet's empowering effects and the state's efforts to control it.[2] Accordingly, scholars often study online expression from the perspective of digital contention. However, such a perspective downplays the richness of online activism and inappropriately conceptualizes netizen activism within a liberalization–control framework. After all, Chinese cyberspace is pluralized, with the state, its critics, and various citizen groups promulgating distinct beliefs, values, and identities online on daily basis. How, then, do these actors interact with each to shape online expression? How do average netizens, who access the Internet for a variety of reasons, see and react to efforts by the state and other actors to shape online discourse? What are the underlying dynamics that influence the format and content of political expression?

This chapter explores these questions by examining how online expression in China has blurred the boundaries between politics and cyber-culture, resulting in a new form of communicative activism that fuses political content with innovative tactics of expression. Such "pop activism" has three defining features. First, it relies heavily on the creative use of linguistic, performance, and media tools to consume politics. Such expressive tools, however, serve both as a means and an end in themselves—while they are used to convey political messages, they also transform political topics into cultural and entertainment subjects. Second, pop activism is "pop" in that both political content and its expressive instruments are socially constructed through a dynamic process of online interaction among many actors, including the state, regime critics, and various netizen groups. The diversity, creativity, and spontaneity of these actors have rendered online politics and cyber-culture highly fuzzy and highly fluid. Third, pop activism simultaneously represents the pluralization of content and the convergence of format in online expression—while different actors pursue drastically different agendas, they all embrace similar tools for popular expression. Thus, pop activism not only works as a weapon to fuel social activism, but may also enable actors to pursue other political or apolitical goals.

The definition of pop activism centers on a shared formality—the fusion of popular culture and politics—while treating actors' motivations as secondary. In this way, it avoids reducing culture to a political instrument and highlights the mutual transformation of cyber-culture and politics, particularly how the former prescribes both the forms and the substance of the latter. Empirically, such a perspective accommodates a broader spectrum of activities by various actors, and enables a more balanced and accurate assessment of the Internet's impact on Chinese politics. In particular, the concept appreciates the role of ordinary netizens as the main producers, distributors, and consumers of online content, whose diverse beliefs, values, and identities are likely to result in pluralized discourses rather a dichotomous state–society struggle. Indeed, as this chapter shows, pop activism serves as more than a tool of contention for dissidents and resentful citizens. It is driven by dynamics of state control and anti-control, the discourse competition between various online groups (including both pro- and anti-regime groups), as well as netizens' pursuit of fun. Thus, rather than dismissing playful expression as apolitical or interpreting it merely as a form of digital contention, pop activism highlights the fluidity and fuzziness of cyberpolitics. It acknowledges that while playfulness may help people evade state censorship and provide momentum for regime-challenging expression, it may also dilute the political message it carries, thus turning online expression into a purely entertaining experience, or be used to popularize pro-regime voices.

THE CULTURE AND POLITICS OF ONLINE EXPRESSION

According to the sociologist Guobin Yang, "online activism is par excellence activism by cultural means," as "it mobilizes collective action by producing and disseminating symbols, imagery, rhetoric, and sounds."[3] Though evaluating online expression from only a digital-contention perspective is constraining, Yang's point is important in that it recognizes the cultural aspect of online politics. Evidently, culture and politics are indispensable in online expression.[4] Many studies have explored the relationship between political culture and democracy and how changes in political culture or mass culture may affect democracies.[5] Others see culture as an instrument in contentious politics. The social movements expert Sidney Tarrow, for instance, identifies culturalism as a major paradigm explaining social movements, which helps shift the focus from structural explanations to the "framing" of collective action.[6] In his synthesis, culture plays a central role in shaping "repertoires of contention," mobilization consensus, and movement identities. More recent studies have focused on the impact of specific sources of popular culture on protest. For instance, Nan Enstad has explored how dime novels and films motivated working women to engage in political activism in the late nineteenth and early twentieth centuries.[7] Rob Rosenthal and Richard Flacks, taking a structural interactionist approach, have shown how music as a social product helps protesters envision an alternative society, crystalize movement identity, recruit activists and maintain the loyalty of long-term members, and articulate movement goals.[8] China scholars have studied the culture-politics relationship from similar perspectives. Some conduct surveys to measure Chinese citizens' political beliefs, values, and identities to explore the potential implications for China's system of authoritarian rule and the country's prospects for democratization.[9] Others examine contention cultures, centering their analysis on rituals, performances, and rhetoric in popular protests.[10] Though these studies have diverse focuses, they are informative in similar ways, especially in terms of showing how culture may inform and shape political processes.

But depicting culture merely as an instrument for achieving political goals is inappropriate because culture itself is a social product. This point is worth highlighting because the Internet has enabled both state and social actors to experience culture and politics in fundamentally different ways than before. Ordinary citizens who had previously been largely passive recipients of cultural and political influences are now connected and thus more actively engaged in the production, distribution, and consumption of cultural and political constructs in a nonhierarchical, networked fashion. As a result, one may argue that what constitutes "culture" and "politics" is increasingly based less on the "inherent qualities of a particular genre, medium, or topic" and more on how they are socially constructed.[11] This perspective, while seemingly apparent, has not been sufficiently incorporated in current studies on cyberpolitics in China.

Indeed, scholars tend to examine the struggle over online expression from a digital-contention perspective that instrumentalizes cyber-culture as a means of protest. There seems to be an unquestioned assumption that citizens are engaging in online expression primarily to express discontent, lodge complaints, and challenge authoritarian rule. This perspective is further confirmed by studies on the Chinese state's efforts to control online expression.[12] In particular, many scholars are often amazed by netizens' creativity, artfulness, and playfulness, which are interpreted as necessary to evade and resist state control. For instance, a great deal of online expression has been brought under scrutiny as different forms of artful contention or "digital hidden transcripts," ranging from creative counter-censorship tactics to spoofing (*e'gao*), and from dissident-driven spectacles to spontaneous criticisms of the regime.[13] Such innovative expressional tactics, as Guobin Yang puts it, reveal the change in style of contention from the pre–Internet age's epic style, which featured "soaring apparitions and death-defying resoluteness to attain noble ideals," to the rise of "more prosaic and playful styles" characteristic of online activism.[14] By making sense of such light, playful, and low-profile digital contention, such studies go beyond understanding politics as merely direct contests for state power[15] and challenge the viewpoint that the majority of China's Internet population is politically irrelevant.

However, some scholars are skeptical of this digital-contention perspective, which focuses on confrontation between the state and society. For Jens Damm, focusing exclusively on state control versus social resistance ignores the increase in urban consumerism in China, which is rendering Chinese cyberspace fragmented and localized.[16] After all, in general, Chinese netizens are not politically driven, and the overwhelming majority of online expression tends to focus on issues of private life and personal experiences. In fact, according to James Leibold, "the Chinese-language blogosphere is producing the same sort of shallow infotainment, pernicious misinformation, and interest-based ghettos that it creates elsewhere in the world."[17] More recent studies, such as one by Min Jiang, have found that uncivil discourse and behaviors coexist with civil activities online, demonstrating a co-evolution of the Internet, an "uncivil" society, and authoritarianism.[18] These studies not only suggest that seeing online expression as digital contention may lead to an overestimation of the Internet's potential for political change and civic activism, but also imply that popular culture may depoliticize online expression or neutralize its impact on authoritarian rule.

It is clearly inappropriate to assume that netizens are apolitical simply because they play online.[19] After all, online struggles "are diffuse, fluid, guerilla-like, both organized and unorganized, and networked both internally and externally, online with offline."[20] However, assuming online activism to be subversive has its limitations in that creative and artful expression is often reduced to being viewed only as a means of resistance. Even when there is no direct linkage to censorship or state repression, online expression is often interpreted as a "venting machine" or a "weapon of the weak," implying that netizens adopt innovative expressional tactics only to defend the discursive space against state intrusion.[21] In this regard, the skeptics have a valid point about the risk of overestimating the significance of online expression.

The literature suggests conflicting views on the political implications of online expression in China. Are scholars reading too much into online activism by taking a digital-contention perspective? Should we dismiss online activism because the majority of netizens are not politically driven most of the time? This chapter attempts to bridge these seemingly incompatible possibilities and decipher the politics and culture of online expression from a perspective that emphasizes both formality and content. It reveals that the dynamics of state control, discourse competition, and netizens' pursuit of fun have driven the fusion and mutual transformation of politics and cyber-culture in online expression, contributing to the rise of pop activism. This form of communicative activism consists of several reciprocal, intertwined, and interactive processes. First, by embedding digital contention in popular cyber-culture, pop activism helps regime critics evade state censorship and protest themselves against the authoritarian regime.[22] Second, pop activism serves as a shared tool for political actors—regime critics, the state and its supporters, as well as ordinary netizens—to promulgate their preferred discourses. Its popularity and appeal are particularly crucial in this discourse competition because netizens' attention is a scarce resource on the information-rich Internet. Third, since not all netizens are politically motivated, pop activism often serves the function of turning political topics into a special type of consumer good for the purpose of entertainment. In this way, politics becomes an organic component of popular cyber-culture. By analyzing these interrelated processes, the chapter highlights that politics and culture are so fluid and fuzzy in Chinese cyberspace that we should neither dismiss online expression as apolitical, nor view formats of creative expression merely as digital hidden transcripts.

The fusion of politics and popular culture is not a new phenomenon. But pop activism is worth noting because it is genuinely popularly produced, distributed, and consumed thanks to the interactive, open, and participatory nature of online communication. Moreover, in the online environment, the processes of production, distribution, and consumption may unwind simultaneously in an interconnected manner, thus enabling a shared popular cyber-culture and context-specific practices, values, and identities. As a result, any attempt to develop a simplified monolithic view of cyber-culture or cyberpolitics is destined to be futile. The following sections will discuss how pop activism functions as an effective weapon against state censorship and why online expression should be understood in a broader sense, as a process through which political content is produced, distributed, and consumed for various purposes.

POP ACTIVISM AS DIGITAL CONTENTION

Guerrilla Warfare Against Censorship

Though taking many different forms, much online activism is driven by the necessity of combating censorship. Facing the world's most sophisticated censorship system,[23] dissidents and resentful netizens have been fighting a guerrilla war with the authoritarian state at unexpected times, on unexpected platforms, and in unexpected ways. Chinese netizens have creatively exploited the weakness of state censorship. Netizens' ultimate strategy to evade censorship is to "exit" by going beyond the Great Firewall. Circumventing the Great Firewall—"wall-climbing" (fanqiang, 翻墙) as it is called by netizens—has been a routine practice for many. Using proxy servers, penetrating software, and virtual private network (VPN) services, they are able to access sites blocked by the Party-state.

Netizens have also learned about and exploited the loopholes in the operation of censorship. Though automatic filtering systems often run around the clock, the intensity of manual surveillance varies at different times of the day.[24] For instance, NewSmth users have noticed that around midnight is a good time to discuss boundary-spanning topics because manual surveillance by forum managers is often weak then, allowing sensitive topics to survive long enough to be discussed.[25]

Another strategy is to discuss politically sensitive topics on forums or discussion boards that attract little surveillance. Large forums that focus on public affairs are typically watched more closely by the state and forum management. Yet, politically sensitive discussions emerge frequently on forums or boards that are thematically apolitical. For instance, when the civil rights activist and law professor Xu Zhiyong was jailed in July 2009, discussion of him was heavily censored on the BBS of his home institution, Beijing University of Posts and Telecommunications, and other popular boards such as NewSmth's "NewExpress." But one thread on "BUPT@NewSmth," a Beijing University of Posts and Telecommunications alumni board that attracts less traffic, survived for days.[26]

Netizens also take advantage of forum functions to reduce the risk of being censored. For instance, many forums allow users to edit their own posts. Thus, one can post a perfectly innocuous post and then later edit it to add more sensitive content.[27] Baidu Tieba users have turned a similar strategy into an everyday practice. Many start a thread with the first post containing only "Baidu on the first floor" (*yilou baidu*, 一楼百度) or "First floor to Lady Baidu" (*yilou xiangei duniang*, 一楼献给度娘). They do so because the first post of a thread is the most heavily censored, and the whole thread may therefore be deleted if the first post is not verified by the system.[28]

The censorship system hinges on numerous keywords. As a result, one central task for netizens engaging in political activism is to fight against and circumvent these keywords. Adding an asterisk or some other symbol within taboo words is the most common and simple way to circumvent keyword filtering. In some cases, random symbols are used to replace the taboo word, leaving audiences to guess the meaning based on the context.[29] Netizens have also found that reformatting text,[30] converting text from an HTML or TXT format into a picture format may be effective because censorship software cannot search for keywords in picture files.

Expressive Resistance to Censorship

If the coping tactics described so far may be considered largely passive, silent, and defensive, netizens' expressive activism may be considered to present a more aggressive challenge, partly because it is more visible and thus "public." Such expressive tactics imply a new type of "digital hidden transcript"—embodied in the creative use of language codes, narrative genres, and multiple performative forms and media formats—that relies less on invisibility and more on a shared cyber-culture to fend off state censorship. It is in this realm that netizens' creativity is fully displayed. In addition to mocking official discourse, language codes, and propaganda rituals, they have developed an entirely new cyber-language to circumvent censorship and protest the regime.

First, netizens have used official discourse as a means of challenging state censorship. For instance, after Premier Wen Jiabao's statement about the government should create "favorable conditions for the people to criticize the government," his words were frequently cited online by netizens, but those posts were subsequently deleted.[31] An even more interesting case occurred after the official takeover of Smth, in which many users quoted Chairman Mao's words from *Xinhua Daily* reports from the 1940s before the Chinese Communist Party took power, which advocated strongly for civil liberties and democracy.[32] Such activism is more provocative than what Guobin Yang describes as online "rightful resistance" in which activists seek to "avoid repression and to widen the channels of communication,"[33] because netizens who engage in this activity are fully aware that the Party-state will not stop censoring their posts. They are clearly challenging and denying the regime's legitimacy, not simply attempting to avoid repression.

Netizens have also challenged the authoritarian regime by parodying familiar tropes of state propaganda.[34] For instance, in June 2010, a group of Tianya users began creating a series of short weekly videos that mocked China Central Television's (CCTV's) *Evening News* (*Xinwen Lianbo*, 新闻联播) and responded to hot-button issues not being covered by state-run media outlets. The videos parody the *Evening News* style, format, and language, and cover topics such as inflation, soaring housing prices, and rampant corruption. In the producers' words, "Put simply, we will cover whatever topics the 'fartizens' (*pimin*, 屁民) are concerned with."[35] The series is very critical of the regime, and its title, *The Emperor Looks Happy* (*Longyan Dayue*, 龙颜大悦) echoes the nickname of the *Evening News*, the *Happy Evening News* (*Xiwen Lianbo*,

喜闻联播), thus satirizing CCTV's inclination to please top leaders rather than meet the needs of ordinary citizens.[36] As an interviewee once said, the message of the CCTV *Evening News* is that "everything in China is great, and all foreign countries are suffering" (*guonei xingshi yipian dahao, guowai shuishen huore*; 国内形势大好,国外水深火热).[37]

In addition to parodying state propaganda, netizens have created numerous cyber-vocabularies using homophones (e.g., "river crab" stands for the official ideology of "harmony" because both terms are pronounced *hexie* in Chinese), homonyms (e.g., Kim Il-sung and Kim Jong-Il are called "King Fucked" and "King Fucking" because the Chinese character "日" in their names can be understood either as "the sun" or "fuck" depending on the context), nicknames (owing to his ideological construct of the "harmonious society," President Hu Jintao is referred to as the "Crab Emperor" [*xiedi*, 蟹帝]), metaphors, and even the so-called Martian language (*huoxingwen*, 火星文).[38] It is fair to say that Chinese netizens have created a complete cyber-vernacular corresponding to all major political figures and events. Table 4.1 provides some further examples of political cyber-speak.

With this wide vocabulary, Chinese netizens are able to comment on political affairs without resorting to keywords that may trigger state censorship. Take the Bo Xilai incident of early 2012 for example. Bo, a high-ranking official and "princeling" (a term often used in a derogatory manner to describe descendants of prominent Party officials), was removed from the post of party secretary of Chongqing Municipality, which caused great political turmoil among the top leadership. A report on Sina.com on the marketing war between two instant noodle producers caught netizens' attention as a political metaphor.[39] The report was titled "Master Kang Intensifies Its Conflict with Uni-President, and a Fierce Fight Over Instant Noodle Marketing Channels Is Imminent." To those in the know, the piece described a rumor about Politburo Standing Committee member Zhou Yongkang ("Master Kang") disputing the handling of Bo Xilai with other Politburo members ("Uni-President"; "统一," *tongyi*, meaning unity or consensus).

The corruption scandal surrounding former premier Wen Jiabao clearly illustrates the dynamics between state censorship and the evolution of netizens' creative expression. When Wen's name became a

TABLE 4.1 Selected Examples of Political Cyber-Vocabulary

English	Cyber-Vocabulary
China	天朝 (tianchao, Heavenly Dynasty)/天朝(tianchao)[a]
The government	朝廷 (chaoting, Royal Court)
The Chinese Communist Party	土共 (tugong, Bandit Communist Party)/TG[b]
The Politburo and its members	长老团 (zhanglaotuan, Council of Elders)/长老 (zhanglao, Elders)
Mao Zedong	太祖 (Taizu, Emperor Taizu), 腊肉 (larou, Bacon)[c]
Deng Xiaoping	笑贫 (Xiaopin, Laughing at the Poor)/Shopping/286[d]
Jiang Zemin	才帝 (caidi, Emperor the Talented)/江Core (Jiang Core)/386[e]
Hu Jintao	团团 (tuantuan, Round and Round)/面瘫帝 (miantandi, Emperor the Face-Paralyzed)/蟹帝 (xiedi, Emperor the Crab)[f]
Wen Jiabao	宝宝 (baobao, Baby)/影帝 (yingdi, the Best Actor)[g]
Li Changchun	长春真人 (changchun zhenren, Ever-Spring Immortal)[h]
Zhou Yongkang	康师傅 (Kang Shifu, Master Kang)[i]
Bo Xilai	平西王 (pingxiwang, the King Who Pacified the West)[j]

[a] Netizens use the dynastic system to mock today's Chinese regime in negative, positive, and neutral senses depending on the context. The character "天" has the same pronunciation and meaning as "天" (tian, heaven). It is intentionally used here because it is composed of "王" and "八," which together mean "tortoise," an offensive term similar to "son of a bitch" in English.

[b] The term tugong (abbreviated "TG") sounds disparaging to many. But it also conveys a sense of affinity to the Chinese Communist Party. For many netizens, the Party's yokel nature lessens its distance to the masses at the grassroots level.

[c] "Emperor Taizu" means the founding emperor of a dynasty. Mao is referred to as "Emperor Taizu" because he was the founding leader of People's Republic of China. Those who hate him call him "Bacon" because his body is still preserved in the memorial hall in Tiananmen Square.

[d] Deng Xiaoping is nicknamed "Laughing at the Poor" because China's economic reform has widened the country's income gap and left the poor behind. He is called "286" (a reference to Intel's 80286 central processing unit [CPU]) because he was the core (hexin, 核心) of the People's Republic of China's second-generation leadership. He is called "Shopping" because this word in English has a similar pronunciation to "Xiaoping." There is a joke about this: While visiting the United States, Deng was interviewed in English while waiting for his interpreter. The reporter asked him, "What's your next stop?" Deng couldn't understand but thought the reporter might be asking about his surname. So he replied in his Sichuan dialect accent, "Wo xing deng," which sounds like "Washington." The reporter then asked, "What do you plan to do?" Again, Deng could not understand but guessed this question might be about his given name. So he replied, "Xiaoping," which sounds like "shopping." The reporter continued with a few questions about Taiwan's leadership after Chiang Ching-Kuo, to which Deng replied, "Ni deng hui er" ("Wait a moment") and "Suibian" ("whoever"), which sound like "Li Teng-Hui" and "Chen Suibian," respectively.

[e] Jiang Zemin is called "Jiang Core" or "386" because he was the core of China's third-generation leadership. He is called "Emperor the Talented" because he likes showing off his versatility in front of international media.

[f] Hu Jintao is called "Tuantuan" because of his Communist Youth League experience, as "tuan" means "league." Netizens call him "Emperor the Face-Paralyzed" because he always keeps a straight face in public. He is named "Emperor the Crab" (recall that the Chinese pronunciations of "river crab" and "harmony" are the same) because of his official ideology of the "harmonious society."

[g] Wen Jiabao got the nickname "Baby" during his 2008 Sichuan earthquake as a result of highly regarded performance. He became "Best Actor" soon after because some thought he was merely acting and would never fulfill the promises he made.

[h] Li Changchun was a Politburo Standing Committee member in the Hu-Wen era. He is named "Ever-Spring Immortal" because his first name literally means "ever-spring," which is also a monastic name in Taoist history.

[i] Zhou Yongkang was another Politburo Standing Committee member in the Hu-Wen era and was in charge of the police and court system. "Master Kang" is a brand of instant noodles.

[j] Bo Xilai, Party Chief of Chongqing, became the target of censorship in the spring of 2012, when he lost his position following the scandal over the death of the British businessman Neil Heywood. "The King Who Pacified the West" was the title given to a general in the early Qing period, Wu Sangui, who surrendered to the Manchurians. Netizens call Bo the "King Who Pacified the West" for two reasons: Chongqing is located in southwest China, geographically close to Wu's fief in Yunnan Province, and, like Wu, Bo was not trusted by the central government.

taboo word after the *New York Times* reported on his family's hidden wealth,[40] nicknames like "Best Actor" (*yingdi, 影帝*) and "Teletubby" (*tianxian baobao, 天线宝宝*) were used to refer to him. In response, the state started censoring these terms, which only pushed netizens to innovate further: They started to call Wen "Starry Sky" (*xingkong, 星空*) because he had once composed a poem titled "Looking up to the Starry Sky."[41] Netizens' messages were conveyed in ways such as, "Looking up to the starry sky, there are 2.7 billion stars, and the brightest one is Sinovel."[42] This sentence appeared completely apolitical but delivered a clear message to anyone who could decipher it: Wen's family had accumulated $2.7 billion of hidden wealth and made their biggest fortune from Sinovel, China's largest maker of wind turbines.[43] Netizens also used the scandal to enrich their cyber-language by inventing new terms to refer to Wen, including "Wen27" (*温27*), "271," and "Aunt 27" (*27姨*). The latter two nicknames are both pronounced as "2.7 billion" in Chinese). Baidu Knows, a user-generated knowledge base, explains why Wen is called "Best Actor,"[44] what "271" stands for,[45] and what "2.7 billion" refers to.[46]

Indeed, netizens have developed a whole cyber-narrative to engage in politics using various linguistic and rhetorical tools and many performative and media forms. They have not only mocked official propaganda, developed cyber-vocabularies, crafted jokes, and composed poems, prose, and parables, but they have also created multimedia commentary, using text, audio, graphic, and video elements in their online expression.[47] The most well-known case of this kind is the "grass mud horse" (*cao ni ma, 草泥马*) meme (a unit of cultural transmission whose role is similar to that of a gene in the biological sphere).[48] The pronunciation of "grass mud horse" in Chinese is similar to "fuck your mother" and was once used simply as a dirty pun. However, it was then politicized by netizens who constructed stories about the grass mud horse (actually a type of alpaca) fighting the river crab (i.e., the official ideology of harmony), which alluded to the fight over state censorship. The story was produced, told, and retold in numerous formats, including text, picture, song, video, and even comic.[49] Similarly, to protest the Green Dam software, which the Ministry of Industry and Information Technology attempted to have pre-installed on all computers sold in

China to filter unapproved information, netizens created a comic figure of the "Green Dam Lady," performed costume plays featuring the character,[50] and even crafted the "Song of the Green Dam Lady."

Netizens are not simply creative in discussing political topics. They often politicize playful topics by mixing a discussion of them with discursive protests. For instance, when one Tianya user asked fellow netizens about what they would put on their tombstone, many complained about social ills such as rising housing prices and forced demolition through humorous, though often satirical, replies. One user said sarcastically, "Thanks to the government for solving my 'housing' problem."[51] Others added satirical elements by writing "Land claimed by government; [burial plot] must be demolished,"[52] and "Soon after you are buried, your precious piece of land will be claimed by a real estate developer, and urban management officers (*chengguan*, 城管) will come with bulldozers."[53] An even richer and more straightforward satire of high housing prices goes as follows:

> It would be a very tall tombstone, and my name would be tiny, only readable with a microscope, followed by 'XXX, lives on XXXX floor of Tomb No. 20349. It is a studio, 90,000 yuan per square feet.' Below that: 'Developed by Poor-Don't-Bother Tomb Estate Developing Company. New villa-style tombs by our company are on sale. Book right now!' At the bottom: 'Burying yourself arbitrarily or secretly is against the law and will be punished severely!'[54]

Some attacked the family planning policy as well as rising housing costs; for example, "[You] will die without a burial place. Where do you put the epitaph if you cannot even afford a burial place?" and "[You] have only a daughter, and she will marry away (*jia chuqu*, 嫁出去). So [you] won't need a grave since no one will visit [you]!"[55] (In China, a woman is often considered only a member of her husband's family after marriage).

Indeed, netizens are good at weaving hot-button issues into short, funny passages (*duanzi*, 段子) to express discontent.[56] In the thread about epitaphs, one *duanzi* parodied the alleged epitaph of the most unfortunate man ever who had failed at everything in his life and died tragically, and this appeared several times.[57] Satirically titled "Records of the Grand Historian: A Biography of the Post-1980 Generation,"[58] the passage is as follows:

> (He) studied literature early on, reached twenty-six with a debt of over 100,000 yuan. He then tried hard to earn a living and took no rest for a decade. Finally he accumulated 100,000 yuan but still could not afford a house. He invested his wealth in the stock market, and it shrank to 10,000 yuan in a year. He was very depressed and got sick. But the health care system refused to cover him because he was ineligible for the major diseases insurance.[59] He spent all he had to get into a hospital for a week but then recovered without any treatment. A friend pitied him and gave him a bag of Sanlu milk powder.[60] He drank it and died.[61]

This single piece of *duanzi* targets the education system, inequality, unaffordable housing costs, stock market volatility, the health care system, and food safety issues, all of which are major social concerns in today's China. As a parody of the epitaph of the most unfortunate man in history, it serves as a poignant self-portrait of the post-1980 generation, their life opportunities, outlook, and discontent. The pervasiveness of such a mentality among netizens helps explain the rise of the *diaosi* (屌丝, literally means "penis hair") culture among young netizens who mock themselves as "losers" as an implicit protest against the dominant state and mainstream culture.[62]

POP ACTIVISM BEYOND DIGITAL CONTENTION

It is fair to say that Chinese netizens have developed pop activism as a means of countering state censorship and challenging authoritarian rule. However, not all netizens engaging in pop activism practices are political—both the format and content of political expression can be entertaining and fun for their own sake; thus, many netizens simply join in for fun rather than out of political motivation. Moreover, in addition to dissidents and resentful citizens, other political actors such as the state and various pro-regime netizen groups also embrace popular cyber-culture to shape discourse to their advantage.

Wall-climbing (i.e., circumventing the Great Firewall) serves as an unlikely example of engaging in politics without being political. The action constitutes an explicit and direct, though passive, challenge to state censorship. But wall-climbers have mixed and complicated motivations. Though resisting censorship is a serious concern for many wall-climbers,[63] it is a secondary concern or even irrelevant to others who motivated simply by the fun or "coolness factor" involved. In addition to the sense of achievement gained and the heroic sentiment of fighting the formidable state apparatus involved, netizens adept in the art of wall-climbing are often perceived as tech savvy and envied by people around them, thus generating a certain degree of self-esteem.[64]

Many netizens do not view wall-climbing as a form of resistance or struggle for freedom. Instead, they see it as an action to overcome a politically neutral obstacle to get what they need and want. For instance, some interviewees with whom I spoke admitted that they circumvented the Great Firewall primarily to access porn.[65] Though it could be argued that it is normal for single men to access porn, these individuals accept that the state prohibition is morally justified. Moreover, some wall-climbers still actively support the state and distance themselves from the dissident groups that help them circumvent the Great Firewall. A netizen using Freegate, the Great Firewall–breaching software developed by the controversial spiritual group Falun Gong and spread secretively among wall-climbing netizens, stated, "Recently, I have been using the wheels' [Falun Gong's] Freegate to access porn sites. No more work finding proxy servers. It is very convenient. The wheels, after all, have produced some benefits."[66] The use of the term "wheels" (*lunzi*, 轮子), is a sign of disrespect.[67] This particular case is even more telling, and ironic, considering that these same porn-site visitors actually sided with state on its censorship of Google.[68]

In comparison, online expressions using semantic and rhetorical tactics are more typical cases of netizens engaging in political expression with apolitical purposes because they are by nature more popular, more entertaining, and more controversial. Take the case of the grass mud horse as an example. The short video of the grass mud horse fighting the river crab went viral online not only because of its pro-test message, but also because of the image of a cute alpaca and the lovely voices of a children's choir that were used.[69] The same case also demonstrates how an apolitical meme can be politicized. When it first appeared on forums, "grass mud horse" was simply an expedient term to bypass forum regulations prohibiting dirty words. Even when it was selected as one of the "Top Ten Holy Animals" in late 2008 and early 2009, it was still more playful than contentious and was not linked explicitly to censorship.[70] This becomes obvious when looking at the rest of the holy animals, all of which are homophones of profane or vulgar terms.[71] These terms were at best social and cultural resistance rather than political contention, not to mention that many just use them for fun. But "grass mud horse" was immediately politicized when it was linked to the state discourse on harmony, as in "The Song of the Grass Mud Horse" (*Cao Ni Ma Zhige*, 草泥马之歌).[72]

Evidently, politics is highly fluid in cyberspace, as content can be perceived as political or apolitical depending on timing and context.[73] But even when content is political—that is, when it carries explicit political messages—online expression is much more than a form of state–society struggle. Indeed, netizens often mix their creativity and artfulness with criticisms of the regime as well as other political actors, including foreign countries, regime critics, and other netizen groups. For instance, the *Emperor Looks Happy* series emphasizes its entertain-ment purpose as much as its intent to criticize the Party-state.[74] Yet, the series is often imbued with nationalism, supporting Johan Lagerkvist's argument that Chinese cyber-nationalism does not always express "an upset or angry tone," but sometimes calls for "jubilant and cheery cel-ebrations."[75] In one clip, a news story jokes about the Japanese, saying that the legendary Chinese goddess Nü Wa (女娲), who created human beings, has made an apology and resigned from her post for creating malfunctioning humans on the Japanese islands.[76] The case becomes more interesting when we consider the producer's response to a user who suggested that the show should not target other countries:

Interests and conflicts between countries are the concerns of lead-ers. As an ordinary person, I hate what the Japanese did in the past.

We have limited time in our program, so we cannot cover all opinions. However, I feel that since *The Emperor Looks Happy* can criticize our own government, why can't we also reproach the Japanese?[77]

Pro-regime netizens have also mobilized to promote their interests in a playful way. For instance, on military forums, users have created their own vernaculars and narratives, not so much to evade censorship as to entertain themselves and their audiences. For example, China is often called "Bunny" or "Panda"; Russia is often called "Polar Bear"; and the United States is often called "Hawk" or "Lighthouse." Such vocabularies also include the term "pussy values" for "universal values," because the English word "pussy" has a similar pronunciation to the Chinese for "universal" (*pushi*, 普世). Other terms include "underworld-ocracy" (*mingzhu*, 冥主) for "democracy" (*minzhu*, 民主) and "persimmon oil" (*shiyou*, 柿油) for "freedom" (*ziyou*, 自由).[78]

Based on this wordplay, netizens on these forums develop particular types of narratives, the best example of which is the serial called "The Glorious Past of the Little White Bunny."[79] This is essentially a playful recounting of modern Chinese history with a focus on the role of the Chinese Communist Party in unifying and building the nation. Initially gaining momentum from the military forum Cjdby (cjdby.net), the serial has been turned into comics and videos and has achieved incredible popularity and stimulated great support for the regime.[80] For instance, after China's first aircraft carrier, Liaoning, was presented to the public, the author of the comic serial soon came up with a new segment called "The Aircraft Carrier Dream." The segment starts by showing a picture of Admiral Liu Huaqing's visit to the U.S. carrier Ranger (CV-61) in 1980 (figure 4.1).[81] Many regard Liu, who served as vice-chief of the General Staff, vice-chair of the Central Military Commission, and People's Liberation Army Navy commander, as the "father of the Chinese aircraft carrier."[82] In the picture, as one Mitbbs user commented, Liu looks like a "kid staring at a toy in a toy store."[83] The work conveys nationalistic emotion so well that it attracted 561 replies in less than two days on NewSmth's "MilitaryJoke" board alone, and over eighty respondents claimed to be "moved to tears."[84]

FIGURE 4.1 Former PLAN commander Liu Huaqing visiting CV-61

Notes: "1980 Nian Liu Huaqing Shouci Dengshang Meiguo Hangmu" (Liu Huaqing Boarded U.S. Carrier for the First Time in 1980), http://news.xinhuanet.com/mil/2014-04/10/c _126375342_3.htm, retrieved March 10, 2017.

It is quite ironic that nationalistic netizens often borrow popular cultural elements from the hostile countries they target. Many are fans of Hollywood movies, Korean television dramas, Japanese anime, and adult videos. For instance, Cjdby users claim themselves to be a trinity of "military, porn, and otaku" (*jun zhai huang*, 军宅黄).[85] This fusion of online military, porn, and otaku subcultures is embodied in the "Moé translation" (*meng fanyi*, 萌翻译) of *Area 11 News* in which netizens translate Japanese news reports into Chinese using cyber-slang, anime jargon, and porn vocabulary. For example, they refer to Japan as "Area 11" based on the setting of the popular Japanese anime series *Code Geass: Lelouch of the Rebellion.*[86] In these posts, China and the United States are often described as a gay couple, Japan as a maid abused by the two powers, and the relationship between the United States and Japan as an incestuous father–daughter relationship.[87]

Another example is the popularity of the Japanese adult film model and actress Sora Aoi among Chinese netizens. When Sino–Japanese disputes over the Diaoyu Islands (called the Senkaku Islands by the Japanese) arose in August 2012, netizens started to joke about the popular actress, who has over 13 million followers on the Twitter-like Sina

FIGURE 4.2 Declare war on Japan and capture Sora Aoi alive

Notes: Zhifeng, "Zhongguo Wangluo Guancha: Cangjing Kong Hen Meng" (China Internet Watch: Sora Aoi is Moe), http://www.voachinese.com/content/china-web-watch-20120921 /1512730.html, retrieved May 20, 2015. Photograph courtesy of Voice of America, http:// www.voachinese.com.

Weibo.[88] After the death of Shinichi Nishimiya, the newly appointed envoy to China, Chinese netizens fabricated stories that the Japanese prime minister had appointed Sora Aoi instead.[89] Figure 4.2 shows demonstrators holding a banner saying, "Declare War on Japan, Capture Teacher Aoi!" This bizarre fusion of nationalism and popular cyberculture with Japanese cultural elements embodies the nature of pop activism better than any other example.

UNDERSTANDING POP ACTIVISM: SPONTANEITY, ENTREPRENEURS, AND REVENGE

The fusion of politics and popular cyber-culture is driven by several mechanisms that speak to the realities of online politics in China. First, to engage in politics, netizens and regime critics often have to circumvent highly sophisticated state censorship. In other words, political expression must be guarded, implicit, or innovative.[90] Thus, it is not surprising that netizens and regime critics would disguise their political messages with playful expressional formats. Second, online expression in China is pluralized, as various actors—that is, the state, its critics, and various netizen groups—are involved in the production, distribution, and consumption of online content while competing with each other to promulgate preferred discourses.[91] Such discourse competition drives the actors to use popular cyber-culture to attract an audience before attempting to win their hearts and minds. Third, most Chinese netizens are not politically motivated. Rather, they tend to be more interested in material and lifestyle topics than political debates.[92] But politics can be made fun, and apolitical netizens can be politicized; for example, in 2008, events such as the Lhasa riot, the Sichuan earthquake, and the Beijing Olympics quickly drew apolitical netizens into discussions of politics. The combination of fun and politics, as these examples illustrate, was a major contributor to the evolution of pop activism.

In effect, within the relatively free discursive space enabled by the Internet, the struggle over online expression in a way resembles a market in which various actors attempt to "sell" their ideas. Since the audience—who are also the potential redistributors and reproducers—vote with their attention, the sellers then must not only produce messages, but also provide an attractive packaging to attract potential consumers.[93] Moreover, sellers cannot control their potential buyers, who may consume the products—the messages and the packaging—at their discretion. Politically motivated buyers may take the message but throw away the packaging. Others, however, may enjoy the packaging more and disregard the message that comes with it. Moreover, since consumers can actively engage in reproduction and redistribution, they may take the original message out of its packaging and replace it with a new one. Such a rapid switch in the roles of producer, distributor, and consumer makes online expression an extremely fluid and dynamic process.

Indeed, participants in pop activism often improvise. A random netizen may become a key player by coining a phrase to describe a certain event, inventing a story, or creatively using a rhetorical tool. Building on such creativity, pop activism gains momentum, as numerous motivated and even unmotivated netizens spread, interpret, and re-create online messages. This process is indeed a networked one.[94] Such spontaneity explains why pop activism seldom involves systematic attention to a particular political agenda, as the rise and fall of many pop activism memes demonstrates. This echoes the media and communications scholar Meng Bingchun's perception of online spoofs, which "neither qualify as rational debates aiming to achieve consensus nor have produced any visible policy consequences," but serve as a "component of civic culture that offers both political criticism and emotional bonding for all participants."[95]

The impulsive nature of pop activism partially explains why the popularity of topics changes so fast online. However, this is not to say that netizens do not have any political consciousness. A few consistent themes sustain pop activism, including concerns about disadvantaged social groups, criticism of corruption, patriotism, and the pursuit of freedom, justice, and democracy. Changing views of Mao's grandson, Mao Xinyu, reveal how netizens' shared concern over corruption has influenced the evolution of pop activism. Mao Xinyu has been frequently satirized because of his corpulence and because he is a high-profile example of nepotism in the Chinese Communist Party. However, popular opinion of him changed a bit in 2012 during the National People's Congress and Chinese People's Political Consultative Conference. Whereas other representatives wore luxury brands, particularly other princelings such as former premier Li Peng's daughter, Li Xiaolin, he wore a military uniform and carried a paper bag. Netizens started to juxtapose photos of him with those of representatives wearing designer clothes. Comments on Mitbbs hailed him as "a pollution-free, all-natural organic person compared to those official and rich offspring bastards" or someone who "not only is harmless, but also brings laughter to us people."[96]

The Role of Activism Entrepreneurs and the Revenge of Pop Activism

Pop activism is not always spontaneous. Motivated actors such as dissidents and opinion leaders play an important role in producing, interpreting, and politicizing the content of pop activism. Take the artist and activist Ai Weiwei as an example. Though the state media have tried to describe him as a deviant, a plagiarist, and a tool of Western political interference,[97] dissident groups, Western media, and his supporters often see him as a one-man hero courageous enough to question the repressive state.[98] Ai has created a series of first-rate online spectacles that have challenged the Party-state.[99] For instance, in 2010, in response to the demolition order of his Shanghai studio, Ai hosted a river crab feast for over one thousand guests.[100] As the river crab represents the state ideology of "harmony," and thus state censorship, the feast was clearly an act of protest. The feast quickly became a hot topic online and was widely viewed by Ai's supporters as an open but creative challenge to censorship.

Ai's contribution to the politicization of the grass mud horse provides a clear example of the role of the "activism entrepreneur." In one of his pieces of performance art, he took a number of pictures of himself in which he was naked except for a toy alpaca in front of his crotch. The message conveyed was "Fuck your mother, CCP Central Committee" because the alpaca is the grass mud horse, which, as mentioned, is a homonym for "fuck your mother," and "center of the crotch" is a homonym for the Party's Central Committee.[101] This highly provocative performance politicized the grass mud horse meme significantly by going beyond targeting the censorship system to challenge the Party-state regime directly. Furthermore, when Ai was charged with tax evasion in 2011, he and his friends again made the incident a cyberspectacle by launching an Internet fundraising campaign to pay his unpaid taxes and fines.[102] Ai added to the episode in November 2011 by singing "The Song of Grass Mud Horse" in jail at the request of creditors who had donated money to his fundraising campaign.[103] This could be viewed as a large-scale performance that expressed not only his but also his supporters' protest against state censorship and repression.

Ai Weiwei is fairly unusual, given his international reputation and artistic creativity, compared with ordinary netizens and other dissidents. But he is not singular in taking advantage of pop activism to disseminate his discourse of dissent. For instance, when sex videos purported to feature the actress Li Xiaolu went viral in May 2014, dissidents immediately turned the incident into a vehicle for anti-regime mobilization by inserting messages commemorating the Tiananmen Square protests of 1989 into the video clips.[104] Cases like this demonstrate how regime critics can exploit popular elements of cyber-culture to spread their messages.

Pop activism sometimes backfires, however. The spontaneous playfulness of pop activism sometimes dilutes its message, as creativeness, artfulness, and intentional obscurity can make it difficult for an audience to receive the intended message. Moreover, pop activism sometimes challenges accepted lifestyles, habits, modes of thinking, and moral standards, causing antipathy toward posters. Thus, although pop activism may be effective in mobilizing some netizens, it may well at the same time offend others. For instance, in contrast to his international reputation and popularity among his supporters, Ai Weiwei is controversial among many Chinese netizens who do not appreciate his art or are suspicious of his motivations, particularly when his "grass mud horse" series appeared to evolve from criticizing the Party-state ("grass mud horse the Chinese Communist Party Central Committee") to China itself (the "grass mud horse Motherland").[105] Though his supporters argued that Ai was targeting the regime, not the nation, many netizens thought he was going too far.[106] The backfiring is evident in the following comment: "So far as 'Ai wee wee' (Ai Weiwei) is anti-CCP, even his shit would smell sweet to someone!"[107]

Similarly, controversial political intentions may result in a severe backlash. For instance, a known dissent activist on Mitbbs once forwarded a false suicide report of a local girl to the forum's joke board.[108] The post immediately attracted criticism as some users did not see the message as funny at all. Similar conflicts between supporters and protesters of Falun Gong material appear frequently on Mitbbs and other overseas forums, and in some cases force board managers to impose limitations on such postings.[109] The backfiring of certain messages partially explains the rise of pro-regime voices that actively discredit regime critics online, as will be discussed in the following chapters.

CONCLUSION

The Internet has enabled resentful netizens and regime critics to resist and protest against state censorship and authoritarian rule in creative, artful, and humorous ways. Yet, online expression is more than digital contention. Through an examination of how political messages are produced, circulated, and consumed online, this chapter highlights the pluralization of Chinese cyberspace and reveals the entangled relationship between politics and popular cyber-culture. It argues that the dynamics of state control, discourse competition, and the pursuit of fun have together contributed to the rise of pop activism, in which the content of expression becomes extremely fluid and fuzzy when formats converge. In short, though various actors—the state, its critics, and different netizen groups—may have distinct agendas for their online expression, which may be political or apolitical, anti-regime or pro-regime, they all engage in the production and circulation of a shared Internet culture that centers on the format of expression. This is the key to deciphering political expression in China.

The analysis in this chapter reveals that a liberalization–control perspective runs the risk of downplaying the richness of political expression and implies a narrow view of the relationship between the state and society online. Pop activism as a tool has empowered social resistance to state censorship and authoritarian rule. In particular, motivated activism entrepreneurs such as dissident activists can play an important role in the production, distribution, and interpretation of pop activism content. But pop activism challenges not only the Party-state,[110] but also political actors such as regime critics and foreign countries. Official ideologies, such as communism, "Three Represents," and the harmonious society, have been confronted and deconstructed by many netizens, but so have alternatives to such Party-state ideologies, such as universal values. Moreover, pop activism is a double-edged sword for actors pursuing a political agenda. Though it may be effective in popularizing political information, it sometimes backfires when playfulness dilutes the message and when controversial political ideas cause antipathy among netizens wishing to stay away from politics and simply have a good time online.

This chapter also suggests a new perspective toward Internet politics, particularly with regard to the nature of online expression and its impact on authoritarian rule. Given the diverse actors, complex motivations, and dynamic processes involved, it is critical to examine how political expression is produced, circulated, and interpreted in specific online contexts. Evidently, the struggle is far beyond one between the state and society and is much richer than a story of censorship versus counter-censorship. Thus, the following chapters shift focus from the struggle over censorship to discourse competition by exploring how the state, regime critics, and ordinary netizens shape online discourse through innovative PR tactics, rich rhetorical tools, and creative expression.

5

TROLLING FOR THE PARTY

State-Sponsored Internet Commentators

In the realm of ideological and public opinion, there are roughly three zones: the red, the black, and the gray. The red zone is our main front, and we must hold it. The black zone is primarily negative; we should dare to confront and greatly compress its domain. The gray zone is what we should try to win over so that it turns red.[1]

XI JINPING

Many studies of Internet politics in authoritarian regimes—including those discussed in the first half of this book—choose to focus on the state–society struggle over content control; that is, what can and cannot be expressed online.[2] These studies offer valuable insights into the dynamics of state control and social resistance in the digital era. As the previous three chapters have shown, the state, intermediary actors, and netizens have wrestled over the limits of online expression in China. Despite its legal, administrative, and technical efforts, the Chinese state has barely succeeded in controlling online expression, with discontented but compliant intermediary actors taking a fence-sitting stance while rebellious netizens regularly circumvent censorship in creative ways. However, focusing exclusively on censorship and counter-censorship is limiting. This perspective implies a cohesive group of netizens fighting unanimously against the state, which is inaccurate, and overlooks certain aspects of state adaptation. High-capacity authoritarian regimes such as those of China and Russia not only enjoy considerable popular support,[3] but also demonstrate a strong adaptability to reform and cope with new challenges.[4] To accurately gauge the resilience of authoritarianism in the digital era, we must look at how authoritarian states adapt beyond censorship, and how various actors interact with each other within the state-stipulated boundaries of expression.

This and the following two chapters focus on discourse competition in Chinese cyberspace by exploring the pluralization of online expression. They place special emphasis on how the state, its critics, and various netizen groups engage each other in ways other than through censorship and counter-censorship. Unlike the cat-and-mouse censorship game in which the state dominates with its coercive power, these chapters reveal a discourse competition in which involved actors rely more on expressive tactics and identity mobilization to shape online discourse. Seeing online expression as a discourse competition helps us understand Internet politics in China from the perspective of the public sphere, while also shedding light on how regime legitimacy is maintained or weakened through public debates in virtual space.

This chapter examines state adaptation beyond censorship. By demonstrating how the state has deployed paid Internet commentators—popularly known as the "fifty-cent army" (*wumao dang*, 五毛党)—to manufacture seemingly spontaneous pro-regime voices online, this chapter reveals authoritarian adaptability in the digital era. Given that old-fashioned propaganda has increasingly become ineffective, the introduction of Internet commentators represents an innovative adaptation of the state to promulgate its preferred messages and guide online opinion. However, this seemingly smart move has produced mixed results: Although the fifty-cent army may have managed to increase the state's PR effectiveness on specific issues, it often backfires. This is because the adaptation is embedded in the apparatus of state propaganda and thought work, which though still powerful and resourceful, functions according to a logic that offers little incentive for Internet commentators to excel at their job and often leads to the exposure of their existence. The mixed results of the fifty-cent army strategy suggest that it is necessary to problematize "state capacity" and "state adaptability" in the digital age, as the Chinese state has been struggling to translate its despotic and infrastructural power of the pre–Internet era appropriately to shape online expression.

STATE ADAPTATION BEYOND CENSORSHIP

Relatively free expression online empowers social actors to challenge authoritarian regimes in many ways. In China, the Internet not only serves as an emerging public sphere, but has also promoted the development of civil society and facilitated collective action, online activism, and dissident mobilization. [5] Thanks to the Internet, Chinese citizens now enjoy some agenda-setting power,[6] are able to question state agents more effectively,[7] and can even influence state policies.[8] In response, the Party-state has adapted to tame the Internet by constructing a comprehensive censorship system to control the flow of information online.[9]

However, the state has neither the capacity[10] nor the intention to completely shut down the Internet or eliminate all political expression online.[11] In fact, perfect censorship may actually be undesirable for authoritarian regimes. On one hand, because much political expression takes place on popular web platforms, imposing overly strict censorship or shutting down such platforms may cause collateral damage, provoking public protests quite unnecessarily.[12] On the other hand, freer online expression may work to the advantage to the authoritarian regime as a form of policy feedback, at least by helping the state discipline its local agents.[13] This logic is nothing new to China scholars, who have commented on the Party-state using village elections or popular unrest as a means of holding local officials accountable.[14] Likewise, the state may selectively censor online expression and adjust the level of censorship in response to social tensions so it can harness the benefits of free information.[15] The strategic censorship consideration, together with capacity constraints, may explain why the state tolerates critical online expression to a considerable degree except in the case of some well-patrolled "forbidden zones."[16]

There is one problem with the strategic censorship logic. It assumes an omnipotent state that can differentiate online content according to the threat it poses and exercise its censorship perfectly. This is unrealistic, even given the strong capacity of the Chinese Party-state. As discussed in chapter 2, state censorship is at best semi-successful, with netizens and dissent groups still capable of penetrating its limits. Moreover, even limited freedom of expression can be risky for the Party-state. By breaking the state's monopoly on mass media, the Internet, with its freer expression, enables citizens to contest the regime's authority, propagate social discontent, and diffuse protest tactics. In this way, it calls the Party-state to account for discrepancies between its own views and those of the public.[17] Freer expression may also expose the pervasiveness of social ills and official misconduct, thus promoting a shared awareness among currently scattered citizens about the need for fundamental change.[18]

What, then, can the state do to offset these detrimental effects of online expression on its authoritarian rule? In addition to enhancing and refining the censorship system, the Chinese Party-state has attempted to expand its online presence and reinvigorate state propaganda online. To increase its online presence, the Chinese state has promoted e-government platforms, pushed state media online, and penetrated popular social media sites. First, to enhance its administrative capacity, improve public services, and expand citizen outreach, the state has pushed government agencies at all levels to set up e-government sites. This "Government Online Project," launched in 1999, has resulted in the creation of 53,546 government websites as of December 2016.[19] Though scholars debate the effectiveness of such platforms, they have indeed become a channel for the state to engage citizens.[20]

Second, the Party-state has pushed state media, such as the *Xinhua News Agency* and the *People's Daily*, to occupy cyberspace[21] and has granted them exclusive rights to produce news reports that other online news services are only allowed to "reprint."[22] In fact, in addition to setting up their own online outposts, state media have also populated major social media platforms. For instance, as of October 2013, the two major microblogging service providers in China, Sina Weibo and Tencent, hosted at least 23,449 and 14,148 verified, official accounts respectively for traditional media outlets, including ones run by the state.[23] The increased online presence of state media has clearly allowed the state to respond to hot-button issues more quickly with its own voice.

Third, the state has attempted to engage the public directly on popular social media platforms.[24] For instance, as of December 2016, there were 164,522 verified, official accounts, representing 125,098 government agencies and 39,424 individual officials on Sina Weibo alone.[25] Some popular ones among the official Weibo accounts, such as that of Chinese Communist Youth League Central Committee, attract millions of followers and thus play a critical role in online agenda setting and issue framing.

Meanwhile, the Party-state has also updated its offline and online propaganda strategies to make state propaganda more appealing and effective. According to the political scientist Anne-Marie Brady, since the early 1990s, "China's propaganda leadership has embraced new modern methods of social control and persuasion and introduced the use of new technology into propaganda work. In doing so, they have made a major contribution toward creating the conditions for ongoing CCP rule in China."[26] In the realm of traditional media, commercialization is a highly salient feature. Scholars such as Yuezhi Zhao have observed that by introducing market mechanisms into Party journalism, China's media system has gradually evolved into a "propagandist/commercial model" that performs more subtle ideological work for the Party.[27] Mixed-method research by Daniela Stockmann has also found that media commercialization promotes regime stability, rather than destabilizing authoritarian rule, because it allows the state to tell more convincing and sophisticated stories while at the same time offering the leadership better information about what citizens think.[28] Alongside media commercialization and globalization, a recent study by Maria Repnikova has found that official influence still looms large in elite journalism training.[29] The state continues to place ideological teachings at the core of journalism curricula and employs control mechanisms, such as structural oversight, ad hoc surveillance, and coercion, to ensure journalism training does not deviate from official ideology. But since educators and students have been able to exploit limited openings to reinterpret some aspects of the Party's ideology, the Party-state has merely achieved a "hegemony of form."

Making state propaganda appealing online is a much more challenging task because the state can have no control over how particular topics are produced, distributed, or consumed without resorting
to censorship, which reduces its success and often causes antipathy.
Indeed, the state now finds itself in a new battlefield in which the
power of beliefs, values, and identity, rather than coercive power, tri-
umphs. It has to employ more innovative strategies to win the hearts
and minds of netizens against competing discourses. According to the
China specialist Johan Lagerkvist, one strategy the state employs to
counter perceived enemies, to win over public opinion, and to shore up
legitimacy is "ideotainment"—the use of popular expressional formats
as vehicles to promulgate state ideological constructs.[30] For instance,
both President Xi Jinping and Premier Li Keqiang published official
cartoon images of themselves in early 2014, making them look more
approachable to the public.[31] In fact, all seven of the new Politburo
Standing Committee members had already been partially "cartoonized"
as early as October 2013 for a video clip comparing how China, the United
States, and the United Kingdom select top leaders.[32] The five-minute
video, using many popular cyber-cultural elements to convey the message that the Chinese Communist Party's rule is justified, immediately
went viral online.[33] According to Youku.com, the Chinese version of
the video recorded more than 1.5 million views within two days.[34] Such
efforts suggest that the Chinese Party-state may have shifted its focus
from ideological indoctrination to a more subtle management of public
attention in the norms competition with regime critics.[35]

Even strategies such as ideotainment cannot prevent the regime
from losing its ideational leadership, however. Netizens are so wary of
state propaganda that any government connection to online content
may be seen as an "instant negative."[36] Thus, hiding the "government
connection" seems to be a natural strategy for the state and its agencies in order to exert influence over online opinion. In this sense, using
"Internet commentators" to troll online expression represents a significant propaganda innovation. At least by deploying the fifty-cent
army to fabricate pro-regime voices under the guise of ordinary netizens, the state can avoid a backlash over outright state propaganda and
manufacture consent more effectively. The following sections examine

this important yet understudied innovation with the purpose of examining and assessing this seemingly smart adaptation by the Chinese Party-state.

POLITICAL ASTROTURFING AND IDENTIFYING INTERNET COMMENTATORS

The Internet not only empowers average citizens to circumvent state control and engage public expression, but also potentially provides a way for any motivated actor to shape public opinion in more subtle and effective ways. Instead of directly promoting certain agendas, motivated actors can manipulate other users, who are vulnerable to such manipulation because they are not embedded in real-life accountability networks. For example, using multiple ghost accounts, a single manipulator can "stir up" (*chaozuo*, 炒作) a topic into a hot one. Public opinion is manipulated in this process not only because the initial momentum comes from a created "public," but also because the "dominant" view of the "public" can be engineered through purposeful framing and information input, which in turn influences innocent users' perceptions and their subsequent input. Such a trolling practice is essentially "astroturfing," a widely used PR technique in politics and marketing in which incentivized actors (often paid) display apparent grassroots support for a product, policy, or event to shore up wider and more genuine support.[37] The tactic allows sponsors to hide their identity—to avoid associated negativity or maintain "plausible deniability"—and enhances the credibility of the message through the false impression of personal testimonies and widespread support.[38] The Internet serves as a natural platform for astroturfing given the anonymity of online expression. In the realm of politics, actors across the globe have used this PR tactic to their advantage. Authoritarian and illiberal regimes, such as those of China, Egypt, Kenya, Russia, Saudi Arabia, Syria, and Venezuela, have all recruited "electronic armies" to conduct political astroturfing.[39] Even in democracies, there are reports of political actors using astroturfing to gain an advantage over competitors.[40]

Though political astroturfing is quite common, in-depth studies on the phenomenon are rare, largely owing to the secretiveness and sensitivity of the practice, especially in repressive regimes. Fortunately, a few existing studies may help us navigate the topic in the Chinese context. Chin-fu Hung, one of the first scholars in the field, has explored how Internet commentators were mobilized to pacify the Weng'an riot in Guizhou after the suspicious death of a 16-year-old girl.[41] But Hung's research does not investigate how Internet commentators actually operate on the ground. Based on the analysis of real fifty-cent army posts leaked from a district government, the political scientist Gary King and his colleagues have developed a sophisticated method to identify Internet commentators on social media.[42] Finding that state astroturfing efforts often focus on cheerleading rather than confronting regime critics or controversial topics, they argue that the state's strategy is not to engage but to distract the public. But this methodologically rigorous research is primarily based on data from one specific local government, making external validity a concern. To address this, Blake Miller, who studies the use of technology in state propaganda, proposes to detect Internet commentators using network and social metadata such as IP addresses and linkages to government accounts.[43] This approach overcomes the external validity problem and shows promise for better appreciating the nuances in online commentating. However, it is also limited, in that just like the work of Gary King's group, it focuses exclusively on Internet commentators' online activities without a holistic examination of how the whole system works, particularly how the Party-state mobilizes Internet commentators.

The existing studies are helpful, particularly in terms of how to identify state astroturfing online. But they are insufficient to assess the state's intentions and capacity in this adaptive move. To fill the gap, it is necessary to situate the Internet commentator system into the broader context of state adaptation to the digital age and examine how it works systemically. The following section draws on many sources of data to show how Internet commentators were first introduced online; how they are recruited, trained, and rewarded; and how they operate in the online environment. Three primary sources of data are especially worth noting here. First, state propaganda directives and other official communication logs are direct evidence of how the system functions. These "internal" documents are not publicly available but may be exposed as a result of system glitches in the state propaganda platforms where they are stored or obtained from officials who leak them because of incompetence, carelessness, or disaffection. Though such incidences are rare, when available they provide rich data for researchers to peek into the "black box" of the state propaganda apparatus. Second, official media and government websites sometimes openly report on their Internet commentators because local authorities and propaganda agencies deem online commentating as a part of their routine work and thus boast rather than hide their achievements.[44] These reports confirm the existence of Internet commentators and are particularly valuable for studying how they are introduced online, trained, and rewarded. Third, in-depth online ethnographic work produces additional data to analyze how the fifty-cent army functions in the online environment. Based on long-term observation, I have established a scheme to differentiate state-sponsored Internet commentators from regular users with quite some confidence. This scheme, which resembles that adopted in both the work of King and his colleagues and Miller, has been developed through learning from netizens, who are extremely sensitive to and thus cognizant of state astroturfing,[45] as well as by comparing expressional traits: Internet commentators tend to make only pro-regime comments on certain restricted political topics using official language codes and generally do not interact with other netizens. In-depth online ethnography also pays in that it exposes the researcher to many leaked official documents first discovered by netizens. I have even observed someone who used to work in the system talking about his or her experiences on Mitbbs.[46]

TROLLING FOR THE PARTY: THE FIFTY-CENT ARMY

The expansion of the Internet has clearly broken the state's monopoly over the media and rendered outright propaganda increasingly ineffective.[47] For instance, in a report on Libya's response to the French-led airstrike in 2011, CCTV attempted to pass off an interpretation of local

Libyans as Kaddafi supporters protesting French intervention. CCTV deliberately mistranslated their "Vive la France" banner as "French, go home."[48] The deliberate misrepresentation was caught by critical netizens and attracted heavy criticism from many Internet forums. Facing such challenges, it is only natural for the state to resort to new propaganda tools and strategies. Introducing Internet commentators represents such an effort of state adaptation. In the political scientist Chin-fu Hung's words, the state has been "revitalizing the propaganda apparatus through the utilization of these commentators."[49] However, as my analysis will show, this seemingly smart adaptation is not as successful as the state may have expected, largely because the system is geared more toward pleasing upper-level state officials than engaging and persuading ordinary citizens.

The Introduction of Online Commentators

There is little solid evidence showing when, why, or how the Internet commentator system was first created. It was in late 2004 when the term "Internet commentator" first appeared in an official report and online. Changsha, in the Hunan Province; the supervision department of the Chinese Communist Party Central Commission for Discipline Inspection; and Nanjing University are possibilities for the first local government, central state agency, and higher education institution, respectively, to deploy Internet commentators.[50] The first group of Internet commentators quickly earned the nickname of "fifty-cent army" because it is believed that they were paid 50 cents per post, plus a base monthly salary of 600 yuan (less than US$75 in 2005) in the Hunan case.[51]

Though some argue that Internet commentators were introduced by the state primarily to combat "Internet spies" sponsored by hostile foreign forces (*wangte*, 网特),[52] the argument is not strongly supported. In fact, the adaptation was initiated by a few state agencies independently, suggesting that it was likely a local or departmental initiative rather than a centrally coordinated policy. That being said, the fact that state agencies in different sectors at different levels adapted this practice at around the same time implies that officials at all levels more or less simultaneously started to realize the potential of Internet commentators to shape public opinion.

Today, the deployment of Internet commentators is a systematic nationwide practice. On one hand, numerous state agencies, including all levels of authorities from counties to ministries, schools, and state-owned enterprises, sponsor their own fifty-cent armies.[53] On the other hand, the central government, through the propaganda system and the Communist Youth League, also controls a direct force of the trolling army. Unlike traditional news commentators who are often media professionals working at state-run media, Internet commentators undertaking astroturfing tasks are mostly employees of the sponsoring agency, whose trolling assignments are part of their regular duties.[54] Recruiting from within the system makes sense because it not only reduces the cost of recruitment, but also ensures a minimal level of accountability of Internet commentators, particularly in terms of their loyalty to the system. Only in rare cases are Internet commentators directly recruited from the general public. In such cases, recruiting agencies often stipulate certain criteria such as political loyalty and basic computer skills.[55] The vague and general nature of such criteria implies that they are mostly official clichés and thus unlikely to be strictly enforced. Indeed, universities often recruit employees from the student body as a form of financial aid, and recruitment is open to all.[56]

In recent years, the state has turned college students into a "fifty-cent army reserve." In 2014, the Chinese Communist Youth League Central Committee decreed universities across the country to set up student Internet propaganda troops to engage in online expression and monitor the "ideological trends" (*sixiang dongtai*, 思想动态) among students.[57] In this massive recruitment, student cadres in local Communist Youth League branches, student unions, campus media outlets, and student news media organizations, were given priority.[58] This again confirms the state's emphasis on the political loyalty of fifty-cent army members.

Official reports indicate that Internet commentators often receive some training, but evidence suggests that such training is likely quite basic in most cases. Mostly, it would involve attending lectures by propaganda officials and media professionals, as well as exchanging experiences with each other.[59] For instance, in October 2009, officials in the Jiangdong district of Ningbo, Zhejiang Province, held a training session for 102 newly appointed online commentators, which included lectures from the local Internet administrative center and Public Security Bureau Internet monitoring branch directors and peer experience exchange.[60] While there are no data on the specific techniques taught at these sessions, the training is likely quite basic and ultimately of no consequence, as will be discussed shortly. Leaked internal training documents suggest that Internet commentators are taught such basic skills as how to register an account and how to post or reply to threads. The only "technique" they are taught is how to create multiple ghost accounts to make their astroturfing activities less apparent.[61] Such minimal requirements betray the low expectations of sponsoring state agencies, suggesting they may not care whether Internet commentators can effectively engage in public debates or sway the opinions of netizens.

Internet commentators tend to be poorly rewarded and are thus often unmotivated. Sponsoring agencies often provide them with monetary compensation, promotion opportunities, and recognition, but none of these constitutes a strong incentive. Monetary compensation is minimal in most cases—sometimes as little as 10 cents per post.[62] Even when they are paid better—for example, a base salary of 600 yuan per month and 50 cents per post, as in the case of Hunan—the compensation is still far from the average for government employees. In some cases, Internet commentators are rewarded with opportunities. This is especially the case for politically ambitious college students, because working as Internet commentators helps open doors to state-sponsored organizations such as student unions or the Communist Youth League. But since there are many alternative options to get into those organizations, becoming an Internet commentator is not particularly attractive. Occasionally, top-performing Internet commentators are selected to receive honors and rewards, showing that their efforts have been recognized by the state.[63] Yet, such recognition is unlikely a strong motivator for most Internet commentators, because only a small percentage of them are eligible for such recognition, and, further, such recognition is not something to be proud of publicly.

Internet Commentators in Action

Since Internet commentators are mobilized by different agencies, it is logical to expect them to fulfill quite different tasks. For instance, Internet commentators in Zhengding, Hebei Province, have been asked to create positive publicity and promote the official agenda, spread state-approved information and suppress rumors, interpret and defend official positions and pacify netizens, and help manage online information.[64] This guideline is quite broad in terms of defining the responsibilities of the Internet commentators. But it is evident that their paramount task is to manipulate public opinion, though they are also expected to monitor online opinion for the sponsoring agency.

Internet commentators are often mobilized for crisis management to defuse collective mobilization online and to maintain the image of their sponsoring agencies. Such cases include social protests such as those that occurred during the 2008 Weng'an riot and the removal of top-ranking officials such as Bo Xilai in 2012. The Weng'an riot was a massive one in which protesters in Weng'an County, Guizhou, thronged the streets and set fire to government buildings and vehicles as a demonstration of outrage over the suspicious death of a young girl and the allegedly official efforts to cover it up.[65] The Bo Xilai case is an example of the central mobilization of Internet commentators. The ousting of Bo—formerly the party chief of Chongqing and a Politburo member—triggered a legitimacy crisis, because it revealed the corruption of a high-ranking Party official, the power struggle among the top leadership, and the ideological conflicts present in Chinese society. As a result, it was unsurprising to see Internet commentators flooding all major online platforms to justify the trial of Bo and to praise the system for championing the rule of law.[66]

The following intercept from an official report authored by the director of the Internet Administration Center of Wenzhou, Zhejiang Province, outlines the conditions that trigger the mobilization of Internet commentators:[67]

> So far, the "Working Procedure of Online Public Opinion Guidance for Wenzhou Municipal Departments" has been implemented among

99 municipal agencies. Meanwhile, [Wenzhou] has established a 173-member liaison team for Internet commentating. The working plan of online public opinion guidance will be activated . . . *when emergency and sensitive issues occur within the municipal departments or agencies that may arouse widespread concern and discussion online, thus producing a negative impact, or when there are emergency and sensitive events involving Wenzhou spreading online that may affect Wenzhou's image or disrupt social stability.*

The italicized section of this statement implies that local authorities are highly concerned with crises under their own jurisdiction and the subsequent impact on their image. This is confirmed by an internal report from the Communist Youth League's Shanghai branch, which listed its several major "achievements" in 2009. According to the report, Internet commentators were mobilized to defuse the following online crises: building collapses,[68] the pre-installation of Green Dam censorship software,[69] violent law enforcement for city management officials in Putuo District,[70] controlling the spread of the H1N1 influenza virus, the case of self-immolation caused by forced eviction in Minhang District,[71] the entrapment of illegal cabs,[72] and glitches in the subway system. All these events but two—the pre-installation of Green Dam and controlling the spread of H1N1—were local crises, indicating the priorities of local authorities. That being said, Internet commentators at all levels can be centrally mobilized by the state when it deems necessary, as in the cases of Green Dam, H1N1, and the Bo Xilai trial. In other words, the Internet commentator system is both fragmented and centrally coordinated. While local propaganda agencies and the Internet commentators they sponsor primarily serve local interests, they must also answer to calls from higher levels.

In addition to defusing online crises, Internet commentators are also mobilized to promote propaganda campaigns at both central and local levels. For instance, authorities in Hengyang, Hunan Province, mobilized Internet commentators in late 2008 to engage the "Liberate Thinking and Develop Hengyang" propaganda campaign. They were asked to participate in thematic discussions, post comments on local and national online platforms, and even fake online interviews with local officials.[73]

One specific assignment was to post one thousand comments to the "Hengyang Municipality Propaganda Branch 'Liberate Thinking Big Discussion' Special Thread."[74] Hengyang is not an exception. For example, Internet commentators from Ganzhou, Jiangxi Province, were deployed to manipulate an online interview of the local Party chief in January 2014. They were asked to leave at least one comment "like average netizens" and report content and links to the Internet Propaganda Office.[75]

Central state agencies also mobilize Internet commentators, often through their local branches, to facilitate propaganda initiatives. In May 2013, the entire propaganda system coordinated to promulgate President Xi Jinping's idea of the "Chinese Dream." In mid-2013, Internet commentators at all levels were mobilized to denigrate "public intellectuals" (*gongzhi*, 公知).[76] In December 2014, to promote the first "National Memorial Day for Nanjing Massacre Victims," the Chinese Communist Youth League Central Committee mobilized college students across the country to comment on and repost designated Weibo entries. Leaked internal communications from the Communist Youth League's Shanghai branch reveal how universities responded to the call. For instance,

> By 12:00 PM, the Shanghai Business College Internet Propaganda Team had completed the following number of reposts and comments: The Oriental Wealth Media and Management School has 347 reposts and 96 comments; the School of Foreign Languages has 593 reposts and 254 comments; the School of Tourism and Food has 651 reposts and 529 comments; the School of Management has 508 reposts and 195 comments; the School of Information and Computer Science has 438 reposts and 147 comments; the School of Arts and Law has 289 reposts and 99 comments; the School of Arts and Design has 324 reposts and 139 comments; the School of Finance and Economics has 862 reposts and 397 comments. In total, our college has produced 4,012 reposts and 1,856 comments.[77]

Not all universities are equally active, however. For instance, Shanghai Normal University produced 2,178 comments and reposts in total; the Shanghai Institute of Health Sciences contributed 816 reposts and 321 comments; the Shanghai University of Finance and Economics

FIGURE 5.1 CCYLCC national memorial day Weibo.

Source: http://weibo.com/1459507082/BAuokusLb, last retrieved June 30, 2016.

reported only 216 reposts and 58 comments; and East China Normal University produced 269 reposts and 56 comments.[78] This variation suggests that the call was not treated as a mandatory task and thus each university felt it had considerable leeway. Nonetheless, contributions from student Internet commentators have made a huge splash online. As figure 5.1 shows, one Weibo entry by the Communist Youth League accumulated over 210,000 reposts and 31,000 comments within a matter of days. Table 5.1 provides an English translation.[79]

TABLE 5.1 Weibo Post from the Chinese Communist Youth League Central Committee School Department

CCYLCC School Department	+Follow

2014-12-12 14:43 from 360 Safe Browser

#National Memorial Day Student Awareness and Action# December 13 is the first National Memorial Day for the Nanjing Massacre Victims. We hereby launch the Weibo Relay theme of "remembering the national calamities through a national memorial with three lines of oration to express heartfelt emotions." Pals, please forward this Weibo post and write three lines of oration with your most sincere feelings to commemorate our deceased compatriots and memorialize the national history. For example: Tens of thousands of martyrs died on the battlefield, whose patriotic mission will never fade, as millions of compatriots commemorate their great deed.

Bookmark	Forwards: 210218	Comments: 31130	Likes: 3377

Since Xi Jinping came to power, the state has made more aggressive efforts to regain ideational leadership. In particular, the propaganda machinery has worked hard to project and maintain a positive image of Xi as the new icon of the regime. Numerous Internet commentators have been mobilized to glorify Xi online. Such blatant praise of Xi by the fifty-cent army is quite easy to recognize: They "smell" official, are highly repetitive, and look similar to each other (figure 5.2, with translation provided in table 5.2). Moreover, the comments come in waves, with a large number of consecutive ones posted from the same city within a very short period of time. A check of user profiles reveals that Internet commentators making such comments tend to comment only on Xi Jinping, use official language codes, and never interact with other netizens (figure 5.3, with translation provided in table 5.3).

An analysis of comments on randomly selected news reports on Xi Jinping, Li Keqiang, Hu Jintao, and Wen Jiabao shows that Internet commentators are indeed much more active in the Xi Jinping era (table 5.4). The results are telling in that the coding scheme is likely to underestimate the pervasiveness of the fifty-cent army, particularly in the case of Xi Jinping, as many anonymous comments regarding him are likely made by Internet commentators. With only location information available (in the following format: Netease User from X Province Y City ip: xxx.xxx.*.*), these anonymous comments are admittedly quite difficult to code. But as figure 5.2 shows, these comments came in waves, with several or even dozens of consecutive comments from the same locality. This discernable pattern, together with the language traces, suggests that these comments are likely not genuine.

In addition to manipulating online opinion, Internet commentators often also function as a bridge connecting the state and the public by helping proliferate and clarify state policies and, more importantly, by reporting public concerns to the authorities. This function, though hardly appreciated by most netizens, is deemed beneficial by some to counterbalance unfounded rumors and to improve governance.[80] In particular, monitoring online discussion provides the state with references for policy-making and implementation. For instance, online commentators are said to have contributed to the *Changsha Public Opinion Express* (*Changsha Yuqing Kuaibao*, 长沙舆情快报), which is edited

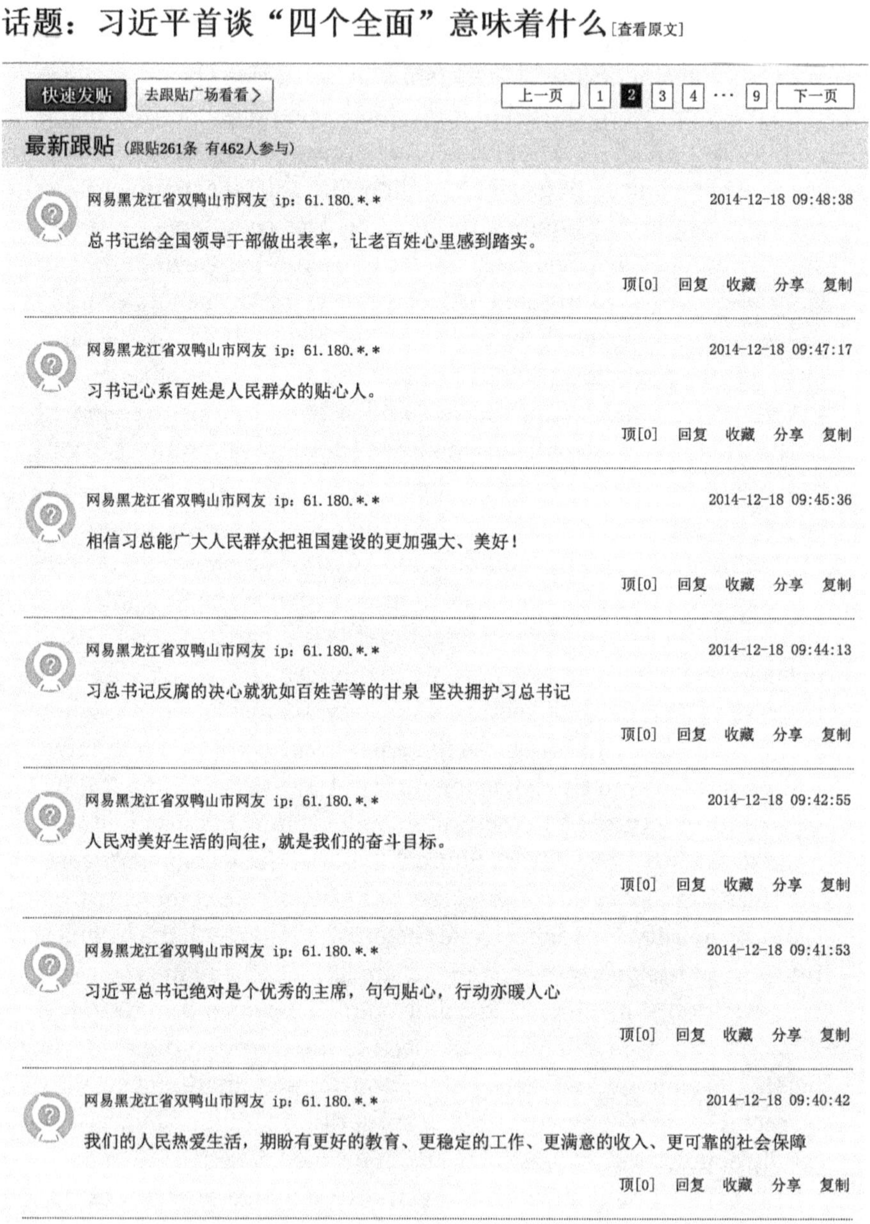

话题：习近平首谈“四个全面”意味着什么[查看原文]

快速发贴 去跟贴广场看看>   上一页 1 2 3 4 … 9 下一页

最新跟贴（跟贴261条 有462人参与）

网易黑龙江省双鸭山市网友 ip：61.180.*.* 2014-12-18 09:48:38
总书记给全国领导干部做出表率，让老百姓心里感到踏实。
顶[0] 回复 收藏 分享 复制

网易黑龙江省双鸭山市网友 ip：61.180.*.* 2014-12-18 09:47:17
习书记心系百姓是人民群众的贴心人。
顶[0] 回复 收藏 分享 复制

网易黑龙江省双鸭山市网友 ip：61.180.*.* 2014-12-18 09:45:36
相信习总能广大人民群众把祖国建设的更加强大、美好！
顶[0] 回复 收藏 分享 复制

网易黑龙江省双鸭山市网友 ip：61.180.*.* 2014-12-18 09:44:13
习总书记反腐的决心就犹如百姓苦等的甘泉 坚决拥护习总书记
顶[0] 回复 收藏 分享 复制

网易黑龙江省双鸭山市网友 ip：61.180.*.* 2014-12-18 09:42:55
人民对美好生活的向往，就是我们的奋斗目标。
顶[0] 回复 收藏 分享 复制

网易黑龙江省双鸭山市网友 ip：61.180.*.* 2014-12-18 09:41:53
习近平总书记绝对是个优秀的主席，句句贴心，行动亦暖人心
顶[0] 回复 收藏 分享 复制

网易黑龙江省双鸭山市网友 ip：61.180.*.* 2014-12-18 09:40:42
我们的人民热爱生活，期盼有更好的教育、更稳定的工作、更满意的收入、更可靠的社会保障
顶[0] 回复 收藏 分享 复制

FIGURE 5.2 Sample comments by Internet commentators.

Source: http://comment.news.163.com/news3_bbs/ADJDQ4OV00014JB5.html, retrieved June 30, 2016.

TABLE 5.2 Translated Comments for Figure 5.2

Topic: Implications for Xi Jinping's first talk on the Four Comprehensives

Netease user from Heilongjiang Shuangyashan   2014-12-18 09:48:38
ip：61.180.*.*

The general secretary sets a good example for cadres across the country, making us ordinary citizens feel assured.

Netease user from Heilongjiang Shuangyashan   2014-12-18 09:47:17
ip：61.180.*.*

General Secretary Xi bears the people in mind and is a close friend of the people.

Netease user from Heilongjiang Shuangyashan   2014-12-18 09:45:36
ip：61.180.*.*

I believe President Xi will lead the people to make our motherland stronger and more prosperous!

Netease user from Heilongjiang Shuangyashan   2014-12-18 09:44:13
ip：61.180.*.*

General Secretary Xi's resolution to fight corruption is the sweet spring that we the masses have been longing for. Firmly support General Secretary Xi.

Netease user from Heilongjiang Shuangyashan   2014-12-18 09:42:55
ip：61.180.*.*

The people's yearning for a good and beautiful life is the goal for us to strive for.

Netease user from Heilongjiang Shuangyashan   2014-12-18 09:41:53
ip：61.180.*.*

General Secretary Xi Jinping is absolutely an excellent chairman. Every sentence of his speech is close to our hearts, and his actions also warm our hearts.

Netease user from Heilongjiang Shuangyashan   2014-12-18 09:40:42
ip：61.180.*.*

Our people love life. They expect better education, more stable jobs, better income, and more reliable social security.

Source: 163.com.

FIGURE 5.3 **Sample user profile of an Internet commentator.**

Source: Netease (news.163.com). Specific URL is not provided to protect the privacy for this user, even though the user is highly likely to be an Internet commentator.

TABLE 5.3 Translated Comments from Figure 5.3

2015-01-23 17:28:20
Well said, President Xi. The people's prosperity, peace, equality, and justice are the core national interests. Strongly support General Secretary Xi.
From: Xi Jinping Inspects Army in Kunming Emphasizing Close-to-Real Training

2015-01-18 12:44:15
His tone is calm and rigorous. He sincerely wants to serve the people. Support President Xi.
From: News Focus on 1/18/2015: Xi'an Starts Food Security Regulation Campaign; Xi Jinping: Grey Income Will No Longer Be Part of Military Officers' Income

2015-01-17 13:25:48
Secretary Xi always prioritizes the masses' interest. He is the people's good secretary!
From: Xi Jinping on the Anti-Corruption Situation: How Can You Demand Others If You Are Not Clean Yourself?

2015-01-17 13:23:16
Every speech and action of President Xi is just so energizing. We support you!
From: Xi Jinping Mentioned Rules More Than Ten Times in Anti-Corruption Speech, Experts Say He Is Trying to Fix the Root

2015-01-17 13:20:12
Support President Xi. Hope China will get better and better.
From: Xi Jinping's Tough Internal Anti-Corruption Talk: Hold Provincial Party Chiefs Accountable

2015-01-17 13:05:42
Under the leadership of General Secretary Xi, China will surely become more prosperous.
From: Xi Jinping on Official Dining and Entertainment: Are You Comfortable Being Drunk All Day?

Source: 163.com

TABLE 5.4 Comparing Internet Commentating Activities on Top Leaders

	Comments Coded	Anonymous	Likely Internet Commentator	Likely Genuine	Unclear
Xi Jinping	1,133	193	786	140	14
	(100%)	(17.03%)	(69.37%)	(12.36%)	(1.24%)
Li Keqiang	446	238	58	138	12
	(100%)	(53.36%)	(13%)	(30.94%)	(2.69%)
Hu Jintao	292	103	9	145	35
	(100%)	(35.27%)	(3.08%)	(49.66%)	(11.99%)
Wen Jiabao	399	140	5	177	77
	(100%)	(35.09%)	(1.25%)	(44.36%)	(19.3%)

Note: News reports sampled from news.163.com. For reports with fewer than one hundred comments, all comments were coded. For reports with more than one hundred comments, the first sixty were coded.

by the local External Propaganda Office and delivered to municipal leaders daily.[81] Li Guanghua, a former deputy director of Hengyang Propaganda Department's Information Office, claimed that he used to organize online commentators to compile netizens' complaints and directly submit them to the local Party chief, who would then push for solutions. Student Internet commentators also assume similar responsibilities, such as collecting and reporting students' suggestions and criticisms.[82]

While "linking the government and the people" sounds like empty self-praise, Internet commentators have indeed helped citizens in some cases. For example, in 2014, in Hukou County, Jiangxi Province, local Internet commenters detected a Weibo entry alleging that a company owed 3 million yuan to more than three hundred migrant workers. Local authorities then looked into it and solved the problem by remunerating the migrant workers.[83] Similar cases are actually quite common, according to leaked internal emails from Zhanggong District, Ganzhou City, Jiangxi Province.

Evaluating the Online Commentator System

As traditional state propaganda becomes increasingly ineffective and inefficient, the fifty-cent army has seemingly come to the regime's rescue. Through astroturfing, Internet commentators serve as the state's covert hand to guide online expression. Compared with coercive measures such as censorship, astroturfing allows state agencies to use identity and rhetorical power—under the guise of being ordinary netizens—to persuade netizens and defend the regime. This is evidently a smart adaptation of the Party-state to the digital age.

The rise and spread of Internet commentators demonstrate the state's strong capacity to learn and mobilize. Initially a local innovation, the practice has not only diffused horizontally across the country, but also become a "national policy," in that it is now an integral part of the state's apparatus of propaganda and thought work. Through existing institutions, such as the propaganda system and the Communist Youth League, the Party-state can mobilize tens of thousands of Internet commentators at any given time. For instance, in March 2014, the Chinese Communist Youth League Central Committee urged colleges and universities to set up a nationwide Internet propaganda troop (*wangluo xuanchuanyuan*, 网络宣传员) of at least 350,000 members, with quotas of the troop assigned to each provincial unit (table 5.5).[84] In February 2015, the Central Committee called for the establishment of an even larger army of "youth Internet civilized volunteers" (*qingnian wangluo wenming zhiyuanzhe*, 青年网络文明志愿者), with a minimum quota of 10.5 million members.[85]

There is no doubt that the Party-state possesses formidable power and resources to institutionally and organizationally restructure itself, to mobilize its agents, and to adapt. But such strong capacity does not automatically guarantee successfully adaptation. Internet commentators have been mobilized for many purposes, including defusing online crises, facilitating state propaganda initiatives, cheerleading for the leaders, and connecting the state and the citizenry. But the state has generally failed in its mission of guiding public opinion online. Like other scholars who have studied this phenomenon, I find that Internet commentators communicate almost exclusively among themselves and

TABLE 5.5 The Chinese Communist Youth League's Provincial Quota for the Internet Propaganda Troop

Province	Quota	Province	Quota
Beijing	20,000	Hubei	20,000
Tianjin	10,000	Hunan	15,000
Hebei	15,000	Guangdong	20,000
Shanxi	10,000	Guangxi	10,000
Inner Mongolia	7,000	Hainan	2,000
Liaoning	20,000	Sichuan	12,000
Jilin	10,000	Chongqing	10,000
Heilongjiang	10,000	Guizhou	6,000
Shanghai	10,000	Yunnan	8,000
Jiangsu	20,000	Tibet	1,500
Zhejiang	15,000	Shaanxi	15,000
Anhui	15,000	Gansu	6,000
Fujian	10,000	Qinghai	2,000
Jiangxi	10,000	Ningxia	2,000
Shandong	20,000	Xinjiang	3,000
Henan	15,000	Bingtuan[a]	500

Total: 350,000

[a] "Bingtuan" refers to the Xinjiang Production and Construction Corporation.

Source: Chinese Communist Youth League Central Committee Office, "Wangluo Xuanchuanyuan Duiwu Jianshe Tongzhi" ("Circular on Establishing an Internet Propaganda Troop"), March 19, 2014.

very rarely interact with netizens.[86] One plausible explanation for this, of course, is that the state intends only to distract rather than engage netizens in online debates.[87] It is also possible that the state's goal is to signal its strength in maintaining social control and political order rather than persuade netizens.[88] But my analysis shows that Internet commentators do not engage in critical online discussion because they are unmotivated to excel at their job. In particular, the state's reliance on the propaganda system, the Communist Youth League, and colleges and universities to mobilize the fifty-cent army betrays how embedded the innovation is in the existing apparatus of propaganda and thought work. Such embeddedness, though able to facilitate the state to more effectively mobilize and control Internet commentators, has captured and bureaucratized the innovative adaptation, thus preventing the fifty-cent army from functioning effectively and, in many cases, rendering its work counterproductive.

First, the existing apparatus of propaganda and thought work is incapable of evaluating and improving the performance of Internet commentators. In fact, as most Internet commentators have been recruited from within the system, with selection criteria that give priority to political loyalty, they often lack proper skills to communicate appropriately with other netizens. As a result, it is not surprising at all that they are not functioning as effectively as the state might have anticipated. According to a former propaganda official in charge of Internet commentators in Hengyang, Hunan Province, Internet commentators vary in terms of their capabilities, and many of their comments "fail to guide public opinion online and even backfire sometimes."[89]

This capacity deficit is made worse by the improper incentive structure, because many Internet commentators simply are unmotivated to excel at their job. Evidently, most Internet commentators are part-time workers trolling for the state and poorly compensated. To many of them, commenting online for their sponsoring agencies is simply extra work. To others, the fact that they are paid makes the job seems to be a cheap "sale of souls" (*chumai linghun*, 出卖灵魂).[90] This is precisely why "fifty-cent army" has become a disgraceful label. As a campus forum commentator confessed,

My friends know that I am working as an online commentator. You cannot hide anything when you all live under the same roof. I remain silent most of the time and only remind them when they are going a little too far. It is not glorious, but they understand.[91]

Second, the embeddedness of the fifty-cent army has made it vulnerable to the problems that plague state propaganda work. While agencies such as the propaganda system and the Communist Youth League can mobilize Internet commentators en masse, their behavior and mindset are not adjusted to fulfill the new task of opinion manipulation.[92] In particular, these agencies have mostly turned political astroturfing into a mundane bureaucratic process of propaganda work, which is often mobilized in a top-down manner, with pleasing higher-ranking officials being the ultimate goal. Subsequently, Internet commentators care more about recognition from above than actually persuading netizens. This explains why Internet commentators have made little effort to hide their distinguishing characteristics or engage other netizens in online discussion. My analysis shows that in addition to being constantly pro-regime and using official language codes, Internet commentators tend to work only during office time, often publicize a large number of consecutive comments in a short period of time, and focus only on tasks assigned to them. Even online commenting on President Xi Jinping—clearly a task with paramount political significance—is implemented in such a crude fashion that any savvy netizen will be able to see through these comments. Apparently, either the entire propaganda system is so incompetent that it does not realize it is doing a bad job, or it could not care less about the actual impact of its work. The latter is more likely considering the incentive structure: For Internet commentators (and propaganda officials), the primary audience is not netizens, but their superiors. In fact, a Hengyang Information Office official admitted that "pleading for achievements" (*yaogong*, 邀功) was one of his goals when mobilizing Internet commentators to interact with the local Party chief in an online interview.[93]

The same rationale explains why the fifty-cent army has also been frequently exposed by state propaganda. In fact, the Party-state, which has repeatedly stressed the importance of strengthening its ideational leadership and maintaining social stability, is unabashed about its intention to control and manage public opinion. For local authorities and propaganda agencies, the fifty-cent army is a means of demonstrating their efforts to upper levels of government. This is why reports on recruiting, training, and rewarding Internet commentators often make their way to online news portals, as well as traditional media such as newspapers and TV channels, which are much more closely watched by the state. For instance, in December 2006, Shanxi Province sponsored its first training session for Internet editors and commentators. The local media outlet, *Jincheng News Online*, which is under the direct management of the Jincheng Propaganda Department, not only reported on this event proudly, but also included in its report links to other influential media platforms that covered the news.[94] Apparently, for local propaganda officials, it is a significant accomplishment to get attention from central media such as *People's Daily Online* (people.cn) and national commercial portals such as QQ.com and 163.com. There are also many other cases of mainstream media reporting on the work of Internet commentators. For example, *Southern Metropolis Daily* reported on Gansu Province's initiative to hire 650 Internet commentators.[95] Similarly, when Guangdong Province planned to set up a new "Internet public opinion guidance troop" of ten thousand members, the news was covered by both *Guangzhou Daily* and the online news portal 163.com (Netease).[96] These examples demonstrate that the propaganda machinery does not intend to keep Internet commentators in the dark, which is clearly a legacy of past approaches to propaganda and thought work.

The fact that the state has failed to keep Internet commentators covert has made what had at first appeared to be a smart state adaptation ineffective. The exposure of the fifty-cent army has only contributed to a growing antipathy toward state propaganda and authoritarian rule, leading to the erosion, rather than consolidation, of the state's ideational leadership. In particular, as netizens learn about the fifty-cent army, it is only natural for them to be doubtful about any pro-regime expression. This explains why voices in favor of the government have become "politically incorrect" among netizens and why any government connection in online expression is seen as an "instant negative."[97] As peer pressure distances netizens from pro-regime stances, potential government supporters are demoralized and silenced. As the Beijing Normal University professor Zhang Shengjun puts it, "Now, the fifty-cent army has become a baton waved toward all Chinese patriots."[98] A flood of criticism has intensified the mutual distrust felt among netizens, exacerbating the labeling wars, as will be further discussed in chapters 6 and 7.

CONCLUSION

The rise of Internet commentators provides an excellent opportunity to examine the capacity and adaptability of the Chinese authoritarian regime. It is clear that the Party-state recognizes that the anonymity of online expression not only frees the flow of information for the citizenry, but also enables itself to covertly shape popular opinion. When the state media lost their credibility, the fifty-cent army could have helped the state "guide" (*yindao*, 引导) popular opinion more effectively to soothe the adverse effects of online crises and spread progovernment voices. Through an analysis of the recruitment, training, rewarding, and functioning of the Internet commentator system, this chapter shows that the Party-state has demonstrated considerable capacity to mobilize its agents and adapt to new challenges. But the seemingly smart strategy has not turned out to be as effective as the state might have anticipated. As this chapter shows, since Internet commentators lack both the incentive and the capability to engage netizens in critical debates, they focus only on cheerleading and demonstrating their loyalty to superiors (ultimately to Xi Jinping), thus failing in their mission. Moreover, relying on the fifty-cent army often backfires because the supposedly invisible force has been made visible for a number of reasons: They are identifiable through their behavior traits, and they have been frequently exposed by netizens, dissidents, and foreign media. Quite ironically, they are often exposed by the state itself because their own sponsoring agencies, incentivized to seek recognition from higher levels of government, attempt to attract rather than avoid publicity. But this outcome is to be expected given that the Internet commentator system is embedded in the existing apparatus of propaganda and thought work, which though quite strong and resourceful, follows a set of institutional rules, procedures, and behavior patterns that are incompatible with the mission of engineering online opinion. The fact that the state has encountered difficulties in trying to translate its pre-Internet power and resources into an effective online trolling machine suggests that it is necessary to problematize state adaptability in the digital age.

The evolution of the Internet commentator system also confirms the fragmented authoritarianism thesis that depicts the Chinese Party-state as divided across different levels and sectors.[99] Begun as a local innovation and spread through imitation and mutual learning, the Internet commentator system was clearly not a policy push from the central government. Central coordination, which exists in some cases today, is still mostly absent, as Internet commentators are sponsored and mobilized by local authorities or specific state agencies for their own purposes. That being said, there are signs of increasing activity among Internet commentators in central-coordinated propaganda campaigns, especially since Xi Jinping came into power. The increased reliance on manufactured pro-regime voices online betrays the new administration's profound sense of insecurity.

The state is not the only actor with the will and capacity to manipulate popular opinion online for political purposes. Other sociopolitical actors such as aggrieved netizens and dissident groups have also been found to employ PR tactics like astroturfing to spread their own voices. To better understand the discourse competition in Chinese cyberspace, nonstate actors' attempts to manufacture discontent and the subsequent implications also deserve close examination. The next chapter explores how online opinion engineering efforts by regime critics have intensified netizens' identity anxiety. Such anxiety fuels discourse wars among netizens, contributing to the rise of a nationalistic narrative that depicts regime critics, pro-liberal media, and foreign countries as national enemies trying to sabotage the rise of China. This explains why the erosion of state discourse has yet to be translated into support for regime-challenging discourse.

6

MANUFACTURING DISTRUST

Online Political Opposition and Its Backlash

Some people said that two hundred died in the Square and others claimed that two thousand died. There were also stories of tanks running over students who were trying to leave. I have to say that I did not see any of that. I don't know [where] those people did [see these things]. I myself was in the Square until six thirty in the morning. I kept thinking, are we going to use lies to attack an enemy who lies? Aren't facts powerful enough? To tell lies against our enemy's lies only satisfies our need to vent our anger, but it's a dangerous thing to do. Maybe your lies will be exposed, and you'll be powerless to fight your enemy.[1]

—HOU DEJIAN, IN *TIANANMEN: THE GATE OF HEAVENLY PEACE*

The Swedish scholar Johan Lagerkvist argues that the struggle in Chinese cyberspace is better viewed as a competition among Party-state, youth/subaltern, and transnational business norms, which is fostering normative change and helping move the nation toward inclusive democracy.[2] This perspective of norms competition is valuable, though many may disagree with the optimistic prediction of a normative move toward inclusive democracy. It is clear that online expression in China is not merely a story of censorship and counter-censorship, but also one of a number of discourses competing with each other for influence. Moreover, the Internet has empowered not only the voices of regime critics, but those of a diverse range of actors, including the state and its supporters. The state is as much a producer and distributor of online content as the censor and repressor, particularly as it begins to embrace innovative propaganda tactics. Meanwhile, netizens are demonstrating diverse political orientations. According to the Chinese scholar Yonggang Li, certain state measures, such as the control of Internet cafés, actually enjoy popular support, which feeds into the state's agenda of content control.[3] Rightist and leftist netizens have been debating each other and have formed stable discursive communities.[4] Cyber-nationalists demonstrate pro-regime tendencies and inclinations to challenge the state's claims to nationalist legitimacy.[5] In a recent study, the communications scholar Min Jiang argues that both civil and uncivil discourses and behaviors co-exist in Chinese cyberspace, resulting in a coevolution of the Internet, uncivil society, and authoritarianism.[6] Such studies break with simplistic state-versus-society or censorship-versus-counter-censorship views of Internet governance, revealing a pluralized cyberspace of multiple public spheres in which various discourses compete with each other for the minds and hearts of netizens, rather than a terrain dominated by state-versus-society confrontation.[7]

While chapter 5 demonstrated how the Chinese Party-state uses astroturfing as a PR tactic to compete with (rather than simply censor and suppress) regime critics, this chapter further complicates the discourse competition perspective by examining how nonstate actors have attempted to engineer popular opinion online. In particular, by revealing how regime critics have ironically fed the popular imagination with the idea of national enemies conducting online sabotage against China, this chapter identifies a mechanism through which nationalist netizens and discourses become highly pro-regime in Chinese cyberspace. This mechanism helps explain the resilience of the Chinese authoritarian regime despite its clumsy efforts to control and shape online expression.

To map the complex dynamics of discourse competition among the diverse actors at the micro-level of cyber-activity, the following sections first explore the online opinion–engineering activities of dissidents and then focus on the rise of pro-regime voices. By highlighting the discursive construction of "national enemies," the chapter

illuminates the process of identity formation and discourse pluralization in Chinese cyberspace and explains why the erosion of state
norms has yet to translate into support for regime critics or a normative transition to inclusive democracy.[8]

WEAPONS OF THE WEAK: POPULAR-OPINION ENGINEERING BY NONSTATE ACTORS

Online opinion manipulation tactics such as astroturfing were not
invented by the state. In fact, BBS users were among the first to employ
such trolling techniques, though seldom for political purposes.[9] In
the early days of BBSs, when the top ten threads on the front page
were selected and ranked according to the total number of participat-
ing accounts, trolling tactics were employed by users to help favored
topics "hit the top ten" (*chong shida*, 冲十大). In addition to inviting
friends to join, users employed multiple ghost accounts to fabricate a
crowd.[10] As the Internet began to penetrate further into Chinese society, and as online expression gained increasing public influence,[11] more
actors, including aggrieved petitioners and businesses,[12] began using
astroturfing to garner attention, to attract media, and to put pressure
on the authorities.[13] Popular platforms such as Tianya's "Free" board
attracted so many petitioners that mutual competition sometimes
drove users to create multiple accounts or recruit relatives and friends
in order to "bump up threads" (*dingtie*, 顶帖).

Opinion manipulation tactics such as astroturfing and rumor-
spreading are natural weapons for disadvantaged social groups like
petitioners or dissidents who have few outlets for dissent in a repressive
regime that controls most media resources.[14] In particular, compared
with petitioners with specific grievances and limited goals, dissident
groups challenging the legitimacy of the entire political system face an
even harsher environment, forcing them to rely on low-profile, everyday forms of resistance. For instance, since the crackdown on Falun
Gong, underground practitioners have been mobilizing through tactics
like posting ads on telephone poles, writing slogans on paper currency
notes, and secretly distributing newspapers and CDs.

With the Great Firewall filtering keywords and blocking suspicious IP addresses, dissidents must hide their identities to bypass state censorship. Meanwhile, many forums also muffle identifiable dissident voices to avoid state repercussions. For instance, Bdwm used to explicitly refuse reposts from Falun Gong sources such as the *Epoch Times*. Similarly, Mitbbs decided to eliminate Falun Gong materials from several boards in order to establish a legitimate mirror site for its domestic Chinese users in 2008. In addition to state and management censorship, dissidents sometimes suffer popular antipathy, making astroturfing a more effective option for them to promulgate their messages. For instance, Falun Gong sources were banned from Mitbbs's "ChinaNews" and "Military" boards by popular demand from users who believed that Falun Gong sources were not credible and were unhappy with Falun Gong practitioners who were flooding these boards with a huge number of posts.[15] Thus, astroturfing tactics protect dissidents' voices from state and management blacklisting, and from potential backlash from other netizens.

Dissident groups have spread their information through email spam and via online forums, as has been documented in a report by the global policy think tank RAND titled *You've Got Dissent*.[16] Falun Gong, for instance, is known for its online campaign efforts, and messages posted by Falun Gong practitioners often carry certain identifying characteristics. An email I received defaming Jiang Zemin, whose administration suppressed the spiritual group, serves as a good example.[17] The email claimed that Jiang had a messy private life and had even asked for sexual services during an official visit to Reno, Nevada, in the 1980s. Though users could not positively identify the sender's identity, the fact that the email was an attempt to defame Zemin points to Falun Gong.

Dissident attempts to delegitimize the regime can be indirect and nuanced. On December 1, 2010, an article titled "Alien Visits Earth: Astonishing Remarks from Martian Boy" was posted on "ChinaNews@Mitbbs," citing an alleged article from *Pravda*, the official newspaper of the Russian Communist Party, regarding a Russian boy who claimed to be a Martian. The post, written in an eschatological tone, claimed that the 2008 Sichuan earthquake was punishment for a "nation lacking belief," prophesied future catastrophes that would cause nearly one million Chinese deaths, and claimed the Martian boy was on a mission to find a China-born "guiding spirit" for humankind. However, none of these points, many of which echo Falun Gong writings, can be found in the *Pravda* article. In addition, while the *Pravda* article was published as early as May 2008, the Chinese post did not start to flood the web until December 2010, with the earliest version found on Minghui.org, a Falun Gong website. Also, Google search results show that it was reposted widely on other Falun Gong websites. The post managed to penetrate popular domestic Chinese forums such as Kdnet, Kds (club. pchome.net), and Xcar (xcar.com). Many netizens suspected the post had Falun Gong origins.[18]

A widely circulated post comparing Chinese and U.S. government buildings provides another case of dissident astroturfing. The post juxtaposes extravagant Chinese city government buildings with austere U.S. city halls, conveying a clear and powerful message: Government agencies and officials in China prioritize their own comfort over the needs of the people. Though the message contains a kernel of truth, watchful netizens uncovered evidence of manipulation. Whereas the photographs of Chinese buildings were correctly identified, most of the photos of the U.S. buildings were distorted; some were simply fake, others were purposefully miniaturized, and still others were photographs from tiny cities with one thousand or so residents, not even as big as some Chinese villages.[19] Many netizens believed that the post was an astroturfing effort by democratic dissidents overseas.[20] Some believed that the same group also fabricated the widely circulated "Rand Opinions on the Chinese People," a falsified document circulated so widely online that Rand was forced to comment on the issue and disown the report. According to the Rand Corporation's official disclaimer, the fabricated report contains "extremely negative comments about Chinese people."[21]

Though it is hard to draw conclusions about the degree of planning behind these online tactics, these examples suggest highly purposeful attempts at evasion by dissidents. Overseas dissident groups, including those made up of Falun Gong practitioners, democratic activists, and people involved with the Tibet and Xinjiang independence movements, are widely believed to be the major actors behind such attempts. One top executive of a major website interviewed for this study suggested that a subversive force was acting behind the scenes to manipulate online opinion.[22] Many other interviewees also commented they would not be surprised if this were true.

IMAGINED ENEMIES AND BACKLASH

Political astroturfing by dissident groups may have helped erode the regime's basis of legitimacy, but these efforts have also generated a backlash. For some netizens, the activities of online dissidents in fact bolster state propaganda identifying a handful of subversive forces, thus creating a counter-espionage atmosphere, at the heart of which is an imagined group of national enemies trying to sabotage China through online opinion manipulation. These enemies include both external hostile forces (especially Western powers) and internal subversive forces such as dissident groups, political and civil rights activists, pro-liberal media professionals, and intellectuals whose interests or values align with those of the external "enemies." It is believed that both the external and internal forces are actively engineering public opinion online in China, not for the good of the Chinese people or the nation as they claim, but for their own benefits or ulterior motives. Thus, their activities should be considered espionage, which patriotic netizens have the responsibility to disclose and counter. Often, the believability and transmission of such counter-espionage ideation is enhanced by netizens' online experiences.

Many Chinese harbor suspicions of Western countries and believe that if they are not conspiring to undermine China's rise, they are at least biased against China and its people.[23] These suspicions are often reinforced when they perceive Western interference with China's domestic affairs. For instance, former Secretary of State Hillary Clinton's involvement in the Google withdrawal case—including her dinner with representatives of IT giants such as Google and Twitter and her later statement on Internet freedom—effectively convinced many netizens that Google was a tool of the U.S. government, driving them to defend the Chinese government even though they disliked censorship.[24]

Similarly, the U.S. ambassador Jon Huntsman's presence at a Jasmine Revolution demonstration in Beijing in February 2011 was taken as evidence of U.S. attempts to destabilize China.[25] And his remarks about reaching out to allies and constituencies within China to "take China down" immediately caught fire among netizens and were thought to be a declaration of America's hostile intentions.[26]

Similarly, Chinese nationalism is often spurred by perceived biases in Western media. A series of events in 2008 is particularly revealing. During the Lhasa riot in March 2008,[27] Rao Jin, a Tsinghua University graduate and NewSmth user, set up a special platform called Anti-CNN.com,[28] which compiled screenshots of distorted Western media coverage of the riot. Such distortions included videos and photos of Nepalese and Indian police forces said to be Chinese police in Lhasa,[29] cropping photos to misguide readers,[30] mistaking rescue efforts as suppression,[31] and other direct manipulations of online opinion.[32] These reports assisted Chinese netizens in "[imagining] the Western world as a collective that has shared perceptions, shared distortions and shared biases towards China," as the Chinese public intellectual Liang Wendao put it.[33] The following poem by an anonymous author, written in response to the Western media coverage of the 2008 Lhasa riot, demonstrates how a particular event may trigger and amplify Chinese netizens' anger toward the West:[34]

WHAT DO YOU REALLY WANT FROM US

When we were the Sick Man of Asia,
We were called the Yellow Peril.
When we are billed as the next Superpower, we are called The Threat.
When we closed our doors, you launched the Opium War to open our
*   markets.*
When we embraced free trade, you blamed us for stealing your jobs.
When we were falling apart, you marched in your troops and demanded your
*   fair share.*
When we tried to put the broken pieces back together again,
Free Tibet, you screamed. It was an Invasion!
When we tried communism, you hated us for being communist.

When we embraced capitalism, you hated us for being capitalist.
When we had a billion people, you said we were destroying the planet.
When we tried limiting our numbers, you said we abused human rights.
When we were poor, you thought we were dogs.
When we lend you cash, you blame us for your national debts.
When we build our industries, you call us polluters.
When we sell you goods, you blame us for global warming.
When we buy oil, you call it exploitation and genocide.
When you go to war for oil, you call it liberation.
When we were lost in chaos, you demanded the rule of law.
When we uphold law and order against violence, you call it a violation of
    human rights.
When we were silent, you said you wanted us to have free speech.
When we are silent no more, you say we are brainwashed xenophobes.
Why do you hate us so much? We asked.
No, you answered, we don't hate you.
We don't hate you either,
But do you understand us?
Of course we do, you said,
We have AFP, CNN and BBC. . .
What do you really want from us?
Think hard first, then answer . . .
Because you only get so many chances.
Enough is Enough, Enough Hypocrisy for This One World.
We want One World, One Dream, and Peace on Earth.
This Big Blue Earth is Big Enough for all of Us.

During these incidents, netizens not only criticized reports from the Western media, but also mobilized to reach out and persuade Western audiences. One Mitbbs user posted a long summary of Australian high school English teacher Mark A. Jones's debate with a pro-Tibet lobbyist as an example of how to effectively communicate with and win over Westerners.[35] A number of similar posts were circulated on Chinese forums such as Mitbbs, NewSmth, and Tianya to facilitate the spread of China's voices. Such efforts took on an even bigger role than the state propaganda machine in publicly defending China's policy in Tibet because of the popularity of the posts and because such posts are not products of the state propaganda machine. In addition, these netizens demonstrated that coverage by Western media can generate considerable backlash, sometimes mobilizing Chinese netizens against the West more effectively than the Chinese state.

Also in 2008, not long after the Lhasa riot, Chinese netizens rallied patriotically during the Olympic torch relay. To show support for the nation, Mitbbs users even donated airfare for those flying from other areas to San Francisco to follow the torch on its U.S. leg.[36] There, they were irritated to find that protesters received far more media coverage than the far larger crowds who gathered in support of China. Furthermore, the CNN commentator and host Jack Cafferty's careless comment—"I think they're basically the same bunch of goons and thugs they've been for the last fifty years"—further infuriated Chinese netizens, who cited his remark as another manifestation of the Western media's stubborn anti-Chinese bias.[37]

In addition to the West, major dissident groups are also commonly portrayed as enemies of the nation or surrogates for hostile foreign powers. Accounts of dissident groups engineering online public opinion are perceived by many netizens as interfering with China's development, thus justifying counter-dissident efforts on the part of both netizens and the regime, even censorship. In fact, the popular perception that democratic activists, Falun Gong practitioners, and separatists (including those involved in the Taiwan, Tibet, and Xinjiang independence movements) are part of a joint force coordinated by the United States and other Western powers is widespread. Rumors about Wang Dan (a student leader in the 1989 Tiananmen Square democratic movement) receiving funds from the independence-leaning Democratic Progressive Party administration in Taiwan are frequently cited as evidence of democratic activists colluding with separatist movements.[38] Furthermore, the awarding of the 2010 Nobel Peace Prize to Liu Xiaobo generated similar backlash among nationalistic netizens. The Noble laureate was accused of "taking money from the National Endowment of Democracy," supporting the U.S. wars in Iraq and Afghanistan, and demeaning China by making statements like "It would take three hundred years of colonization for China to become what Hong Kong is today."[39]

The perception of online dissidence as a threat to national inter-ests has soured many netizens on the democratization movement that sprung up in the 1980s. Democratic activists are perceived as being manipulated by external hostile forces, and nationalistic netizens blame them for being too stubborn to compromise in 1989, for leaving fellow students behind while fleeing Tiananmen, and for escaping the bloody crackdown in China to live an easy life overseas. Such percep-tions, in combination with factional struggles within the democratic movement, have convinced many netizens that the type of democracy advocated by these activists is not a viable alternative to the Chinese Communist Party.[40]

This legacy became evident during the 2011 pro-democracy "Jas-mine Revolution" protests in China. When the democratic activist Wang Juntao posted a tweet urging well-known democratic activists to stay at home to avoid repression,[41] he triggered a wave of jeers aimed at democratic activists. Ranxiang, a popular microblogger on Weibo who calls herself the "Chair of the Fifty-Cent Party,"[42] posted a series of satirical entries, including the following, which were then retweeted by fellow microbloggers and widely circulated in major forums[43]:

> Let democratic elites go first, and you should hide behind them.[44]
>
> Most democratic elites have enjoyed the fruits of China's reform and opening-up and led a good life, so they should be on the fore-front and die for their cause; we common people haven't had enough good days and cannot die now. What's more, your death is different from an elite's death: yours is as light as a swan feather, and theirs is as weighty as Mount Tai.[45]

These passages depict democratic activists as cowards who have been selfishly risking the lives of ordinary citizens for their own agenda. This reminds many netizens of Chai Ling, one of the most noted student leaders of the 1989 Tiananmen movement, who said "You, the Chinese! You are not worth my struggle! You are not worth my sacrifice!"[46]

It is not just dissident groups who are constructed as internal ene-mies, however. Pro-democracy liberal intellectuals, opinion leaders, and media professionals are also lumped together as "elites" (*jingying*, 精英) and "universalists" (*pushipai*, 普世派), or sometimes as "universal elites" (*pushi jingying*, 普世精英).[47] For instance,

> I admire the young people for their courage in pursuing democracy. But in case bloody revolution happens, you must remember that your life is most important. Don't trust those *elites* who talk about liberty above everything . . . . Those with the most adamant revolutionary will like *Zhang Ming, Li Chengpeng, Huang Jianxiang, Xia Yeliang, Tufu, Zhan Jiang,* and *Sanren* should be on the forefront. If they are not, you should try all means to bring them to the forefront and use them as human shields.[48]

The "elites" listed here are all public intellectuals, media professionals, or opinion leaders known for their "universalist" stance. Given their influence on online public opinion, some netizens are justifiably wary about their motivations. For instance, during the Arab Spring, the popular playwright and microblog celebrity Ning Caishen posted a Weibo entry reporting that his friends were stuck in Cairo, Egypt, owing to a slow and inefficient evacuation by the Chinese embassy. The message was retweeted over twenty-eight thousand times before it was deleted by Ning himself, recognizing that the situation was not entirely the embassy's fault. However, his corrective tweet to clarify his overreaction and acknowledge the embassy's work, which was posted just three hours after his first tweet, was retweeted only 491 times in three weeks.[49] This contrast not only shows how criticism of the government easily becomes viral and thus difficult to neutralize, but also convinces many that an "invisible hand" (*mushou heishou*, 幕后黑手) is manipulating online opinion for subversive purposes.[50] In another case, three individuals, Li Chengpeng, Zhang Ming, and Huang Jianxiang, retweeted a Weibo post claiming that a government corruption case involving $25,000 was the biggest in U.S. history (in contrast to corruption cases in China involving much greater sums). Li's retweet alone was subsequently retweeted close to three thousand times by his followers in about a week, few of whom doubted the claim.[51] But critical netizens, while acknowledging China's corruption problem, correctly cast doubt on the figure and also took the tweet as evidence of opinion leaders irresponsibly inciting anti-government sentiment by overstating the honesty of U.S. officials.[52]

Many netizens also believe that pro-liberal media groups such as the Southern Clique (*Nanfang Xi*, 南方系) are motivated by a clandestine agenda.[53] Named after the outspoken Southern Media Group, known for its investigative journalism and pro-liberal standpoint,[54] the Southern Clique is a loose grouping of media outlets and professionals either currently or formerly affiliated with the Southern Media Group. A former *Southern Metropolis Daily* (*Nanfang Dushibao*, 南方都市报) reporter confirmed the group's tendency to report on "issues related to the public interest, especially government misbehavior."[55] The Southern Clique's critical stance is a major part of its reputation, and the group is well respected among many readers. Yet it also invites criticism from both nationalists and politically neutral netizens suspicious of any attempt to guide public opinion. In fact, the Southern Clique is frequently charged online with "smuggling in its own values and beliefs in reports" and "brainwashing" the public.[56] The following blog entry by Liu Yuan—who used to work at *Southern Metropolis Daily* and was editor in chief of *South Morning Post* (*Nanguo Zaobao*, 南国早报)—boasting of the influence of the Southern Media Group only validates netizens' belief that the group is engaged in a subversive conspiracy:

Southern Group's contribution is not limited to the newspapers it directly operates. It has educated countless people who worked there and influenced peer media professionals. When it and *China Youth Daily* become role models, their values are embraced by numerous media professionals. . . .

The Internet provides the most freedom of expression. But interestingly, left voices are rare on major portals, except Sina. . . .

I told my friends, among the four major portals, QQ's editor in chief, Chen Juhong, was from *Southern Weekend* [*Nanfang Zhoumo*, 南方周末]; Sohu's Zhao Mu, who runs the blog sector, was from *Southern Weekend*, and Liu Xinzheng was from the *Beijing News*

[*Xin Jingbao*, 新京报; cofounded by *Guangming Daily* and the Nanfang Group]; Sina has many old friends from *Southern Metropolis Daily* and the *Beijing News*, not to mention *Netease*, whose vice-president, editor in chief, deputy editor in chief, chief inspector, and almost all managing channel editors were from the Southern Group. . . .

No doubt, they play a big role in clamping down extreme nationalism. Pitiful leftists can only curse in their or others' blogs in vain. Internet gurus know that a rational, portal-recommended post would be more influential than ten thousand follow-up, cursing, leftist posts.[57]

For many netizens, self-identified liberals such as Liu Yuan are not practicing freedom of expression. Instead, they are merely trying to establish their own dominance in online expression. And to achieve this goal, they are more than willing to suppress different voices with managerial power. A widely circulated online image demonstrates how some netizens ridicule the pro-liberal media's disdain for nonliberal viewpoints. The image includes the logos of three perceived pro-liberal media outlets: *Southern Weekend*, Netease, and Kdnet. Under each logo is a mission statement for the particular media platform. They read, "We do not allow you to say anything bad about the U.S.!" (*Southern Weekend*); "We do not allow you to say anything good about China!" (Netease); and "We are discussing democracy, and we do not allow you to say anything!" (Kdnet.net).[58]

Such negative views of the pro-liberal media are only reinforced when reports contain misleading factual errors. For instance, after the Polish president's plane crashed in April 2010, QQ (which is popularly believed to be part of the Southern Clique) praised the frugality of the Polish government for owning just one plane. This detail immediately caught netizens' attention, and online accusations of extravagance and waste in Chinese government spending followed. Suspicious fact-checkers, however, soon found that Poland actually has six planes (two Tu-154s and four Yak-40s) and a number of helicopters for its leaders. Once fact-checkers publicized these errors, netizens accused the Southern Clique of deliberately manipulating public opinion to serve its own interests or of at least being blinded by its predispositions.[59]

The social construction of enemies through online discourse evokes strong emotions. When *Southern Weekend* was the only media outlet granted an interview with President Obama during his 2009 visit to China, nationalistic netizens perceived this as a reward for American "agents." When the interview was printed, *Southern Weekend* left the bottom half of its front page blank (*kai tianchuang*, 开天窗) under the Obama interview as a protest against state censorship. The action, while applauded by pro-liberal netizens, was viewed by their nationalistic counterparts as a public humiliation, defaming China by begging for foreign intervention in domestic Chinese affairs.[60] Similarly, online discourse surrounding the case of Yao Jiaxin, who was executed for the stabbing death of a woman following a hit-and-run, strengthened netizens' perception of a pro-Western media. The victim's lawyer posted a microblog entry claiming that a Southern Clique journalist had tried to dissuade him from pursuing the death penalty for Yao in order to promote the abolition of the death penalty in China. Numerous netizens subsequently became incensed at what they perceived as the pro-liberal media being infiltrated by "pussy" (yes, they used the English word, which has a similar pronunciation to the Chinese word for *universalism*: *pushi*, 普世) Western values that are sympathetic to killers but not victims.[61]

TWO TALES: A MULTIPLAYER MODEL OF ONLINE DISCOURSE COMPETITION

Online PR practices like astroturfing by both the state and its challengers have exacerbated confusion and distrust among netizens. On one hand, as discussed in chapter 5, many netizens are wary of state PR efforts to cover up failures and manipulate public opinion. In this framing, online discourse competition can be viewed as a story of netizens defending their freedoms against state censorship and manipulation. On the other hand, the discussion in this chapter illustrates the popular suspicion of mass opinion–engineering efforts by dissident groups and other regime challengers. This framing promotes a view of online discourse competition between pro-state and anti-state actors. Each viewpoint presents a distinctive perspective. Netizens either see themselves as freedom-loving fighters—allied to a degree with dissidents, other suppressed domestic actors, and foreign powers pushing for China's liberalization and democratization—struggling against state agents and brainwashed regime-defenders, or as patriots allied with the state against subversive actors, including netizens "brainwashed" by a pro-liberal media bias.

In anonymous online expression, both framings reveal anxiety about the political stance and true identity of others netizens. Widespread labeling wars—netizen groups attacking each other with derogatory labels—demonstrate these anxieties. Binary "us-versus-them" labels, as shown in table 6.1, reflect competing framings of online discourse without clearly defined or self-conscious group identities.

These labels often intentionally carry negative and even highly offensive connotations. For instance, in place of the Chinese character 愤 (angry) for "angry youth," its homonym, 粪 (shit), is often used. Similarly, the word "pussy" is often used to refer to universalism and universalists because the English pronunciation of the word is similar to that of the Chinese term 普世. These labeling confrontations often

TABLE 6.1 Labels and Labeling Wars

Two Dominant Framings in Online Political Expression in China

The Struggle-for-Freedom Tale		The Counterespionage Tale
		Net spies (*wangte*, 网特; foreign agents)
Fifty-cent army (*wumao dang*, 五毛党)	vs.	U.S. cents (*meifen dang*, 美分党)
		Road-leading party (*dailu dang*, 带路党)
		Dog food party (*gouliang dang*, 狗粮党)
Angry youth (*fengqin*, 愤青)	vs.	Elites (*jingying*, 精英)
Patriotic traitor (*aiguo zei*, 爱国贼)	vs.	Universalists (*pushipai*, 普世派)
		Western slaves (*xinu*, 西奴)
Little red guards (*xiaojiang*, 小将)	vs.	Old generals (*laojiang*, 老将)

serve only to reinforce netizens' existing biases and thus trap both sides into identities from which they are incapable of escaping. This devolution of labeling wars into conflicts between opposing parties comes up again in the next chapter when we will look more closely at the "voluntary fifty-cent army."

It is worth noting that these denigrating labels sometimes are reinterpreted differently and even internalized by the victims of the labeling war. For instance, the "road-leading party" (*dailu dang*, 带路党; the term literally means people that lead the way for invaders; it is used by nationalist netizens as an equivalent to betrayers of the nation) is depicted positively in an online image of a peasant giving directions to a United Nations (UN) solider.[62] The individual pictured has an honest face and invokes the image of an elderly farmer willingly assisting Chinese soldiers during China's anti-Japanese War. Behind the farmer and the UN solider is a flag, on which is written, "Leading the way [for foreign intervention] is glorious" and "Liberate China." It appears that the graph is meant to convey a more sympathetic than critical image of the road-leading party, which believes that China needs to be liberated again, possibly through foreign intervention.

The appendix provides an example of a dialogue typical of a labeling war, with the users anonymized. The thread, captured from Mitbbs, was initiated by "X18," a Xiaojiang (小将, "little red guard," often referring to pro-Chinese government users) user deriding Falun Gong practitioners ("wheels") for failing to seek political asylum status after destroying their Chinese passports upon arrival in the United States. In a condescending tone, he mocked these people because the United States had denied their appeal for political asylum and the Chinese government had refused to reissue them Chinese passports. "LBK," a Laojiang (老将, "old general," users that are against the Chinese government and the Party) user known for his anti-Party stance, replied immediately, jeering that XI8 might end up practicing Falun Gong in order to stay in the United States because he had not found a job yet— rather than a factual claim, such an accusation was meant to demean X18 as a jobless loser. XI8's follow-up reply showed that he actually had got a job and implied that LBK was a traitor and a loser by labeling him as an agent of the National Endowment for Democracy, which is

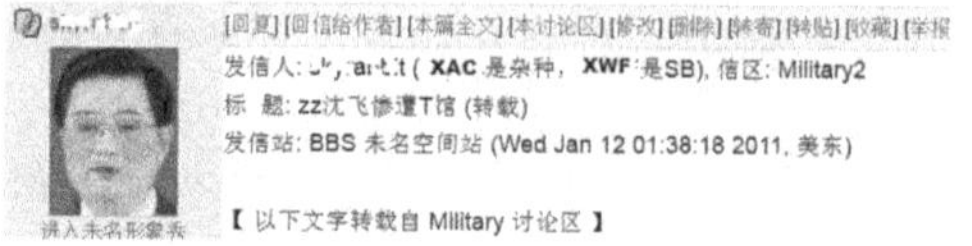

FIGURE 6.1 Avatar of an MITBBS User.

Source: mitbbs.com. Usernames are redacted to protect privacy of the users.

often perceived by nationalist netizens as a proxy of the United States government to subvert other countries. In return, LBK charged XI8 with being a Party-state proxy. As more users became involved, the discussion quickly devolved into attacks between Xiaojiang and Laojiang users blaming each other for being cheap, trashy, and selling their souls to either the Party-state or foreign enemies.

This kind of mutual antagonism sometimes escalates. For instance, a Laojiang user—whose political inclination is clear from his posts as well as his avatar (an uglified image of then president Hu Jintao; figure 6.1)—showed his hatred toward two Xiaojiang users, "XAC" and "XWF," by nicknaming himself "XAC is a bastard and XWF is a son of a bitch." Such hatred sometimes drives personal attacks to a vitriolic level; for example, an alleged Laojiang cursed some Xiaojiang users from Mitbbs and another overseas Chinese forum, 6park.com (implying that he was active on both forums), by creating an online graveyard. And on each gravestone was written, "The grave of the son-of-a-bitch fifty-cent dog XXX@YYY [ID@forum]'s stinky bitch mother, who died of AIDS." Below that was the national flag of the People's Republic of China with the stars replaced by the Chinese character "Mao" (毛) to symbolize the fifty-cent army. And on the left and right sides of the gravestone was text reading, "Listen to the Party, serve as the Party's dog, and pretend to be a human and yell out," and "Bite whoever the Party wants you to bite, and bite as many times as ordered."[63]

In contrast, like-minded users interact much more amicably among themselves, for purposes of both exchanging ideas and performative expression. Sharing similar values and opinions, these users sometimes ridicule discussions like cross-talk masters chiming back and forth to each other. Again, let's take the labeling war presented in the appendix as an example. "XWF" asked whether unsuccessful Falun Gong asylum-seekers without valid passports might have to stay underground for their entire lives. Another user, "XWR," quickly replied that he shouldn't worry because the U.S. government respects human rights. XWF then asks, "Won't illegal immigrants be thrown in jail?" XWR then explained his logic: Yes, illegal immigrants would be thrown in jail, but food and accommodation would be provided, thus demonstrating U.S. human rights. This dialogue clearly distorts the concept of human rights and makes little sense, unless viewed as purposeful performative behavior through which a common identity is strengthened and rival netizens are mocked.

There are two different framings reflected in labeling wars. In Xiao-jiang users' eyes, the Laojiang group comprises democratic activists, Falun Gong practitioners, and traitors, as well as their supporters.[64] For Laojiang users, Xiaojiang users are either members of the fifty-cent army or angry youth brainwashed by the Chinese state. Laojiang users on Mitbbs have even created a list of those they accuse of being part of the fifty-cent army, most of whom are Xiaojiang. Similarly, Xiaojiang users have identified a list of "China-betrayers" (*hanjian*, 汉奸). The confrontation spills over into the struggle for forum management: Mitbbs managers of the "ChinaNews" and "Military" boards are frequently criticized for taking one side and suppressing the other.[65]

Although the examples presented here are primarily from Mitbbs, similar phenomena occur on almost all major forums both inside and outside China, to varying degrees and with variations in the labels used.[66] However, whatever labels are deployed, the same dyadic pattern holds: Netizens on both sides, either intentionally or unintentionally, seek moral positionality in a binary framework by claiming they are speaking for the people, or on behalf of the truth, and blaming the other side for immorality, insincerity, or serving as either state or foreign agents. Given the different framings, netizens often resort to distinctive norms and facts in their debates, thus making online discussion unconstructive, with netizens primarily speaking with like-minded others rather than interacting constructively across opposing frameworks.[67]

The two framings analyzed here complicate the story of discourse competition in Chinese cyberspace beyond the narrative of social norms challenging Party-state norms. As the next section demonstrates, a complex and dynamic process of persuasion and dissuasion involving multiple actors with diverse beliefs, values, and identities permeates both framings, resulting in intriguing and sometimes unexpected implications for discourse competition.

COMPLICATIONS WITH THE MULTIPLAYER MODEL

The 2011 Japanese earthquake provides a chance to examine the complicated mechanisms at work in online discourse competition. After the quake, Chinese nationalism and anti-Japanese sentiment were stimulated by Japanese netizens, whose cynical reactions to China's assistance were translated and widely circulated on Chinese forums.[68] This was unexpected by a number of actors, including the governments and many netizens from both countries.[69] Chinese netizens were obviously not the intended audience when Japanese netizens expressed their views. Yet, the whole process traces back to a chain reaction that actually began much earlier when the Chinese media projected a largely negative image of China to its domestic audience, which then spread overseas. In fact, terms used by Japanese netizens, such as "poisonous milk powder" (*du naifen*, 毒奶粉) and "paper-filled buns" (*zhi baozi*, 纸包子), were all first disclosed by the Chinese media. This image reinforced Japanese netizens' already negative impression of China owing to longstanding historical animosity and territorial disputes. So when the Chinese responded to the Japanese earthquake and tsunami with good intentions,[70] some Japanese netizens revealed their distrust, which then was translated into Chinese and circulated in Chinese cyberspace. The contrast between the good intentions of the Chinese and hostility from the Japanese reinforced the image of an ungrateful Japan, reminding Chinese netizens of unpleasant historical experiences.[71] Through such complicated multi-actor dynamics, the impression of external hostility was strengthened, adding credibility to the counter-espionage narrative.

Interestingly, both the freedom-struggle and counter-espionage framings may backfire, further complicating the model. The mixed responses of Chinese netizens to Google's withdrawal from the country provide a good example of this. Though many framed the withdrawal as a counter-espionage story by imagining the company as a tool of the U.S. government,[72] netizens in general were divided on the issue. When one Ccthere user ("User A"), a website developer, expressed his sympathy for Google and dissatisfaction with state censorship, he was immediately criticized for being hijacked by Google:

> . . . This shows that "doggy" (a slighting homophone of "Google") has already abducted some of our nationals. No wonder "doggy" feels confident enough to challenge *tugong* [±工, a pet name for the Chinese Communist Party]. Mrs. Clinton is now taking charge, and "doggy" cannot quit the game now. Propping up compradors, cultivating elites, and hijacking public opinion, imperialist America has numerous means and is indeed the number-one empire.[73]

Infuriated, User A replied,

> Alright! I am a comprador. I am elite. I am a fifth-column agent planted in China by imperialists. I am the gun used by others. I have been manipulated and abducted. I should not have spoken my grievances because behind me stands imperialism. I should not have raised opinions toward website management because I am fooled, brainwashed, with my mind full of institutions and rules. . . . For small potatoes in the country like me, does it mean I am manipulated and attempt to attack the government when I talk about housing demolition? Does it mean I side with Western environmental fascists and attempt to attack the government when I talk about environmental protection? Does it mean I bind myself with American imperialists and attempt to attack the government when I talk about Internet governance and sympathize with Google? Does it mean I attempt to stimulate riots, create trouble, and point the spear toward the government when I sympathize with petitioning masses? Standing on the commanding heights of "For the rise of China" and criticizing others is easy. Others are deceived or manipulated, if not driven by bad intentions. . . . Please don't categorize me as being manipulated, abducted, or ignorant. I have my own judgment and thoughts.[74]

While the counter-espionage framing may persuade some netizens to adopt a nationalistic stance, User A's response demonstrates that such an approach may backfire: when one is portrayed as an enemy, one might get irritated and fight back. Clearly, User A's background as a web developer mattered.[75] Google not only provides services that benefit Internet users, but also has been a role model for IT professionals: Its decision to withdraw from China and the slogan "Do no evil" are shining symbols against state censorship and repression. Meanwhile, what discouraged netizens from further nationalistic mobilization were widespread rumors about how baidu.com, the Chinese search engine giant, gained market share through unfair competition and cooperation with regime censorship objectives.

CONCLUSION

This chapter demonstrates how regime critics, such as Western powers, dissident groups, and even pro-liberal intellectuals and media professionals, can suffer from a loss of credibility, just as the state can, in online discourse competition. Though the perception of regime critics as national enemies conducting online espionage by many netizens may be unfair, erroneous, or based on stereotypes, some netizens believe that a counter-espionage framing of their opponents has merit or at least makes more sense than a framing of a struggle for freedom. For these netizens, the paramount task is to defend China against these hostile forces rather than to fight for civil liberties or democracy.

The analysis in this chapter shows that online discourse competition in China is much more complicated than what Lagerkvist depicts as the state and the society interacting with an "uneasy social contract on control and freedom."[76] Thus, netizens' support of the regime is not merely a result of their deference to authoritarian rule or about seeking psychological coherence for the current political status quo. Rather, it represents a coherent and solid logic: They support a pro-state discourse not because the state is doing well, but because regime critics are not trustworthy and have failed to live up to their expectations.[77] For many netizens who buy into the counter-espionage framing, the

Chinese Party-state is a necessary evil for defending national interests and delivering prosperity.

To a large extent, imagining enemies is a process through which netizens form fragmented and unsystematic pieces of information into a stereotype. This is often done in a collective manner through interactions among like-minded netizens who echo and reinforce each other's views in online discussions. These like-minded netizens tend to form stable online communities in which they share common values, adopt a uniform behavioral code, and interact to sustain a preferred discourse.[78] Through repeated interactions with comrades, a common memory of online experiences is constructed, and collective identity is strengthened.

The next chapter examines the formation and maintenance of online communities by focusing on the so-called voluntary fifty-cent army, a group that claims to defend the regime on a voluntary basis. While this chapter emphasizes the process of netizens constructing a counter-espionage framing to make sense of discourse competition, chapter 7's study of the voluntary fifty-cent army highlights the group's identity formation, community building, and discourse production through daily interactions among themselves and against imagined enemies.

7

DEFENDING THE REGIME

The "Voluntary Fifty-Cent Army"

As chapter 5 revealed, the Party-state has turned to Internet commentators, commonly referred to as the "fifty-cent army," to produce seemingly spontaneous pro-state commentary. Such astroturfing efforts often backfire because netizens have wised up to this propaganda tactic, which has resulted in a pandemic of criticism of the state and its fifty-cent army agents. However, struggles for control in the competitive terrain of online discourse are not simply binary interactions between the state and those representing "society." Chapter 6 argued that through imagining "online enemies of the Chinese nation," a constituency of netizens has been persuaded by a counter-espionage framing that depicts regime challengers and their sympathizers as saboteurs of the nation rather than fighters for freedom and democracy. This suggests a multi-actor model of online discourse competition that involves the state, its critics, as well as fragmented netizen constituencies with diverse values, beliefs, and identities.

This chapter explores the fragmentary politics of online expression by looking at online communities, especially the "voluntary fifty-cent army" (*zidai ganliang de wumao*, 自带干粮的五毛). These netizens openly disagree with more radical netizens who directly challenge the regime or even pursue a regime-change agenda. In fact, they have emerged with a stated cause of defending the authoritarian regime on an unpaid basis. This is quite unusual given the liberal-leaning environment of online expression. By examining a selection of their tactics, this chapter reveals not only how members of the voluntary fifty-cent army maintain their identity through constant rhetoric battles with their opponents and amicable interactions among themselves, but also how their daily activities have created online communities in which a regime-defending discourse prevails. My study suggests a more balanced picture of China's Internet politics than previously available and also illustrates a complex pattern of state–society interaction in a reforming authoritarian regime. The anonymous discourse competition illustrates a struggle in which uncoercive power dominates and provides a chance to demonstrate empirically how creativity, art, and identity spill over into the realm of politics.

FRAGMENTED CYBERSPACE: TOWARD A PUBLIC SPHERE OR A BALKANIZED PUBLIC?

Scholars of Western and Chinese politics have drawn quite diverse conclusions about the impact online expression has on civic participation and politics in general. Given China's oppressive authoritarian regime, observers of Chinese Internet politics have understandably emphasized the liberalizing and empowering effects of the technology, as well as the state's efforts to constrain its impact. For instance, the sociologist Guobin Yang argues that the Internet has contributed to the rise of a public sphere, which in his conception is more about "free spaces" than "spaces for rational debate in the Habermasian sense."[1] In fact, with only a few exceptions,[2] concerns about the detrimental impact of the Internet on civil society and civic participation are largely nonexistent. Johan Lagerkvist puts this rationale most succinctly; acknowledging that the Internet in China has yet to evolve into a "public sphere," he sees online communities coalescing around shared affinity and interests as "public sphericules" that represent progress in unlocking the public sphere and serve as "bases for public opinion, social organizing, and the occasional stirring of political mobilization."[3] Although in his 2010 book, *After the Internet, Before Democracy*, Lagerkvist depicts the Internet as a platform for norms competition, he still frames the regulation, influence, and control of online expression as a "control-and-freedom" struggle between the Party-state and rising subaltern norms. More recent studies have started to focus on the varieties of online activism,[4] though few have truly gone beyond the state-versus-social dichotomy to fully appreciate the richness, diversity, and complexity of online expression in China.[5] In general, they still tend to implicitly or explicitly assume that the Internet is inherently regime-challenging.

While observers of Chinese Internet politics have hailed the technology for empowering society within an authoritarian regime,[6] people who study cyberpolitics elsewhere are less convinced. In addition to studies that question the Internet's empowering effects,[7] many have emphasized its detrimental effects. Matthew Hindman, for example, argues that instead of the Internet making public discourse more accessible, political advocacy communities and blogs follow a "winner-takes-all" distribution with a small number of sites getting most of the resources and attention, turning blogs into a new elite media.[8] Others argue that the Internet does not necessarily promote the critical exchange of ideas. For example, Barry Wellman and Milena Gulia have found that many online communities are composed of relatively homogenous groups with similar interests, concerns, and opinions. Such online communities, which are characterized by homophily, tend to foster an empathetic understanding and mutual support rather than encouraging the critical evaluation of each other's claims.[9] A content analysis of posts from BBS forums[10] and Usenet newsgroups,[11] in which more political discussions take place, also finds high concentrations of like-minded individuals. Thus, the media and politics scholar Lincoln Dahlberg argues that online interaction is fragmented into exclusive groups of similar values and interests.[12] In fact, according to Cass Sunstein, rather than simply encouraging group exclusivity, online discussions may even encourage polarization on issues that involve diverse opinions, leading to a "Balkanized public" with users interacting in "information cocoons, or echo chambers of their own design,"[13] leading to the entrenchment of various discourses in different communities.

In addition to the state–society confrontation, online expression in China has shown distinctive yet discernible patterns that confirm the

perspective of a "fragmented cyberspace." Some studies have characterized China's Internet as reflecting China's fragmented society and
have characterized netizens as apolitical,[14] tending to withdraw rather
than fight for free speech when encountering state censorship.[15] Even
when taking up explicitly political topics, netizens are divided in terms
of their identities, political orientations, and discourse preferences.
For instance, the Chinese new media scholar Fang Tang, analyzing
posts from randomly sampled users of the "Qiangguo" and "Maoyan"
forums, found that more than 82 percent of "Qiangguo" users identify as moderate or ultra-left (43 percent and 39 percent, respectively),
whereas 73 percent of "Maoyan" users identify as moderate or ultra-
right (63 percent and 10 percent, respectively).[16] A content analysis
of posts from the same two forums by the Internet researchers Yuan
Le and Boxu Yang resulted in similar results ("Qiangguo": 75 percent
left versus 9.5 percent right; "Maoyan": 21.6 percent left versus 48.4
percent right).[17] Debates between leftists and rightists and the rise
of cyber-nationalism targeting minority groups and foreign actors[18]
suggest that online expression in China is pluralized and not always
regime-challenging. Moreover, the formation of exclusive online communities of individuals with internally coherent political orientations
means that open deliberation among diverse netizen groups may be
obstructed. Evidently, according to these studies, Chinese cyberspace
is better viewed as a "force field in which different social forces and
political interests compete"[19] than simply as an emerging public sphere
that fosters civic engagement and challenges the Party-state.

Will online expression in China precipitate the formation of a public sphere, or instead create "information cocoons" or even result in a
"Balkanized public"? What are the potential implications for authoritarian rule? It is clear that a binary conceptualization of online politics
as a confrontation between the state and society neglects external factors that condition and influence online political participation. After
all, it makes little sense to ignore factors found in open societies simply because China is an authoritarian regime, particularly since the
country has evolved into a much more pluralized society after nearly
four decades of economic reform. Moreover, as the content analysis
approach[20] often falls short of revealing the character of and changing

trends in online expression, a closer examination of the dynamics of discourse production and the role of online communities is necessary. This chapter makes such an attempt by tracing how online groups such as the voluntary fifty-cent army engage in political expression, thus incorporating netizens, online communities, and discourse competition into a dynamic model. And, by casting light on how an opposition to regime critics has developed, my analysis seeks to inform and inspire those primarily concerned with the Internet's "democratizing" effects.

This chapter focuses on the voluntary fifty-cent army for a few reasons. First, this strategy provides analytical continuity with the analysis of chapter 6 while avoiding the near-impossible task of assessing an exhaustive list of possible online groups. Second, it offers a perspective on public opinion in Chinese cyberspace that differs greatly from that which emerges from a static content analysis of state versus society or right versus left. And, finally, aside from a few accounts of cybernationalism and online commentators suggesting that pro-regime voices can be state-sponsored,[21] few studies have systematically analyzed the dynamics of pro-regime expression online. Studying such a force thus may enable a better understanding of why China's authoritarian regime still enjoys popular support.

THE VOLUNTARY FIFTY-CENT ARMY: IDENTITY, COMMUNITY, AND DISCOURSE

Online interactions tend to encourage the formation of relatively homogeneous user communities. Though seemingly a fluid and unreal space with anonymous users constantly logging in and out and commenting on diverse topics, online forums often allow users to develop closer online and sometimes offline ties, stronger mutual trust, and a shared group identity that differentiates them from others. Such netizen groups, with their distinctive language and behavioral codes, shared values and political inclinations, often promote discourse with a "communitarian subject constituted within, and bound by, an ethically integrated community."[22] Thus, homogeneous online communities become "information cocoons" in which a relatively stable discourse will be sustained and reinforced through frequent online and offline interactions.

But why would netizens take up the unpopular mission of defending the authoritarian regime and even name themselves after the notorious fifty-cent army? Are they truly voluntary in the first place? There are solid reasons to believe that members of the voluntary fifty-cent army are not state agents. First, they are not unthinking tools of the state; their opinions diverge from official discourse and are critical of the regime on a wide scope of issues, from censorship and policies regarding minorities to official ideology and discourse. For instance, they debate the merits and faults of current and past leaders, a practice discouraged by the state, and they frequently disparage the propaganda system as incompetent and corrupt. They even adopt the idioms and critiques of dissidents, such as referring to former premier Wen Jiabao as China's "best actor."[23] Second, members of the voluntary fifty-cent army are often active on overseas, smaller-scale, or less popular boards and forums, which are not at the heart of the state's efforts to control and shape public opinion. If they were actually state agents, it is likely that they would be active mainly on popular domestic platforms. Third, unlike the state-deployed Internet commentators who generally avoid arguing with netizens on controversial topics, the voluntary fifty-cent army has become adept at using creative online expressive tactics and more actively engages in online debates. Moreover, I also personally know several active voluntary fifty-cent army members who are clearly not state agents and who, to all appearances, are sincere in their beliefs. All these reasons suggest that at least some regime defenders are not paid state agents.

The very existence of the voluntary fifty-cent army was, in fact, an accidental discovery of my guerrilla ethnography.[24] When exploring online forums, I found netizens demonstrating a strong sense of territory. I frequently observed adversarial comments like "Go back to the military boards where you can keep each other warm!" and "Go back to your angry youth home, Kdnet!" By following these cues, and noting the associations among users, expressive behavior patterns, and certain platforms, I located the home bases of the voluntary fifty-cent army, and these became my primary data collection sites. These sites included military-related discussion boards on NewSmth and Mitbbs, the military enthusiasts' forums Cjdby and Sbanzu, the "Outlook" board of the popular forum Tianya, as well as the overseas Chinese forum Ccthere. Aside from Mitbbs and Ccthere, all these sites are domestic forums located inside China's Great Firewall. Moreover, though they vary dramatically in popularity, all the selected forums attract stable traffic flows—even the smaller ones claim a simultaneous user population of one thousand or more during peak periods. As a result, even though this selection of sites is not representative of the full range of political discourse across the entire Chinese cyber-sphere, it is sufficient to study the voluntary fifty-cent army.

The Voluntary Fifty-Cent Army: The Formation of Group Identity

To understand why "innocent" netizens would associate with the fifty-cent army, it is important to examine how the group identity of the voluntary fifty-cent army has come into being. Largely a reaction to pervasive criticism and rumors targeting the regime, identification with the voluntary fifty-cent army is both externally imposed and actively chosen. In the first place, online antagonism, such as that seen in the labeling wars, provides the initial momentum for identity formation by imposing the fifty-cent army label on some netizens. Censorship and opinion-guiding efforts by the state often spark netizens' fury toward a lurking fifty-cent army such that any voice supportive of the state comes to be viewed as a state agent regardless of any "accidental causalities."[25] Although many of those labeled fifty-cent army simply retreat or keep silent, some fight back. In this sense, many netizens become the voluntary fifty-cent army involuntarily: They fall into this camp because they are labeled fifty-cent army (bei wumao, 被五毛) by others who dislike their pro-government stance. The confrontation often further amplifies enmity, which in turn promotes the imagined threat of enemies and consolidates the voluntary fifty-cent army identity.

The external imposition of the fifty-cent army label has been complemented by the active construction of a group identity, thus promoting a voluntary acceptance of the label. Once labeled as a member of the fifty-cent army, some netizens somehow subvert the pejorative label and turn it into a badge of honor and superiority: They believe they are demeaned only because they are more patriotic and rational than their opponents. For instance, Zhang Shengjun, a professor of international politics at Beijing Normal University, explicitly links the fifty-cent army to the concept of patriotism by arguing that the label has become a "baton waved at all Chinese patriots."[26] It is not purely a coincidence that voluntary fifty-cent army members often evince nationalistic opinions. Nationalistic netizens view the West skeptically and tend to see the regime as playing a critical role in unifying and industrializing the nation. As a result, they are more likely to support the regime.

But the voluntary fifty-cent army is not just a group of cyber-nationalists. Members of the group claim that they emphasize evidence and logic over more emotional, nationalistic claims in debates. The association with rationality justifies acceptance of the group identity. The following example is telling. By pointing out the unequal growth rates of Han and non-Han populations (2.03 percent versus 15.88 percent, respectively) in China's 2005 One-Percent Population Survey and its 2000 census, many nationalistic netizens argue that family planning regulations—which impose birth control on Han Chinese but not on ethnic minority groups—is tantamount to the "genocide" of Han Chinese. In response to this, one Ccthere user explained away Han versus non-Han disparities in population growth as a result of statistical error. Before his rebuttal, he added,

> I have heard about the job of paid Internet commentators, which I have always wanted. But I don't know who is in charge of recruiting. Since I have been longing for the job, let me try to explain this "genocide policy" by *Tugong* [土共, the "Bandit Communist Party"].[27] Take it as my effort to clean up the mess for *Tugong*, and count it as my application for the Internet commentator position. So please feel free to forward. You may get a referral bonus.[28]

Claiming that scientific rationality distinguishes the voluntary fifty-cent army from other nationalist and far-left-wing groups who are commonly perceived as anti-West (and sometimes pro-regime).[29] For them, what one argues for is an issue of standpoint (*lichang wenti,* 立场问题), and how one advances an argument is an issue of intelligence (*zhishang wenti,* 智商问题). The standpoint may be critical, but it must be backed with intelligence, or else it will only make one look like a fool.

The Tactics of the Voluntary Fifty-Cent Army

Taking on the identity of the voluntary fifty-cent army does not mean these netizens build online communities. Community-building occurs through a process similar to that of identity formation, and thus is driven by confrontations with netizens who disagree with each other and amicable interactions among those who are like-minded. Indeed, members of the voluntary fifty-cent army engage in a rich array of rhetorical games in their everyday online activities. Through such regular interactions, they consolidate their identity, build community, and sustain a pro-regime discourse. This section examines the interactive tactics that are employed by the voluntary fifty-cent army. These tactics share a playful quality, a nationalistic orientation, and most importantly, an emphasis on rationality.

Labeling Wars

Labeling refers to the practice of imposing a disgraceful label on opponents in online debates. Labeling wars provided the initial momentum for the formation of the voluntary fifty-cent army in that some of its members acquired the identity because they had been labeled as members of the state-sponsored fifty-cent army. The same mechanism continues to reinforce this identity in online debates. In addition, a labeling war is never unidirectional. If being labeled fifty-cent army helps a person to passively define who they are, labeling others, particularly enemies, constitutes a more active seeking of identity by defining who they are *not*. Members of the voluntary fifty-cent army use many labels to describe their opponents, including the "U.S. cents party" (*meifen dang,* 美分党; i.e., agents hired by the United States), the "dog food party" (*gouliang dang,* 狗粮党; i.e., those begging foreign powers for food like dogs), and the "road-leading party" (*dailu dang,*

带路党; i.e., those who lead the way for invaders). These counter-labels recast their accusers as aligning with foreign governments. Not all counter-labels are nationalistic, however. For instance, the labels of "elite" (*jingying*, 精英) and "public intellectual" (*gongzhi*, 公知) are often used by the voluntary fifty-cent army to demean pro-liberal intellectuals and media professionals.[30] Such labels carry strong negative connotations that these groups are detached from the public, lack common sense and professional knowledge, and, most importantly, prioritize standpoint over logic and facts owing to ignorance or their attempts to manipulate public opinion. These labels further demonstrate that the voluntary fifty-cent army is not a group of run-of-the-mill nationalists. The use of diverse labels also reflects a variety of political inclinations among members of the voluntary fifty-cent army, with many emphasizing their national identity and others adopting a more class-oriented perspective.

Face-Slapping

Given the symbolic significance of face (*mianzi*, 面子), referring to reputation, in Chinese society, "face-slapping" (*dalian*, 扇脸) is considered quite radical and directly confrontational. In online discussion, face-slapping is an effective way to impair an opponent's reputation by challenging a point ruthlessly and pointing out logical errors, factual mistakes, or discrepancies. For instance, Internet regulation efforts by liberal democracies have often been cited as a way to "slap the face" of those advocating for Internet freedoms in China. The goal of the voluntary fifty-cent army is not to defend censorship, but rather to rebut those who fail to differentiate regulation from censorship and to criticize "road-leaders" for turning a blind eye to their masters' "censorship" and highlighting Western hypocrisy.[31]

In many cases, face-slapping serves to defend the regime more directly. For instance, after the March 2010 Japanese earthquake, a Cjdby user explicitly stated, "Those claiming that earthquakes can be forecasted after the Wenchuan earthquake, I am here to slap your face!!!!"[32] The post defended the regime by suggesting that many criticisms are unfounded and unfair. This same logic held when the "face" of the Southern Clique—a loose grouping of pro-liberal media outlets and professionals connected to the Southern Media Group and a long-imagined enemy of the voluntary fifty-cent army—was slapped over the same incident. When reports by the group appeared on forums praising the Japanese for being orderly and lauding its government for transparency, the voluntary fifty-cent army immediately countered with news about looting in earthquake-stricken areas and criticism of Tokyo Electric Power and the Japanese government.[33] They argued that media outlets such as the Southern Clique held the Japanese and Chinese governments to different standards and attributed the Southern Clique's critical portrayal of the Chinese state's response to the Sichuan earthquake to its malicious, anti-regime intentions.

Cross-Talk

Unlike labeling wars and face-slapping, both of which require direct confrontation, cross-talk (*xiangsheng*, 相声) involves the collective ridicule of enemies. The popular linguistic art of Chinese cross-talk uses exaggeration, irony, or parody to highlight the illogical, laughable, or ridiculous nature of an opponent's views. For instance, when China's first aircraft carrier started its maiden sea trials in August 2011, one Ccthere user commented, "Ah, we don't want a floating coffin. We want a star destroyer."[34] Fellow community members knew immediately that this comment was intended to poke fun at those who condemned China's aircraft carrier as "a coffin floating on the sea."[35] Similarly, when voluntary fifty-cent army members on Mitbbs repeated slogans like "Heaven condemns the CCP" (*tianmie zhonggong*, 天灭中共)[36] or "It is all because of the Three Gorges Dam"[37] after earthquakes shook New York and Washington, DC, they were not condemning the Chinese Communist Party or blaming the Three Gorges Dam project, but practicing cross-talk.[38] Such comments were intended to ridicule and parody the tendency of some netizens (and dissidents) to attribute all disasters to the Chinese Communist Party.

Fishing

"Fishing" (*diaoyu*, 钓鱼) is one of the most popular tactics of the voluntary fifty-cent army. Unlike phishing practices that attempt to obtain users' sensitive information under the guise of trustworthy entities, fishing takes advantage of netizens' tendency to believe what they want to believe by "hooking" them with fabricated information, thus revealing their gullibility or inherent biases. The game has four stages: (1) bait preparation, which is the fabrication of a message as bait; (2) bait spreading, which involves posting the message to targeted platforms; (3) hooking, which involves collecting evidence that netizens are spreading the false information; and (4) celebration, which consists of laughing at those who were gullible enough to fall for the false message.

A classic case of fishing started at sbanzu.com, a military forum in which voluntary fifty-cent army members concentrate. Mainly to demonstrate the superficiality, ignorance, and bad intentions of Kuomintang fans (*guofen*, 果粉 or 国粉) and the "truth discovery party" (*zhenxiang dang*, 真相党),[39] the user "Muhaogu" forged a handwritten receipt by Mao Zedong (figure 7.1). This "receipt" states that Mao had received 350 million gold rubles from the Comintern (an international organization advocating world communism). The document contains historical anachronisms and handwriting errors and also explicitly states at the bottom that it was "made by the Pollen Institute and specially designed for the Truth Discovery Party."[40] However, when posted on Kdnet, one of the perceived bases of Kuomintang fans and members of the "truth discovery party," it was taken by many netizens to be a piece of newfound "truth" about the Chinese Communist Party's inglorious history. The highlight of the story for "Muhaogu" was that a

FIGURE 7.1 Forged receipt by Mao Zedong to the Comintern. Image courtesy of Mr. Muhaogu.

Kdnet user and student of Chinese Communist Party history cited the document in her Master's thesis and was expelled from her program as a result. This was an unexpected and delectable "fish" for many in the voluntary fifty-cent army. Catching such a "fish" so easily further convinces the voluntary fifty-cent army that many of their opponents are ignorant and intellectually incurious.

A more influential case of fishing made it into China's print media. Mimicking a report on Huang Wanli, a hydrologist known for his opposition to the Three Gorges Dam project, a Mitbbs user fabricated a story of an imaginary environmental scientist called Zhang Shimai who had proposed a theory that high-speed trains will cause massive geological disasters.[41] Two key concepts defined at length in the fabricated theory, the "Charles Chef Force" and the "Stephen King Effects," were actually named after two popular Mitbbs users, "xiaxie" and "Stephen-King." Widely reproduced online, the article hooked many unsuspecting readers despite efforts by netizens and the Chinese Academy of Sciences to debunk the story.[42] More astonishingly, the nonexistent Professor Zhang was "quoted" by *China Business News (diyi caijing ribao,* 第一财经日报) after a high-speed train accident on July 23, 2011.[43] The newspaper was forced to make an apology when netizens started to "slap its face" by commenting on the report. However, even after that, Zhang continued to be quoted by a *Xinhua News Agency* reporter in her microblog.[44] Such events only serve to feed the deeply held belief among the voluntary fifty-cent army that some media groups are either unprofessional or harbor ulterior motives that blind them from simple facts.[45]

Positive Mobilization

Like other online activists, the voluntary fifty-cent army sometimes mobilizes shared beliefs, values, or emotions directly. For instance, as mentioned in chapter 4, a serial entitled "The Glorious Past of the Little White Bunny"—the playful narrative praising the Communist Party for unifying and building the nation—is very popular among the voluntary fifty-cent army. On Cjdby alone, the serial has attracted over 4.5 million views and 14,000 replies.[46] The following alternative lyrics by a Cjdby user to the "Ode to the Motherland," the song sung at the opening ceremony of the Beijing Olympics, serves as another good example of positive mobilization:[47]

The Flag of Five Stars is fluttering in the wind (The Flag of Five Stars is the Chinese national flag and is clearly a symbol of nationalism),

The Song of CNMD is so sound (The abbreviation "CMND," which stands for "Chinese National Missile Defense," is a pun on the phrase "fuck your mother"),

We are singing for our "black-belle" TG (" 'Black-belle' TG" is jargon used by military enthusiasts meaning "evil Communist Party" and is an affectionate nickname the voluntary fifty-cent army often uses to refer to the regime),

And the Fucking Two Holes is even more shameless and rogue ("Fucking Two Holes" is again an obscene pun, in this instance referring to the first Chinese stealth fighter, the J-20).

We are clean and honest,

We are nice and kindhearted,

The white bunny and the panda are the role models of our kind (These lines project an innocent and "cute" image of China and the regime),

How many times we've being looked down upon we cannot count,

And today we finally can be proud and unbridled (These lines clearly attempt to evoke nationalism through past memories of humiliation),

We love river crabs (As discussed in chapter 4, the river crab symbolizes state censorship; this, this line demonstrates that the voluntary fifty-cent army supports the regime),

We love keeping accounts (jizhang, 记账; some members of the voluntary fifty-cent army claim that they are "keeping accounts," or keeping a record of enemies' misdeeds, to ensure payback in the future),

Whoever owes us money and refuses to pay back will be eliminated!

Long live our motherland, our mighty and powerful motherland!

(Although this is not an alternative lyric, it demonstrates blunt nationalist sentiment.)

These alternative lyrics demonstrate an ostensible nationalistic stance and support for the regime among the voluntary fifty-cent army. The mixture of national symbols, combined with elements of a particular military forum's subculture (including the profanity), appealed to fellow community members and made the post very popular.[48] Posted right after China's stealth fighter J-20 made its first public flight in January 2011, the post attracted more than one thousand replies within two weeks, most echoing the message of and lauding the original post.

Other popular tactics among the voluntary fifty-cent army include onlooking (*weiguan*, 围观), playing undercover (*wujiandao*, 无间道), and keeping accounts (*jizhang*, 记账). *Onlooking* refers to large crowds surrounding and watching spectacles. Although often deployed by regime critics to demonstrate public opinion and question the regime,[49] this tactic is also used by the voluntary fifty-cent army to bully their opponents. By bombarding a target with repeated replies saying "onlooking" or "onlooking, too," they signal to other netizens that the target is voicing an unpopular or even absurd opinion.[50] In "playing undercover," members of the voluntary fifty-cent army hide their true opinions and support the opposite side in an exaggerated and parodied fashion, recasting opponents as unpersuasive and untrustworthy. *Keeping accounts* refers to keeping a record of what perceived enemies have said or done as evidence of their bad deeds or inconsistency. For instance, a Ccthere user compiled a collection of BBC reports about the Chinese Internet over eight years in which one photo was repeatedly used but interpreted differently. In its earliest appearance in 2000, the photo was used as an illustration of "authorities wary of the web." But, in 2008, right before the Beijing Olympics, the photo was interpreted as "China enhancing its surveillance of Olympic guests."[51]

Not all these expressive tactics are exclusively deployed by the voluntary fifty-cent army. Some, such as labeling wars, onlooking, and positive mobilization, are common among netizens generally. Others, such as face-slapping, fishing, and keeping accounts, are more specific to the voluntary fifty-cent army. However, these rhetorical games all help define the group identity and share certain features. In particular, they vary along two important dimensions: the degree of confrontation and the type of persuasive power (table 7.1). In terms of confrontation, some games rely primarily on facts and reasoning to persuade others or to mock opponents, whereas others resort to emotional and normative appeals. The more distinctive rhetorical tactics employed by the voluntary fifty-cent army—face-slapping, fishing, and keeping accounts—are used to demonstrate that its members prioritize logic and factual evidence in debates, in contrast to other cyber-nationalists and regime supporters. In terms of persuasive power, some games involve direct attacks on opposing opinions, whereas others are more like playful ripostes among voluntary fifty-cent army members themselves, and still others fall somewhere in between. Through antagonistic interactions with other netizens, the voluntary fifty-cent army shapes and defines its group identity, demonstrating that its members are unified in their opposition to a perceived set of regime critics or foreign-agent "enemies." Mutual cooperation and more amicable interactions within the group further strengthen group identity by reinforcing shared values and behavioral codes.

The categorization in table 7.1 is not definitive, but rather contextualized. On one hand, the factual/rational and normative/emotional divide exists but is far from clear-cut. For instance, in both of the positive mobilization cases discussed, readers' attention was directed toward a series of historical events imbued with nationalistic sentiment. In fact, nationalism and rationality serve as major forces in defining the identity of the voluntary fifty-cent army. Nationalism provides the normative imperative: to defend the nation against online

TABLE 7.1 Categorizing the Rhetorical Tools of the Voluntary Fifty-Cent Army

	Confrontational ◄——► Amicable		
Factual/Rational	Face-slapping	Fishing	Cross-talk
↕			
Normative/Emotional	Labeling war		Positive mobilization

sabotage by enemies from within and without. Rationality, however, justifies the group's accusation that much online criticism is unfounded or biased, thus reinforcing the belief among its members that they are enlightening netizens who are otherwise deceived, ill informed, or unreflective.[52] Thus, both factual/rational and normative/emotional persuasive techniques provides the voluntary fifty-cent army with a sense of fulfillment and superiority.

On the other hand, the antagonism inherent in these tactics largely depends on who is using them and the context in which they are used. For instance, when deployed in the presence of other voluntary fifty-cent army members and supportive netizens, tactics like cross-talk, which involve subtle satire, are often echoed and appreciated. When deployed in the presence of opposing netizens, they frequently escalate into direct confrontation. Similarly, the degree of antagonism can vary at each stage in a multi-stage battle depending on changes in context or participants. Take fishing as an example. While bait preparation and celebration generally consist of amicable interactions within the voluntary fifty-cent army group, hooking often involves direct confrontation to humiliate the hooked (often on perceived enemy sites, which are seen as "fish ponds" by the voluntary fifty-cent army). In fact, many voluntary fifty-cent army members refer to this step as face-slapping.

Despite the variation in degree of antagonism and pattern of persuasive power, these rhetorical tactics consolidate the collective experiences of the voluntary fifty-cent army into a cohesive group identity, strengthening community ties, and producing a pro-regime discourse. The fishing tactic discussed earlier in this chapter, which involves multiple community members at different stages, is a perfect example. Although it takes only one creative member to devise the bait, others may contribute by offering comments and suggestions or by producing adaptations of the message or even derivative stories.[53] Community members also play a larger role in spreading the bait, especially initially.[54] "Setting a hook" often involves collective confrontation with those who get hooked, thus promoting group identity through solidarity against a common enemy. Celebration enhances the collective imagination of a common enemy; against a "them," members of the voluntary fifty-cent army actively project an image of an "us." Moreover, by employing shared behavioral codes and championing similar values and beliefs, the voluntary fifty-cent army has effectively established independent online colonies, or public sphericules, with a fairly stable regime-defending discourse.

The rhetorical games can backfire, though. Fishing, for instance, can effectively discredit opponents, but the tactic is a double-edged sword. To counter criticism of China's aircraft carrier project, a Mitbbs user wrote a post titled "For a country without human rights, what's the point of building aircraft carriers?"[55] In the post, the author states,

> Recently, in one of its northern cities, a power has been speeding up construction of an aircraft carrier, which has symbolic significance.
>
> . . .
>
> However, under the glossy surface of being an Olympic Games host and aircraft carrier owner is a different picture—at the same time the carrier is being built, a growing number of "mass incidents" [*quntixing shijian*, 群体性事件, referring to public protests and other forms of collective dissent] are imposing huge pressure on the country's stability maintenance apparatus. They have introduced strict control over the Internet, manipulated public opinion, deployed legions of police to disperse assemblies, and are ready to arrest netizens spreading "inharmonious" information.
>
> Canada's *Vancouver Sun* commented on [August] 10 that the society is "sick." French commentator Agnes Poirier even told the BBC that this country remained one of the most "unequal societies" [in Europe].

Though the user confessed that he intended to mock Great Britain, both those critical and those supportive of the regime took the bait. This example reveals the dilemma faced by the voluntary fifty-cent army: When people prove unable or unwilling to recognize the barbs in the bait, hooking a fish can turn into feeding a fish and involuntarily add to the volume of rumors and criticism that the voluntary fifty-cent army is trying to fight.[56]

The Reach and Influence of the Voluntary Fifty-Cent Army

Owing to the subjectivity of its members' identities and the fluidity of cyberspace, it is impossible to estimate the size of the voluntary fifty-cent army. However, there are indicators of the reach of the group, which suggest that the voluntary fifty-cent army has become a significant force in online expression.

Although representing a small portion of netizens, the voluntary fifty-cent army has firmly established itself in cyberspace, with certain platforms such as military forums tending to serve as initial bases. This is by no means an accident, as these forums often attract nationalistic netizens with a realistic view of international politics. As nationalists, they appreciate the regime's role in unifying, industrializing, and strengthening the nation. For them, despite all its problems, the current regime contrasts well with the pre-1949 Kuomintang regime that not only failed to establish domestic order, but also failed to protect China from external threats. They are convinced that the nation is on the right track and that maintaining stability is necessary. Their realist or even hawkish inclination makes them susceptible to the counter-espionage framing that imagines domestic and foreign regime critics as national enemies engineering online expression to sabotage China's revival. As these like-minded netizens naturally gravitate to military forums, they gradually turn these platforms into virtual colonies in which they intensify their interactions with each other and exchange ideas, which in turn further shapes and consolidates their identity.

The voluntary fifty-cent army has occupied not only small-scale forums that attract nationalistic netizens or military enthusiasts, but also popular boards on major forums such as Mitbbs, NewSmth, and Tianya. Tianya is the largest online forum in China, attracting millions of visitors daily, whereas Mitbbs and NewSmth are the most popular student forums, each with more than thirty thousand simultaneous users.[57] Not all users identify with the voluntary fifty-cent army, but the group has gained traction on these platforms, demonstrating its capacity to reach a wide audience, as netizens "vote" with their attention and continue to visit platforms where they are prominent.[58] How the "Military" board has replaced "ChinaNews" as the most popular board on Mittbbs is a good example here. Before 2008, most netizens frequented "ChinaNews" to discuss Chinese politics, whereas the "Military" board attracted only military enthusiasts. But a series of events in 2008—the Lhasa riot, the Sichuan earthquake, and the Beijing Olympics—triggered a mass exodus from "ChinaNews" as users became dissatisfied with the anti-regime orientation that dominated the board. They turned to "Military," where the voluntary fifty-cent army is based, for more "neutral" and more positive discussions of China. Since then, the "Military" board has often attracted ten times the traffic of "ChinaNews."[59] This shift reveals the growing influence of the voluntary fifty-cent army in online expression.

The influence of the voluntary fifty-cent army is not limited to the isolated virtual colonies they occupy. As a reaction to what they feel are unreflective criticisms of the regime, its members confront opponents both at their bases and on "battlefields" where they are not dominant. Such battlefields include other forums, blogs, and more recently, the Twitter-like Weibo. For instance, the concentration of voluntary fifty-cent army members on Tianya's "Outlook" board does not prevent some members from entering debates on "Free," the second-most popular board of the forum. Through labeling wars, cross-talk, and fishing, they try to exert influence beyond the locations they dominate.

The voluntary fifty-cent army has also built deeper and broader ties beyond their base platforms. Many of its members have established close contact using QQ or WeChat groups and have even developed real-life friendships with each other.[60] These ties expand their reach and also link members of the voluntary fifty-cent army together. In addition, cross-community connections are established, linking relatively isolated voluntary fifty-cent army communities together. Just as like-minded websites cross-link more so than differently minded websites,[61] voluntary fifty-cent army members based across different sites weave connections among the various sites they frequent. For instance, on NewSmth's military boards, one can often find posts from Mitbbs's "Military" board, Ccthere, and Cjdby, or Weibo entries from other voluntary fifty-cent army comrades. Fishing initiatives from Mitbbs may inspire similar ones on NewSmth.[62] Some netizens even consciously advocate an alliance of communities that share similar political inclinations and face a common enemy. A Ccthere user explicitly argued that the voluntary fifty-cent army should support WYZX

乌有之乡 (*wyzxsx.com*, an ultra-left website) against the common enemy of "universalists" (*pushi pai*, 普世派).[63] Forums such as April Media (*siyue chuanmei*, 四月传媒; formerly Anti-CNN.com) and more serious news platforms such as the Observer (*guanchazhe*, 观察者; guancha.cn) show that the voluntary fifty-cent army, which has largely been reactive, may be growing into a more self-conscious group with a clearly defined mission to execute.[64] Through this transition, at least some of its members have turned into political activists who strive to disseminate their political beliefs online.

In fact, the voluntary fifty-cent army has grown from an online phenomenon into a group with political momentum. For instance, after the Taiwanese election in early 2016, many Chinese netizens flooded the Facebook page of President-Elect Tsai Ing-wen to defend the "One China" principle, many of whom claimed to be members of the voluntary fifty-cent army.[65] Though not all such self-appointed members likely fit in the definition of a voluntary fifty-cent army member outlined in this chapter, this case nonetheless demonstrates the political influence of the group.

As a political force, the voluntary fifty-cent army is now also recognized by the Party-state. On October 15, 2014, at the highly prominent and symbolic Forum on Literature and Art in Beijing, President Xi Jinping openly praised two "online writers"—Zhou Xiaoping and Hua Qianfang—who are viewed as representatives of the voluntary fifty-cent army.[66] Since not one of the many more influential cyber-celebrities or public intellectuals was invited to the event, the state's promotion of Zhou and Hua was clearly intended to bring the voluntary fifty-cent army under its banner.[67] However, this move backfired among both the voluntary fifty-cent army and ordinary netizens. For the voluntary fifty-cent army, Zhou and Hua are not considered their true representatives: They are considered to be overtly pro-regime, and their comments tend to be logically and factually weak. For ordinary netizens, the association with the state immediately turned the voluntary fifty-cent army from a relatively neutral group into the state's convenient mouthpiece.

Indeed, the popularity and influence of the voluntary fifty-cent army appears to fluctuate over time depending on factors such as state behavior. Take NewSmth's "MilitaryJoke" board as an example. As figure 7.2

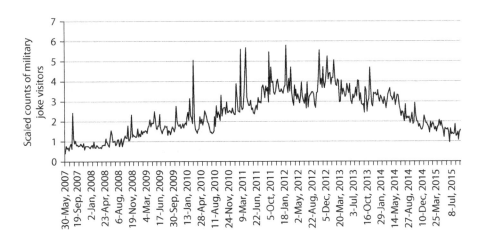

FIGURE 7.2 Weekly military joke visits in relation to NewSmth average.

Source: newsmth.net.

shows, the board's influence grew significantly from 2007 to 2011, after which it suffered a temporary stagnation before starting to decline steadily after a brief period of revival in late 2012. The changes in the trend correspond well with the leadership succession in China. The period of stagnation overlapped with the power struggle before the Chinese Communist Party's Eighteenth National Congress, and the continuous decline started quickly after Xi Jinping assumed power—both time periods that witnessed tightened state control over online expression. Since "MilitaryJoke" is only a small board and generally features pro-regime expression, the decline was unlikely the result of direct state censorship. Instead, it may well be that enhanced state control delegitimized the group, making it less appealing among ordinary netizens.

CONCLUSION

Cyberspace is not a monolithic medium. Instead, it consists of fragmented fields that serve either as frontiers at which opponents meet or colonies occupied by certain communities. The analysis of the voluntary fifty-cent army in this chapter details how group identity has been shaped through repeated rhetorical interactions with both opposing netizens and fellow community members. Such interactions have turned some online platforms into voluntary fifty-cent army bases in which a particular pro-regime discourse is produced and reproduced.

Though they represent just a small portion of netizens, the voluntary fifty-cent army influences public opinion in significant ways. An experimental study with Facebook users, for example, found evidence of emotion contagion on a massive scale; that is, emotions expressed by others influence our own.[68] Other researchers have found that social consensus can effectively be influenced or even reversed by a minority of committed agents who "consistently proselytize the opposing opinion and are immune to influence."[69] Here, members of the voluntary fifty-cent army compose just such a "committed minority" in Chinese cyberspace. Their relatively neutral stance, calls for nationalism, emphasis on facts and rationality, as well as their sense of humor, all make them more effective in persuading netizens than state agents. In fact, a Ccthere user openly claimed that given the incompetence of state propaganda bodies, the voluntary fifty-cent army has started to play a larger role in maintaining the regime's stability.[70]

Rather than denying the efforts of researchers, observers, and activists to "push China's limits on the web," the chapter aims to highlight the complicity and plurality of opinions on the Internet and the subsequent implications.[71] Such a perspective helps take our understanding of cyberpolitics in China beyond the state-versus-society models—subaltern norms versus state norms, an expanding public sphere versus state censorship, a rising civil society versus an authoritarian regime, and empowered social actors versus state suppression—to one that recognizes conflict among social actors themselves.[72] In this way, it contributes to the authoritarian resilience literature by highlighting that in addition to variables such as state capacity and adaptability,[73] groups such as the voluntary fifty-cent army help stabilize the regime, not so much by legitimizing it, but by undermining the moral and factual grounds of regime challengers.

8

AUTHORITARIAN RESILIENCE ONLINE

Mismatched Capacity, Miscalculated Threat

The relationship between digital media and authoritarian rule in China is intriguing.[1] In this book, I have aimed to look at the topic from a distinctive perspective with several counterintuitive arguments. The struggle over online expression is both a censorship game and a form of discourse competition. In the censorship game, the Chinese Party-state, intermediary actors, and netizens constantly engage each other in numerous boundary-spanning battles that define the taboo zones, gray zones, and free zones of online expression. In the discourse competition, all actors play within the boundaries prescribed by the state, but the struggle centers not so much on what is expressed, but on how information is effectively conveyed, spread, and manipulated. It is clear that the struggle is not simply one between the authoritarian state and digitally empowered social forces. The boundaries and landscape of online expression are shaped by internal fragmentation within the Party-state, the diverse capacities and agency of intermediary actors, and the heterogeneity of netizen groups. Such a pluralized terrain of online politics complicates the apparent authoritarian resilience in the digital age and at the same time undermines any technological-deterministic view of a democratizing Internet.

What I hope sets this book apart from current studies on Internet politics in China are two significant features. First, it examines several understudied but crucial elements in the struggle over online expression in China. The role of forum administrators in mediating state–society interaction online, for instance, is often overlooked. Considering that Facebook and Twitter facilitated mobilization in the Arab Spring, the state's control over intermediary actors may have contributed to authoritarian resilience in China, and probably beyond (for example, in Russia).[2] The phenomenon of the fifty-cent army, despite frequent mentions in Western media, is rarely studied. An analysis of this phenomenon provides an opportunity to evaluate state adaptation in the digital era and examine the internal dynamics of China's fragmented authoritarian regime. Moreover, the book explores the pluralization of online expression by studying the voluntary fifty-cent army. Freer online expression is not only helping to erode state norms, but also—counterintuitively—discounting the impact of regime critics by creating their opponents.

Second, this book provides a fresh and provocative explanation of authoritarian resilience in the digital age. Current studies either suggest a "mutual empowerment" situation that strengthens both the state and society[3] or imply an omnipotent state capable of optimally adapting to harness the benefits of free expression without risking overthrow.[4] I have aimed to debunk the myth of state adaptation and problematize state capacity by demonstrating that the state's efforts to shape online expression are at best quasi-successful. The fact that the Chinese authoritarian regime survives, and the fact that Arab Spring countries fell despite serious control efforts,[5] together suggest that state adaptability alone is likely neither a sufficient nor necessary condition for authoritarian resilience. But ineffective state control does not automatically lead to democratization. Regime critics in China have yet to win the hearts and minds of netizens. In other words, authoritarianism can coexist with relatively free expression provided that the regime still enjoys popular support and/or that those criticizing the regime are popularly discredited, as in the cases of China and Russia.

AUTHORITARIAN RESILIENCE IN THE DIGITAL AGE

The central question of this book is how the Chinese authoritarian regime remains resilient despite the profound sociopolitical challenges brought about by the Internet. The Chinese Party-state was quite successful adapting itself to new challenges before the Internet age.[6] Since the death of Mao and the end of the devastating Cultural Revolution, the Chinese Communist Party has undertaken a fundamental socioeconomic reformation[7] and shifted its primary source of legitimacy from communist ideology and revolutionary rhetoric to economic development and improved governance.[8] The Party-state has also transformed itself politically in the reform era since 1978.[9] In addition to routinizing leadership change and improving cadre management, the Party has embraced institutional and organizational adaptations such as legal reforms, grassroots elections, and the introduction of intra-party democracy.[10] Moreover, contentious politics scholars find that the Chinese Party-state has significantly enhanced its capacity to suppress and defuse popular unrest,[11] not only to preserve social stability,[12] but also to maintain an image of benevolent and responsive authoritarianism.[13] As the "rightful resistance" framework suggests, the Party-state actually has managed to reinforce its rule and legitimacy by accommodating or even encouraging citizen complaints targeting local officials based on state-sanctioned claims, channels, and strategies.[14] In this way, popular contention becomes "constructive noncompliance."[15]

However, some scholars question the resilience of China's authoritarian rule.[16] Even former champions of the idea, such as the known Chinese politics experts Andrew Nathan and David Shambaugh, have somewhat shifted their view. In 2009, the *Journal of Democracy* published a special issue on the challenges facing the Party-state since Tiananmen. In his concluding essay to the collection, Nathan argued that the Party-state suffers from a fundamental legitimacy deficit, and thus a robust plurality of disaffected citizens, a catalytic event, and a leadership split may together contribute to a regime transition.[17] In a March 2015 *Wall Street Journal* article, David Shambaugh asserted that "the endgame of communist rule in China has begun, and Xi Jinping's ruthless measures are only bringing the country closer to a breaking point."[18] This claim echoes research by Cheng Li, another long-term observer of elite politics in China. After identifying the major tensions within the regime, including nepotism, rampant corruption, growing oligarchic power, and factional struggle, Li concludes that while China as a nation may be resilient, the Party-state's capacity and legitimacy are fragile and perhaps even in the midst of a serious decline.[19]

Existing studies suggest two inherently conflicting but both well-reasoned images of the Chinese authoritarian regime. One image depicts the regime as resilient with a strong capacity to control its population and adapt to new challenges. Along this line, it is predicted that "China will continue to rise, not fade. Its leaders will consolidate the one-party model and, in the process, challenge the West's smug certainty about political development and the inevitable march toward electoral democracy."[20] The other image depicts the regime as fragile, facing increasing challenges with declining and degenerating capacity. From this angle, the scholar Yasheng Huang states that China faces a "democratize-or-die" situation, and "what has held China back is not any lack of demand for democracy, but a lack of supply."[21] Both perspectives provide valuable insights into China's authoritarian rule, its strengths and weaknesses, and its democratic prospects. However, what is missing in the debate is a closer examination of state capacity in relation to the challenges faced by the state and a subtler reflection on the nature of those challenges.

Many challenges have been brought about by the Internet, and the Party-state's agility in adapting to digital challenges is impressive. Yet, the state's strong capacity is a mismatch to the new tasks of information control and manipulation, rendering its adaptive efforts ineffective and even counterproductive. In other words, state adaptability is insufficient to explain resilient authoritarianism, at least in the Chinese case. In this regard, the real question is not how the state has successfully tamed the Internet, but why the Internet has so far failed to scuttle authoritarian rule in China, as many had expected. It turns out that the pluralization of online expression has ironically contributed to authoritarian resilience. The identity anxiety and animosity among netizens in online interactions have provided room for "state allies" such as nationalistic netizens and the voluntary fifty-cent army to sustain pro-regime discourses, who, in turn, have helped convert and neutralize regime criticism.

Strong State, Mismatched Capacity

The expansion of the Internet has broken down the state's monopoly over the media, which has brought about two broad empowering effects on particular threats to the Chinese Party-state, namely facilitating collective mobilization and spreading general criticism.[22] The first empowering effect is primarily concerned with expanding the political opening and enriching the mobilization resources that allow citizens to more actively participate in sociopolitical activities and to resist authoritarian rule. But as contentious politics scholars suggest, the Chinese Party-state has rich experience and sufficient capacity to deal with collective mobilization.[23] Moreover, online mobilization may have actually made it easier for the state both to observe and interfere with citizen activism.[24] This was precisely why the police force was ready when China's pro-democracy "Jasmine Revolution" took place.

The second empowering effect is essentially an ideational and cultural war, or what can be considered a norms competition.[25] The Party-state, no matter how resilient it once was, must now "account for the anomalies between its view of events and the public's"[26] and combat dissenting discourses for citizens' hearts and minds. This is more detrimental for the Party-state, as the collapse of the Soviet Union started with a similar challenge. It was the "intellectual and moral quest for self-respect and pride that, beginning with a merciless moral scrutiny of the country's past and present," quickly "hollowed out the mighty Soviet state, deprived it of legitimacy, and turned it into a burned-out shell that crumbled in August 1991."[27]

The Chinese Party-state has attempted to shape online expression through massive censorship and innovative PR tactics such as astroturfing, as discussed in chapters 2 and 5, respectively. How the state has implemented such adaptations not only demonstrates the regime's adaptability, but also provides as an excellent opportunity to assess its capacity. The Party-state's censorship and manipulation efforts confirm its formidable despotic and infrastructural power to regulate and control intermediary actors as well as to mute and punish dissidents and deviant netizens. In particular, with its organizational capacity, the Party-state has been able to mobilize tens of thousands of state agents at different levels in different sectors to enforce the daunting tasks of censorship and astroturfing. Take astroturfing as an example. Initially a local innovation, this tactic has now been incorporated into the state's routine propaganda work, particularly in the Xi Jinping era. Through apparatuses such as the propaganda system and the Chinese Communist Youth League—the latter alone controls an army of at least 350,000 Internet propagandists and 10.5 million youth Internet civilized volunteers—the Party-state can potentially flood cyberspace with manufactured pro-regime content at any time.[28] In fact, according to King, Pan, and Roberts, the state fabricates an estimated 448 million posts every year.[29]

But there is a mismatch between the state's capacity and the challenges it faces in the digital age. The hard-to-control features of online expression—anonymity, creativity, and the volume of content—have made censorship an almost impossible mission. The censorship system, which relies exclusively on taboo-word filtering and intermediary actors, is ill equipped to counter creative expression. Using creative and playful tactics, regime critics and ordinary netizens have successfully circumvented state censorship and, at the same time, turned it into a target of online activism. In discourse competition, persuasive power builds on expressive, interactive, and cultural qualities, none of which is a strength of the Party-state. After all, the state does not speak the cyber-language, nor can it full-heartedly embrace popular cyber-culture or cyber-norms. Even when it attempts to incorporate popular expressive formats or to exploit the anonymity of online expression, its innovations often prove ineffective, as discussed in chapters 4 and 5.

The Party-state has encountered tremendous difficulty in translating its offline power into effective control over the online world. Through its massive apparatus, the state has mobilized sizable institutional, organizational, administrative, and technical resources to build the most sophisticated censorship system in the world. But the system suffers from the state's internal fragmentation, which is driven by conflicts of interest, the division of labor among bureaucratic responsibilities, and intra-party ideological discrepancies. In particular, while the central state appears to be more concerned with the regime's overall legitimacy, local authorities often use censorship to cover up their own scandals and to maintain their own images. Similarly, its strong organizational capacity has enabled the state to mobilize the massive fifty-cent army. However, the state agents undertaking the army's delegated tasks are often not properly motivated or skilled enough to engage in and guide online discussion. Moreover, local authorities often expose the supposedly covert force as an achievement of their propaganda work. Apparently, for local officials, the priority is not to persuade netizens, but to demonstrate competence to their superiors. In other words, the state's thought work apparatus, including the propaganda system and the Chinese Communist Youth League, are no longer effective tools of ideological indoctrination. They have increasingly become vehicles through which state agents seek promotion and rewards in exchange for political loyalty, which explains the "nauseating displays of loyalty" characteristic of local state agencies.[30]

The mismatch between the state's capacity and the challenges it faces suggests that adaptations by the Chinese Party-state thus far are not optimal for authoritarian resilience. In fact, the state's control and manipulation efforts may even have exacerbated the regime's legitimacy and governance crises. First, state censorship provokes digital contention and substantiates criticism of regime repressiveness. In particular, rigid and arbitrary censorship often disturbs communications that are not politically sensitive at all. Such "collateral casualties" have resulted numerous complaints among netizens on Internet forums, blogs, microblogs, and other social media platforms, thus politicizing and alienating many otherwise indifferent netizens. Even innovative PR tactics like astroturfing by the fifty-cent army can backfire. Thanks to the state's attempt to manipulate popular opinion, any voice supporting the government now becomes dubious. Indeed, the cases of netizens being labeled as the fifty-cent army and the "grass mud horse" fighting the "river crab" are vivid examples of how state censorship and opinion manipulation efforts have incensed netizens and fed online contention.

The Party-state's control over online expression also jeopardizes its relationship with IT business entrepreneurs. Internet service providers and other intermediary actors, who are delegated censorship responsibilities, play a pivotal role in online content control. As chapter 3 showed, intermediary actors generally demonstrate "discontented compliance" toward censorship, which implies a pattern of state–business relations different from what is depicted in the literature. Earlier studies suggested a rosy picture of mutual dependence between the Party-state and business: The Party-state promotes business, as economic development has become its source of legitimacy, while business elites are closely tied to and dependent on the current regime both economically and politically, thus maintaining the status quo or even allying with the authoritarian state.[31] The scenario is different in the censorship system. State censorship is often at odds with business interests (and those of other intermediary actors) because it increases operational costs, political risks, and market uncertainty. Thus, the compliance of intermediary actors is less a voluntary choice than the result of a fear of being punished.

By controlling and manipulating the flow of information online, the Chinese Party-state has also impaired its capacity to respond to citizen complaints and improve governance. As in village elections and rightful resistance,[32] online expression can serve as a safety valve,[33] provide a channel for policy feedback,[34] and help discipline local agents.[35] However, as state censorship clearly prioritizes repressing online expression over responding to popular demands,[36] it prevents the Party-state from turning online citizen complaints into "constructive noncompliance," which thus hurts its image as a benevolent, responsive regime. Likewise, the deployment of the fifty-cent army distorts the policy-feedback function of online expression; given the state's internal fragmentation and local officials' priority of pleasing their superiors, top officialdom may have difficulty distinguishing manufactured expression from genuine opinions from ordinary citizens.

What is particularly worth highlighting is that state control may disable the fire-alarm function of online expression and weaken its capacity to discipline local agents by delegating too much power to local authorities. Local officials have been trying their best to suppress citizen complaints, to cover up local scandals, and to please their superiors. State censorship and online opinion manipulation efforts provide them with convenient tools to do so. In particular, since local authorities mostly target tangible grievances, which tend to provoke citizens' wrath more than abstract issues, their control efforts are ultimately detrimental to regime legitimacy and social stability. Considering that tangible grievances can be addressed relatively easily by accommodating limited demands and disciplining local officials, local control initiatives only decrease citizens' trust in both the local officialdom and the regime as whole. After all, allowing local governments to block online petitioning indicates the central government's failure, or even worse, its lack of intention, to discipline local agents. And, as China scholars have discovered, trust in the central government's intention to side with citizens and punish deviant local cadres is critical for the regime's survival.[37]

Empowering Expression, Miscalculated Threat

The Internet, with its inherently uncontrollable characteristics, has been thought to empower social actors to challenge authoritarian regimes. Though social media platforms such as Twitter and Facebook indeed played a crucial role in the Arab Spring, optimism about the Internet's political impact is challenged by cases such as Singapore and China. In fact, though observers find the new technology empowering as a tool for public expression, social connection, and collective mobilization in China, expectations for its democratizing effects have not played out. Existing studies offer different explanations: The state has achieved sufficient control over the Internet;[38] cyberspace is a forum only for everyday resistance, which slowly expands the public sphere and transforms norms;[39] and the Internet has contributed to liberalization, but not democratization.[40] I argue that we should consider an alternative explanation: The struggle over online expression is not a two-player game between the state and society. Rather, to assess the Internet's empowerment effects, we need to understand online politics in a broader sense, acknowledge the diversity of social actors, and examine how society is empowered.

Though the Internet has undoubtedly provided opportunities for political activism, not all of the population using the Internet may be politicized. It is inappropriate to assume that all Chinese netizens are preoccupied with resisting the authoritarian regime. As Mark Priors argues, "lack of motivation, not lack of skills or resources," may be the main obstacle to active political participation in an environment characterized by a great deal of choice.[41] Indeed, scholars find that "political content comprises only an extremely tiny portion of China's cyber-cacophony,"[42] and "the Chinese Internet is more a playground for leisure, socializing, and commerce than a hotbed of political activism."[43] The analysis of pop activism in chapter 4 confirms such findings to a large extent by revealing apolitical motivations in online expression and online activism, as well as a fusion of popular entertainment with politics. In short, one should neither dismiss apolitical uses of the Internet, nor overestimate the political impact of online activism.

Moreover, social actors may be empowered to engage in politics, but not necessarily in ways or to an extent that will bring about democratizing effects. Many observers argue that freer online expression has contributed to the rise of a public sphere[44] in which citizens can express opinions and deliberate public affairs despite state constraints, which in turn erodes the Party-state's legitimacy. However, the conception of the public sphere in these studies is often imperfect, emphasizing its lack of control rather than its deliberative features. In fact, online experience may well have increased cynicism among netizens, since expressions of dissatisfaction or political engagement are often restricted to cyberspace, where there are no tangible implications. This is why netizens often refer to online dissenters in a negative sense as "keyboard freedom fighters."[45] They argue against investing too much into online debates because "you will only lose if you are serious" (*renzhen ni jiu shu le*, 认真你就输了). Moreover, labeling wars among netizen groups and the polarization of ideas witnessed in online discussions suggest that Chinese cyberspace is far from being a public sphere characterized by rational debate.[46] Instead, it is highly fragmented, with a number of relatively independent and isolated communities that sustain widely different discourses, both civil and uncivil.

Since netizens go online for a range of purposes, with varying concerns and prior beliefs, any theoretical framework that focuses exclusively on the state–society interaction is inadequate to fully capture the dynamics of online politics. As this book has shown, some netizens have even developed a particular identity that leads them to attack regime critics and defend the authoritarian regime. In other words, the discourse competition in cyberspace is not only fought between "young subaltern norms" and "state norms,"[47] but also among various ideational camps among netizens. This perspective, though quite novel in the field of Internet politics, is in accordance with scholarship on Chinese politics: Despite its legitimacy deficit, the Party-state still enjoys considerable popular support. In fact, survey studies repeatedly reveal that the Chinese Party-state enjoys one of the highest degrees of political support in the world.[48]

It is quite intriguing that many netizens support or passively tolerate a regime that is nondemocratic and suppressive. According to Johan Lagerkvist, there are two possible explanations for Chinese citizens' tacit acquiescence to state control of freedom of expression: They may hold "private truths" while telling "public lies" by repeating official discourse, or they may be seeking psychological coherence to rationalize the current political status quo.[49] Yet, the backlash against regime critics and the rise of the voluntary fifty-cent army suggest that Chinese netizens' support of the regime can also be genuine and rational. Indeed, netizens may side with the state in discourse competition for nationalistic causes. Though nationalist activists and intellectuals may have "espoused democracy as a means to defending the nationalist interest,"[50] popular nationalism in China today is often positioned against democracy and democratization. Why? Chapter 6 showed that it is not that the state has successfully co-opted nationalism. Rather, it is because regime critics, including democratic activists, pro-liberal media professionals and intellectuals, and Western powers have lost their appeal among nationalistic netizens. Given such a nationalistic framing, dissenting expression is then not about defending the citizenry against the repressive state, but about patriotic netizens allying with the state against subversive actors.

Similarly, the voluntary fifty-cent army is not a group of true believers in the Party-state or communism. They harbor their own critiques of the regime but choose to defend it because they have doubts about the intentions and competence of regime critics. These netizens acknowledge the historical role of the Communist revolution and the

Party-state, and, more importantly, they trust the state's intentions and capacity to cope with current governance and development problems. They believe China needs a strong government to continue the country's revival and that a transition will not solve all problems, but instead may cause some to worsen or possibly lead to social turmoil. In contrast, they see regime critics as having an overly hypercritical "anti-establishment" tendency when criticizing the government, which renders their criticism meaningless or even harmful.[51] In their eyes, it is unfair to attribute all social ills to the regime, and regime critics' call for regime transition is considered morally dubious, factually slippery, and logically flawed. They question regime critics' ability to establish and run the democratic government they promise. They also see regime critics as being impatient and intolerant of netizens who disagree with them. In fact, some have claimed that they decided to join the voluntary fifty-cent army because they got sick of regime critics.

The voluntary fifty-cent army phenomenon suggests that though authoritarian regimes may suffer from a legitimacy deficit, fighting autocrats does not automatically win the hearts and minds of the people. In China, regime critics have yet to provide the people with a viable alternative to the current regime. Such a depiction is not entirely unfounded, as democratic activist organizations, such as the Federation for a Democratic China (FDC), suffer from a number of internal plagues. As the veteran sinologist Jean-Philippe Béja has insightfully pointed out,

> Finding a basis for cooperation proved difficult, however, and the FDC's status as an exile group unavoidably left it cut off from ground-level Chinese realities. Debates among its members were abstract and had no impact on developments in China. Competition for the support of foreign political forces provoked fierce inner struggles, and the dream of the emergence of a new Sun Yat-sen evaporated. . . . The exiles' greatest achievements have been to help keep the memory of the 1989 movement alive and to inform foreign governments, publics, and media outlets about violations of human rights in China.[52]

In sum, despite the repression of the authoritarian state, online expression has empowered Chinese citizens to contest authoritarian rule in a number of ways. In particular, freer online expression has challenged the state's monopoly over information and, ultimately, its ideational leadership. Some studies even claim that the state has already lost the war of position in cyberspace.[53] However, the state's loss is not regime critics' gain. Those attempting to bring democracy to China via online expression have thus far failed to convince the populace that democratic change would be an improvement. For many netizens, the risks and uncertainties of regime transition far outweigh its potential benefits. They worry about a possible decline in social stability, economic growth, and national security, as well as the possibility of achieving a nonfunctional democracy. Such fears, together with netizens' suspicion of the intention and credibility of regime critics, explain why the erosion of state legitimacy—as observed by many scholars[54]—has thus far failed to move China toward inclusive democracy. In this sense, the pluralization of online expression has worked to the advantage of the Chinese authoritarian regime.

THE INTERNET AS A CHALLENGE OR AN OPPORTUNITY

The Chinese Party-state faces two distinct challenges or crises. The first challenge, which might be called a legitimacy crisis, calls into question the right of the Party-state to rule its population. The regime's image as a "people's republic" and socialist state collapsed after it crushed the democratic movement of 1989, and its ideological foundation, communism, has been eroded by the ever-expanding market economy and proliferation of liberal democratic values.[55] In Patricia Thornton's words, China, like all other nondemocracies, "suffers from a birth defect that it cannot cure: the fact that an alternative form of government is by common consent more legitimate."[56]

But, in many cases, Chinese citizens do not directly question the Party-state's right to rule. They instead contest how the state and its agents exercise power in specific cases and seek immediate remedies to their grievances. This explains why popular unrest in China has been highly localized and compartmentalized, with "hardly any sign of mobilization that transcends class or regional lines."[57] This second challenge, which might be called a governance crisis, demands that the state improve its provision of services and address social ills. There can be many reasons why citizens choose not to negate the regime's legitimacy entirely: Rapid economic and sociopolitical developments in the reform era have helped the regime to accumulate some performance-based legitimacy, and focusing on specific issues rather than pursuing fundamental regime change may be more effective for citizens looking to address issues of immediate concern. Even political dissidents may choose to prioritize governance deficits and addressable problems as entry points for bigger political changes. For instance, Huang Qi, a human rights activist and the creator of the "June 4 Heavenly Web" website (*Liusi Tianwang*, 六四天网; www.64tianwang.com/), once commented,

> I think it has to start with protecting ordinary people's rights to petition and oppose corruption without being arrested. If that can happen then it's really a significant improvement. You can oppose the Communist Party, but someone will rule the country—and even if they call themselves the "Democracy Party," without a change in structures it'll be the same. . . . If all we do is call out "down with the Communist Party" or whatever slogan you want, it isn't as good as actually doing something.[58]

The distinction between the challenges of governance and legitimacy is crucial to an accurate assessment of the impact of online expression on the authoritarian regime. With most citizens more concerned with governance deficits than regime legitimacy,[59] the authoritarian state finds it more essential to demonstrate its ability and intent to solve governance problems than to limit criticism or engage in debates about its own legitimacy.

My findings suggest that the Chinese Party-state has been overreacting to online expression. Though online criticism sometimes challenges the regime's legitimacy, it is far from effective in mobilizing a revolution. The Internet first and foremost serves as safety valve that allows netizens to vent their anger concerning both personal and social grievances. In this regard, state censorship has done more harm than good to the regime's resilience, and reducing censorship would not be a disaster for the regime. In particular, less, but more accurate, censorship may lead to less critical, more supportive voices in cyberspace. After all, censorship has been the major source of grievance for many apolitical netizens and intermediary actors, and reducing it would certainly alleviate such complaints. Further, netizens who still trust the regime will be able to defend it with more confidence. After all, state censorship has effectively muted supportive voices, as it both justifies resistance to and dampens supporters' enthusiasm for the regime. In fact, rigid state censorship has often resulted in the indiscriminate elimination of both supportive and challenging voices. The irony—that the regime does not allow netizens to defend it—is disheartening for regime supporters. As Hu Ping, editor in chief of the New York–based dissident magazine *Beijing Spring*, has commented,

> Currently, the Chinese Communist Party is suppressing voices from both liberals and leftists and Maoists. Under such a circumstance, it is ridiculous for someone who perceives himself as a leftist, whose voice [is] suppressed, to defend the repressive regime.[60]

Instead of censorship, the Party-state could have used freer online expression as an opportunity to improve its governance. As David Shambaugh points out, the Chinese Party-state "is in the simultaneous state of atrophy and adaptation."[61] The survival of the regime to a large extent depends on whether its adaptations will outpace its atrophy. Systematic political reform will of course be crucial,[62] but so will the state's efforts to address specific governance deficits. The Internet and other new communication technologies can be convenient tools for the state. Of late, it appears the state may be recognizing this point by signaling its intention to improve government efficiency, transparency, accountability, and responsiveness by taking advantage of the Internet.[63] Recent speeches by top leaders, the "government online project," various local e-government trials, and efforts to engage citizens on popular social media platforms all seem to point, at least generally, in this direction.[64]

But more serious action needs to be taken, particularly in terms of responding to popular demands related to specific governance issues. Although Premier Wen Jiabao has urged "creat[ing] conditions that allow the people to criticize and supervise the government,"[65] heavy-handed censorship and punishment of outspoken netizens make it hard for citizens to believe the government's sincerity. Even if the state is still primarily concerned with stability and would prefer to continue censoring the web, it needs to tolerate complaints about governance issues and show its commitment to solving such problems by responding to netizens rather than habitually covering problems up.

CHINA IN THE WORLD

Findings in China certainly have broader implications when put in a comparative context. Authoritarian and illiberal regimes across the globe have adapted to the digital era and employed control tactics highly similar to those of China.[66] In addition to censorship, regimes such as those of Kenya, Russia, Syria, Turkey, and Venezuela have all deployed their own versions of the fifty-cent army.[67] A study on China— a most-likely case of strong state and authoritarianism—could thus lead to a better understanding of these cases, as well as digital authoritarianism in general, by providing a theoretical framework that could be adapted to similar situations. In fact, anecdotal evidence suggests that although Russian government-sponsored trolls are more dedicated, more professional, and better paid than Internet commentators in China, they have an equal lack of motivation, morale, and skill in implementing their tasks.[68] Similarly, the rise of spontaneous regime-defenders in China echoes studies on Putin's popularity and its political implications in Russia,[69] highlighting the necessity of examining the competing beliefs, values, and identities in authoritarian regimes.

Moreover, the finding that online expression has done more to delegitimize the regime than to spread civic and democratic norms in China may contribute to the literature on democratization. In particular, it provides a possible explanation for the resurgence of authoritarianism in some Arab Spring countries, as well as in many other countries that have experienced a democratic transition yet have failed to consolidate the new democratic regime.[70] After all, the pluralization of online discourses is as much a sign of authoritarian pullback as the erosion of social trust or social capital, which is crucial for democracy.[71] In other words, the findings presented in this book imply that certain problems that plague new democracies may relate to the legacy of the liberalization process rather than authoritarian rule.[72] For democratic activists anywhere, including those in China, this is a reminder that construction (of civic norms and democratic values) is at least as important as destruction (of state norms) in order to achieve an inclusive democracy.

APPENDIX

A LABELING WAR EXAMPLE

> ### THREAD: WHEELS TORE THEIR PASSPORTS UP FOR POLITICAL ASYLUM
>
> [Board: Military][OP: XI8], April 2, 2011, 14:38:49 [Page:1]
>
> Sender: XI8 (XI8 Nickname), Board: Military
> Now foreigners don't want them [Falun Gong practitioners], so they are crying and yelling to go back [to China]. The [Chinese] embassy refuses to issue passports because their identities cannot be verified. So each of them is crying and yelling, shamelessly hanging around outside the embassy, and [I] saw quite a few thrown out by security guards.
>
> —
>
> Sender: LBK (LBK Nickname), Board: Military
> You haven't found a job. You may practice FLG [Falun Gong] one day.
> 【Quoted from XI8 (XI8 Nickname)'s Post:】
> : Now foreigners don't want them, so they are crying and yelling to go back. . . .
>
> —
>
> Sender: XI8 (XI8 Nickname), Board: Military
> I guess you don't even know what a 401K is. NED [National Endowment for Democracy] will never provide social welfare for you, right?
> >>Sender: XI8 (XI8 Nickname), Board: Working
> >>[You're] truly an inexperienced, unenlightened guy.
> >>Our company deposits 3 percent without our contributing a single penny.
> 【Quoted from LBK (LBK Nickname)'s Post:】
> : You haven't found a job. You may practice FLG one day.
>
> —

Sender: XWR (XWR Nickname), Board: Military
Joining the older generals [Laojiang] when you are at a dead end? So you Laojiang have many such precedents [that became Laojiang because they were at a dead end]?
　【Quoted from LBK (LBK Nickname)'s Post:】
: You haven't found a job. You may practice FLG one day.

—

Sender: XWF (XWF Nickname), Board: Military
Then what do they do? Without passports and their identities unable to be verified? Stay underground here in the U.S. for their entire lives?
　【Quoted from XI8 (XI8 Nickname)'s Post:】
: Now foreigners don't want them, so they are crying and yelling to go back. . . .

—

Sender: LBK (LBK Nickname), Board: Military
The [Chinese] embassy has been nice to you then, even provided this [401K] for you.
　【Quoted from XI8 (XI8 Nickname)'s Post:】
: I guess you don't even know what a 401K is. NED will never provide social welfare for you, right? . . .

—

Sender: LBK (LBK Nickname), Board: Military
There are many such precedents among young generals [Xiaojiang].
　【Quoted from XWR (XWR Nickname)'s Post:】
: Join the older generals [Laojiang] when you are at a dead end? . . .

—

Sender: XWR (XWR Nickname), Board: Military
The U.S. government respects human rights, so you don't have to worry about that.
　【Quoted from XWF (XWF Nickname)'s Post:】
: Then what do they do? Without passports and their identities unable to be verified? . . .

—

Sender: XWR (XWR Nickname), Board: Military
Unpromising young generals turn into old generals. No wonder old generals are of low quality.
　【Quoted from LBK (LBK Nickname)'s Post:】
: There are many such precedents among young generals [Xiaojiang].

—

Sender: XI8 (XI8 Nickname), Board: Military
If that doesn't happen, they can be shipped to India and herded [like animals] with Dalai Lama and his supporters. Though they may suffer in terms of their material life, they should enjoy a spiritual life under the sunshine of democracy.
　【Quoted from XWF (XWF Nickname)'s Post:】
: Then what do they do? Without passports and their identities unable to be verified? . . .

—

Sender: XWF (XWF Nickname), Board: Military
Aren't illegal immigrants thrown in jail?
　【Quoted from XWR (XWR Nickname)'s Post:】
: The U.S. government respects human rights, so you don't have to worry about that.

—

Sender: XMD (XMD Nickname), Board: Military
If the U.S. is smart, they should take measures to prevent these people from becoming anti-U.S. terrorists.
　【Quoted from XI8 (XI8 Nickname)'s Post:】
: Now foreigners don't want them, so they are crying and yelling to go back. . . .

—

Sender: XWR (XWR Nickname), Board: Military
[Verified] illegal immigrants [are sent to] jail and provided with food and accommodation. This is human rights.
　【Quoted from XWF (XWF Nickname)'s Post:】
: Aren't illegal immigrants thrown in jail?

—

Sender: XWR (XWR Nickname), Board: Military
Chinese people won't. One American guy in my company who visits Asia frequently told me frankly [that] Chinese people are either good or bad. Easy to tell that. The good guys have a diverse attitude toward the U.S., and the bad guys all love the U.S.
　【Quoted from XMD (XMD Nickname)'s Post:】
: If the U.S. is smart, they should take measures to prevent these people from becoming anti-U.S. terrorists.

—

Sender: XJS (XJS Nickname), Board: Military
Not many wheels would tear up their passports. Those who do are mostly illegal immigrants.
　【Quoted from XI8 (XI8 Nickname)'s Post:】
: Now foreigners don't want them, so they are crying and yelling to go back. . . .

—

Sender: XI8 (XI8 Nickname), Board: Military
These wheels are as cheap as boneless pugs, and they don't even have the balls to become terrorists.
　【Quoted from XMD (XMD Nickname)'s Post:】
: If the U.S. is smart, they should take measures to prevent these people from becoming anti-U.S. terrorists.

—

Sender: XMD (XMD Nickname), Board: Military
[The] Laojiang hate the CCP. So they can hate the U.S. as well when the U.S. abandons them. That's very normal.
　【Quoted from XI8 (XI8 Nickname)'s Post:】
: These wheels are as cheap as boneless pugs, and they don't even have the balls to become terrorists.

—

Sender: XTL (XTL Nickname), Board: Military
You practiced?
　【Quoted from LBK (LBK Nickname)'s Post:】
: You haven't found a job. You may practice FLG one day.

—

Sender: XCI (XCI Nickname), Board: Military
I glanced at NTDTV [a Falun Gong media outlet] yesterday, and they were stirring this up. Through this, we further see wheels are the trash among the trash.
　【Quoted from XI8 (XI8 Nickname)'s Post:】
: Now foreigners don't want them, so they are crying and yelling to go back. . . .

—

Note: The users' names have been anonymized to protect their privacy.

Source: "Wheels Tore Their Passports Up for Political Asylum," *Mitbbs*, April 2, 2011, http://www.mitbbs.com/article_t/Military/35576285.html.

NOTES

PREFACE

1. We had computer classes, but the computers on the Changping campus were not connected to the Internet. We learned typing and programming in those classes.
2. Guobin Yang, "Contention in Cyberspace," in *Popular Protest in China*, ed. Kevin J. O'Brien (Cambridge, MA: Harvard University Press, 2008), 135
3. "The Trial of Xu Zhiyong: A New Citizen," *Economist*, no. 8871 (2014): 52.
4. Some Smth administrators moved their user data off campus and with these data established NewSmth.

1. INTRODUCTION: PLURALISM AND CYBERPOLITICS IN CHINA

1. See Philip N. Howard and Muzammil M. Hussain, *Democracy's Fourth Wave? Digital Media and the Arab Spring* (Oxford: Oxford University Press, 2013); Gilad Lotan, Erhardt Graeff, Mike Ananny, Devin Gaffney, Ian Pearce, and Danah Boyd, "The Revolutions Were Tweeted: Information Flows During the 2011 Tunisian and Egyptian Revolutions," *International Journal of Communication* 5 (2011): 1375–1405; Clay Shirky, "The Political Power of Social Media," *Foreign Affairs* 90, no.1 (2011): 28–41; Mohamed Zayani, *Networked Publics and Digital Contention: The Politics of Everyday Life in Tunisia* (Oxford: Oxford University Press, 2015); Nahed Eltantawy and Julie B. Wiest, "Social Media in the Egyptian Revolution: Reconsidering Resource Mobilization Theory," *International Journal of Communication* 5 (2011): 1207–24; Ethan Zuckerman, "The First Twitter Revolution?" *Foreign Policy*, January 15, 2011.

2. See Ian Johnson, "Activists Call for a 'Jasmine Revolution' in China," *New York Times*, February 24, 2011.

3. James Fallows, "Arab Spring, Chinese Winter," *Atlantic*, September 2011; Tania Branigan, "China's Jasmine Revolution: Police but No Protesters Line Streets of Beijing," *Guardian*, February 27, 2011; Jeremy Page, "Call for Protests Unnerves Beijing," *Wall Street Journal*, February 21, 2011; Austin Ramzy, "State Stamps Out Small 'Jasmine' Protests in China," *Time*, February 21, 2011, http://content.time.com/time/world/article/0,8599,2052860,00.html.

4. Lisa Anderson, "Demystifying the Arab Spring," *Foreign Affairs* 90, no. 3 (2011): 2–7.

5. See Fallows, "Arab Spring, Chinese Winter"; Gady Epstein, "A Revolution Is Not a Tweetup: Jasmine Revolution and the Limits of China's Internet," *Forbes*, February 22, 2011, http://www.forbes.com/sites/gadyepstein/2011/02/22/a-revolution-is-not-a-tweetup-jasmine-revolution-and-the-limits-of-chinas-internet/print/.

6. Andrew Nathan, "Authoritarian Resilience," *Journal of Democracy* 14, no. 1 (2003): 6–17; David L Shambaugh, *China's Communist Party: Atrophy and Adaptation* (Berkeley: University of California Press, 2008).

7. See Kevin J. O'Brien and Lianjiang Li, *Rightful Resistance in Rural China* (New York: Cambridge University Press, 2006); Kevin J. O'Brien, ed., *Popular Protest in China* (Cambridge, MA: Harvard University Press, 2008); Yongshun Cai, *Collective Resistance in China: Why Popular Protests Succeed or Fail* (Stanford, CA: Stanford University Press, 2010); Jianrong Yu, *Kangzhengxing Zhengzhi: Zhongguo Zhengzhi Shehuixue Jiben Wenti (Contentious Politics: Basic Questions of Chinese Political Sociology)* (Beijing: People's Publishing House, 2010).

8. Guobin Yang, *The Power of the Internet in China: Citizen Activism Online* (New York: Columbia University Press, 2009); Johan Lagerkvist, *After the Internet, Before Democracy: Competing Norms in Chinese Media and Society* (Bern, Switzerland: Peter Lang, 2010); Yongnian Zheng, *Technological Empowerment: The Internet, State, and Society in China* (Stanford, CA: Stanford University Press, 2008); Ashley Esarey and Qiang Xiao, "Political Expression in the Chinese Blogosphere," *Asian Survey* 48, no. 5 (2008): 752–72.

9. Barbara Demick, "Protests in China Over Local Grievances Surge, and Get a Hearing," *Los Angeles Times*, October 8, 2011, http://articles.latimes.com/2011/oct/08/world/la-fg-china-protests-20111009. The report suggests that Chinese demonstrators "have a narrow agenda and concrete demands: Farmers want a stop to confiscations of their land or to get better compensation for lost property. Homeowners want to stop demolitions. People want cleaner air and water and safer food. Truckers and taxi drivers want relief from soaring fuel prices."

10. Sheri Berman, "Civil Society and the Collapse of the Weimar Republic," *World Politics* 49, no. 3 (1997): 401–29.

11. Taylor C. Boas, "Weaving the Authoritarian Web: The Control of Internet Use in Nondemocratic Regimes," in *How Revolutionary Was the Digital Revolution: National Responses, Market Transitions, and Global Technology*, ed. John Zysman and Abraham Newman (Stanford, CA: Stanford Business Books, 2006), 365.

12. Zeynep Tufekci and Deen Freelon, "Introduction to the Special Issue on New Media and Social Unrest," *American Behavioral Scientist* 57, no. 7 (2013): 843.

13. Philip N. Howard, Aiden Duffy, Deen Freelon, Muzammil M. Hussain, Will Mari, and Marwa Maziad, "Opening Closed Regimes: What Was the Role of Social Media During the Arab Spring?" *SSRN* (2011), https://ssrn.com /abstract=2595096, http://dx.doi.org/10.2139/ssrn.2595096; W. Lance Bennett and Alexandra Segerberg, *The Logic of Connective Action Digital Media and the Personalization of Contentious Politics* (New York: Cambridge University Press, 2013); Zeynep Tufekci, "Social Movements and Governments in the Digital Age: Evaluating a Complex Landscape," *Journal of International Affairs* 68, no. 1 (2014): 1–18; Zeynep Tufekci and Christopher Wilson, "Social Media and the Decision to Participate in Political Protest: Observations from Tahrir Square," *Journal of Communication* 62, no. 2 (April 2012): 363–79; Emily Parker, *Now I Know Who My Comrades Are: Voices from the Internet Underground* (New York: Farrar, Straus and Giroux, 2014).

14. Howard et al., "Opening Closed Regimes."

15. Howard and Hussain, *Democracy's Fourth Wave?*

16. Guobin Yang, "The Internet and the Rise of a Transnational Chinese Cultural Sphere," *Media, Culture & Society* 24, no. 4 (2003): 469–90; Guobin Yang and Craig Calhoun, "Media, Civil Society, and the Rise of a Green Public Sphere in China," *China Information* 21, no. 2 (2007): 211–36; Yang, *The Power of the Internet in China: Citizen Activism Online*; Johan Lagerkvist, *The Internet in China: Unlocking and Containing the Public Sphere* (Lund, Sweden: Lund University Publications, 2007); Yong Hu, *Zhongsheng Xuanhua: Wangluo Shidai de Geren Biaoda Yu Gonggong Taolun (The Rising Cacophony: Personal Expression and Public Discussion in the Internet Age)* (Nanning: Guangxi Normal University Press, 2008). Xu Wu also argues that the Internet has nurtured cyber-nationalism by creating a public sphere beyond state control. See Xu Wu, *Chinese Cyber Nationalism: Evolution, Characteristics, and Implications* (Lanham, MD: Lexington Books, 2007).

17. Esarey and Xiao, "Political Expression in the Chinese Blogosphere"; Qiang Xiao, "The Battle for the Chinese Internet," *Journal of Democracy* 22, no. 2 (2011): 47–61; Yang, *The Power of the Internet in China*.

18. Guobin Yang, "The Co-evolution of the Internet and Civil Society in China," *Asian Survey* 43, no. 3 (2003): 124–41; Guobin Yang, "The Internet and Civil Society in China: A Preliminary Assessment," *Journal of Contemporary China* 12, no. 36 (2003): 453–75; Guobin Yang, "How Do Chinese Civic Associations Respond to the Internet? Findings from a Survey," *The China Quarterly*, no. 189

(2007): 122–43; Zixue Tai, *The Internet in China: Cyberspace and Civil Society* (London: Routledge, 2006).

19. Zheng, *Technological Empowerment*; Yongnian Zheng and Guoguang Wu, "Information Technology, Public Space, and Collective Action in China," *Comparative Political Studies* 38, no. 5 (2005): 507–36; Patricia Thornton, "Manufacturing Dissent in Transnational China: Boomerang, Backfire or Spectacle?" in *Popular Protest in China*, ed. Kevin J. O'Brien (Cambridge, MA: Harvard University Press, 2008), 179–204; Chin-Fu Hung, "Citizen Journalism and Cyberactivism in China's Anti-PX Plant in Xiamen, 2007–2009," *China: An International Journal* 11, no. 1 (2013): 40–54; Chin-Fu Hung, "The Politics of Cyber Participation in the PRC: The Implications of Contingency for the Awareness of Citizens' Rights," *Issues and Studies* 42, no. 4 (2006): 137–73; Li Gao and James Stanyer, "Hunting Corrupt Officials Online: The Human Flesh Search Engine and the Search for Justice in China," *Information, Communication, & Society* 17, no. 7 (2014): 814–29; Michael S. Chase and James C. Mulvenon, *You've Got Dissent! Chinese Dissident Use of the Internet and Beijing's Counter-Strategies* (Santa Monica, CA: RAND, 2002).

20. Lawrence Lessig, *Code and Other Laws of Cyberspace* (New York: Basic Books, 1999); Jack Goldsmith and Tim Wu, *Who Controls the Internet? Illusions of a Borderless World* (New York: Oxford University Press, 2006).

21. Yang, *The Power of the Internet in China*; Yonggang Li, *Women de Fanghuoqiang: Wangluo Shidai de Biaoda Yu Jianguan (Our Great Firewall: Expression and Governance in the Era of the Internet)* (Nanning: Guangxi Normal University Press, 2009); Eric Harwit and Duncan Clark, "Shaping the Internet in China: Evolution of Political Control Over Network Infrastructure and Content," *Asian Survey* 41, no. 3 (2001): 377–408; Ronald Deibert, John Palfrey, Rafal Rohozinski, and Jonathan Zittrain, eds., *Access Denied: The Practice and Policy of Global Internet Filtering* (Cambridge, MA: MIT Press, 2008); Ronald Deibert, John Palfrey, Rafal Rohozinski, and Jonathan Zittrain, eds., *Access Contested: Security, Identity, and Resistance in Asian Cyberspace* (Cambridge, MA: MIT Press, 2011); Ronald Deibert, John Palfrey, Rafal Rohozinski, and Jonathan Zittrain, eds., *Access Controlled: The Shaping of Power, Rights, and Rule in Cyberspace* (Cambridge, MA: MIT Press, 2010).

22. He Qinglian, *The Fog of Censorship: Media Control in China* (New York: Human Rights in China, 2008); Chase and Mulvenon, *You've Got Dissent*; Jonathan Zittrain and Benjamin Edelman, "Internet Filtering in China," *IEEE Internet Computing*, 2003, 70–77; Greg Walton, "China's Golden Shield: Corporations and the Development of Surveillance Technology in the People's Republic of China" (Montreal: International Centre for Human Rights and Democratic Development, 2001), accessed April 20, 2012, http://www.dd-rd.ca/site /_PDF/publications/globalization/CGS_ENG.PDF; Lena L. Zhang, "Behind the

'Great Firewall': Decoding China's Internet Media Policies from the Inside," *Convergence: The International Journal of Research into New Media Technologies* 12, no. 3 (2006): 271–91; Gary King, Jennifer Pan, and Margaret E. Roberts, "How Censorship in China Allows Government Criticism but Silences Collective Expression," *American Political Science Review* 107, no. 2 (2013): 1–18; Gary King, Jennifer Pan, and Margaret E. Roberts, "Reverse-Engineering Censorship in China: Randomized Experimentation and Participant Observation," *Science* 345, no. 6199 (2014): 1–10; Lokman Tsui, "An Inadequate Metaphor: The Great Firewall and Chinese Internet Censorship," *Global Dialogue* 9, no. 1/2 (2007): 60–68.

23. See Walton, "China's Golden Shield"; Tsui, "An Inadequate Metaphor." It is worth noting that the Great Firewall is not equivalent to the Golden Shield Project started by the Ministry of Public Security. The latter, attempting to "informatize" the ministry's workflow, is "better described as an effort to network the police, rather than police the network." See Dave Lyons, "China's Golden Shield Project: Myths, Realities and Context" (paper presented at the 7th Chinese Internet Research Conference, University of Pennsylvania, Philadelphia, PA, May 27–29, 2009).

24. Andrew Jacobs, "China Requires Censorship Software on New PCs," *New York Times*, June 8, 2009.

25. See Jens Damm, "The Internet and the Fragmentation of Chinese Society," *Critical Asian Studies* 39, no. 2 (2007): 273–94

26. Guobin Yang, "Technology and Its Contents: Issues in the Study of the Chinese Internet," *The Journal of Asian Studies* 70, no. 4 (2011): 1043–50; Bingchun Meng, "Moving Beyond Democratization: A Thought Piece on the China Internet Research Agenda," *International Journal of Communication* 4 (2010): 501–8; Damm, "The Internet and the Fragmentation of Chinese Society."

27. Yang, "Technology and Its Contents," 1044.

28. Lagerkvist, *After the Internet*, Chapter 5 and p. 122.

29. Rebecca MacKinnon, "China's 'Networked Authoritarianism,'" *Journal of Democracy* 22, no. 2 (2011): 32–46; Chin-Fu Hung, "China's Propaganda in the Information Age: Internet Commentators and the Weng'an Incident," *Issues & Studies* 46, no. 4 (2010): 149–81.

30. Johan Lagerkvist, "Internet Ideotainment in the PRC: National Responses to Cultural Globalization," *Journal of Contemporary China* 17, no. 54 (2008): 121–40.

31. Yang, *The Power of the Internet in China*.

32. Paola Voci, *China on Video: Smaller-Screen Realities* (New York: Routledge, 2010); Meng, "Moving Beyond Democratization."

33. Zheng, *Technological Empowerment*.

34. Jonathan Hassid, "Safety Valve or Pressure Cooker? Blogs in Chinese Political Life," *Journal of Communication* 62, no. 2 (2012): 212–30.

35. Among the few studies on intermediary actors, none has examined the role of forum managers who directly interact with netizens. See Rebecca MacKinnon, "China's Censorship 2.0: How Companies Censor Bloggers," *First Monday* 14, no. 2 (2009), http://firstmonday.org/article/view/2378/2089; Lagerkvist, *The Internet in China: Unlocking and Containing the Public Sphere*, 166–76; Ethan Zuckerman, "Intermediary Censorship," in *Access Controlled: The Shaping of Power, Rights and Rule in Cyberspace*, ed. Ronald Deibert, John Palfrey, Rafal Rohozinski, and Jonathan Zittrain, eds., *Access Controlled: The Shaping of Power, Rights, and Rule in Cyberspace* (Cambridge, MA: MIT Press, 2010), 71–85.

36. Kenneth Lieberthal and Michel Oksenberg, *Policy Making in China: Leaders, Structures, and Processes* (Princeton, NJ: Princeton University Press, 1988); Lianjiang Li, "Political Trust in Rural China," *Modern China* 30, no. 2 (2004): 228–58; Andrew Mertha, " 'Fragmented Authoritarianism 2.0': Political Pluralization in the Chinese Policy Process," *The China Quarterly*, no. 200 (2009): 995–1012.

37. See Cass R. Sunstein, *On Rumors: How Falsehoods Spread, Why We Believe Them, What Can Be Done* (New York: Farrar, Straus and Giroux, 2009); Cass R. Sunstein, *Infotopia: How Many Minds Produce Knowledge* (New York: Oxford University Press, 2006); Cass R. Sunstein, *Republic.com* (Princeton, NJ: Princeton University Press, 2002); Matthew Hindman, *The Myth of Digital Democracy* (Princeton, NJ: Princeton University Press, 2009); Barry Wellman and Milena Gulia, "Net-Surfers Don't Ride Alone: Virtual Communities as Communities," in *Networks in the Global Village: Life in Contemporary Communities*, ed. Barry Wellman (Boulder, CO: Westview, 1999), 331–66; Kevin A. Hill and John E. Hughes, *Cyberpolitics: Citizen Activism in the Age of the Internet* (Rowman & Littlefield, 1998); Lincoln Dahlberg, "The Internet and Democratic Discourse: Exploring the Prospects of Online Deliberative Forums Extending the Public Sphere," *Information, Communication & Society* 4, no. 4 (2001): 615–33; Lincoln Dahlberg, "Rethinking the Fragmentation of the Cyberpublic: From Consensus to Contestation," *New Media & Society* 9, no. 5 (2007): 827–47; Anthony G. Wilhelm, "Virtual Sounding Boards: How Deliberative Is Online Political Discussion?" *Information, Communication & Society* 1, no. 3 (1998): 313–38; Lincoln Dahlberg, "Computer-Mediated Communication and the Public Sphere: A Critical Analysis," *Journal of Computer-Mediated Communication* 7, no. 1 (2001): 0, doi:10.1111/j.1083-6101.2001.tb00137.x.

38. Yang, "Technology and Its Contents," 1048.

39. In 2012, all top twenty BBS sites had at least nine hundred simultaneous users online at their peak hours. For eighteen of them, the number exceeded one thousand, and the largest (NewSmth) had over thirty thousand. See "BBS Zhandian Liebiao Qian Ershiqiang (2012 Nian 03 Yue)" ("Top 20 BBS Sites"), *Newsmth*, March 2012, http://www.newsmth.net/bbstcon.php?board=BBSView&gid=45334.

40. See Guobin Yang, ed., *China's Contested Internet* (Copenhagen: Nordic Institute of Asian Studies, 2015).

41. James Leibold, "Blogging Alone: China, the Internet, and the Democratic Illusion?" *The Journal of Asian Studies* 70, no. 4 (2011): 1023–41.

42. For instance, "NewExpress@NewSmth," "Maoyan@Kdnet," "Military@Mitbbs," "Triangle@Bdwm," and "Free@Tianya" are all among the most popular discussion boards of these forums. Qianguo Luntan is primarily a political forum.

43. See "Social Media Dominates Asia Pacific Internet Usage," *Nielsen*, July 9, 2010, http://blog.nielsen.com/nielsenwire/global/social-media-dominates -asia-pacific-internet-usage/.

44. Kevin J. O'Brien, "Neither Transgressive nor Contained: Boundary-Spanning Contention in China," *Mobilization* 8, no. 1 (2003): 51–64.

45. Ron Deibert, "Cyberspace Under Siege," *Journal of Democracy* 26, no. 3 (2015): 64–78; Florian Toepfl, "Managing Public Outrage: Power, Scandal, and New Media in Contemporary Russia," *New Media & Society* 13, no. 8 (2011): 1301–19; Carolina Vendil Pallin, "Internet Control Through Ownership. The Case of Russia," *Post-Soviet Affairs*, 2016, 1–18; Luca Anceschi, "The Persistence of Media Control Under Consolidated Authoritarianism: Containing Kazakhstan's Digital Media," *Demokratizatsiya* 23, no. 3 (2015): 277–95; Çağri Yalkin, Finola Kerrigan, and Dirk vom Lehn, "(Il)Legitimisation of the Role of the Nation State: Understanding of and Reactions to Internet Censorship in Turkey," *New Media & Society* 16, no. 2 (2013): 271–89.

46. For instance, see Calum MacLeod, "Media Controls Leave Most Chinese Unaware of Activist Chen," *USA Today*, May 5, 2012, http://usatoday30.usatoday .com/news/world/story/2012-05-04/China-media-blackout/54773020/1. Authoritarian regimes may only pursue sufficient control for their political, economic, and social goals, rather than perfect control that would prevent even tech-savvy individuals from gaining unfettered access to the Internet. See Boas, "Weaving the Authoritarian Web."

47. For a discussion of rights consciousness in China, see Kevin J. O'Brien, "Villagers, Elections, and Citizenship in Contemporary China," *Modern China* 27, no. 4 (2001): 407–35; Lianjiang Li, "Rights Consciousness and Rules Consciousness in Contemporary China," *The China Journal*, no. 64 (2010): 47–68; Elizabeth J. Perry, "Chinese Conceptions of Rights: From Mencius to Mao— and Now," *Perspectives on Politics* 6, no. 1 (2008): 37–50.

48. See Henrik Serup Christensen, "Political Activities on the Internet: Slacktivism or Political Participation by Other Means?" *First Monday* 16, no. 2 (2011), http://firstmonday.org/article/view/3336/2767; Evgeny Morozov, "The Brave New World of Slacktivism," *Foreign Policy*, May 19, 2009.

49. King, Pan, and Roberts, "How Censorship in China Allows Government Criticism but Silences Collective Expression"; Peter Lorentzen, "China's Strategic Censorship," *American Journal of Political Science* 58, no. 2 (2014): 402–14.

50. Manuel Castells, "A Network Theory of Power," *International Journal of Communication* 5, no. 1 (2011): 779.

51. Evan Osnos, "Angry Youth: The New Generation's Neocon Nationalists," *New Yorker*, July 28, 2008, www.newyorker.com/reporting/2008/07/28 /080728fa_fact_osnos. Also see Li Guang, " 'Siyue Qingnian': Wangluo Minzu Zhuyi Xin Shili" (" 'April Youth': The New Force of Cyber Nationalism"), *Fenghuang Zhoukan (Phoenix Weekly)* 434, no. 13 (May 2012): 24–31; Wang Jiajun, "Cong Caogen dao Jingying–Dalun Wangluo Minzu Zhuyi Liubian" ("From Grassroots to Elitism: The Transformation of Mainland Cyber Nationalism"), *Fenghuang Zhoukan (Phoenix Weekly)* 434, no. 13 (May 2012): 36–38.

52. In fact, Chinese netizens are the most likely in Asia Pacific to post and share negative reviews of products. See "Social Media Dominates Asia Pacific Internet Usage."

53. Manuel Castells, *Communication Power* (New York: Oxford University Press, 2009), 362.

54. In the 2012 Diaoyu (Senkaku) Islands dispute with Japan, several local Chinese media outlets cropped a picture in their reports to conceal the flag of the Taiwan-Based Republic of China, whereas national news agencies such as *Xinhua News Agency* and *Global Times* (*Huanqiu Shibao*, 环球时报) used the original picture. Clearly, local censors imposed tougher constraints to avoid political risks. See Ding Li and Zheng Lingyu, "Diaoyudao Qingtian Bairi Qi, Zhongguo Meiti Nanti, Zaojiazhe Aipi Daoqian" ("The Flag of the Republic of China Over Diaoyu Islands Poses a Dilemma for Chinese Media, and Forgers Apologized After Being Criticized"), *VOA Chinese*, August 20, 2012, www. voachinese.com/content/hk_newspaper_20120820/1491305.html. For a good analysis of different rationales behind the central and local authorities in their responses to collective action, see Cai, *Collective Resistance in China*, 4–8.

55. For more on the safety-valve function of online expression, see Hassid, "Safety Valve or Pressure Cooker?" For more on the backfire effects of the state's censorship and opinion manipulation, see Michael Wines, "China's Censors Misfire in Abuse-of-Power Case," *New York Times*, November 17, 2010.

56. Li, "Political Trust in Rural China"; Lianjiang Li, "Political Trust and Petitioning in the Chinese Countryside," *Comparative Politics* 40, no. 2 (2008): 209–26.

57. Lagerkvist, *The Internet in China.*

58. Yang, "Technology and Its Contents," 1044.

59. James C. Scott, *Weapons of the Weak : Everyday Forms of Peasant Resistance* (New Haven, CT: Yale University Press, 1985).

60. See Yanqi Tong and Shaohua Lei, "War of Position and Microblogging in China," *Journal of Contemporary China* 22, no. 80 (2013): 292–311; Esarey and Xiao, "Political Expression in the Chinese Blogosphere"; He Qinglian, " 'Renmin Luntan' Diaocha Cuihuile Beijing de Zhidu Zixin" ("People's Forum

Survey Defeats Beijing's Confidence in System"), *VOA Chinese*, April 15, 2013, www.voachinese.com/content/public-opinion-survey-20130415/1641814 .html.

61. Damm, "The Internet and the Fragmentation of Chinese Society"; Leibold, "Blogging Alone."

62. "Chai Ling Jiaochu le Toumingzhuang" ("Chai Ling Has Proved Her Allegiance [to Foreign Powers]"), *Mitbbs*, September 28, 2011, www.mitbbs.com /article_t/Military/36507361.html (link expired).

63. "Wang Dan zai Fating Chengren: Shoudao Chen Shui-Bian de 40 Wan Meiyuan" ("Wang Dan Confesses in Court: He Received US$400,000 from Chen Shui-Bian"), *Mitbbs*, April 15, 2011, www.mitbbs.com/article_t/Military/35644205 .html (link expired); "Wang Adan Na le Chen A-bian 40 Wan Meijin" ("Wang A-Dan Took US$400,000 from Chen A-Bian"), *Mitbbs*, April 15, 2011, www .mitbbs.com/article_t/Military/35642545.html (link expired).

64. Political ambition carries negative implications among netizens because it implies that the struggle is not between the citizenry and the repressive state, but instead between political power contenders who are concerned only with their own interests rather than public welfare.

65. Lagerkvist, *After the Internet*, 39.

66. Guillermo O'Donnell and Philippe C. Schmitter, *Transitions from Authoritarian Rule* (Baltimore, MD: Johns Hopkins University Press, 1986), 8.

67. Zheng, *Technological Empowerment*.

68. Samuel P. Huntington, *Political Order in Changing Societies* (New Haven, CT: Yale University Press, 1968), 1.

69. Austin Ramzy, "China's Alarming Spate of School Knifings," *Time*, April 30, 2010, http://content.time.com/time/world/article/0,8599,1985834,00.html.

70. See Robert D. Putnam, *Making Democracy Work: Civic Traditions in Modern Italy* (Princeton, NJ: Princeton University Press, 1993); Robert D. Putnam, *Bowling Alone: The Collapse and Revival of American Community* (New York: Simon and Schuster, 2001). Alexis de Tocqueville viewed civic associations as the key to American democracy and defined egoism as "a passionate and exaggerated love of oneself," which "blights the germ of all virtue," including that of public life. See Alexis de Tocqueville, *Democracy in America*, volume 2 (New York: Vintage, 1840), 98–99.

71. Netizens label experts (zhuanjia, 专家) as "brick owners" (zhuanjia, 砖家, "charlatans"), professors (jiaoshou, 教授) as "shouting beasts" (jiaoshou 叫兽), and journalists (jizhe, 记者) as "prostitutes" or "jorkalists" (jizhe, 妓者). Even "public intellectuals" (gonggong zhishi fenzi, 公共知识分子) are popularly denigrated among netizens. See Rongbin Han, "Withering Gongzhi: Cyber Criticism of Chinese Public Intellectuals," *International Journal of Communication* (forthcoming).

72. For a brief review and critique of the democratic consolidation literature, see Andreas Schedler, "What Is Democratic Consolidation?" *Journal of Democracy* 9, no. 2 (1998): 91–107. For a collection of discussions on the quality of democracy, see Larry Diamond and Leonardo Morlino, *Assessing the Quality of Democracy* (Baltimore, MD: Johns Hopkins University Press, 2005).

73. Guobin Yang, "The Internet and the Rise of a Transnational Chinese Cultural Sphere," *Media, Culture & Society* 24, no. 4 (2003): 471.

74. See James C. Scott, *Seeing Like a State: How Certain Schemes to Improve the Human Condition Have Failed* (New Haven, CT: Yale University Press, 1998).

75. The representativeness of online expression is a potential problem because, besides everything else, not all citizens are online, and not all netizens are equally active. But the term *representative* is used here in a narrow sense, referring only to the degree to which online voices are included in this study.

76. They both offer telnet access, a defining technical feature of many early campus forums.

77. For example, Admin5.com, which targets developers and managers of small and medium-size websites.

78. For example, NewSmth's "BBSview Board," which attracts campus BBS managers.

79. QQ is an instant messenger service platform. QQ chat groups are similar to online chat rooms.

80. See "Shanxisheng Shoupi Wangluo Bianji he Wangluo Pinglunyuan Peixunban Xueyuan Zhengshi Zai Bing Jieye" ("Commencement of the First Training Class of Internet Editors and Commentators of Shanxi Province"), *Jincheng News*, December 20, 2006, www.jcnews.com.cn/Html/guondongtai/2006-12/20/120854983.html.

81. OpenNet Initiative, "Internet Filtering in China in 2004–2005: A Country Study," *OpenNet Intiative*, 2005, https://opennet.net/sites/opennet.net/files/ONI_China_Country_Study.pdf.

2. HARMONIZING THE INTERNET

1. Ronda Hauben, Jay Hauben, Werner Zorn, and Anders Ekeland, "The Origin and Early Development of the Internet and of the Netizen: Their Impact on Science and Society," in *Past, Present and Future of Research in the Information Society*, ed. Wesley Shrum, Keith Benson, Wiebe Bijker, and Klaus Brunnstein (Boston: Springer, 2007), 47–62; Werner Zorn, "How China Was Connected to the International Computer Networks," *The Amateur Computerist Newsletter* 15, no. 2 (2007): 72–98.

2. Rongbin Han, "Cyberactivism in China: Empowerment, Control, and Beyond," in *The Routledge Companion to Social Media and Politics*, ed. Axel Bruns, Gunn Enli, Eli Skogerbo, Anders Olof Larsson, and Christian Christensen (New York: Routledge, 2016), 268–80.

3. Jesper Schlæger and Min Jiang, "Official Microblogging and Social Management by Local Governments in China," *China Information* 28, no. 2 (2014): 189–213; Ashley Esarey, "Winning Hearts and Minds? Cadres as Microbloggers in China," *Journal of Current Chinese Affairs* 44, no. 2 (2015): 69–103.

4. Johan Lagerkvist, "Internet Ideotainment in the PRC: National Responses to Cultural Globalization," *Journal of Contemporary China* 17, no. 54 (2008): 121–40.

5. Yongnian Zheng, *Technological Empowerment: The Internet, State, and Society in China* (Stanford, CA: Stanford University Press, 2008); Lena L. Zhang, "Behind the 'Great Firewall': Decoding China's Internet Media Policies from the Inside," *Convergence: The International Journal of Research Into New Media Technologies* 12, no. 3 (2006): 271–91.

6. Zheng, *Technological Empowerment*, 50–53.

7. Min Jiang, "Authoritarian Informationalism: China's Approach to Internet Sovereignty," *SAIS Review of International Affairs* 30, no. 2 (2010): 71–89.

8. See, for instance, Zheng, *Technological Empowerment*; Yongnian Zheng and Guoguang Wu, "Information Technology, Public Space, and Collective Action in China," *Comparative Political Studies* 38, no. 5 (2005): 507–36; Guobin Yang, *The Power of the Internet in China: Citizen Activism Online* (New York: Columbia University Press, 2009); Patricia Thornton, "Manufacturing Dissent in Transnational China: Boomerang, Backfire or Spectacle?" in *Popular Protest in China*, ed. Kevin J. O'Brien (Cambridge, MA: Harvard University Press, 2008), 179–204; Susan Shirk, *China: Fragile Superpower* (New York: Oxford University Press, 2007); Susan Shirk, ed., *Changing Media, Changing China* (New York: Oxford University Press, 2011); Ashley Esarey and Qiang Xiao, "Political Expression in the Chinese Blogosphere," *Asian Survey* 48, no. 5 (2008): 752–72; Guobin Yang, "The Internet and Civil Society in China: A Preliminary Assessment," *Journal of Contemporary China* 12, no. 36 (2003): 453–75; Johan Lagerkvist, *The Internet in China: Unlocking and Containing the Public Sphere* (Lund, Sweden: Lund University Publications, 2007).

9. Lawrence Lessig, *Code and Other Laws of Cyberspace* (New York: Basic Books, 1999); Jack Goldsmith and Tim Wu, *Who Controls the Internet? Illusions of a Borderless World* (New York: Oxford University Press, 2006).

10. Eric Harwit and Duncan Clark, "Shaping the Internet in China: Evolution of Political Control Over Network Infrastructure and Content," *Asian Survey* 41, no. 3 (2001): 377–408.

11. He Qinglian, *The Fog of Censorship: Media Control in China* (New York: Human Rights in China, 2008); Jonathan Zittrain and Benjamin Edelman, "Internet

Filtering in China," *IEEE Internet Computing*, 2003, 70–77; Gary King, Jennifer Pan, and Margaret E. Roberts, "Reverse-Engineering Censorship in China: Randomized Experimentation and Participant Observation," *Science* 345, no. 6199 (2014): 1–10; Michael S. Chase and James C. Mulvenon, *You've Got Dissent! Chinese Dissident Use of the Internet and Beijing's Counter-Strategies* (Santa Monica, CA: RAND, 2002); Freedom House, "Freedom on the Net: A Global Assessment of Internet and Digital Media," *Freedom House*, April 1, 2009, https://freedomhouse.org/sites/default/files/Freedom%20OnThe%20Net _Full%20Report.pdf.

12. Edward Wong, "Xinjiang, Tense Chinese Region, Adopts Strict Internet Controls," *New York Times*, December 11, 2016.

13. The Ministry of Industry and Information Technology responded promptly to popular criticism, claiming that the software does not monitor users' online activities and can be uninstalled. See Bao Ying, "Xin Diannao Xuzhuang Guolü Shangwang Ruanjian" ("Filtering Software to Be Installed on New Computers"), *Xin Jingbao (Beijing News)*, June 10, 2009.

14. King Wa Fu, Chung Hong Chan, and Michael Chau, "Assessing Censorship on Microblogs in China: Discriminatory Keyword Analysis and the Real-Name Registration Policy," *IEEE Internet Computing* 17, no. 3 (2013): 42–50; Johan Lagerkvist, "Principal–Agent Dilemma in China's Social Media Sector? The Party-State and Industry Real-Name Registration Waltz," *International Journal of Communication* 6 (2012): 2628–46; Tamara Renee Shie, "The Tangled Web: Does the Internet Offer Promise or Peril for the Chinese Communist Party?" *Journal of Contemporary China* 13, no. 40 (2004): 523–40.

15. Zheng, *Technological Empowerment*.

16. Yang, *The Power of the Internet in China*, 47–51.

17. Yonggang Li, *Women de Fanghuoqiang: Wangluo Shidai de Biaoda Yu Jianguan (Our Great Firewall: Expression and Governance in the Era of the Internet)* (Nanning: Guangxi Normal University Press, 2009), 117–26. Yang and Li differ in their assessment of when the third stage started. Yang believes the third stage began in 2003 and was marked by the power transition from Jiang Zemin to Hu Jintao. Li argues that the third stage began in 2004, when the state concluded its policy learning process with the release of important documents such as *Opinions on Further Strengthening the Administration of the Internet*.

18. Zheng, *Technological Empowerment*, xviii.

19. See Michael D. Cohen, James G. March, and Johan P. Olsen, "A Garbage Can Model of Organizational Choice," *Administrative Science Quarterly* 17, no. 1 (1972): 1–25.

20. Li, *Women de Fanghuoqiang*, 117–26.

21. There are agencies peripherally involved in Internet control. For instance, the State Administration for Industry and Commerce joined seven other

ministries to launch a campaign to restrict the presence of undesirable information online in 2002. See Zheng, *Technological Empowerment*, 55. Also, as the Internet has become an increasingly important channel for publicity, many state agencies have established their own information services or Internet offices.

22. The term may also refer to censoring agencies as a whole.

23. See David Shambaugh, "China's Propaganda System: Institutions, Processes and Efficacy," *China Journal*, no. 57 (2007): 25–58. The Fifth Bureau of the State Council Information Office (i.e., the Internet Bureau) has been delegated the power to supervise and approve Internet news information services and to intervene in the dissemination of routine online news reports through decrees. The Ninth Bureau of the State Council manages Internet culture and also has the authority to exert control over online forums, blogs, and microblogs. See Su Yongtong, "Guoxinban 'Kuobian,' Wangluo Guanli Jusi Yi Bian Er" ("State Council Information Office Expansion: One Internet Administration Bureau Becomes Two"), *Nanfang Zhoumo (Southern Weekend)*, May 20, 2010; Tao Xizhe, "Jiekai Zhongguo Wangluo Jiankong Jizhi de Neimu" ("Uncovering Inside Stories of China's Internet Censorship Regime"), Reporters *Without Borders*, October 10, 2007, http://archives.rsf.org/IMG/pdf/China_Internet _Report_in_Chinese.pdf.

24. Michael Wines, "China Creates New Agency for Patrolling the Internet," *New York Times*, May 4, 2012.

25. See Jack Linchuan Qiu, "Virtual Censorship in China: Keeping the Gate Between the Cybersapces," *International Journal of Communications Law and Policy*, no. 4 (2000): 1–25. Qiu argues that the government has come to play a more significant role as the Party has moved into the background. See also Tao, "Jiekai Zhongguo Wangluo Jiankong Jizhi de Neimu."

26. The Internet Police perform multiple functions, with online content surveillance being one of them. See Li, *Women de Fanghuoqiang*, 96–98.

27. For news reports, see Xing Jun, Chen Wei, Ji Yu, and Zhang Gaofeng, ".cn Geren Yuming Shenqing Bei Jiaoting, Wangyou Zhiyi Tuixie Jianguan Zeren" ("Individuals' Applications to .cn Domain Name Suspended, Netizens Criticize It as Shirking Regulating Responsibility"), *Netease*, December 15, 2009, http://news.163.com/09/1215/08/5QIHRTVE0001124J.html; Hou Zhenwei, "Geren Weihe Bei Jin Zhuce '.cn'" ("Why Individuals Are Forbidden to Register for .cn Domains"), *Beijing Wanbao (Beijing Evening News)*, December 24, 2009.

28. Cui Qingxin, "Woguo Yi Chubu Jianli Hulianwang Jichu Guanli Zhidu" ("Our Country Has Established a Basic Internet Regulation System"), *Xinhua Net*, May 2, 2010, http://news.xinhuanet.com/fortune/2010-05/02/c_1269514 .htm.

29. The state has never released an official list of taboo words, forcing forums to maintain their own lists. This is according to group discussions at the National Campus Bulletin Board System Managers Conference in Suzhou, October 24, 2012, and interviews with BBS managers in Suzhou, October 23–24, 2009: interviews RSZ 2009–21, RSZ 2009–23, RSZ 2009–24, RSZ 2009–25, RSZ 2009–29, and RSZ 2009–30.

30. For instance, see Shanghai Municipal Government, "Shanghai Shi Wangluo yu Xinxi Anquan Shijian Zhuanxiang Yingji Yu'an" ("Special Emergency Plan for Internet and Information Security Crises of Shanghai Municipality"), *Shanghai Emergency Response Center for Information Security*, February 20, 2014, http://www.sercis.cn/html/30254986.html; Fengxian County Party Committee Office and Fengxian County Government Office, "Fengxian Xinxi Anquan Tufa Shijian Yingji Yu'an" ("Emergency Plan for Information Security Crises of Fengxian County"), *Government Website of Fengxian County*, September 25, 2012, www.sxfx.gov.cn/?viewinfor-199-0-11518.htm.

31. "Guoxinban Fuzeren: Liyong Hulianwang Zaoyao Chuanyao shi Weifa Xingwei" ("Cyberspace Administration of China Officials: Using the Internet to Fabricate and Spread Rumors Is Against the Law"), *Xinhua Net*, April 12, 2012, http://news.xinhuanet.com/politics/2012-04/12/c_111772774.htm.

32. Wang Xin, "Xinlang Tengxun Weibo Zanting Pinglun San Tian" ("Sina and Tencent Suspend Comment Function of Microblog Services for Three Days"), *Chengdu Ribao (Chengdu Daily)*, April 1, 2012.

33. Cheng Shuwen, "Woguo Wangluo Fanfu Chuxian 'Duanyashi Jiangwen'" ("Online Anticorruption Cools Down Dramatically"), *Nanfang Dushibao (Southern Metropolis Daily)*, December 26, 2014.

34. See Tao, "Jiekai Zhongguo Wangluo Jiankong Jizhi de Neimu."

35. Jasper Schlæger, *E-Government in China: Technology, Power and Local Government Reform* (Abingdon, UK: Routledge, 2013); Kathleen Hartford, "Dear Mayor: Online Communications with Local Governments in Hangzhou and Nanjing," *China Information* 19, no. 2 (July 1, 2005): 217–60.

36. In August 2000, the *People's Daily* urged state media to conquer "online commanding heights of thought and public opinion." See "Dali Jiaqiang Woguo Hulianwang Meiti Jianshe" ("Strengthen the Construction of Our Internet Media"), *People's Daily*, August 9, 2000. In December 2000, the State Council Information Office approved nine key online news providers, all of which were mouthpiece agencies, such as People's Daily Online, Xinhua Net, and CCTV Online.

37. Schlæger and Jiang, "Official Microblogging"; Liang Ma, "The Diffusion of Government Microblogging," *Public Management Review* 15, no. 2 (February 28, 2013): 288–309; Esarey, "Winning Hearts and Minds?"

38. Lagerkvist, "Internet Ideotainment in the PRC"; Rongbin Han, "Manufacturing Consent in Cyberspace: China's 'Fifty-Cent Army,'" *Journal of Current*

Chinese Affairs 44, no. 2 (2015): 105–34; Chin-Fu Hung, "China's Propaganda in the Information Age: Internet Commentators and the Weng'an Incident," *Issues & Studies* 46, no. 4 (2010): 149–81.

39. In 2004, at the Fourth Plenum of the Chinese Communist Party's Sixteenth National Congress, then president Hu Jintao proposed the idea of a "harmonious society" as a strategic goal for China's development. This idea soon became the official rhetoric that the state, particularly its local agents, would use to justify its efforts to maintain social stability, suppress popular mobilization, and censor online expression. This is why netizens have used the term *harmony* to refer to state censorship. Chapter 4 discusses netizens' reactions to the idea of a "harmonious society" and state censorship in greater detail.

40. Shie, "The Tangled Web," 538.

41. See Li, *Women de Fanghuoqiang*, 126–30.

42. State Council Information Office, *Hulianwang Shangwang Fuwu Yingye Changsuo Guanli Tiaoli (Regulations on the Administration of Business Sites of Internet Access Services)*, September 29, 2002.

43. The Cybersecurity Law, passed in November 2016, explicitly requires network operators, including online service providers, to verify users' true identity. This law has resulted in greater implementation of real-name registration. Forums such as Baidu Tieba and NewSmth now force users to provide cellphone numbers before allowing them to post. But as of June 6, 2017, Tianya still allows users to post without going through identity verification.

44. For instance, see Gady Epstein and Lin Yang, "Sina Weibo," *Forbes Asia* 7, no. 3 (March 2011): 56–60.

45. Interview RSZ 2009–25, with a campus BBS manager, Suzhou, October 24, 2009; interview RBJ 2009–18, with an unofficial forum campus BBS manager, Beijing, October 22, 2009; interview OBE 2011–53, phone interview with a private BBS manager, February 9, 2011.

46. As indicated by the numerous ads online, helping online businesses with the registration and licensing process is actually a lucrative business.

47. See John Steinbruner, *The Cybernetic Theory of Decision: New Dimensions of Political Analysis* (Princeton, NJ: Princeton University Press, 2002).

48. Gary King, Jennifer Pan, and Margaret E. Roberts, "How Censorship in China Allows Government Criticism but Silences Collective Expression," *American Political Science Review* 107, no. 2 (2013): 1–18.

49. Li Shao, "The Continuing Authoritarian Resilience Under Internet Development in China: An Observation of Sina Micro-Blog" (master's thesis, University of California, Berkeley, 2012), 1-51, http://oskicat.berkeley.edu/record=b21909970~S1; Ian Bremmer, "Why China's Leaders Fear the Teletubbies," *Foreign Policy*, June 13, 2012, http://eurasia.foreignpolicy.com/posts/2012/06/13/why_china_s_leaders_fear_the_teletubbies.

50. King, Pan, and Roberts, "How Censorship in China Allows Government Criticism but Silences Collective Expression."

51. For instance, see "Lüba Pingce Baogao" ("Technique Review of Green Dam Software"), *Southern Weekly Web*, June 11, 2009, http://www.infzm.com/content/29952 (link expired).

52. Hong Sha, "Liu Xiaobo 'Ruanjin' Bairi yu Qizi Dierci Jianmian" ("After One-Hundred-Day House Arrest, Liu Xiaobo Sees His Wife Again"), *Sina North America*, March 20, 2009, http://news.sina.com/ch/dwworld/102-000-101-105/2009-03-20/04163726082.html; Nick Amies, "Europe Praises, China Condemns Liu Xiaobo Choice for Nobel Peace Prize," *Deutsche Welle*, October 8, 2010, www.dw-world.de/dw/article/0,,6093118,00.html; "Liu Xiaobo Bei Kong Shandong Dianfu Guojia Zhengquan Zui" ("Liu Xiaobo Accused of Inciting Subversion of State Authority"), *BBC Chinese*, June 24, 2009, http://news.bbc.co.uk/chinese/trad/hi/newsid_8110000/newsid_8116000/8116019.stm.

53. Jim Yadley, "Detained AIDS Doctor Allowed to Visit U.S. Later, China Says," *New York Times*, February 17, 2007.

54. Interview RBJ 2010–41, with a forum manager of a large commercial website, Beijing, May 21, 2010.

55. Qin Wang, "Zhuli Zhe de Xin Jianghu" ("New Rivers and Lakes for Profit Seekers"), *Nandu Zhoukan (Southern Metropolis Weekly)*, no. 3 (2010): 36.

56. See Kenneth Lieberthal and Michel Oksenberg, *Policy Making in China: Leaders, Structures, and Processes* (Princeton, NJ: Princeton University Press, 1988); Kenneth Lieberthal and David M. Lampton, eds., *Bureaucracy, Politics, and Decision Making in Post-Mao China* (Berkeley, CA: University of California Press, 1992); Kevin J. O'Brien and Lianjiang Li, *Rightful Resistance in Rural China* (New York: Cambridge University Press, 2006); Andrew Mertha, " 'Fragmented Authoritarianism 2.0': Political Pluralization in the Chinese Policy Process," *The China Quarterly*, no. 200 (2009): 995–1012.

57. See Zheng, *Technological Empowerment*, 50. An understanding of the distinction between regulatory and control regimes is insightful. Note that the regulatory regime may facilitate content control.

58. See Austin Ramzy, "China's Domain-Name Limits: Web Censorship?" *Time*, December 18, 2009, www.time.com/time/world/article/0,8599,1948283,00.html; Zhang Yi, "Zhuce CN Yumin Jin Qi Ju Geren" ("CN Domain Name Registration Closed for Individuals from Today Onward"), *Xin Jingbao (Beijing News)*, December 14, 2009. In 2006, the China Internet Network Information Center campaigned to rectify domain name registration, but more for regulatory than control purposes. See "Xinxi Chanye Bu Jiang Zhengdun Yumin Zhuce" ("The Ministry of Industry and Information Technology Will Start Rectifying Domain Name Registration), *Xinhua Net*, November 2006, http://news.xinhuanet.com/politics/2006-11/06/content_5297176.htm. There have

also been discussions on loosening policy restrictions. See "Zhuceliang Die Zhi Disi, CN Yuming Ruhe Shoufu Shidi?" ("Registration Rate Falling to Number 4; How Will CN Domain Name Reclaim the Loss?"), *Zhongguo Xin Tongxin (China New Telecommunications)*, no. 14 (2010): 27–28.

59. This may be inaccurate, as another source suggests that three major telecommunication giants together shut down around 136,000 unregistered websites. See Wang Yunhui, "Gongye he Xinxihua Bu: Shouji Saohuang 'Shenhoushi'" (The Ministry of Industry and Information Technology: The Aftermath of the Mobile Phone Anti-pornography Campaign"), *Nanfang Zhoumo (Southern Weekend)*, January 21, 2010.

60. Wang, "Zhuli Zhe de Xin Jianghu," 36.

61. "Gongxin Buzhang Fouren Fengsha Geren Wangzhan, Cheng Zhili Yao Jiada Lidu" ("Ministry of Industry and Information Technology Minister Denies Banning Personal Websites, Asserting that Rectification Will Be Strengthened"), *Netease*, March 9, 2010, http://news.163.com/10/0309/09/61ASVNQK000146BD .html.

62. Interview RBJ 2009–34, with a PR manager of a multinational corporation, Beijing, April 23, 2010.

63. Xi Yihao and Zhang Wei, "Wangjing Huilu Wangjing: Ti Lingdao Shantie" ("Internet Police Bribing Internet Police: Deleting Posts for Local Leaders"), *Nanfang Zhoumo (Southern Weekend)*, April 17, 2014.

64. See "Zhongyang Waixuanban Yuan Fujuzhuang Gao Jianyun Shouqian Shantie Beicha" ("Former Deputy Bureau Director of Central International Communication Office Gao Jianyun Under Investigation for Taking Bribes to Delete Online Postings"), *Xinhua Net*, January 21, 2015, http://news.xinhuanet .com/legal/2015-01/21/c_1114076120.htm.

65. See Johan Lagerkvist, *After the Internet, Before Democracy: Competing Norms in Chinese Media and Society* (Bern, Switzerland: Peter Lang, 2010), 49. Helen Sun has discussed the struggle between the Ministry of the Electronics Industry and the Ministry of Posts and Telecommunications over the formation of China Unicom as a competitor of China Telecom. See Helen Sun, *Internet Policy in China: A Field Study of Internet Cafés* (Lanham, MD: Lexington, 2010), 148–49.

66. See Chen Hanci, "Xinwen Chunban Zongshu Zaici Qiangdiao Wangluo Youxi Shenpiquan Guishu" ("The General Administration of Press and Publication Reasserts Its Authority of Online Gaming Approval"), *Diyi Caijing Ribao (China Business News)*, October 12, 2009.

67. See "Guangdian Zongju he Gongxinbu Qiajia, Haisi Putong Wangmin he Wangzhan Zhanzhang" ("Fight Between the State Administration of Radio, Film, and Television and the Ministry of Industry and Information Technology Damaging to Ordinary Netizens and Website Administrators"), *PC Online*, December 13, 2009, http://itbbs.pconline.com.cn/diy/topic_10477883 -10849950.html. The competition between the State Administration of Radio,

Film, and Television and the Ministry of Industry and Information Technology has been widely acknowledged and reported, even in the mainstream media. See Chen Xuedong, "Liang Buwei Boyi Hulianwang Dianshi" ("The Struggle Between the State Administration of Radio, Film, and Television and the Ministry of Industry and Information Technology Over Internet Television"), *Xin Kuaibao (New Express News)*, August 27, 2009.

68. Tao, "Jiekai Zhongguo Wangluo Jiankong Jizhi de Neimu."
69. The First National Campus Bulletin Board System Managers Conference, Suzhou, Jiangsu Province, October 23–25, 2009.
70. An example here is the former high-ranking Xinhua News Agency official Xu Jiatun, who defected after the 1989 democratic movement. See Zhou Nan, "Zhou Nan Koushu: Xu Jiatun Pantao" ("Zhou Nan's Account: The Defection of Xu Jiatun"), *Lingdao Wencui (Leadership Digest)*, no. 16 (2010): 109–112.
71. See the Constitution of the People's Republic of China (1982; amended 1988, 1993, 1999, 2004), Article 35. A most recent example is the "Open Letter to the National People's Congress," written by a group of former officials headed by Li Rui, a former deputy director of the Central Organization Department, advocating for freedom of speech and freedom of the press. See David Bandurski (trans.), "Open Letter from Party Elders Calls for Free Speech," *China Media Project*, October 11, 2010, http://chinamediaproject.org/2010/10/13/translation-the-october-11-letter-from-party-elders/. The message even spread within the Great Firewall. See "Jiang Ping, Li Rui, Hu Jiwei, deng Zhi Quanguo Renda Gongkaixin" ("Open Letter to the National People's Congress from Jiang Ping, Li Rui, Hu Jiwei, et al."), *NewSmth*, October 12, 2010, http://www.newsmth.net/bbstcon.php?board=Law&gid=78794.
72. Oiwan Lam, "China: Censoring the Red and Bo Xilai's Supporters," *Global Voices*, March 16, 2012, http://advocacy.globalvoicesonline.org/2012/03/16/china-censoring-the-red-and-bo-xilais-supporters/.
73. Lagerkvist, *After the Internet*, 272–73.
74. Ibid., 265.
75. Interview RBE 2008–02, with a former journalist from *Guangzhou Daily*, Berkeley, California, October 25, 2008; interview RBJ 2009–08, with a former journalist, Beijing, January 9, 2009; interview OBE 2010–52, phone interview with a junior faculty member at a communications school who had once been a CCTV reporter, September 4, 2010.
76. Lagerkvist, "Principal–Agent Dilemma in China's Social Media Sector?"
77. Lagerkvist, *After the Internet*, 49–50.
78. An investigative report suggests that websites registered in Beijing are more tightly controlled than those registered in Shenzhen. See Mr. Tao [pseud.], *China: Journey to the Heart of Internet Censorship* (Paris: Reporters Without Borders, 2007), http://www.refworld.org/docid/47fcdc630.html. See also Rebecca MacKinnon, "China's Censorship 2.0: How Companies

Censor Bloggers," *First Monday* 14, no. 2 (2009), http://firstmonday.org/article/view/2378/2089.

79. Maria Edin, "State Capacity and Local Agent Control in China: CCP Cadre Management from a Township Perspective," *The China Quarterly*, no. 173 (2003): 35–52; Maria Edin, "Remaking the Communist Party-State: The Cadre Responsibility System at the Local Level in China," *China: An International Journal* 1, no. 1 (2003): 1–15; Yuhua Wang and Carl Minzner, "The Rise of the Chinese Security State," *The China Quarterly*, no. 222 (2015): 339–59; Kevin J. O'Brien and Lianjiang Li, "Selective Policy Implementation in Rural China," *Comparative Politics* 31, no. 2 (1999): 167–86.

80. See "Wang Shuai Yihuo Guojia Peichang, Gong'an Juzhang Dengmen Daoqian" ("Wang Shuai Receives State Compensation, Police Chief Visits His House and Apologizes"), *Fuzhou Ribao—Xin Dushi* (*Fuzhou Daily—New Metropolitan*), April 20, 2009.

81. Wang Junxiu, "Yipian Tiezi Huanlai Bei Qiu Bari" ("One Online Posting Resulted in Eight Days in Detention), *Zhongguo Qingnian Bao* (*China Youth Daily*), April 8, 2009; Zhang Dongfeng, "Fatie 'Feibang' Bei Panxing Shijian Wangshang Taolun Relie" ("Hot Discussion Arises Among Netizens on Being Jailed for Online 'Libel' "), *Nanfang Dushibao* (*Southern Metropolis Daily*), April 21, 2009. The story is also available in English; see "*Ordos* Becomes Nationally Known Word," *EastSouthWestNorth Blog*, April 21, 2009, http://www.zonaeuropa.com/200904a.brief.htm.

82. For studies on stability maintenance, see Yue Xie and Wei Shan, "China Struggles to Maintain Stability: Strengthening Its Public Security Apparatus," in *China: Development and Governance*, ed. Gungwu Wang and Yongnian Zheng (Singapore: World Scientific, 2012), 55–62; Wang and Minzner, "The Rise of the Chinese Security State"; Jonathan Hassid and Wanning Sun, "Stability Maintenance and Chinese Media: Beyond Political Communication?" *Journal of Current Chinese Affairs* 44, no. 2 (2015): 3–15; Yue Xie, "Rising Central Spending on Public Security and the Dilemma Facing Grassroots," *Journal of Current Chinese Affairs* 42, no. 2 (2013): 79–109; Jie Gao, "Political Rationality vs. Technical Rationality in China's Target-Based Performance Measurement System: The Case of Social Stability Maintenance," *Policy and Society* 34, no. 1 (March 2015): 37–48.

83. Brook Larmer, "In China, an Internet Joke Is Not Always Just a Joke. It's a Form of Defiance—and the Government Is Not Amused," *New York Times Sunday Magazine*, October 30, 2011.

84. The uncertainty of the censorship system may encourage self-censorship. See Rachel E. Stern and Jonathan Hassid, "Amplifying Silence: Uncertainty and Control Parables in Contemporary China," *Comparative Political Studies* 45, no. 10 (2012): 1230–54.

3. TO COMPLY OR TO RESIST?

1. Chinese citizens are adept at boundary-spanning contention. See Kevin J. O'Brien, "Neither Transgressive nor Contained: Boundary-Spanning Contention in China," *Mobilization* 8, no. 1 (2003): 51–64.

2. For instance, see Vivienne Shue, *The Reach of the State: Sketches of the Chinese Body Politic* (Stanford, CA: Stanford University Press, 1988).

3. Kenneth Lieberthal and David M. Lampton, eds., *Bureaucracy, Politics, and Decision Making in Post-Mao China* (Berkeley: University of California Press, 1992); Jean Oi, *Rural China Takes Off: Institutional Foundations of Economic Reform* (Berkeley: University of California Press, 1999); Marc Blecher and Vivienne Shue, "Into Leather: State-Led Development and the Private Sector in Xinji," *The China Quarterly*, no. 166 (2001): 368–93; Thomas. P Bernstein and Xiaobo Lü, *Taxation Without Representation in Rural China* (New York: Cambridge University Press, 2003); Kevin J. O'Brien and Lianjiang Li, *Rightful Resistance in Rural China* (New York: Cambridge University Press, 2006); Kevin J. O'Brien, ed., *Popular Protest in China* (Cambridge, MA: Harvard University Press, 2008).

4. Andrew Mertha, "'Fragmented Authoritarianism 2.0': Political Pluralization in the Chinese Policy Process," *The China Quarterly*, no. 200 (2009): 995–1012. Also see Yuan Yao and Rongbin Han, "Challenging, But Not Trouble-Making: Cultural Elites in China's Urban Heritage Preservation," *Journal of Contemporary China* 25, no. 98 (2016): 292–306.

5. Shanthi Kalathil, "China's New Media Sector: Keeping the State In," *The Pacific Review* 16, no. 4 (2003): 489–501.

6. The intelligent contrast between "just doing business" and "doing just business" is borrowed from the title of the following article: Gary Elijah Dann and Neil Haddow, "Just Doing Business or Doing Just Business: Google, Microsoft, Yahoo! and the Business of Censoring China's Internet," *Journal of Business Ethics* 79, no. 3 (2008): 219–34.

7. Sarah Lai Stirland, "Cisco Leak: 'Great Firewall' of China Was a Chance to Sell More Routers," *Wired*, May 20, 2008, www.wired.com/threatlevel/2008/05/leaked-cisco-do/.

8. Rebecca MacKinnon, "Shi Tao, Yahoo!, and the Lessons for Corporate Social Responsibility," *RConversation Blog*, December 30, 2007, http://rconversation.blogs.com/YahooShiTaoLessons.pdf.

9. Jedidiah R. Crandall, Masahi Crete-Nishihata, Jeffrey Knockel, Sarah McKune, Adam Senft, Diana Tseng, et al., "Chat Program Censorship and Surveillance in China: Tracking TOM-Skype and Sina UC," *First Monday* 18, no. 7 (2013), http://firstmonday.org/ojs/index.php/fm/article/view/4628/3727.

10. Microsoft remained cooperative with the Chinese state even after Google's withdrawal. See Joshua Rhett Miller, "Microsoft to Continue Censorship in

China as Google Opens Up," *Fox News*, March 16, 2010, www.foxnews.com /scitech/2010/03/16/google-reportedly-ends-censorship-china/; Rebecca MacKinnon, "Flatter World and Thicker Walls? Blogs, Censorship and Civic Discourse in China," *Public Choice* 134, no. 1–2 (2008): 31–46.

11. Clive Thompson, "Google's China Problem (and China's Google Problem)," *New York Times*, April 23, 2006.

12. See Ethan Zuckerman, "Intermediary Censorship," in *Access Controlled: The Shaping of Power, Rights and Rule in Cyberspace*, ed. Ronald J. Deibert, John Palfrey, Rafal Rohozinski, and Jonathan Zittrain (Cambridge, MA: MIT Press, 2010), 82–83.

13. See Yonggang Li, *Women de Fanghuoqiang: Wangluo Shidai de Biaoda Yu Jianguan (Our Great Firewall: Expression and Governance in the Era of the Internet)* (Nanning: Guangxi Normal University Press, 2009), 141.

14. See Johan Lagerkvist, *After the Internet, Before Democracy: Competing Norms in Chinese Media and Society* (Bern, Switzerland: Peter Lang, 2010), 146–47. Intermediary actors such as forums take preemptive measures to prevent content that may trigger state censorship from being posted. In this sense, they are censoring themselves.

15. Rebecca MacKinnon, "China's Censorship 2.0: How Companies Censor Bloggers," *First Monday* 14, no. 2 (2009), http://firstmonday.org/article /view/2378/2089.

16. Johan Lagerkvist, "Principal–Agent Dilemma in China's Social Media Sector? The Party State and Industry Real-Name Registration Waltz," *International Journal of Communication* 6 (2012): 2628–46.

17. Lagerkvist, "Principal–Agent Dilemma," 2628.

18. See for instance, An Chen, "Capitalist Development, Entrepreneurial Class, and Democratization in China," *Political Science Quarterly* 117, no. 3 (September 15, 2002): 401–22; Kellee S. Tsai, *Capitalism Without Democracy: The Private Sector in Contemporary China* (Ithaca, NY: Cornell University Press, 2007); Bruce J. Dickson, *Red Capitalists in China: The Party, Private Entrepreneurs, and Prospects for Political Change* (Cambridge: Cambridge University Press, 2003); Jie Chen and Bruce J. Dickson, *Allies of the State: China's Private Entrepreneurs and Democratic Change* (Cambridge, MA: Harvard University Press, 2010).

19. For instance, see Jean-Jacques Laffont and David Martimort, *The Theory of Incentives: The Principal-Agent Model* (Princeton, NJ: Princeton University Press, 2009).

20. Interview RBJ 2009–09, January 11, 2009; interview RBJ 2010–37, May 14, 2010, interview RBJ 2010–38, May 14, 2010; with Bdwm system administrators, board managers, and users, all in Beijing.

21. Interview RBJ 2010–42, interview RBJ 2010–47, and interview RBJ 2010– 49, with several unofficial campus BBS managers, Beijing, May 22, 2010.

For stories about of how website owners have suffered state censorship, see Zhu Xiaokun, "Baozhengshu de Shijie" ("In the World of Affidavits"), *Diyi Caijing Zhoukan (CBN Weekly)*, no. 43 (November 22, 2010): 56–64.

22. Xiong Li, "Ma Huateng deng Si Gaoguan Baoyuan Hulianwang Jianguan Yidaoqie" ("Four Senior Internet Executives, Including Ma Huateng, Complain About One-Size-Fits-All Internet Censorship), *Netease*, March 28, 2010, http://tech.163.com/10/0328/01/62R0RT6B000947HQ.html. For an English translation, see www.danwei.org/net_nanny_follies/net_censorship _complaints.php.

23. Rachel E. Stern and Jonathan Hassid, "Amplifying Silence: Uncertainty and Control Parables in Contemporary China," *Comparative Political Studies* 45, no. 10 (February 23, 2012): 1230–54.

24. See "Caifang Kaidi Wangluo Chuangshiren" ("An Interview with the Founder of Kdnet"), *Zhanzhang Zixun (Information for Webmasters)*, January 4, 2006, www.chinahtml.com/0601/11363423773006.html.

25. See Article 17 of "Shuimu Shequ Guanli Guize" ("NewSmth Community Management Regulations"), *NewSmth*, November 11, 2012, www.newsmth .net/nForum/#!reg.

26. Large commercial or mouthpiece forums had no problem, as they were either already registered or could easily obtain registration.

27. Many registered by paying brokers who claimed to have connections with local Ministry of Information Industry subsidiaries. Many also moved their websites to overseas servers and registered international domain names with the hope of solving the problem once and for all and to avoid future campaigns.

28. The system translated users' online activities (based on the history of the account and the degree of account activity) into points, and only those with more than two thousand points were allowed to post on "NewExpress." In October 2011, the forum lowered the requirement to five hundred points.

29. China is not a unique case in this regard. For instance, see Christopher Soghoian, "The Spies We Trust: Third Party Service Providers and Law Enforcement Surveillance," (Ph.D. dissertation, Indiana University, 2012): 1–107, http://files.dubfire.net/csoghoian-dissertation-final-8-1-2012.pdf. In fact, IT giants such as Google and Facebook now release their records of government data requests annually.

30. See Article 5.1 of "Tianya Shequ Yonghu Zhuce Xieyi" ("Terms and Conditions of Tianya Community Account Registration"), http://service.tianya.cn /guize/regist.do.

31. See Article 6 of "Shuimu Shequ Baohu Yinsiquan zhi Shengming" ("NewSmth Community Statement of Privacy"), *NewSmth*, www.newsmth.net/about /privacy.html.

32. Some forums have also been asked to provide surveillance reports on popular opinion. Interview RBJ 2010–42, with the forum manager of an unofficial campus BBS, Beijing, May 22, 2010.

33. See Li Shao, "The Continuing Authoritarian Resilience Under Internet Development in China: An Observation of Sina Micro-Blog" (master's thesis, University of California, Berkeley, 2012), 1–51, http://oskicat.berkeley.edu /record=b21909970~S1. In some cases, the post will still be "published," but visible only to the user him- or herself.

34. Rebecca MacKinnon, "China's Censorship 2.0"; Yongming Zhou, *Historicizing Online Politics: Telegraphy, the Internet, and Political Participation in China* (Stanford, CA: Stanford University Press, 2005), 179.

35. MacKinnon, "China's Censorship 2.0."

36. All major commercial forums included in this study (e.g., 163, Kdnet, Sina, Sohu, and Tianya) have established such a system. Tianya has both board managers and content editors, with the content editors in charge of content control. Board managers are often selected from among a forum's users, and their responsibilities include moderating discussions, compiling digests, and organizing online and offline activities.

37. For instance, on March 6, 2012, the welcome page of the forum provided a link to the following article: Zhang Lei, "Wang Jingguan, Wo Xiang Bao Nin Yixia" ("Officer Wang, I Want to Hug You"), *Fazhi Wanbao (Legal Evening News)*, February 23, 2012. The article praises a police officer from the Haidian branch of the Beijing Municipal Police Bureau.

38. Lagerkvist, *After the Internet*, 147; see also Lagerkvist, "Principal–Agent Dilemma in China's Social Media Sector?"

39. Many BBS managers in Beijing envy BYR, the official campus BBS of the Beijing University of Posts and Telecommunications because its administrators have maintained a positive relationship with university authorities. Interview RBJ 2010–48, with a forum manager, Beijing, May 22, 2010.

40. Interview RBJ 2010–43, with a university faculty member who supervises student BBSs, Beijing, May 22, 2010. Though impossible to completely fend off state intervention, trust from university supervisory bodies may enable freer online discussion by reducing the need for self-censorship.

41. Interview RBJ 2010–44, interview RBJ 2010–45, interview RBJ 2010–48, and interview RBJ 2010–48, with forum managers, Beijing, May 22, 2010.

42. Interview RBJ 2009–18, with an unofficial forum campus BBS manager, Beijing, October 22, 2009.

43. Lagerkvist, "Principal–Agent Dilemma in China's Social Media Sector?"

44. These low-profile strategies resemble what James Scott calls "weapons of the weak." See James C. Scott, *Weapons of the Weak: Everyday Forms of Peasant Resistance* (New Haven, CT: Yale University Press, 1985).

45. Interview OBJ 2009–13, online interview with a state-run forum administrator, August 28, 2009.

46. Interview RBJ 2010–44, with a forum manager, Beijing, May 22, 2010.

47. None of the officials at the meeting responded to the complaints.

48. For instance, the following thread was first posted on April 15 and attracted fifty replies by May 3 before being deleted. See "'Bai Jia Hei'— Zhongguo Diyibu Miaoxie Liusi Yundong de Zizhuanti Xiaoshuo" ("'Black and White'—China's First Autobiographical Novel on the June Fourth Movement"), *NewSmth*, April 23, 2016, http://ar.newsmth.net/thread -1ac547bdd085e31-1.html.

49. See Li Liang and Yu Li, "14 Buwei Lianhe Jinghua Hulianwang" ("Fourteen Ministries and Commissions Jointly Cleanse the Internet"), *Nanfang Zhoumo (Southern Weekend)*, August 18, 2005.

50. See Ministry of Information Industry, "Xinxi Chanyebu Guanyu Zuohao Hulianwang Wangzhan Shiming Guanli Gongzuo de Tongzhi" ("Ministry of Information Industry Circular on Effectively Enforcing Real-Name Administration of Websites"), July 19, 2007.

51. Qin Wang, "Zhuli Zhe de Xin Jianghu" ("New Rivers and Lakes for Profit Seekers"), *Nandu Zhoukan (Southern Metropolis Weekly)*, no. 3 (2010): 34–37; Zhou Peng, "Zhongxiao Wangzhan Handong 'Duanwang'" ("Small and Medium-Size Websites 'Down' in Freezing Winter"), *Nandu Zhoukan (Southern Metropolis Weekly)*, no. 3 (2010): 26–30.

52. Interview RBJ 2010–42, with the forum administrator of an unofficial campus BBS, Beijing, May 22, 2010. A number of campus BBS sites started to implement the policy under pressure from their home universities as a result of the Ministry of Education's 2005 mandate to transform campus forums into internal communication platforms.

53. Interview RBJ 2010–36 with the forum manager of a large commercial website, Beijing, May 6, 2010.

54. Xiao Qiang, "1984bbs Wangzhan Guanbi you Chongkai Shuoming le Shenme?" ("What Can We Learn from the Shutdown and Resurrection of 1984bbs?"), *Radio Free Asia*, October 26, 2010, www.rfa.org/mandarin/pinglun/xiaoqiang /xq-10262010171852.html. The forum based its server outside China, although its founder and owner, Jiannan Zhang (a.k.a. SecretaryZhang), lives in Beijing. The forum suffered many hacker attacks, and Zhang himself was harassed and threatened by the authorities. The forum was finally forced down in October 2010 after allowing a discussion of the Nobel Peace Prize being awarded to jailed dissident Liu Xiaobo. An interesting question here is why the Great Firewall failed to block 1984bbs before its closure. Zhang and his group claimed that it was because they had outsmarted the firewall. However, someone (likely an Internet security expert) challenged this claim, suggesting

that Great Firewall authorities turned a blind eye to the forum because it was compromised by the state. Another netizen suggested that it might be that the forum appeared controllable to the state. See Huo Ju and Ayue A, "He SecretaryZhang Jiufen Shimo" ("The Whole Story of My Controversy with SecretaryZhang"), *Google Buzz*, November 1, 2010, https://profiles.google.com/109778955150081671489/buzz/c5E5GfefCpR. It is also worth noting that 1984bbs here refers exclusively to 1984bbs.com, not to 1984bbs.org, which was established after the closure of 1984bbs.com.

55. For more information about the scandal, see "Wangbao Shaanxi Ankang Huanyun Qi Yue Yunfu Qiangzhi Yinchan" ("Internet Disclosed Seven-Month Pregnant Women Forced to Abort in Ankang, Shaanxi"), *Netease*, June 12, 2012, http://news.163.com/12/0612/18/83QP5TAI00011229.html.

56. Interview RBJ 2009–09, January 11, 2009; interview RBJ 2010–37, May 14, 2010; interview RBJ 2010–38, May 14, 2010; with Bdwm system administrators, board managers, and users, all in Beijing. Also interview RBJ 2009–17, with veteran forum users, Beijing, September 23, 2009. The takeover took place on January 1, 2003, in a very dramatic way. The university authorities summoned all system administrators for a meeting while working with some of them to move the BBS server from the computer center to the Youth Research Center of the university's Communist Youth League Committee. Those who cooperated with the university justified their choice by arguing that the takeover would grant official status to the BBs and thus ensure more support from the university.

57. Interview RBE 2008–01, with a former forum manager from Tsinghua University, Berkeley, California, September 23, 2008; interview RBJ 2009–12, with a Smth user who was familiar with the Smth system administrators involved in the struggle in Beijing. For a brief introduction to the event, see "Weishenme You Liangge Shuimu? 3.16 Shi Shenme?" ("Why Are There Two Smth Sites? What Is March 16?"), *NewSmth*, March 16, 2006, www.newsmth.net/bbscon.php?bid=313&id=9466&ftype=11.

58. See Albert O. Hirschman, *Exit, Voice, and Loyalty: Responses to Decline in Firms, Organizations, and States* (Cambridge, MA: Harvard University Press, 1970).

59. Later, Nanjing University authorities and forum administrators actually compromised and restored Lily, though with more restrictions imposed.

60. The two based in China—Yjrg (yjrg.org) and Lqqm (lqqm.net)—were significantly depoliticized, but still allowed former Ytht users to grumble. A third forum was re-established in the United States, also named Ytht. All three forums were based on backup data from the original forum. Anecdotally, when Ytht was forced down, authorities attempted to destroy its hard drives. Yet, some hard drives survived because forum administrators at the scene claimed them to be personal belongings. Interview RBJ 2009–07, with

a former Ytht board manager, Beijing, January 6, 2009; interview RBJ 2010–38, with a Bdwm administrator who was also a veteran user and board manager of Ytht, Beijing, May 14, 2010.

61. See "Renminwang Qiangguo Shequ Xinban Shangxian Youjiang Huodong Huojiang Gonggao" ("Winning Announcement of People's Daily Online Qiangguo Community New Version Launch Awards Event"), *People's Daily Online*, July 27, 2012, www.people.com.cn/n/2012/0727/c345746-18613565.html.

62. Interview OBJ 2009–13, online interview with a state-run forum administrator, August 28, 2009.

63. Gary King, Jennifer Pan, and Margaret E. Roberts, "How Censorship in China Allows Government Criticism but Silences Collective Expression," *American Political Science Review* 107, no. 2 (2013): 1–18; Gary King, Jennifer Pan, and Margaret E. Roberts, "Reverse-Engineering Censorship in China: Randomized Experimentation and Participant Observation," *Science* 345, no. 6199 (2014): 1–10.

64. For instance, see Gady Epstein and Lin Yang, "Sina Weibo," *Forbes Asia* 7, no. 3 (March 2011): 56–60.

65. Ethan Zuckerman, "Cute Cats to the Rescue? Participatory Media and Political Expression," in *From Voice to Influence: Understanding Citizenship in a Digital Age*, ed. Danielle Allen and Jennifer S. Light (Chicago: University of Chicago Press, 2015), 131–54.

66. State Council Information Office Internet Bureau, "Guanyu Tengxun Wang Weigui Qingkuang de Tongbao" ("Circular on Tencent's Violations of Regulations"), leaked internal censorship directive communication, March 3, 2009. According to the *Administrative Provisions of Internet News Information Services*, the company is not qualified to produce its own news reports. It can only reprint reports from state-sanctioned sources.

67. Yawei Liu, "A Long Term View of China's Microblog Politics" (paper presented at the 10th Annual Chinese Internet Research Conference, University of Southern California, Annenberg, Los Angeles, CA, May 21–22, 2012).

68. See "Jinji Tongzhi: Zongheng Sousuo Kaifang Guanliyuan Sousuo Jinci Quanxian" ("Emergency Notice: Zongheng Search Enables Administrators to Search for Taboo Words"), *Discuz!*, April 10, 2012, www.discuz.net/thread-2755103-1-1.html. For an English translation of the notice, see "Censorship Instructions for Online Forums," http://chinadigitaltimes.net/2012/10/censorship-instructions-for-online-forums/.

69. See "Ni Zenme Kandai Google Tuichu Zhongguo Shichang" ("Your Opinions on Google's Withdrawal from China"), *Admin5*, January 13, 2010, www.a5.net/thread-1546443-1-1.html. Of survey respondents, 330 (86.61 percent) stated that Google had provided convenience to Chinese users, Google should not exit China, and the government should support Google.

70. Most campus forums are hosted on university servers, use university bandwidth, and are exempt from or have obtained Internet content provider registration with university facilitation. Official campus forums can generate revenue but are not designed to be profit seeking. Some forums earn good money by selling advertising spots: Bdwm's ad revenue, for example, was estimated to be over 200,000 RMB in 2009. But since they normally cannot spend the money directly, forums have no incentive to increase revenue. Interview RBJ 2009-19 and interview RBJ 2009-20, with campus forum managers, Beijing, October 21, 2009.

71. Interview RBJ 2009-18, interview RBJ 2009-19, and interview RBJ 2009-20, with campus forum managers, Beijing, October 21, 2009; interview RSZ 2009-26, with a BBS manager, Suzhou, October 24, 2009; interview RBJ 2010-46, with a BBS manager, Beijing, May 22, 2010. At one university, there were four student forums whose managers competed for a scholarship from a tech company to advance the development of campus Internet platforms.

72. Earlier campus forums, whether official or not, were primarily driven by nonprofit motivations. Ytht, for instance, relied on donations from its administrators and users; however, this was not sustainable in the long run. Recognizing this, forum administrators began to discuss ways to generate greater revenue. Unfortunately, they did not have a chance to try out their plans before the site was shut down in 2004. See "lovemeandyou Huida mgzf Tiwen" ("lovemeandyou Responds to mgzf's Questions"), *hkday.net*, October 26, 2003, www.hkday.net/ytht/SM_Election/8/3/7/1.html (link expired); "[Huida mgzf Wangyou Tiwen] Guanyu Yitahutu de Fazhan Fangxiang" ("[Responses to mgzf's Questions] About the Direction of Ytht's Future Development"), *hkday.net*, October 26, 2003, http://hkday.net/ytht/SM_Election/8/3/3/1.html (link expired).

73. Being an unofficial BBS run primarily by Peking University students, Ytht attempted to maintain a liberal discussion environment because its administrators and active users believed in freedom of expression. The founder of NewYtht is also a Peking University graduate. He and a few friends set up the new site with the goal of maintaining the spirit of Ytht. Interview RBJ 2009-18, with the forum manager of an unofficial campus BBS, Beijing, October 22, 2009.

74. Ethan Michelson finds that bureaucratic, instrumental, or affective ties to the Party-state and its agents can help lawyers in their everyday difficulties. See Ethan Michelson, "Lawyers, Political Embeddedness, and Institutional Continuity in China's Transition from Socialism," *American Journal of Sociology* 113, no. 2 (2007): 352–414.

75. Kalathil, "China's New Media Sector."

76. Lagerkvist, "Principal–Agent Dilemma in China's Social Media Sector?" The state has used a similar strategy to control the traditional commercial media. See Ashley Esarey, "Cornering the Market: State Strategies for Controlling China's Commercial Media," *Asian Perspective* 29, no.4 (2005): 37–83.

77. Certain channels on those platforms can be shut down under state pressure. For instance, in 2009, Tianya suspended its "Grassroots Voices" board, which allows netizens to complain about issues including government misconduct, for weeks for the People's Republic of China's sixtieth anniversary.

78. Wang, "Zhuli Zhe de Xinjiang Hu"; Zhou, "Zhongxiao Wangzhan Handong 'Duanwang'"; "Gongxin Buzhang Fouren Fengsha Geren Wangzhan, Cheng Zhili Yao Jiada Lidu" ("Ministry of Industry and Information Technology Minister Denies Banning Personal Websites, Asserting that Rectification Will Be Strengthened"), *Netease*, March 9, 2010, http://news.163.com/10/0309/09/61ASVNQK000146BD.html.

79. For instance, Ccthere attempted to depoliticize itself in early 2012 by posting a notice on its front page in which its owner and administrator, Tieshou (a.k.a. the Iron Hand) stated, "You are welcome to use herewp.com. Those who feel constrained on Ccthere or Cchere, consider herewp.com. Cchere will not address politically controversial topics. Ccthere will also gradually clean up these topics, particularly topics on Chinese domestic politics." See Laowantong, "Jubao Tieshou" ("A Complaint Against Tieshou"), *Ccthere*, July 26, 2012, www.ccthere.com/article/3761371.

80. For stories on forums geared toward ideological and intellectual expression, see Ji Tianqin and Tang Ailin, "BBS Wangshi" ("The Legend of BBS"), *Nandu Zhoukan (Southern Metropolis Weekly)*, no. 20 (May 28, 2012): 56–63.

81. Daniela Stockmann, *Media Commercialization and Authoritarian Rule in China* (Cambridge: Cambridge University Press, 2013), 51.

4. POP ACTIVISM: PLAYFUL NETIZENS IN CYBERPOLITICS

1. Mao Tse-Tung, "On Protracted War," in *Selected Works of Mao Tse-Tung*, vol. 2 (Peking: Foreign Languages Press, 1965), 143–44.

2. Guobin Yang, ed., *China's Contested Internet* (Copenhagen: Nordic Institute of Asian Studies, 2015).

3. Guobin Yang, *The Power of the Internet in China: Citizen Activism Online* (New York: Columbia University Press, 2009), 14.

4. For instance, see Gabriel A. Almond and Sidney Verba, *The Civic Culture: Political Attitudes and Democracy in Five Nations*, (Princeton, NJ: Princeton University Press, 1963); Stuart Hall, "Cultural Studies: Two Paradigms," *Media, Culture & Society* 2, no. 1 (1980): 57–72; Jean-François Lyotard, *The Postmodern Condition: A Report on Knowledge, Theory and History of Literature*, vol. 10 (Minneapolis: University of Minnesota Press, 1984); Emile Durkheim, "The Cultural Logic of Collective Representations," in *Social Theory: The Multicultural, Global, and Classic Readings*, ed. Charles Lemert (Boulder, CO: Westview, 1993), 98–108; Edward W. Said, *Culture and Imperialism* (New York:

Vintage, 1993); Max Weber, *The Protestant Ethic and the Spirit of Capitalism* (London: Penguin, 2002); Max Horkheimer and Theodor W. Adorno, *Dialectic of Enlightenment: Philosophical Fragments*, ed. Gunzelin Schmid Noeri (Stanford, CA: Stanford University Press, 2002); Liesbet van Zoonen, *Entertaining the Citizen: When Politics and Popular Culture Converge* (Lanham, MD: Rowman & Littlefield, 2005).

5. Gabriel Almond and Sidney Verba, *The Civic Culture* (Thousand Oaks, CA: Sage, 1963); Ronald Inglehart, *Culture Shift in Advanced Industrial Society* (Princeton, NJ: Princeton University Press, 1990); Robert D. Putnam, *Making Democracy Work: Civic Traditions in Modern Italy* (Princeton, NJ: Princeton University Press, 1993); Bob Franklin, *Packaging Politics: Political Communications in Britain's Media Democracy*, 2nd ed. (London: Bloomsbury Academic, 2004); van Zoonen, *Entertaining the Citizen*; Todd Gitlin, *Media Unlimited: How the Torrent of Images and Sounds Overwhelms Our Lives* (New York: Henry Holt, 2007).

6. Sidney Tarrow, *Power in Movement: Social Movements and Contentious Politics* (New York: Cambridge University Press, 1998), 16–18.

7. Nan Enstad, *Ladies of Labor, Girls of Adventure: Working Women, Popular Culture, and Labor Politics at the Turn of the Twentieth Century* (New York: Columbia University Press, 1999).

8. Rob Rosenthal and Richard Flacks, *Playing for Change: Music and Musicians in the Service of Social Movements* (Abingdon, Oxon: Routledge, 2016).

9. Tianjian Shi, "Cultural Values and Political Trust: A Comparison of the People's Republic of China and Taiwan," *Comparative Politics* 33, no. 4 (2001): 401–19; Tianjian Shi, "China: Democratic Values Supporting an Authoritarian System," in *How East Asians View Democracy*, ed. Larry Diamond, Andrew J. Nathan, and Doh Chull Shin (New York: Columbia University Press, 2008), 209–37; Wenfang Tang, *Populist Authoritarianism: Chinese Political Culture and Regime Sustainability* (New York: Oxford University Press, 2016).

10. Jeffrey N. Wasserstrom and Elizabeth J. Perry, eds., *Popular Protest and Political Culture in Modern China* (Boulder, CO: Westview, 1994).

11. Michael X. Delli Carpini, "The Political Effects of Entertainment Media," in *The Oxford Handbook of Political Communication*, ed. Kate Kenski and Kathleen Hall Jamieson (New York: Oxford University Press, 2014).

12. Gary King, Jennifer Pan, and Margaret E. Roberts, "How Censorship in China Allows Government Criticism but Silences Collective Expression," *American Political Science Review* 107, no. 2 (2013): 1–18; Ronald Deibert, John Palfrey, Rafal Rohozinski, and Jonathan Zittrain, eds., *Access Denied: The Practice and Policy of Global Internet Filtering* (Cambridge, MA: MIT Press, 2008); Ronald Deibert, John Palfrey, Rafal Rohozinski, and Jonathan Zittrain, eds., *Access Controlled: The Shaping of Power, Rights, and Rule in Cyberspace* (Cambridge, MA: MIT Press, 2010); John Sullivan, "China's Weibo: Is Faster Different?" *New Media & Society* 16, no. 1 (2014): 24–37.

13. Bingchun Meng, "From Steamed Bun to Grass Mud Horse: E Gao as Alternative Political Discourse on the Chinese Internet," *Global Media and Communication* 7, no. 1 (2011): 33–51; Paola Voci, *China on Video: Smaller-Screen Realities* (New York: Routledge, 2010); Christopher G. Rea, "Spoofing (E'gao) Culture on the Chinese Internet," in *Humour in Chinese Life and Culture*, ed. Jessica Milner Davis and Jocelyn Chey (Hong Kong: Hong Kong University Press, 2013), 149–72; David Kurt Herold and Peter Marolt, "Online Society in China: Creating, Celebrating, and Instrumentalising the Online Carnival," *Media, Culture and Social Change in Asia* (New York: Routledge, 2011).

14. Yang, *The Power of the Internet in China*, 85.

15. Guobin Yang, "Technology and Its Contents: Issues in the Study of the Chinese Internet," *The Journal of Asian Studies* 70, no. 4 (2011): 1043–50.

16. Jens Damm, "The Internet and the Fragmentation of Chinese Society," *Critical Asian Studies* 39, no. 2 (2007): 285.

17. James Leibold, "Blogging Alone: China, the Internet, and the Democratic Illusion?" *The Journal of Asian Studies* 70, no. 4 (2011): 3.

18. Min Jiang, "The Coevolution of the Internet, (Un)Civil Society, and Authoritarianism in China," in *The Internet, Social Media, and a Changing China*, ed. Jacques DeLisle, Avery Goldstein, and Guobin Yang (Philadelphia: University of Pennsylvania Press, 2016), 28–48.

19. Yang, "Technology and Its Contents."

20. Yang, *The Power of the Internet in China*, 63.

21. Rea, "Spoofing (E'gao) Culture on the Chinese Internet."

22. Shaohua Guo, "Ruled by Attention: A Case Study of Professional Digital Attention Agents at Sina.com and the Chinese Blogosphere," *International Journal of Cultural Studies* 19, no. 4 (2016): 407–23.

23. OpenNet Initiative, "Internet Filtering in China in 2004–2005: A Country Study" (OpenNet Intiative, 2005), https://opennet.net/sites/opennet.net/files/ONI_China_Country_Study.pdf.

24. This may be why Qiangguo Luntan, the forum run by people.com.cn, used to close down at 10:00 PM and reopen at 10:00 AM before its new version came online on July 1, 2012.

25. It is also easier to bump a post to the top-ten list then because traffic is usually much lighter.

26. A discussion of Xu also took place in a private club on Bdwm where a few members knew him personally.

27. Netizens not only use this strategy to avoid censorship, but also for other, sometimes mischievous, purposes. For instance, one Mitbbs user trolled forum users by putting up a post promising 10 Mitbbs yuan (a virtual currency that can be used for a variety of forum functions) to everyone who replied. After attracting hundreds of replies, he altered his original post by adding pornographic photos.

28. See "Weishenme zai Tieba Yilou Yao Gei Baidu?" ("Why Dedicate the First Floor to Baidu?"), *Baidu Knows*, January 29, 2012, http://zhidao.baidu.com /question/371559846.html.

29. See Yang, *The Power of the Internet in China*, 61.

30. Tech-savvy netizens have even developed software that automatically breaks down words or reformats texts so that filtering software cannot recognize taboo words. For an example of such software, see "Wangluo Fayan Fang Hexie Qi" ("Anti-censorship Software for Online Expression"), *SourceForge*, November 13, 2011, http://fanghexie.sourceforge.net/.

31. See Yue Sheng, "Ruhe Rang Quanli zai Yangguang Xia Yunxing" ("How to 'Exercise Power Under the Sun'"), *BBC Chinese*, March 8, 2010, www.bbc .co.uk/zhongwen/simp/china/2010/03/100308_china_media_liu.shtml.

32. See "Shuimu Qinghua BBS Zhannei Xianqi Xuexi, Yinyong Maozhuxi Yulu Rechao" ("Smth BBS Users Started the Upsurge of Learning and Citing Chairman Mao's Quotations"), *Oh My Media*, March 20, 2005, http://ohmymedia .com/2005/03/20/315/; "Guanshuiji de Zhonglei" ("Varieties of Automatic Posting Software"), *Smthbbs.blogspot.com*, April 21, 2005, http://smthbbs .blogspot.com/2005/04/post2005-04-21_21.html.

33. See Yang, *The Power of the Internet in China*, 57. Yang borrowed the idea of rightful resistance from Kevin O'Brien and Lianjiang Li, who studied how peasants use laws, policies, and officially promoted values to resist misconduct by local authorities. See Kevin J. O'Brien and Lianjiang Li, *Rightful Resistance in Rural China* (New York: Cambridge University Press, 2006).

34. Ashley Esarey and Qiang Xiao, "Political Expression in the Chinese Blogosphere," *Asian Survey* 48, no. 5 (2008): 752–72.

35. See "'Longyan Dayue' 2011 Quanji" ("*The Emperor Looks Happy* 2011 Collection"), *Tianya*, January 17, 2011, www.tianya.cn/publicforum/content/funinfo /1/2447177.shtml. The term *pimin*, which literally means "fart citizen," conveys a sense of political powerlessness.

36. The boundary-spanning program was sometimes censored by the state. For instance, one episode that criticized "official-center-ness" (*guanbenwei*, 官本位, the official rank-oriented political culture that prioritizes political power and status over other merits or achievements) by mocking the five-bar Young Pioneer in Wuhan was banned by the state according to a Falun Gong source. See "[Jinwen] Longyan Dayue Xinqu Egao Wudaogang" ("Forbidden News: New Song by *The Emperor Looks Happy* Spoofs Five-Bar"), YouTube video, 3:45, posted by "ntdtvchinese3," May 10, 2011, www.youtube .com/watch?v=Mrgd5PZZLvg. A 13-year-old boy in Wuhan, Hubei Province, became one of the hottest topics in Chinese cyberspace in May 2011 after he posted a picture of himself wearing a five-bar Young Pioneer badge on Weibo. The Chinese Young Pioneers are a mass organization of elementary school students run by the Chinese Communist Party. Student officers of the Young

Pioneers wear white badges with red bars to indicate their position, with two bars indicating a class monitor and three bars indicating a grade-level leader. There has never been a five-bar ranking, and Huang's five-bar badge, indicating his status as chief of Wuhan's Young Pioneers, was a local invention.

37. Interview OBE 2011–61, online interview with a veteran netizen from Beijing, October 18, 2011.

38. "Martian language" (*huoxingwen*) refers to an unconventional presentation of Chinese characters, which can be extremely hard to decode. For instance, after the Ministry of Education mandated campus forums to reform into internal communications platforms and restrict off-campus access, netizens on Smth, the official BBS of Tsinghua University, replaced the forum's name, "水木," with "困困." By putting the characters "水木" into squares, they were attempting to convey the message that the forum had been restricted and was trapped.

39. See "Xinhuawang Shouye shang Kangshifu Zuixin Xiaoxi" ("The Latest News on Master Kang on the Front Page of Xinhua Net"), *Mitbbs*, May 7, 2012, http://www.mitbbs.com/article_t/Military/37741563.html.

40. David Barboza, "Billions in Hidden Riches for Family of Chinese Leader," *New York Times*, October 26, 2012.

41. Wen Jiabao, "Yangwang Xingkong" ("Looking Up to the Starry Sky"), *Renmin Ribao (The People's Daily)*, September 4, 2007.

42. See "Yangwang Xingkong, 27 Yi Ke Xingxing, Zuiliang de Yike Shi Huarui Fengdian" ("Looking Up to the Starry Sky. There Are 2.7 Billion Stars, and the Brightest One Is Sinovel"), *Guba*, June 18, 2013, http://guba.eastmoney.com/news,601558,80317545.html.

43. According to open reports, New Horizon Capital, a private equity firm cofounded by Wen's son, made over 10 billion yuan through capital operations in three years with an initial investment of 75 million yuan. Hu Zhongbin, "Huarui Fengdian Ziben Chuanqi Xintianyu Sannian Huibao 145 Bei" ("Legendary Capital Operations of Sinovel New Horizon Capital Earned a 145-Times Return in Three Years"), *Jingji Guanchabao (Economic Observer)*, January 10, 2011.

44. See "Wen Weishenme Jiao Yingdi" ("Why Is Wen Called Best Actor?"), *Baidu Knows*, February 26, 2014, http://dwz.cn/iJbdt.

45. See "271 Daibiao Shenme Yisi?" ("What Does 271 Stand For?"), *Baidu Knows*, July 22, 2013, http://dwz.cn/iJavX.

46. See "27 Yi Shi Shui" ("Who Is 2.7 Billion?"), *Baidu Knows*, January 19, 2014, http://dwz.cn/iJ9Sz.

47. Guobin Yang provides a wonderful summary of some of the genres of digital contention. According to Yang, two popular genres are confessional/autobiographical genres, including diaries, letters, essays, and personal photographs, and parody/travesty genres, including jokes, doggerel (*dayoushi* 打油诗),

slippery jingles (*shunkouliu*, 顺口溜), and Flash videos. He argues that the second category embodies the playful style of digital contention. See Yang, *The Power of the Internet in China*, 76–82, 89.

48. Richard Dawkins, *The Selfish Gene* (Oxford: Oxford University Press, 1989).

49. See "Cao Ni Ma Zhige" ("The Song of the Grass Mud Horse"), YouTube video, 1:23, posted by "ideacm," February 4, 2009, https://youtu.be/01RPek5uAJ4. The video has had over 1.1 million views. For a version with English subtitles, see "Song of the Grass-Mud Horse (Cao Ni Ma)," YouTube video, 1:24, posted by "skippybentley," March 12, 2009, https://youtu.be/wKx1aenJK08.

50. Costume play (or cosplay) is a type of performance art in which actors dress up to role-play characters from movies, comics, or games.

51. See "Bainian Zhihou, Nide Muzhiming hui Zenme Xie?" ("What Would Be Your Epitaph After You Pass Away?"), *Tianya*, December 25, 2006, www.tianya .cn/publicforum/content/free/1/842556.shtml.

52. Ibid.

53. Ibid.

54. Ibid. The post not only complains about housing prices, but also mocks developers and the government. The developer is called "Poor-Don't-Bother" and develops only tombs for the rich; the government, by prohibiting the poor from constructing their own tombs, forces them to buy from developers.

55. See "Bainian Zhihou, Nide Muzhiming hui Zenme Xie?" The entry has been censored. One should note that to "die without a burial place" is considered one of the most unfortunate scenarios in life for Chinese people, and the phrase is often used as a severe curse.

56. Guobin Yang and Min Jiang, "The Networked Practice of Online Political Satire in China: Between Ritual and Resistance," *International Communication Gazette* 77, no. 3 (2015): 215–31.

57. The epitaph goes like this: "[He] studied literature early on and failed exams three times; [he] switched to martial arts, shot the drummer when taking the exam and thus was kicked out of the field; [he then] tried medicine with limited success, gave himself a prescription, took the medicine, and died." The populist passage was cited multiple times in the thread. See "Bainian Zhihou, Nide Muzhiming hui Zenme Xie?"

58. The title is also a parody of *Records of the Grand Historian*, which is considered one of the most prestigious, important, and trustworthy history books of ancient China.

59. Major diseases insurance is a government-sponsored health care system that covers the expenses associated with major diseases.

60. In 2008, milk and infant formula produced by several producers in China were found to have been adulterated with melamine, affecting thousands of victims, including several babies who died. The scandal started with the Sanlu Group. For a collection of reports in English, see "Sanlu Milk Sickens Babies,"

China Daily, 2008, http://www.chinadaily.com.cn/china/china_2008sanlu
_page.html.

61. See "Gaoxiao yu Zhongguo Zhengzhi" ("Spoofing and Chinese Politics"),
    Ccthere, December 10, 2008, www.ccthere.com/article/1933680.

62. Marcella Szablewicz, "The 'Losers' of China's Internet: Memes as 'Struc-
    tures of Feeling' for Disillusioned Young Netizens," *China Information* 28, no. 2
    (2014): 259–75.

63. Netizens complained about the difficulty of accessing services like Google
    and Facebook, especially when there is no Chinese counterpart, as is the case
    with Google Scholar. Such instrumental reasons explain why Google's with-
    drawal triggered huge waves of criticism of state censorship.

64. Interview RBJ 2008-04, with a veteran forum user, Beijing, December 29,
    2008; interview RBJ 2009-16, online interview with a veteran forum user,
    September 22, 2009.

65. Interview RBJ 2009-06, with a board manager and veteran forum user, Bei-
    jing, January 6, 2009; interview RBJ 2009-10, with a veteran forum user,
    Beijing, August 21, 2009; interview RBJ 2009-17, with a veteran forum user,
    Beijing, September 23, 2009. Users of the overseas democratic activist forum
    "Free China" had a conversation about this. See "Dui Ziyoumen Gongsi de
    Jianyi" ("Suggestions to the Freegate Company"), *Free China*, April 8, 2010,
    http://zyzg.us/archiver/tid-207519.html.

66. See "Zhongguo Guge Bei Hei le Ma? Quanshi Zhexie Xinwen" ("Google.cn
    Got Hacked? News About It Everywhere"), *Long de Tiankong (Dragon's Sky)*,
    November 8, 2008, http://lkong.cn/thread/204283.

67. "Falun Gong" literally means "Dharma [Law] Wheel Practice." Netizens call
    its practitioners "wheels" to satirize their beliefs.

68. This was before Google's withdrawal. The thread was started by an Lkong
    user who accidentally found news reports from the *Epoch Times*, a Falun Gong
    media outlet, via Google.cn, which should likely have been filtered by the
    search engine.

69. See "Cao Ni Ma Zhige."

70. See Li Bin, "Wangyou Chuangzao 'Shida Shenshou'" ("Netizens Create Top
    Ten Holy Animals"), *Xinxi Shibao (Information Times)*, January 6, 2009.

71. The other nine holy animals are the stretch-tailed whale (*wei sheng jin*, 尾申鲸,
    "sanitary pad"); the hidden fiery crab (*qian lie xie*, 潜烈蟹, "prostate"); the
    intelligent, fragrant chicken (*da fei ji*, 达菲鸡, "male masturbation")' the lucky
    journey cat (*ji ba mao*, 吉跋猫, "pubic hair"); the singing field goose (*yin dao
    yan*, 吟稻雁, "vaginitis"); the chrysanthemum silkworm (*ju hua can*, 菊花蚕,
    "broken anus"); the small, elegant butterfly (*ya mie die*, 雅蠛蝶, "Yamete,"
    meaning "stop," a reference to rape scenes in Japanese porn videos); the
    French–Croatian squid (*fa ke you*, 法克鱿, "fuck you"), and the quail pigeon or
    spring pigeon (*chun ge*, 鹑鸽, "Brother Chun," which mocks the androgynous

appearance of the popular singer Li Yuchun). For some basic information in English, see "Baidu Ten Mythical Creatures," *Wikipedia*, last modified August 9, 2017, http://en.wikipedia.org/wiki/Baidu_10_Mythical_Creatures.

72. See "Cao Ni Ma Zhige"; Michael Wines, "A Dirty Pun Tweaks China's Online Censors," *New York Times*, March 12, 2009.

73. For a discussion on being political and apolitical, see Maria Repnikova and Kecheng Fang, "China's New Media: Pushing Political Boundaries Without Being Political," *Foreign Affairs*, October 12, 2016, www.foreignaffairs.com /articles/china/2016-10-12/chinas-new-media.

74. The producers expressed their hope that the title could be a symbol that their program would bring "endless happiness to the audience." See "'Longyan Dayue' 2011 Quanji."

75. Johan Lagerkvist, *The Internet in China: Unlocking and Containing the Public Sphere* (Lund, Sweden: Lund University Publications, 2007), 46.

76. See "Longyan Dayue 037 Qi: Longyan Buluo Hao" (*The Emperor Looks Happy*, Issue 37: The Volume of the Long Yan Tribe"), *Tianya*, February 28, 2011, www. tianya.cn/publicforum/content/funinfo/1/2503694.shtml.

77. See "'Longyan Dayue' 2011 Quanji."

78. Netizens using the terms are not necessarily against universal values, democracy, or liberties. Rather, many are simply targeting individuals or groups that they believe are opportunists trying to profit from a disruptive transition in China while leaving average people to suffer.

79. See "Xiaobaitu de Guangrong Wangshi" ("The Glorious Past of the Little White Bunny"), *Cjdby*, February 24, 2011, http://lt.cjdby.net/thread-1066806-1-1 .html.

80. For the comic serial, see "Nanian Natu Naxie Shier" ("Year, Hare, Affair"), *Cjdby*, June 19, 2011, http://lt.cjdby.net/thread-1163825-1-1.html. For the videos, see "Nanian Natu Naxie Shier" ("Year, Hare, Affair"), YouTube channel, www.youtube.com/channel/UCIyiOC9sDtnuZTVdZBU9bGw.

81. While many netizens believe that the picture was taken on the USS Kitty Hawk (CV-63), one picture in the collection shows the mark "CV-61."

82. For the role of Liu in China's aircraft carrier dream, see Andrew S. Erikson and Andrew R. Wilson, "China's Aircraft Carrier Dilemma," *Naval War College Review* 59, no. 4 (2006): 13–45. Also see Li Jun, "Cisheng Wukui 'Zhongguo Hangmu Zhifu,' Zhi Han Weineng Qinjian Zhongguo Hangmu Xiashui" ("He Is Worthy of Being Considered the 'Father of China's Aircraft Carrier,' His Only Regret Is Not Seeing China's Aircraft Carrier in Service"), *Yangzi Wanbao (Yangtse Evening News)*, January 15, 2011.

83. "Xinsuan Ah, Kanle Ni Jiu Mingbai Zhongguo Weishenme Yao Jian Hangma Le" ("So Bitter! You Will Understand Why China Needs an Air Carrier After Seeing this Picture"), *Mitbbs*, September 26, 2012, http://www.mitbbs.com /article_t/Military/38453741.html.

84. See "[Heji] [Zhuan] Nanian Natu–Liaoning Jian" ("[Compiled] [Forwarded] Year, Hare–Carrier Liaoning"), *Newsmth*, September 27, 2012, www.newsmth. net/bbstcon.php?board=MilitaryJoke&gid=221488. The thread made its way into the top-ten list, which is rare for the "MilitaryJoke" board, as it normally attracts only a small amount of traffic.

85. *Otaku* is a Japanese term referring to people obsessed with Japanese anime, manga, or video games.

86. "Moé" is an idea closely related to the Japanese anime subculture. Chinese anime fans and netizens use the term to refer to a particular type of "adorable" or "cute" content.

87. For instance, see "[Zongbu Shisheng HGCG Meng Fanyi Xilie] 11 Qu Chan-jing: Ji Er Shenme De Doushi Tubalu Wangtu Mabi Huangjun Douzhi de Guiji" ("[Headquarter Porn-Saint HGCG Moé Translation Serial] Economic News from District 11: Talking about G2 Is Only a Scheme of the Eighth Route Army to Lull the Will of Imperial Army"), *Cjdby*, November 16, 2009, http://lt.cjdby .net/thread-723428-1-1.

88. "Can't We All Just Get It On?" *Economist* 404, no. 8803 (2012): 54. The article reads too much into the slogan "The Diaoyu Islands belong to China; Sora Aoi belongs to the world." It is not so much a contradiction as an example of pop activism that mixes nationalistic sentiment with fun.

89. Similar messages spread widely online. See "Lubian Kuaixun: Ri Xiang Yetian Jiayan Timing Cangjing Kong wei Xinren Zhuhua Dashi" ("Road-side Express: Japanese Prime Minister Yoshihiko Noda Nominates Sora Aoi as New Ambassador to China"), *Tianya*, September 16, 2012, http://www .tianya.cn/publicforum/content/worldlook/1/565840.shtml.

90. Esarey and Xiao, "Political Expression in the Chinese Blogosphere"; Guobin Yang, "China Since Tiananmen: Online Activism," *Journal of Democracy* 20, no. 3 (2009): 33–36; Yang and Jiang, "The Networked Practice of Online Political Satire in China."

91. Johan Lagerkvist, *After the Internet, Before Democracy: Competing Norms in Chinese Media and Society* (Bern, Switzerland: Peter Lang, 2010); Rongbin Han, "Defending the Authoritarian Regime Online: China's 'Voluntary Fifty-Cent Army,'" *The China Quarterly*, no. 224 (2015): 1006–25; Rongbin Han, "Manufacturing Consent in Cyberspace: China's 'Fifty-Cent Army,'" *Journal of Current Chinese Affairs* 44, no. 2 (2015): 105–34.

92. Damm, "The Internet and the Fragmentation of Chinese Society"; Leibold, "Blogging Alone."

93. Guo, "Ruled by Attention."

94. Yang and Jiang, "The Networked Practice of Online Political Satire in China."

95. Meng, "From Steamed Bun to Grass Mud Horse," 35.

96. See "Shaojiang Zheme Meng, Nimen Buxu Chaoxiao Ta" ("Major General Is So Moé, You Should Not Laugh at Him"), *Mitbbs*, March 26, 2012, www.mitbbs .com/article_t1/Military/37501841_0_2.html. See also "Shaojiang Zheme Meng, Nimen Buxu Zai Quxiao Ta" ("Major General Is So Moé, You Should Make Fun of Him"), *Tianya*, March 12, 2012, www.tianya.cn/publicforum /content/free/1/2425719.shtml.

97. Liu Yiheng, "Ai Weiwei Zhen Mianmu: Wu Wan Yishu Jia—Wudu Juquan" ("Ai Weiwei's True Colors: A Five-Play Artist—Full of Evil"), *Wenweipo*, April 15, 2011. Though based in Hong Kong, *Wenweipo* is long recognized as a pro-Chinese Communist Party media outlet. See also Jin Yi, "Zhongguo Dangdai Yishujia Aiweiwei Zuopin 'Tonghua' Bei Zhi Chaoxi" ("Chinese Contemporary Artist Ai Weiwei's Work 'Fairy Tale' Charged with Plagiarism"), *Xinhua Net*, June 21, 2007, http://news.xinhuanet.com/shuhua/2007-06/21/content _6272614.htm; "Xifang Zongxiang Gei Zhongguo Fayuan 'Pi Tiaozi'" ("The West Always Wants to Issue Directives to the Chinese Court"), *Global Times*, June 24, 2011. For a rebuttal, see Geremie R. Barmé, "A View on Ai Weiwei's Exit," *China Heritage Quarterly*, no. 26 (2011), www.chinaheritagequarterly .org/articles.php?searchterm=026_aiweiwei.inc&issue=026.

98. See *Ai Weiwei Never Sorry*, directed by Alison Klayman (2012; United Expression Media).

99. See Meng Bingchun, "Mediated Citizenship or Mediatized Politics? Political Discourse on Chinese Internet" (paper presented at the 10th Annual Chinese Internet Research Conference, University of Southern California, Annenberg, Los Angeles, CA, May 21–22, 2012).

100. Lu Yang, "Ai Weiwei Hexie Yan Zhuizong Baodao" ("Follow-Up Reports on Ai Weiwei's River Crab Feast"), *VOA Chinese*, November 7, 2010, www.voachinese .com/content/article-20101107-ai-weiwei-106847008/772266.html. Ai Weiwei himself was not present because at the time, he was under house arrest.

101. Liu Qing, "Ai Weiwei Wangluo Xingwei Yishu Biaoda Yuanfen" ("Ai Weiwei Expresses Resentment Through Online Performance"), *Radio Free Asia*, July 7, 2009, www.rfa.org/mandarin/pinglun/teyuepinglun-07072009112454.html.

102. Andrew Jacobs, "Lawyer for Released Chinese Artist Seeks Review on Taxes," *New York Times*, June 29, 2011, www.nytimes.com/2011/06/30/world/asia /30artist.html?_r=1; "Ai Weiwei China Tax Bill Paid by Supporters," *BBC*, November 7, 2011, www.bbc.co.uk/news/world-asia-pacific-15616576.

103. See "Ai Weiwei Xuechang Cao Ni Ma Zhige" ("Ai Weiwei Learns to Sing 'The Song of the Grass Mud Horse'"), YouTube video, 2:50, posted by "译者," November 12, 2011, www.youtube.com/watch?v=oL57X4GcyTs.

104. "Yi Li Xiaolu Seqingpian Cang Liu Si Guanggao Wangshang Fengchuan" ("June 4 Ads Found in Suspected Li Xiaolu Sex Videos and Went Viral Online"), *DW News*, May 11, 2014, china.dwnews.com/news/2014-05-11/59470725.html.

In his interview with VOA, Wen claimed that he did the same thing using the sex scandal of the pop star Edison Chen to spread a Tiananmen Square documentary in 2008. See "Shishi Dajiatan: Buya Shipin 'Touliang Huanzhu', Duifu Baozheng Bushe Dixian?" ("Roundtable on Politics: Infiltrating Sex Videos with Political Messages, No Bottom Line Fighting Against Tyranny?") *VOA*, May 14, 2014, www.voachinese.com/a/1914392.html.

105. For the video clip, see www.flickr.com/photos/winterkanal/3967547911 /, posted by "MotherLand_2," September 30, 2009.

106. See "Ai Weiwei: 'Cao Ni Ma Zuguo'—Tamen Zheyang 'Wenhou' Zuguo" ("Ai Weiwei: Grass Mud Horse Motherland—They Greet the Motherland in this Way"), Dingsheng *China*, October 4, 2009, http://top81.org/show .php?f=1&t=879418&m=6002706. See also "Ai Weiwei Meiyou Shuoguo Cao Ni Ma Zuguo" ("Ai Weiwei Did Not Say 'Grass Mud Horse Motherland'"), *Mitbbs*, April 15, 2011, www.mitbbs.com/article_t/Military/35644267.html.

107. See "Ai Weiwei Meiyou Shuoguo Cao Ni Ma Zuguo." It is worth noting that "wee wee" was used intentionally.

108. Netizens learn about each other's political orientations through repeated interactions. This user constantly and exclusively posted anti-regime materials. He used to post daily reports on Feng Zhenghu, a dissident stranded at Narita Airport in Tokyo between November 2009 and January 2010 because Chinese authorities refused his re-entry into China. When Ai Weiwei was jailed, the same user changed his nickname to "I am not the hero; I am a creditor of the hero," to illustrate that he had donated money to Ai.

109. The policy is pinned to the top of the board. See "Benban Bu Huanying Zhengzhilei Ticai de Fei Xiaohua" ("This Board Does not Welcome Political Topics that Are not Funny"), *Mitbbs*, November 10, 2011, www.mitbbs.com /article_t2/Joke/32046745.html. It is worth noting that forums inside China may also explicitly or implicitly discourage political jokes to avoid censorship pressure, though users' antipathy toward such "not-so-funny" topics also matters.

110. Lagerkvist, *After the Internet, Before Democracy*.

5. TROLLING FOR THE PARTY

1. Xi Jinping, "Zai Quanguo Dangxiao Gongzuo Huiyi Shangde Jianghua" ("Talk at the National Party School Work Meeting"), *Qiushi*, April 30, 2016, www .qstheory.cn/dukan/qs/2016-04/30/c_1118772415.htm.

2. For instance, see Taylor C. Boas, "Weaving the Authoritarian Web: The Control of Internet Use in Nondemocratic Regimes," in *How Revolutionary Was the Digital Revolution: National Responses, Market Transitions, and Global Technology,*

ed. John Zysman and Abraham Newman (Stanford, CA: Stanford University Press, 2006), 361–78; Eric Harwit and Duncan Clark, "Shaping the Internet in China: Evolution of Political Control Over Network Infrastructure and Content," *Asian Survey* 41, no. 3 (2001): 377–408; Ronald Deibert et al., Ronald Deibert, John Palfrey, Rafal Rohozinski, and Jonathan Zittrain, eds., *Access Denied: The Practice and Policy of Global Internet Filtering* (Cambridge, MA: MIT Press, 2008); Ronald Deibert, John Palfrey, Rafal Rohozinski, and Jonathan Zittrain, eds., *Access Controlled: The Shaping of Power, Rights, and Rule in Cyberspace* (Cambridge, MA: MIT Press, 2010); Ronald Deibert, John Palfrey, Rafal Rohozinski, and Jonathan Zittrain, eds., *Access Contested: Security, Identity, and Resistance in Asian Cyberspace* (Cambridge, MA: MIT Press, 2011); Guobin Yang, *The Power of the Internet in China: Citizen Activism Online* (New York: Columbia University Press, 2009); Johan Lagerkvist, *The Internet in China: Unlocking and Containing the Public Sphere* (Lund, Sweden: Lund University Publications, 2007); Ashley Esarey and Qiang Xiao, "Political Expression in the Chinese Blogosphere," *Asian Survey* 48, no. 5 (2008): 752–72; Gary King, Jennifer Pan, and Margaret E. Roberts, "How Censorship in China Allows Government Criticism but Silences Collective Expression," *American Political Science Review* 107, no. 2 (2013): 1–18.

3. For instance, see Richard Rose, William Mishler, and Neil Munro, *Popular Support for an Undemocratic Regime: The Changing Views of Russians* (Cambridge: Cambridge University Press, 2011); Tianjian Shi, "Cultural Values and Political Trust: A Comparison of the People's Republic of China and Taiwan," *Comparative Politics* 33, no. 4 (2001): 401–19; Jie Chen and Bruce J. Dickson, *Allies of the State: China's Private Entrepreneurs and Democratic Change* (Cambridge, MA: Harvard University Press, 2010); Lianjiang Li, "The Magnitude and Resilience of Trust in the Center: Evidence from Interviews with Petitioners in Beijing and a Local Survey in Rural China," *Modern China* 39, no. 1 (2013): 3–36; Barbara Geddes and John Zaller, "Sources of Popular Support for Authoritarian Regimes," *American Journal of Political Science* 33, no. 2 (1989): 319–47; Wenfang Tang, *Populist Authoritarianism: Chinese Political Culture and Regime Sustainability* (New York: Oxford University Press, 2016); Bruce J. Dickson, *The Dictator's Dilemma: The Chinese Communist Party's Strategy for Survival* (New York: Oxford University Press, 2016); Teresa Wright, *Accepting Authoritarianism: State-Society Relations in China's Reform Era* (Stanford, CA: Stanford University Press, 2010).

4. Andrew Nathan, "Authoritarian Resilience," *Journal of Democracy* 14, no. 1 (2003): 6–17; Xiaojun Yan, "Engineering Stability: Authoritarian Political Control Over University Students in Post-Deng China," *The China Quarterly*, no. 218 (2014): 493–513; Eva Bellin, "The Robustness of Authoritarianism in the Middle East: Exceptionalism in Comparative Perspective," *Comparative Politics* 36, no. 2 (2004): 139–57; Steven Heydemann and Reinoud Leenders,

"Authoritarian Learning and Authoritarian Resilience: Regime Responses to the 'Arab Awakening,'" *Globalizations* 8, no. 5 (2011): 647–53; Karrie J. Koesel and Valerie J. Bunce, "Diffusion-Proofing: Russian and Chinese Responses to Waves of Popular Mobilizations Against Authoritarian Rulers," *Perspectives on Politics* 11, no. 3 (2013): 753–68; Florian Toepfl, "Blogging for the Sake of the President: The Online-Diaries of Russian Governors," *Europe-Asia Studies* 64, no. 8 (2012): 1435–59.

5. Patricia Thornton, "Manufacturing Dissent in Transnational China: Boomerang, Backfire or Spectacle?" in *Popular Protest in China*, ed. Kevin J. O'Brien (Cambridge, MA: Harvard University Press, 2008), 179–204; Michael S. Chase and James C. Mulvenon, *You've Got Dissent* (Santa Monica, CA: RAND, 2002); Esarey and Xiao, "Political Expression in the Chinese Blogosphere"; Yang, *The Power of the Internet in China.*

6. Jonathan Hassid, "Safety Valve or Pressure Cooker? Blogs in Chinese Political Life," *Journal of Communication* 62, no. 2 (2012): 212–30; Lijun Tang and Helen Sampson, "The Interaction Between Mass Media and the Internet in Nondemocratic States: The Case of China," *Media, Culture & Society* 34, no. 4 (2012): 457–71.

7. Li Gao and James Stanyer, "Hunting Corrupt Officials Online: The Human Flesh Search Engine and the Search for Justice in China," *Information, Communication, & Society* 17, no. 7 (2014): 814–29.

8. Yongnian Zheng, *Technological Empowerment: The Internet, State, and Society in China* (Stanford, CA: Stanford University Press, 2008); Yongnian Zheng and Guoguang Wu, "Information Technology, Public Space, and Collective Action in China," *Comparative Political Studies* 38, no. 5 (2005): 507–36.

9. Gary King, Jennifer Pan, and Margaret E. Roberts, "Reverse-Engineering Censorship in China: Randomized Experimentation and Participant Observation," *Science* 345, no. 6199 (2014): 1–10; King, Pan, and Roberts, "How Censorship in China Allows Government Criticism but Silences Collective Expression"; Rebecca MacKinnon, "China's Censorship 2.0: How Companies Censor Bloggers," *First Monday* 14, no. 2 (2009), http://firstmonday.org/article/view/2378/2089; Boas, "Weaving the Authoritarian Web"; Harwit and Clark, "Shaping the Internet in China"; Lena L. Zhang, "Behind the 'Great Firewall': Decoding China's Internet Media Policies from the Inside," *Convergence: The International Journal of Research Into New Media Technologies* 12, no. 3 (2006): 271–91.

10. The state-imposed boundaries of online expression have numerous loopholes. For instance, see Yang, *The Power of the Internet in China*; Esarey and Xiao, "Political Expression in the Chinese Blogosphere"; Lagerkvist, *The Internet in China.* See also chapter 2 of this book.

11. For instance, see David Barboza, "China Leader Encourages Criticism of Government," *New York Times*, January 27, 2011; Fareed Zakaria, "Interview

with Wen Jiabao," *CNN Global Public Square*, October 3, 2010, http://transcripts.cnn.com/TRANSCRIPTS/1010/03/fzgps.01.html.

12. Ethan Zuckerman, "Cute Cats to the Rescue? Participatory Media and Political Expression," in *From Voice to Influence: Understanding Citizenship in a Digital Age*, ed. Danielle Allen and Jennifer S. Light (Chicago: University of Chicago Press, 2015), 131–54.

13. See Gao and Stanyer, "Hunting Corrupt Officials Online"; Keith B. Richburg, "China's 'Netizens' Holding Officials Accountable," *Washington Post*, November 9, 2009, www.washingtonpost.com/wp-dyn/content/article/2009/11/08/AR2009110818166_pf.html.

14. See Kevin J. O'Brien and Lianjiang Li, *Rightful Resistance in Rural China* (New York: Cambridge University Press, 2006); Peter Lorentzen, "Regularizing Rioting: Permitting Public Protest in an Authoritarian Regime," *Quarterly Journal of Political Science* 8, no. 2 (2013): 127–58.

15. Peter Lorentzen, "China's Strategic Censorship," *American Journal of Political Science* 58, no. 2 (2014): 402–14; King, Pan, and Roberts, "How Censorship in China Allows Government Criticism but Silences Collective Expression"; King, Pan, and Roberts, "Reverse-Engineering Censorship in China."

16. Rachel E. Stern and Kevin J. O'Brien, "Politics at the Boundary: Mixed Signals and the Chinese State," *Modern China* 38, no. 2 (2011): 174–98.

17. Clay Shirky, "The Political Power of Social Media," *Foreign Affairs* 90, no.1 (2011): 28–41

18. Nathan, "Authoritarian Resilience"; Lorentzen, "China's Strategic Censorship."

19. China Internet Network Information Center, *Di 39 Ci Zhongguo Hulian Wangluo Fazhan Zhuangkuang Tongji Baogao (The 39th Statistical Report on Internet Development in China)*, January 22, 2017.

20. Kathleen Hartford, "Dear Mayor: Online Communications with Local Governments in Hangzhou and Nanjing," *China Information* 19, no. 2 (2005): 217–60; Xia Li Lollar, "Assessing China's E-Government: Information, Service, Transparency and Citizen Outreach of Government Websites," *Journal of Contemporary China* 15, no. 46 (2006): 31–41; Jesper Schlæger, *E-Government in China: Technology, Power and Local Government Reform* (Abingdon, UK: Routledge, 2013).

21. See "Dali Jiaqiang Woguo Hulianwang Meiti Jianshe" ("Strengthen the Construction of Our Internet Media"), *People's Daily*, August 9, 2000.

22. See State Council Information Office and Ministry of Information Industry, *Hulian Wangzhan Congshi Dengzai Xinwen Yewu Guanli Zanxing Guiding (Interim Provisions for the Administration of News Publication by Internet Sites)*, November 6, 2000; State Council Information Office and Ministry of Information Industry, *Hulianwang Xinwen Xinxi Fuwu Guanli Guiding (Administrative Provisions for Internet News Information Services)*, September 25, 2005.

23. Tang Xujun, Wu Xinxun, Huang Chuxin, and Liu Ruisheng, eds., *Zhongguo Xinmeiti Fazhan Baogao No. 5 (Annual Report on the Development of New Media in China, 2014)* (Beijing: Social Science Academic Press, 2014), 18–19.

24. Jesper Schlæger and Min Jiang, "Official Microblogging and Social Management by Local Governments in China," *China Information* 28, no. 2 (2014): 189–213; Liang Ma, "The Diffusion of Government Microblogging," *Public Management Review* 15, no. 2 (2013): 288–309; Ashley Esarey, "Winning Hearts and Minds? Cadres as Microbloggers in China," *Journal of Current Chinese Affairs* 44, no. 2 (2015): 69–103; Nele Noesselt, "Microblogs and the Adaptation of the Chinese Party-State's Governance Strategy," *Governance* 27, no. 3 (2014): 449–68.

25. China Internet Network Information Center, *Di 39 Ci Zhongguo Hulian Wangluo Fazhan Zhuangkuang Tongji Baogao.*

26. Anne-Marie Brady, *Marketing Dictatorship: Propaganda and Thought Work in Contemporary China* (Lanham, MD: Rowman & Littlefield, 2008).

27. Yuezhi Zhao, "Toward a Propaganda/Commercial Model of Journalism in China? The Case of the Beijing Youth News," *International Communication Gazette* 58, no. 3 (1997): 143–57.

28. Daniela Stockmann, *Media Commercialization and Authoritarian Rule in China* (New York: Cambridge University Press, 2013); see also Daniela Stockmann and Mary E. Gallagher, "Remote Control: How the Media Sustain Authoritarian Rule in China," *Comparative Political Studies* 44, no. 4 (2011): 436–67.

29. Maria Repnikova, "Thought Work Contested: Ideology and Journalism Education in China," *The China Quarterly* (2017): 1–21, https://doi.org/10.1017/S0305741017000583.

30. Johan Lagerkvist, "Internet Ideotainment in the PRC: National Responses to Cultural Globalization," *Journal of Contemporary China* 17, no. 54 (2008): 121–40.

31. See Chang Meng, "Xi's Cartoon Depiction Breaks Taboo," *Global Times*, February 20, 2014, www.globaltimes.cn/content/843632.shtml; "Li Joins Xi in Viral Cartoon Celebrity," *Global Times*, February 28, 2014, www.globaltimes.cn/content/845260.shtml. This was the first time the Chinese state had published official cartoon images of top leaders, although non-state sanctioned cartoon images of top leaders like Deng Xiaoping had appeared much earlier. See Zhang Wu, "Lingdaoren Manhua Youxue Yourou, Baozhi Shichang Chuxian" ("Vivid Cartoon Images of Top Leaders Have Appeared in Newspapers Often"), *Xinwen Chenbao (Shanghai Morning Post)*, February 20, 2014.

32. See "How Leaders Were Tempered?" YouTube video, 5:28, posted by "ministryoftofu," October 16, 2013, https://youtu.be/6BosGD5Bk98. The producer, Studio on Fuxing (Revival) Road, is not well known. However, the former CCTV headquarters were located on Fuxing Road, Beijing. In addition, the

term "Revival Road" echoes the state propaganda of the national revival of China.

33. The video concludes, "Whether by a single ballot that gets the whole nation out to vote or by a meritocratic screening that requires years of hard work like the making of a Kung Fu master, as long as the people are satisfied and the country develops and progresses as a result, it's working."

34. Youku Quanshijiao, "5 Fenzhong Xianqi Quanmin Da Taolun Lingdaoren Zheyang Liancheng" ("Five-Minute Video Inspired Nationwide Discussion, and This Is How Leaders Were Tempered"), Youku video, 3:47, posted by "Seven News," October 15, 2013, http://v.youku.com/v_show/id_XNjIzMTM4ODI0 .html; "[Xi Da Pu Ben] Lingdaoren Shi Zenyang Liancheng De" ("[Exhilarating News that Everyone Is Celebrating and Spreading] How Leaders Were Tempered"), Youku video, 5:02, posted by "Fuxing Road," October 14, 2013, http://v.youku.com/v_show/id_XNjIxNTg1NzI0.html.

35. Johan Lagerkvist, *After the Internet, Before Democracy: Competing Norms in Chinese Media and Society* (Bern, Switzerland: Peter Lang, 2010), 122, and chapter 5.

36. Yanqi Tong and Shaohua Lei, "War of Position and Microblogging in China," *Journal of Contemporary China* 22, no. 80 (2013): 292–311; see also Xueyi Chen and Tianjian Shi, "Media Effects on Political Confidence and Trust in the People's Republic of China in the Post-Tiananmen Period," *East Asia* 19, no. 3 (2001): 84–118; Jiangnan Zhu, Jie Lu, and Tianjian Shi, "When Grapevine News Meets Mass Media: Different Information Sources and Popular Perceptions of Government Corruption in Mainland China," *Comparative Political Studies* 46, no. 8 (2012): 920–46.

37. Dexter Roberts, "Inside the War Against China's Blogs," *BusinessWeek*, June 12, 2008; Zhou Chunlin, "Jiekai Wangluo Tuishou Zhizao 'Zuimei Nüjiaoshi' Beihou Neimu" ("Uncovering How Internet Spin Doctors Crafted 'The Most Beautiful Female Teacher'"), *Xinhua Net*, July 28, 2007, http://news .xinhuanet.com/2007-07/28/content_6441463.htm; Zhang Shunhe, "Wangluo Tuishou Jiemi Chaozuo Neimu: Yige Fengjie Ke Fu Yige Tuandui " ("Internet Spin Doctor Discloses Inside Story of Spinning: A Sister Phoenix Can Make a Whole Group Rich"), *Sina*, April 15, 2010, http://tech.sina.com.cn/i/2010 -04-15/11484061901.shtml; Kong Pu, "Jiemi Wangluo Weiji Gongguan" ("Deciphering Online Crisis Management"), *Xin Shiji Zhoukan (Century Weekly)* 340, no. 28 (October 2008): 62–63. Astroturfing wars are often fought among market competitors. See "The Chinese Dairy Wars," *EastSouthWestNorth Blog*, October 20–25, 2010, http://www.zonaeuropa.com/20101021_1.htm.

38. See David Streitfeld, "The Best Reviews Money Can Buy," *New York Times*, August 26, 2015.

39. Ron Deibert, "Cyberspace Under Siege," *Journal of Democracy* 26, no. 3 (2015): 64–78.

40. Tom Cahill, "Pro-Clinton Super PAC Spending $1 Million Hiring Online Trolls," *U.S. Uncut*, April 21, 2016, http://usuncut.com/politics/clinton-super-pac -busted/; Olga Khazan, "Russia's Online-Comment Propaganda Army," *Atlantic*, October 9, 2013, www.theatlantic.com/international/archive/2013/10/russias -online-comment-propaganda-army/280432/.

41. Chin-Fu Hung, "China's Propaganda in the Information Age: Internet Commentators and the Weng'an Incident," *Issues & Studies* 46, no. 4 (2010): 149–81.

42. Gary King, Jennifer Pan, and Margaret E. Roberts, "How the Chinese Government Fabricates Social Media Posts for Strategic Distraction, Not Engaged Argument," *American Political Science Review* 111, no.3 (2017): 484–501.

43. Blake Andrew Phillip Miller, "Automatic Detection of Comment Propaganda in Chinese Media," *SSRN Electronic Journal*, 2016, 1–38, doi:10.2139/ssrn.2738325.

44. See "Shanxisheng Shoupi Wangluo Bianji he Wangluo Pinglunyuan Peixunban Xueyuan Zhengshi Zai Bing Jieye" ("Commencement of the First Training Class of Internet Editors and Commentators of Shanxi Province"), *Jincheng News*, December 20, 2006, www.jcnews.com.cn/Html/guondongtai /2006-12/20/120854983.html.

45. This is similar to what Stern and O'Brien advocate as the "state reflected in society approach." See Stern and O'Brien, "Politics at the Boundary."

46. See "Jinian Tuoli Wumaodang Liang Zhounian" ("Memorial of the Two-Year Anniversary of Quitting the Fifty-Cent Army), *Mitbbs*, March 8, 2010, http:// mitbbs.com/article_t/NKU/31204643.html.

47. Scholars debate the effectiveness of state propaganda and the state's capacity to control the propaganda system. See Chen and Shi, "Media Effects on Political Confidence and Trust in the People's Republic of China in the Post-Tiananmen Period"; Stockmann, *Media Commercialization and Authoritarian Rule in China*; Stockmann and Gallagher, "Remote Control"; David Shambaugh, "China's Propaganda System: Institutions, Processes and Efficacy," *China Journal*, no. 57 (2007): 25–58; John James Kennedy, "Maintaining Popular Support for the Chinese Communist Party: The Influence of Education and the State-Controlled Media," *Political Studies* 57, no. 3 (2009): 517–36; Tong and Lei, "War of Position and Microblogging in China"; Lagerkvist, *After the Internet*; Maria Repnikova, *Media Politics in China: Improvising Power Under Authoritarianism* (Cambridge: Cambridge University Press, 2017); Jonathan Hassid, *China's Unruly Journalists: How Committed Professionals Are Changing the People's Republic* (New York: Routledge, 2015).

48. See "CCAV, Laozi Dong Fayu, Ni pian Gui Ah?" ("CCAV, Your Daddy Knows French, So You're Cheating the Ghost!"), *Huashang Forum*, March 28, 2011, http://bbs.hsw.cn/a/t249/2677249.html. (CCAV is the derogatory nickname used by Chinese Internet commentators for CCTV; the "AV" refers to "adult video.")

49. Hung, "China's Propaganda in the Information Age."

50. According to *Changsha Yearbook 2006*, the launch of Changsha's Internet commentator system could have been as early as August 2004. See Gong Jian, "Jianchi Sanjiehe, Zujian Wangluo Pinglunyuan Duiwu" ("Stick to the Three-in-One Combination and Establish the Troop of Online Commentators"), in *Changsha Yearbook 2006*, ed. Changsha Municipal Office of Local Chronicles (Beijing: Fangzhi Chubanshe, 2006), 55–56; "Zhongyang Jiwei Gaodu Zhong shi Wangluo Pinglun Gongzuo" ("Central Commission for Discipline Inspection Attaches Much Importance to Online Commentary Work"), *CCP Hubei Provincial Commission for Discipline Inspection*, January 1, 2005, www.hbjwjc.gov .cn/wzlm/info/18944.htm; David Bandurski, "China's Guerrilla War for the Web," *Far Eastern Economic Review* 171, no. 6 (July 2008): 41–44; Wen Yunchao, "Shouquan Fabu: Dalu Wangluo Pinglunyuan Jianru Gongzhong Shiye" ("Authorized Release: China's Internet Commentators Gradually Gaining Public Sight"), *Zuiren Yiyu Blog*, July 17, 2007, https://wenyc1230.wordpress. com/2008/07/17/授权发布：大陆网络评论员渐入公众视野/.

51. "Guanyu Nanchang, Changsha, Zhengzhou Xuanchuan Wenhua Gongzuo de Kaocha Baogao" ("Research Report on Propaganda and Cultural Work of Nanchang, Changshang, and Zhengzhou"), *CCP Hefei Municipal Committee Propaganda Department*, May 24, 2006, http://swxcb.hefei.gov.cn/ContentDir /20065/24124915293.shtml.

52. See Wen, "Shouquan Fabu."

53. China's largest oil and gas producer, Sinopec, mobilized its employees to justify rising gas prices through online astroturfing. See Wang Xing, "Zhongshihua Beibao Zuizhi Renyuan zai Wangshang Xuanchuan Zhangjia Heli" ("Sinopec Exposed for Organizing Personnel to Justify Price Increase Online"), *Nanfang Dushibao (Southern Metropolis Daily)*, February 13, 2011.

54. Zhang Lei, "Invisible Footprints of Online Commentators," *Global Times*, February 5, 2010, http://special.globaltimes.cn/2010-02/503820_2.html.

55. See Shandong University of Traditional Chinese Medicine, "Guanyu Jianli Shandong Zhongyiyao Daxue Wangluo Pinglunyuan Duiwu de Tongzhi" ("Circular on Establishing an Internet Commentator Troop at the Shandong University of Traditional Chinese Medicine"), November 27, 2008, http://xcb .web.sdutcm.edu.cn/htm/tz/646.html; Dingtao No. 1 Middle School, "Guanyu Zujian Dingtao Yizhong Wangluo Pinglunyuan Duiwu de Yijian" ("Opinions on Establishing Internet Commentator Troops at Dingtao No. 1 Middle School"), December 21, 2009, www.sddtyz.cn/web/pro/detail.php?tid=1450; "'Dangxiao Zhendi' Wangpingyuan Guanli Banfa" ("Regulations on the Internet Commentator Management of the 'Party School Front'"), *Hengyang Party Building Net*, January 8, 2010, http://dx.hydjnet.gov.cn/News_View .asp?NewsID=28290; Chinese Communist Party Zhengding County Committee

Propaganda Department, "Guanyu Zhaopin Hulianwang Wangluo Xuanchuan Pinglunyuan de Tongzhi" ("Circular on Recruiting Internet Commentators"), June 18, 2009, www.zd.gov.cn/ReadNews.asp?NewsID=12226&BigClass
Name=%B9%AB%B8%E6%C0%B8&SmallClassName=%B9%AB%B8%E6%C0%B8
&SpecialID=0.

56. Observation at the First Conference of National Campus Bulletin Board
System Managers, Suzhou, Jiangsu Province, October 23–25, 2009.

57. Qiao Long, "Heike Baoguang Wumao Shujuku Dangju Jiankong Yuqing Fenbu
Zhuangkuang" ("Hacker Exposes Database of the 'Fifty-Cent Army' and How
Authorities Monitor Public Opinion"), *Radio Free Asia*, May 20, 2015, www.rfa
.org/mandarin/yataibaodao/renquanfazhi/ql1-05202015101938.html.

58. Chinese Communist Youth League Central Committee Office, "Wangluo
Xuanchuanyuan Duiwu Jianshe Tongzhi" ("Circular on Establishing an Internet Propaganda Troop"), March 19, 2014.

59. See Wen, "Shouquan Fabu." The article provides a good description of how
Internet commentators are trained.

60. Hong Yanqing, "Woqu Shouci Zuzhi Wangpingyuan Peixun" ("Our District
Organizes Its First Internet Commentator Training"), *Jinri Jiangdong (Jiang-
dong Today)*, October 27, 2009. For more examples, see Fuyang Public Health
Bureau, "Woshi Weishengju Jianzhi Wangpingyuan Shanggang" ("Part-Time
Internet Commentators of the Public Health Bureau in Position"), *Fuyang
Public Health Bureau Website*, September 7, 2009, http://wsj.fuyang.gov.cn
/zwdt_8848/20090907226641.shtml.

61. For instance, see "Wangpingyuan Jishu Fudao Tigang" ("Technical Training
Outline for Internet Commentators"), *Hengyang Party Building Net*, January 8,
2010, http://dx.hydjnet.gov.cn/News_View.asp?NewsID=28291.

62. See " 'Dangxiao Zhendi' Wangpingyuan Guanli Banfa."

63. For instance, see "Zhejiang Zaixian 'Shijia Banzhu, Shijia Boke, Shijia Wang-
pingyuan' Pingxuan Huodong" ("Selection of the Top Ten Board Managers,
Top Ten Bloggers, and Top Ten Internet Commentators of Zhejiang Online"),
Zhejiang Online Community, October 14, 2008, http://bbs.zjol.com.cn/zjolbbs
/system/2008/10/14/010026334.shtml; "Dangwang 2009 Niandu Youxiu
Tongxunyuan, Shida Wangpingren' Pingxuan, Huanying Toupiao" ("Please
Vote for Outstanding Correspondents and the Top Ten Internet Commentators of Party Web in 2009"), *July 1st Community*, January 22, 2010, http://71bbs
.people.com.cn/viewthread.php?tid=118294.

64. See "Zhonggong Zhengding Xianwei Xuanchuanbu Guanyu Zhaopin Hulianwang Wangluo Xuanchuan Pinglunyuan de Tongzhi."

65. See Hung, "China's Propaganda in the Information Age."

66. See Rongbin Han, "Manufacturing Consent in Cyberspace: China's 'Fifty-Cent
Army,' " *Journal of Current Chinese Affairs* 44, no. 2 (2015): 119–21.

67. Chen Liangqiu, "Guifan Yindao Liucheng, Zhuangda Wangping Duiwu" ("Standardize Opinion Guidance Procedures and Strengthen the Internet Commentating Troops"), *Zhongguo Xinwen Chuban Bao (China Press and Publishing Journal)*, June 24, 2008.

68. Hou Lei, "Poor Construction Blamed for Shanghai Building Collapse," *China Daily*, June 30, 2009, www.chinadaily.com.cn/china/2009-06/30/content_8338226.htm.

69. In 2009, the Ministry of Industry and Information Technology attempted to require all PC manufacturers to preinstall Green Dam software, which filters out pornography and other "undesirable" content. The policy turned out to be a public relations disaster. See Andrew Jacobs, "China Requires Censorship Software on New PCs," *New York Times*, June 8, 2009; Rebecca Mackinnon, "The Green Dam Phenomenon: Governments Everywhere Are Treading on Web Freedoms," *Wall Street Journal*, June 18, 2009, http://online.wsj.com/article/SB124525992051023961.html.

70. Zhou Kai, "Shanghai Putuoqu Chengguan Guren Baoli Zhifa Shijian Diaocha" ("Investigation of Violent Law Enforcement by Agents Hired by Putuo District Urban Management in Shanghai"), *China Youth Online*, July 3, 2009, http://zqb.cyol.com/content/2009-07/03/content_2739631.htm.

71. Qian Yanfeng, "Shanghai Residents Fight Forced Demolitions," *China Daily*, February 26, 2010, www.chinadaily.com.cn/china/2010-02/26/content_9506528.htm. The report claims that it was not actually a self-immolation incident. Instead, the protestor was fighting the demolition squad with homemade Molotov cocktails.

72. A driver was entrapped by traffic authorities in Pudong District, Shanghai, who were investigating illegal cabs. He was so disturbed that he cut off a finger to prove his innocence. A follow-up investigation found that local traffic authorities had generated millions of yuan in fines using such "entrapment" law enforcement methods over a period of two years. For a collection of reports (translated from Chinese sources) on this issue, see "The Shanghai Illegal Cab Entrapment Case," *EastSouthWestNorth Blog*, October 17–27, 2009, www.zonaeuropa.com/20091025_1.htm. See also Bao Qian, "Shanghai Shizhengfu Jieru Diaoyu Zhifa Shijian, Lüshi Shenqing Xinxi Gongkai" ("Shanghai Municipal Government Steps in in Illegal Cab Entrapment Case, and Lawyer Asks for Information Disclosure"), *Legal Daily (Fazhi Ribao)*, October 19, 2009.

73. See "Gewei Wangpingyuan Zhuyi: Jinji Renwu!!!" ("Attention Online Commentators, Urgent Task!!!"), *Red Net Forum*, October 9, 2008, http://bbs.rednet.cn/a/a.asp?B=339&ID=13937127.

74. See "Hengyangshi Xuanchuan Zhanxian 'Jiefang Sixiang Dajiatan' Taolun Zhuantie" ("Hengyang Municipal Propaganda Branch 'Big Discussion on

Liberating Thoughts' Special Thread"), *Red Net Forum*, September 22, 2008, http://bbs.rednet.cn/a/a.asp?B=339&ID=13937127. When last accessed on February 26, 2011, there were 1,155 comments on the thread. And it is worth noting that the language used in all these comments carries a strong propagandist flavor.

75. Zhanggong District Internet Propaganda Office, "Shi Wenqing Zhongguo Ganzhou Wang Zaixian Fangtan" ("Shi Wenqing's Online Interview with China Ganzhou Net"), internal email communication, January 16, 2014, 12:24 AM.

76. "Cao Guoxing, Guanzhong Kuibao: Zhanggongqu Wangxinban Xinxiang Baoguang Wumao Yunzuo Jizhi" ("Zhanggong District Cyberspace Administration Email Leakage Reveals How the 'Fifty-Cent Army' Operates"), *Radio France Internationale*, May 12, 2014, www.chinese.rfi.fr/中国/20141205 -管中窥豹: 章贡区网信办信箱曝光五毛运作机制.

77. "Shanghai Shangxueyuan Wangxuan Duiwu Fadong Weibo Zhuanfa Pinglun Qingkuang" ("Shanghai Business College Internet Propaganda Team's Efforts to Forward and Comment on Weibo"), leaked internal email, December 13, 2014, 11:22 PM.

78. "Shanghai Shifan Daxue 'Guojia Gongjiri' Xuezi Zhiyuxing Huodong Canyu Qingkuang" ("Shanghai Normal University 'National Memorial Day' Student Awareness and Engagement Activity Report"), leaked internal email, December 13, 2014, 9:26 PM; "Woxiao Shouge 12.13 Guojia Gongjiri Daonian Huodong Zongjie Shanghai Yiyao Gaodeng Zhuanke Xuexiao" ("The First December 13 National Memorial Day Activity Report by the Shanghai Institute of Health Sciences"), leaked internal email, December 16, 2014, 10:22 AM; "Shanghai Caijing Daxue Wangxuanyuan Canyu Tuanzhongyang Gongjiri Huodong Qingkuang" ("The Shanghai University of Finance and Economics Internet Propaganda Team's Participation in the Chinese Communist Youth League Central Committee's National Memorial Day Campaign"), leaked internal email, December 13, 2014, 9:36 PM; "Huashida Gongjiri Huodong Zongjie" ("East China Normal University National Memorial Day Activity Report"), leaked internal email, December 13, 2014, 9:37 PM.

79. The Weibo entry was first posted at 2:43 PM, December 12, 2014, and the last comment it received was posted at 2:39 PM, December 16, 2014, which suggests that there was a precise four-day window within which student commentators engaged.

80. Very few people defended the Internet commentator system. But some interviewees with whom I spoke mentioned this point as one of the few positive implications. Interview RBJ 2010–39, with a veteran forum user and observer, Beijing, May 21, 2010; interview RBJ 2010–40, with a junior media scholar, Beijing, May 21, 2010; interview RBE 2011–58, with a Chinese scholar, Berkeley, May 28, 2011.

81. Zhang Lei, "Wumaodang de Wangluo Jianghu" ("The Cyberspace Rivers and Lakes of the Fifty-Cent Party"), *Changcheng News Digest (Changcheng Yuebao)*, no. 9 (2010).

82. Interview RBJ 2009–18, interview RBJ 2009–19, and interview RBJ 2009–20, with campus forum managers, Beijing, October 21, 2009.

83. "Hukou Xian Guanyu Dui 'Zhongwei Huagong Tuoqian Yuangong Gongzi' Yuqing de Huifu Shuoming" ("Hukou County on the Response to the Public Opinion Event of Arrears of Wages by Zhongwei Chemical Company"), internal e-mail communication to the Internet Propaganda Office of Jiujiang Prefecture, January 27, 2014, 3:17 AM.

84. Chinese Communist Youth League Central Committee Office, "Wangluo Xuanchuanyuan Duiwu Jianshe Tongzhi."

85. Chinese Communist Youth League Central Committee Office, "Gongqing-tuan Zhongyang Guanyu Guangfan Zujian Qingnian Wangluo Wenming Zhiyuanzhe Duiwu, Shenru Tuijin Qingnian Wangluo Wenming Zhiyuan Xingdong de Tongzhi" ("Chinese Communist Youth League Central Committee Office Circular on Widely Establishing a Youth Internet Civilized Volunteers Troop and Deeply Promoting Youth Internet Civilized Action"), February 16, 2015.

86. King, Pan, and Roberts, "How the Chinese Government Fabricates Social Media Posts for Strategic Distraction."

87. Ibid.

88. Haifeng Huang, "Propaganda as Signaling," *Comparative Politics* 47, no. 4 (July 2015): 419–37.

89. Zhang, "Wumaodang de Wangluo Jianghu."

90. See "Zhongguo Gansu Chengren Zujian Wumaodang, Beipi Niuqu Minyi" ("China's Gansu Province Admits Establishing Fifty-Cent Army and Is Criticized for Distorting Public Opinion"), *Voice of America*, January 24, www.voachinese.com/a/china-20100124-82548812/460017.html.

91. Interview RBJ 2009–15, with a student Internet commentator, Beijing, September 21, 2009.

92. Ann Florini, Hairong Lai, and Yeling Tan, *China Experiments: From Local Innovations to National Reform* (Washington, DC: Brookings Institution Press, 2012).

93. Zhang, "Wumaodang de Wangluo Jianghu."

94. "Shanxisheng Shoupi Wangluo Bianji he Wangluo Pinglunyuan Peixunban Xueyuan Zhengshi Zai Bing Jieye."

95. "Gansu Jiang Jian 650 Ren Wangping Duiwu Tixi" ("Gansu Province Will Set Up an Internet Commentator Troop with Six Hundred Members"), *Nanfang Dushibao (Southern Metropolis Daily)*, January 20, 2010; Cai Xiaoquan, "Suqian 26 Wangpingyuan Jin Shanggang" ("Twenty-six Internet Commentators in Position Today"), *Yangzi Wanbao (Yangtse Evening Post)*, April 29, 2005.

96. Liao Jingwen and Yao Wenjun, "Guangdong Jiang Zaijian Wanren Wangluo Yuqing Yindaoyuan Tuandui" ("Guangdong Will Establish Another Ten-Thousand-Member Public Opinion Guidance Troop"), *Netease*, February 21, 2012, http://news.163.com/12/0221/05/7QOTQNCA0001124J.html.
97. Tong and Lei, "War of Position and Microblogging in China."
98. Zhang, "Invisible Footprints of Online Commentators."
99. Kenneth Lieberthal and David M. Lampton, eds., *Bureaucracy, Politics, and Decision Making in Post-Mao China* (Berkeley: University of California Press, 1992); Andrew Mertha, " 'Fragmented Authoritarianism 2.0': Political Pluralization in the Chinese Policy Process," *The China Quarterly*, no. 200 (2009): 995–1012.

6. MANUFACTURING DISTRUST

1. See *Tiananmen: The Gate of Heavenly Peace*, directed by Richard Gordon and Carma Hinton (Boston: Long Bow, 1995). For a complete transcript of the documentary, see www.tsquare.tv/film/transcript.html.
2. Johan Lagerkvist, *After the Internet, Before Democracy: Competing Norms in Chinese Media and Society* (Bern, Switzerland: Peter Lang, 2010).
3. Yonggang Li, *Women de Fanghuoqiang: Wangluo Shidai de Biaoda Yu Jianguan (Our Great Firewall: Expression and Governance in the Era of the Internet)* (Nanning: Guangxi Normal University Press, 2009).
4. See Fang Tang, "Zhengzhi Wangmin de Shehui Jingji Diwei yu Zhengzhi Qingxiang: Jiyu Qiangguo he Maoyan de Tansuoxing Fenxi" ("Political Netizens' Socioeconomic Status and Political Orientations: Exploratory Research on Qiangguo and Maoyan Forums"), *China Media Report* 8, no. 3 (2009): 96–107.
5. Xu Wu, *Chinese Cyber Nationalism: Evolution, Characteristics, and Implications* (Lanham, MD: Lexington, 2007); Simon Shen and Shaun Breslin, eds., *Online Chinese Nationalism and China's Bilateral Relations* (Lanham, MD: Lexington, 2010); Peter Gries, "Chinese Nationalism: Challenging the State?" *Current History* 104, no. 683 (2005): 251–56; James Leibold, "More than a Category: Han Supremacism on the Chinese Internet," *The China Quarterly*, no. 203 (2010): 539–59.
6. Min Jiang, "The Coevolution of the Internet, (Un)Civil Society, and Authoritarianism in China," in *The Internet, Social Media, and a Changing China*, ed. Jacques DeLisle, Avery Goldstein, and Guobin Yang (Philadelphia: University of Pennsylvania Press, 2016), 28–48.
7. Adrian Rauchfleisch and Mike S. Schäfer, "Multiple Public Spheres of Weibo: A Typology of Forms and Potentials of Online Public Spheres in China," *Information, Communication & Society* 18, no. 2 (February 24, 2015): 139–55.

8. Lagerkvist argues that "as long as anonymity on the Internet and online use remains relatively free compared to the offline world, it can be conceived as an institution and cultural form that is facilitating normative change, and transforming China toward its ultimate horizon—inclusive democracy." See Lagerkvist, *After the Internet*, 39.

9. Some users would initiate politically sensitive topics at midnight, not only to evade censorship, but also to make the top-ten list quickly and thus generate a greater impact beyond the particular board.

10. Many forums allow users to have multiple accounts. One's most frequently used account is called the primary ID, and all other accounts are called ghost accounts or jackets. Ghost accounts became so prevalent in determining top-ten lists and other BBS activities that major BBS sites had to change their rules regulating the use of jacket IDs. For instance, both Bdwm and NewSmth changed the top-ten ranking from being ID-based to IP-based because the latter is much more difficult to fabricate. In addition, both sites now stipulate that users cannot have more than three IDs. However, without strict enforcement of real-name registration, forums cannot practically prevent users from using jackets.

11. See Yongnian Zheng, *Technological Empowerment: The Internet, State, and Society in China* (Stanford, CA: Stanford University Press, 2008).

12. Business astroturfing activities are rampant in Chinese cyberspace. In fact, there are crowdsourcing platforms, such as zhubajie.com, which business owners can use to hire people to conduct business astroturfing. State media outlets have widely criticized this phenomenon. See Jing Xiaolei, "The Business of Manipulation," *Beijing Review* 54, no. 2 (2011): 18–19; interview RBJ 2010-36, with a forum manager of a large commercial website, Beijing, May 6, 2010.

13. See Yongshun Cai, "Disruptive Collective Action in the Reform Era," in *Popular Protest in China*, ed. Kevin J. O'Brien (Cambridge, MA: Harvard University Press, 2008), 163–78; Yongshun Cai, *Collective Resistance in China: Why Popular Protests Succeed or Fail* (Stanford, CA: Stanford University Press, 2010).

14. See Michael S. Chase and James C. Mulvenon, *You've Got Dissent* (Santa Monica, CA: RAND, 2002), 1. Dissident groups include Falun Gong, activists in support of independence for Xinjiang and Tibet, and democratic activists, all of whom are regarded as subversive by the Chinese authorities.

15. Even today, posts from identifiable Falun Gong sources still invite antipathy on many forums even when they are not banned. Both state denigration and Falun Gong's association with foreign support contribute to this antipathy, in addition to the backlash of Falun Gong's PR efforts discussed here.

16. Chase and Mulvenon, *You've Got Dissent*.

17. The email was received on December 6, 2010.

18. Some netizens suspected that the post had Falun Gong (FLG) origins. For instance, one user on Xcar replied, "Fuck, FLGer?" See www.xcar.com.cn/bbs /viewthread.php?tid=13568953&extra=&showthread=&page=2. A Kds user also said, "It reads like something written by FLG." See http://club.pchome .net/thread_1_15_5957312.html. Unlike on Xcar, most users expressed doubt here.

19. See "[Kaozheng] Yige Liuchuan le Hao Jinian de Huanghua Tie" ("[Investigation] A Rumor that Circulated for Years"), *Ccthere*, January 28, 2010, www .ccthere.com/topic/2690660#C2690660.

20. In early 2011, a post titled "Old Pictures: Five-Cent Dining Together" was posted to NewSmth's "MilitaryJoke" board, with photos from the Fourth Anniversary Potluck Party at the Chinese Democratic Party U.S. headquarters. The post claimed that one man in the photo was an active online astroturfer ("Director Wang") and charged him with fabricating the post comparing government buildings from the United States and China. See "Laotu: Wumeifen Kaifan le" ("Old Pictures: Five-Cents Dining Together"), *NewSmth*, January 1, 2011, www.newsmth.net/bbscon.php?bid=1031&id=125689.

21. See "Comment on False Web Postings Regarding RAND Work on China," *RAND Corporation*, October 4, 2010 (revised January 20, 2012), www.rand.org/news /announcements/2012/01/20.html.

22. Interview RBJ 2010–32, with a top executive of a portal website, Beijing, April 22 2010.

23. Henry Chiui Hail, "Patriotism Abroad: Overseas Chinese Students' Encounters with Criticisms of China," *Journal of Studies in International Education* 19, no. 4 (January 12, 2015): 311–26.

24. See Cecilia Kang, "Secretary Clinton Dines with High-Tech Titans to Talk Diplomacy," *Washington Post*, January 11, 2010, http://voices.washington-post.com/posttech/2010/01/sec_clinton_dines_high-tech_ti.html; Hillary Rodham Clinton, "Remarks on Internet Freedom," *U.S. Department of State*, January 21, 2010, https://2009-2017.state.gov/secretary/20092013clinton /rm/2010/01/135519.htm.

25. Jeremy Page, "What's He Doing Here? Ambassador's Unusual Protest Cameo," *Wall Street Journal*, February 23, 2011, http://on.wsj.com/17d6nlq. For the reaction of Chinese netizens, see "Tuwen + Shipin Baoliao: Meiguo Dashi Qinfu Wangfujing Wei 'Dailu dang' Zhuwei Daqi!" ("Text, Pictures, and Video Reports: The U.S. Ambassador Showed Up on Wangfujing Street to Encourage 'Road-Leading Party!'"), *April Youth Community*, February 23, 2011, http://bbs .m4.cn/viewthread.php?tid=301579&rpid=4155507&ordertype=0&page =30#pid4155507.

26. Huntsman made the statement at the 2012 South Carolina Republican Party presidential debate. For the reactions of Chinese netizens, see "Wokao, Hong Peibo Huochuqu le" ("Holy Shit! Huntsman Has Thrown Caution to the Wind"),

Mitbbs, November 15, 2011, www.mitbbs.com/article_t/Military/36740857 .html; "Hong Bopei—Meiguo Jiang Jiezhu Zhongguo Wangmin de Liliang lai Jikui Zhongguo" ("Jon Huntsman: The U.S. Will Topple China with Assistance from Chinese Netizens"), *Newsmth*, November 15, 2011, www.newsmth.net /bbstcon.php?board=MilitaryJoke&gid=174754; "Hong Peibo: Women Yao he Zhongguo Neibu de Mengyou Yiqi Yindao Zhongguo de Biange" ("Jon Huntsman: We Should Guide China's Reform with Allies Inside China"), *Ccthere*, November 15, 2011, www.ccthere.com/article/3610243.

27. Wei Cheng, "Shui shi Xizang Saoluan Zhong de Shujia?" ("Who Loses in the Tibet Riots?"), *Financial Times Chinese*, March 31, 2008, www.ftchinese.com /story/001018283.

28. The platform later evolved into a larger and more comprehensive nationalistic website called April Youth Media (m4.cn).

29. According to Anti-CNN.com, such media outlets include bild.de, n-tv.de, rtlaktuell.de, N24, the *Washington Post*, and Fox News.

30. CNN cropped a photo, cutting off the half that depicted Tibetans throwing stones at a truck.

31. The *Berliner Morgenpost website* and the BBC mistook an ambulance for a police vehicle.

32. YouTube is said to have reduced the view counts of a Chinese nationalistic video titled "Tibet Was and Is and Always Be Part of China."

33. Liang Wendao, "Zai Fanhua Langchao yu Kuangre Minzu Zhuyi Zhijian" ("Between China-Bashing and Frenetic Nationalism"), *University Students Online*, April 27, 2008, www.univs.cn/newweb/univs/hust/2008-04-27 /837018.html.

34. "What Do You Really Want from Us?" *Washington Post*, May 18, 2008.

35. "Zongjie Pian—Du Mark A. Jones he Zangdu Bianlun Yougan" ("Summary: Reflections After Reading How Mark A. Jones Debated with Tibet Independence Supporters"), *Mitbbs*, April 21, 2008, www.mitbbs.com/pc /pccon_2306_36397.html.

36. See "Lingqu Buzhu Shouxu Liucheng [4 Yue 24 Ri Gengxin Zanzhu Jipiao Feiyong $11777.41 Meiyuan Juankuan]" ("Procedure to Claim the Subsidies [April 24 Update: Donated Airfare Funding $11,777.41]"), *Mitbbs*, April 8, 2008, www.mitbbs.com/article_t/SanFrancisco/31296057.html.

37. Cafferty made the comment on the April 9, 2008, broadcast of CNN's *The Situation Room*. This resulted in offline protests against CNN and an official apology from CNN. See David Pierson, "Protesters Gather at CNN," *Los Angeles Times*, April 20, 2008, http://articles.latimes.com/print/2008/apr/20/local /me-cnn20; Matthew Moore, "CNN Apologises to Chinese Over Host's 'Goons and Thugs' Outburst," *Telegraph*, April 16, 2008, www.telegraph.co.uk/news /worldnews/1895792/CNN-apologises-to-Chinese-over-hosts-goons-and -thugs-outburst.html.

38. "Wang Dan zai Fating Chengren: Shoudao Chen Shui-Bian de 40 Wan Meiyuan" ("Wang Dan Confesses in Court: He Received US$400,000 from Chen Shui-bian"), *Mitbbs*, April 15, 2011, www.mitbbs.com/article_t/Military/35644205 .html; "Wang A-Dan Na le Chen A-Bian 40 Wan Meijin" ("Wang A-Dan Took US$400,000 from Chen A-Bian"), *Mitbbs*, April 15, 2011, http://www.mitbbs .com/article_t/Military/35642545.html.

39. This accounts for his online nickname "Liu 300." In fact, the Mitbbs military board added a sticky post (a post pinned to the top of the page) titled "NED 2009 Asia Program Highlights," which was not unpinned until April 29, 2011.

40. Ironically, this mechanism is more prevalent on forums outside China, partly because the state bans these groups within the Great Firewall.

41. See Wang Juntao, Twitter post, March 1, 2011, 1:32 AM, http://twitter.com /#!/juntaowang/status/42472321251942401.

42. Netizens later discovered that it was a group account trying to attract attention through controversial topics. This does not affect the analysis here, as the key is not the expression per se, but its popularity.

43. The message was forwarded to all major forums I observed, including Ccthere, m4.cn, Mitbbs, NewSmth, and Tianya. See also "Tuwen + Shipin Baoliao"; "Haishi Kankan Ranxiang de Dianjing Zhiyu" ("Let's See Ranxiang's Perceptive Comments Again"), *Ccthere*, February 24, 2011, https://www.ccthere.com /article/3298313.

44. See Ranxiang's microblog, "Chupai de Xuewen" ("The Art of Positioning In A Card Game"), *Sina Weibo*, February 22, 2011, http://t.sina.com.cn /1671042153/5KD0VOr8xB9.

45. See Ranxiang's microblog, "Kandao Dajia zai Zhuipeng Ranxiang de Zhili Mingyan" ("I Saw People Following Ranxiang's Words of Wisdom"), *Sina Weibo*, February 22, 2011, http://t.sina.com.cn/1654592030/60L0VOrqCZg.

46. *Tiananmen*. The documentary had a negative impact on Chai Ling's image. Many believe that it was her stubbornness and that of a few others that led to the suppression.

47. For more discussion on labeling wars, see the following discussion, especially table 6.1.

48. See Wusuonanyang's microblog, "Wo dui Qingnian men Zhuiqiu Minzhu de Yongqi Biaoshi Zanshang" ("I Admire the Young People for Their Courage to Pursue Democracy"), *Sina Weibo*, February 22, 2011, http://t.sina.com .cn/1671042153/5en0VNP4PIl. However, the entry was deleted by the time I attempted to revisit the site on November 14, 2011.

49. See "The Impact of a Celebrity Microblogger," *EastSouthWestNorth Blog*, January 29, 2011, http://www.zonaeuropa.com/201101a.brief.htm#037. Ning himself felt regret and decided to avoid political topics when possible. See Yang Tingting, "Ningcaishen: Aiji Nashier Huisi Wo le!" ("Ningcaishen: That Egypt Thing Really Ruined Me!"), *Economic Observer*, February 17, 2011, www .eeo.com.cn/Business_lifes/wenhua/2011/02/17/193600.shtml.

50. See "Xiang Zhidao Yulun, Zhenxiang Zenme Zaochulai he Chuanbo de me?" ("Do You Want to Know How Public Opinion and Truth Are Fabricated and Circulated?"), *Newsmth*, January 29, 2011, www.newsmth.net/bbstcon.php? board=MilitaryJoke&gid=129800.

51. See Li Chengpeng's microblog, http://t.sina.com.cn/1189591617/5en0TsZ7hN6; see also "The Biggest Corruption Case in American History," *EastSouthWest North Blog*, February 12, 2011, http://www.zonaeuropa.com/201102a.brief .htm#029.

52. "Wumanlanjiang Jiancai Meihua Miguo Tanfu An Bei Jiechuan Dalian" ("Wumanlanjiang's Face Slapped for Cropping and Beautifying Corruption Case in the U.S."), *jinbushe.org*, February 13, 2011, http://xinu.jinbushe.org /index.php?doc-view-2757.

53. Some netizens call Southern Clique "Southern Lizard" ("Nanfang Xi"). See "Shenshou Xinpian: Nanfang Xi" ("New Holy Animals: Southern Lizard"), *Ccthere*, April 14, 2010, www.ccthere.com/article/2841932. According to an entry created by netizens on the Wikipedia-like site Hudong Baike, Southern Lizards live near the "Tencent Jungle" on the "South Ma-le Desert" (*Male Gebi*, 马勒戈壁; a dirty pun in Chinese). The Southern Lizards have scales that can change color for camouflage. They attract insects and small animals with a "pussy, pussy" sound (mocking "universal values"). The sound attracts a specific type of fly, the "elite" fly (a homophone of "elite" in Chinese). Southern Lizards also have a strange capacity. When encountering a predator, they can drive little insects like elite flies to attack it while they themselves flee. Southern Lizards have sharp teeth with strong poison and they like drinking "persimmon oil" (a homophone of "freedom" in Chinese). So some people cook persimmon oil to attract Southern Lizards and threaten anyone who dislikes persimmon oil that Southern Lizards will bite them to death. See "Nanfang Xi" (Southern Lizard), *Hudong Wiki*, last updated on December 12, 2012, http://www.hudong.com/wiki/南方蜥.

54. This echoes Lagerkvist's observation on *Southern Weekend* as a major driving force of investigative reports in China. See Lagerkvist, *After the Internet*, chapter 3.

55. Interview RBE 2011-54, with a former *Southern Metropolis Daily* journalist, Berkeley, California, February 11, 2011. Many media professionals demonstrate a similar tendency. See interview RBE 2008-02, with a former journalist of the Guangzhou Daily Group, Berkeley, California, October 25, 2008; interview RBJ 2009-08, with a former journalist, Beijing, January 9, 2009; interview OBE 2010-52, phone interview with junior faculty member at a communications school who was a former CCTV reporter, September 4, 2010. For studies on critical journalists, see Maria Repnikova, *Media Politics in China: Improvising Power Under Authoritarianism* (Cambridge: Cambridge University Press, 2017); Jonathan Hassid, *China's Unruly Journalists: How Committed Professionals Are Changing the People's Republic* (New York: Routledge, 2015); H. Christoph

Steinhardt, "From Blind Spot to Media Spotlight: Propaganda Policy, Media Activism and the Emergence of Protest Events in the Chinese Public Sphere," *Asian Studies Review* 39, no. 1 (2015): 119–37; David Bandurski and Martin Hala, eds., *Investigative Journalism in China: Eight Cases in Chinese Watchdog Journalism* (Hong Kong: Hong Kong University Press, 2010).

56. An example of such a conflict can be found in "Lüshi Zhangxian: Nanfang ZM Quan Women Busha Yao Jiaxin" ("Lawyer Zhang Xian: *Southern Weekend* Tries to Persuade Us Not to Pursue Yao Jiaxin's Death Penalty"), *Newsmth*, April 12, 2011, http://wwv.newsmth.net/bbstcon.php?board=Reader&gid=495482.

57. Liu Yuan, "[Zhongguo Bu Gaoxing]: Zuofen de Huanghun" ("China Is Unhappy: The Coming Doomsday of the Shit Leftists"), *Liu Yuan's Blog Sanjiaquan Ye You Xiangchou*, April 10, 2009, http://sohuliuyuan.blog.sohu.com/114075956.html.

58. See Sichuan Xiaoqi, "You Zhihui de Wangyou Zongjie: Nanfang Zhoumo: Buxu Shuo Meiguo Huaihua" ("Summary by Wise Netizens: *Southern Weekend*: We Don't Allow You to Say Anything Bad About the U.S."), *April Youth Community*, November 18, 2011, http://bbs.m4.cn/thread-3244443-1-1.html.

59. For instance, see "Tengxun Shexian Paozhi Jia Xinwen: Sanpian Bolan Zongtong Zhuiji Fangtan Yidoucongsheng" ("Tencent Allegedly Fabricated Facts: Three of Its Interviews on Polish President's Plane Crash Are Suspicious"), *Cjdby*, April 12, 2010, http://lt.cjdby.net/thread-906493-1-1.html; "Lian ge Bolan Zongtong Zhuiji Dou Youren Nong Jia Xinwen" ("Someone Fabricated Facts on Polish President's Plane Crash"), *Newsmth*, April 13, 2010, www.newsmth.net/bbstcon.php?board=MilitaryJoke&gid=87874.

60. To "open a blank window" (*kai tianchuang*, 开天窗) means to leave space on a page blank. The implicit message is that something has been censored. For an English report, see Chris Buckley, "China Demotes Editor After Obama Interview: Sources," *Reuters*, December 13, 2009, www.reuters.com/article/2009/12/13/us-obama-china-censorship-idUSTRE5BC0BM20091213.

61. For instance, see "Yao Jiaxin Sixing Ji Yicheng Dingju Meiti Qiuqing Beiju" ("Yao Jiaxin's Death Penalty Is Almost Certain, Media's Plea for Forgiveness Was Rejected"), *KDS Community*, April 20, 2011, http://club.kdslife.com/t_6249691_0_0.html.

62. The image has been deleted from its original source (weibo.com/2105744042). For an example of nationalistic responses, see "Dailu Dang, Yige Exin de Qunti" ("The Road-Leading Party: A Sick Group of People"), *Tiexue Shequ (The Iron and Blood Community)*, December 10, 2011, http://bbs.tiexue.net/post2_5628039_1.html.

63. See "Biantai Laojiang Zhenshi Xiaoshun Ah, Kuailai Weiguann Laojiang Gei Wolao Gaode Mudi" ("The Psychopathic Laojiang Is So Filial-Hearted: Come and Have a Look at the Graveyard Laojiang Built for Me"), *Mitbbs*, April 20, 2011, http://www.mitbbs.com/article_t/Military/35674583.html.

64. "Yiding Yao Daji Yaoyan Beihou de Laojiang, Minyun, Dailu Dang" ("We Must Strike Old Generals, Democratic Activists, and the Road-Leading Party Behind Those Rumors"), *Mitbbs*, May 6, 2012, http://www.mitbbs.com/article/Military/35464931_3.html.

65. Some users once impeached a board manager of "ChinaNews" because they believed that he or she was an imposter from Laojiang.

66. One major difference between forums inside and outside the Great Firewall is the scope of discussion. Taboo topics such as Falun Gong and the 1989 democratic movement are freely discussed (whether condemned or championed) on overseas forums but not on domestic forums.

67. Yong Hu, *Zhongsheng Xuanhua: Wangluo Shidai de Geren Biaoda Yu Gonggong Taolun (The Rising Cacophony: Personal Expression and Public Discussion in the Internet Age)* (Nanning: Guangxi Normal University Press, 2008).

68. "Shuiyao Zaigei Xiao Riben Juankuan, Wo Duo le Ta! (Zhuanzai)" ("Whoever Donates to the Japanese, I Will Chop!" (forwarded), *Mitbbs*, March 29, 2011, www.mitbbs.com/article_t/Stock/33405813.html; "Zhongguo Juanzeng Bengche Hou Riben Wangmin de Fanying" ("Reactions from Japanese Netizens After China Donates Pump Vehicles to Japan"), *China Net Forum*, March 22, 2011, http://club.china.com/data/thread/1011/2723/93/31/8_1.html; "[Shishi Jujiao] Zhongguo Bengche Zao Baiyan" ("[News Focus] Japanese Disdained Pump Vehicles Donated by China" (forwarded), *Tianya*, March 24, 2011, http://www.tianya.cn/publicforum/content/worldlook/1/333008.shtml; "Riben Wangmin Ruhe Pingjia Zhongguo Juankuan?" ("How Japanese Netizens Responded to Chinese Donations"), *Baidu Tieba Shenzhen Ba*, March 19, 2011, http://tieba.baidu.com/f?kz=1029009252.

69. The state and media elites have lost their monopoly over the dissemination of information to the outside world, which was critical in shaping public perceptions of other countries (or "facts" in a broader sense), as well as of China. See Haifeng Huang and Yao-Yuan Yeh, "Information from Abroad: Foreign Media, Selective Exposure and Political Support in China," *British Journal of Political Science* (2017): 1–26, https://doi.org/10.1017/S0007123416000739.

70. This was not the only mechanism at work. As soon as the earthquake occurred, some netizens proposed not helping Japan because of unpleasant historical memories. See "Xiezai He Chen'ai Shangwei Luoding de Shike" ("At this Time when Nuclear Dust Is Still in the Air"), *Ccthere*, March 15, 2011, https://ccthere.com/article/3326816. The post received more than three thousand "flowers" (an icon indicating support) when last retrieved, making it the third highest-ranking post in the website's history.

71. See "Xiezai He Chen'ai Shangwei Luoding de Shike"; "Shuiyao Zaigei Xiao Riben Juankuan."

72. "Google Fangyan Tuichu Zhongguo, Xilali Yeshi Muhou Tuishou?" ("Google Declares Withdrawal from China; Is Hillary Also Pushing Behind the Scenes?"),

April Youth Community, January 14, 2010, http://bbs.m4.cn/thread-217242-1-1. html; "Google Shitu Yaoxie Zhongguo? Baigong Shitu Zhengzhihua Google?" ("Is Google Attempting to Blackmail China? Is the White House Attempting to Politicize Google?"), *April Youth Community*, January 13, 2010, http://bbs .m4.cn/thread-217168-1-1.html. Similar threads are widely circulated on forums such as Ccthere, Mitbbs, NewSmth, and Tianya.

73. "Yuanlai Gougou Yijing Bangjia le Yixie Guoren~" ("So Google Has Already Hijacked Some of Our Compatriots"), *Ccthere*, January 13, 2010, http://www .ccthere.com/article/2654701.

74. "Meicuo, Wo Shi Maiban, Wo Shi Jingying, Wo Shi Diguozhuyi Fang Zhongguo de Diwu Zhongdui" ("Alright! I Am a Comprador. I Am Elite. I Am a Fifth-Column Agent Planted in China by Imperialists"), *Ccthere*, January 13, 2010, http://www.ccthere.com/article/2654783.

75. "Kuai Yinian le, Huitou Kankan Zhiqian Ziji Fa de Zhepian Tiezi, Yi You Shenme Fenlu Gan le" ("Almost a Year Later, When I Read this Post Again, I Am no Longer Angry"), *Ccthere*, December 27, 2010, http://www.ccthere .com/article/3222301. This may be the reason why the majority of small websites managers sided with Google.

76. Lagerkvist, *After the Internet*, 265–67.

77. The mechanism echoes Haifeng Huang's research. Huang has found that Chinese citizens' attitudes toward the government are conditioned by their perceptions of foreign countries. See Haifeng Huang, "International Knowledge and Domestic Evaluations in a Changing Society: The Case of China," *American Political Science Review* 109, no. 3 (2015): 613–34.

78. For instance, see Anthony G. Wilhelm, "Virtual Sounding Boards: How Deliberative Is Online Political Discussion?" *Information, Communication & Society* 1, no. 3 (1998): 313–38; Lincoln Dahlberg, "Rethinking the Fragmentation of the Cyberpublic: From Consensus to Contestation," *New Media & Society* 9, no. 5 (2007): 827–47; Cass R. Sunstein, *Infotopia: How Many Minds Produce Knowledge* (New York: Oxford University Press, 2006).

7. DEFENDING THE REGIME

A significant portion of this chapter was published as a journal article under the title "Defending the Authoritarian Regime Online: China's 'Voluntary Fifty-Cent Army.'" Reprinted with permission from *The China Quarterly*, no. 224 (2015): 1006–25.

1. Guobin Yang, "The Internet and the Rise of a Transnational Chinese Cultural Sphere," *Media, Culture & Society* 24, no. 4 (2003): 469–90.

2. Min Jiang, "The Coevolution of the Internet, (Un)Civil Society, and Authoritarianism in China," in *The Internet, Social Media, and a Changing China*,

ed. Jacques DeLisle, Avery Goldstein, and Guobin Yang (Philadelphia: University of Pennsylvania Press, 2016), 28–48; Rongbin Han, "Withering Gongzhi: Cyber Criticism of Chinese Public Intellectuals," *International Journal of Communication*, forthcoming.

3. Johan Lagerkvist, *The Internet in China: Unlocking and Containing the Public Sphere* (Lund, Sweden: Lund University Publications, 2007), 151. Lagerkvist borrowed the concept from Todd Gitlin, "Public Sphere or Public Sphericules?" in *Media, Ritual and Identity*, ed. Tamar Liebes and James Curran (London: Routledge, 1998), 68–174.

4. For some excellent works, see Bingchun Meng, "Moving Beyond Democratization: A Thought Piece on the China Internet Research Agenda," *International Journal of Communication* 4 (2010): 501–8; Bingchun Meng, "From Steamed Bun to Grass Mud Horse: E Gao as Alternative Political Discourse on the Chinese Internet," *Global Media and Communication* 7, no. 1 (2011): 33–51; Paola Voci, *China on Video: Smaller-Screen Realities* (Abingdon, Oxon: Routledge, 2010); Christopher G. Rea, "Spoofing (E'gao) Culture on the Chinese Internet," in *Humour in Chinese Life and Culture*, ed. Jessica Milner Davis and Jocelyn Chey (Hong Kong: Hong Kong University Press, 2013), 149–72; David Kurt Herold and Peter Marolt, "Online Society in China: Creating, Celebrating, and Instrumentalising the Online Carnival," *Media, Culture and Social Change in Asia* (Abingdon, Oxon: Routledge, 2011).

5. Jens Damm, "The Internet and the Fragmentation of Chinese Society," *Critical Asian Studies* 39, no. 2 (2007): 273–94.

6. For instance, see Yongnian Zheng, *Technological Empowerment: The Internet, State, and Society in China* (Stanford, CA: Stanford University Press, 2008); Guobin Yang, "The Co-evolution of the Internet and Civil Society in China," *Asian Survey* 43, no. 3 (2003): 124–41; Guobin Yang, "How Do Chinese Civic Associations Respond to the Internet? Findings from a Survey," *The China Quarterly*, no. 189 (2007): 122–43; Guobin Yang, *The Power of the Internet in China: Citizen Activism Online* (New York: Columbia University Press, 2009); Lagerkvist, *The Internet in China*; Yong Hu, *Zhongsheng Xuanhua: Wangluo Shidai de Geren Biaoda Yu Gonggong Taolun (The Rising Cacophony: Personal Expression and Public Discussion in the Internet Age)* (Nanning: Guangxi Normal University Press, 2008).

7. Evgeny Morozov, *The Net Delusion: How Not to Liberate the World* (London: Penguin, 2011); Bruce Bimber, "Information and Political Engagement in America: The Search for Effects of Information Technology at the Individual Level," *Political Research Quarterly* 54, no. 1 (2001): 53–67; Dietram A. Scheufele and Matthew C. Nisbet, "Being a Citizen Online: New Opportunities and Dead Ends," *Harvard International Journal of Press/Politics* 7, no. 3 (2002): 55–75.

8. Hindman measured online traffic and audience share using link density as an effective proxy. See Matthew Hindman, *The Myth of Digital Democracy* (Princeton, NJ: Princeton University Press, 2009), 56.

9. Barry Wellman and Milena Gulia, "Net-Surfers Don't Ride Alone: Virtual Communities as Communities," in *Networks in the Global Village: Life in Contemporary Communities*, ed. Barry Wellman (Boulder, CO: Westview, 1999), 331–66.

10. Kevin A. Hill and John E. Hughes, *Cyberpolitics: Citizen Activism in the Age of the Internet* (Lanham, MD: Rowman & Littlefield, 1998).

11. Anthony G. Wilhelm, "Virtual Sounding Boards: How Deliberative Is Online Political Discussion?" *Information, Communication & Society* 1, no. 3 (1998): 313–38.

12. Lincoln Dahlberg, "The Internet and Democratic Discourse: Exploring the Prospects of Online Deliberative Forums Extending the Public Sphere," *Information, Communication & Society* 4, no. 4 (2001): 615–33; Lincoln Dahlberg, "Computer-Mediated Communication and the Public Sphere: A Critical Analysis," *Journal of Computer-Mediated Communication* 7, no. 1 (2001): 0; Lincoln Dahlberg, "Rethinking the Fragmentation of the Cyberpublic: From Consensus to Contestation," *New Media & Society* 9, no. 5 (2007): 827–47.

13. Cass R. Sunstein, *On Rumors: How Falsehoods Spread, Why We Believe Them, What Can Be Done* (New York: Farrar, Straus and Giroux, 2009), 7. See also Cass R. Sunstein, *Infotopia: How Many Minds Produce Knowledge* (New York: Oxford University Press, 2006).

14. Damm, "The Internet and the Fragmentation of Chinese Society"; James Leibold, "Blogging Alone: China, the Internet, and the Democratic Illusion?" *The Journal of Asian Studies* 70, no. 4 (2011): 1023–41.

15. Cuiming Pang, "Self-Censorship and the Rise of Cyber Collectives: An Anthropological Study of a Chinese Online Community," *Intercultural Communication Studies* VXII, no. 3 (2008): 57–76.

16. See Fang Tang, "Zhengzhi Wangmin de Shehui Jingji Diwei yu Zhengzhi Qingxiang: Jiyu Qiangguo he Maoyan de Tansuoxing Fenxi" ("Political Netizens' Socioeconomic Status and Political Orientations: Exploratory Research on Qiangguo and Maoyan Forums"), *China Media Report* 8, no. 3 (2009): 96–107. Tang first sampled users from the two forums and then analyzed their political inclination by tracing and coding their online posts.

17. Yuan Le and Boxu Yang, "Online Political Discussion and Left–Right Ideological Debate: A Comparative Study of Two Major Chinese BBS Forums" (paper presented at the 7th Annual Chinese Internet Research Conference, University of Pennsylvania, Philadelphia, PA, May 27–29, 2009). Le and Yang sampled posts, which may explain why the left–right ratio is less striking for *Maoyan* than it is in Tang's study. Right-wing netizens can be underrepresented if they are less active in posting.

18. James Leibold, "More Than a Category: Han Supremacism on the Chinese Internet," *The China Quarterly*, no. 203 (2010): 539–59; Peter Gries, "Chinese Nationalism: Challenging the State?" *Current History* 104, no. 683 (2005):

251–56; Simon Shen and Shaun Breslin, eds., *Online Chinese Nationalism and China's Bilateral Relations* (Lexington Books, 2010); Xu Wu, *Chinese Cyber Nationalism: Evolution, Characteristics, and Implications* (Lanham, MD: Lexington, 2007).

19. Johan Lagerkvist, *After the Internet, Before Democracy: Competing Norms in Chinese Media and Society* (Bern, Switzerland: Peter Lang, 2010), 14.

20. For instance, see Hill and Hughes, *Cyberpolitics*; Wilhelm, "Virtual Sounding Boards"; Fang Tang, "Zhengzhi Wangmin de Shehui Jingji Diwei yu Zhengzhi Qingxiang"; Le and Yang, "Online Political Discussion and Left–Right Ideological Debate."

21. Susan Shirk, *China: Fragile Superpower* (New York: Oxford University Press, 2007); Rebecca MacKinnon, "China's 'Networked Authoritarianism,'" *Journal of Democracy* 22, no. 2 (2011): 32–46; Chin-fu Hung, "China's Propaganda in the Information Age: Internet Commentators and the Weng'an Incident," *Issues & Studies* 46, no. 4 (2010): 149–81; Gary King, Jennifer Pan, and Margaret F. Roberts, "How the Chinese Government Fabricates Social Media Posts for Strategic Distraction, Not Engaged Argument," *American Political Science Review* 111, no.3 (2017): 484–501; Blake Andrew Phillip Miller, "Automatic Detection of Comment Propaganda in Chinese Media," *SSRN Electronic Journal*, 2016, 1–38, doi:10.2139/ssrn.2738325.

22. Dahlberg, "The Internet and Democratic Discourse," 618.

23. This derogatory nickname appeared in the title of a book by the dissident Yu Jie. Yu is in exile, and the book is banned in China. See Yu Jie, *Zhongguo Yingdi Wen Jiabao (China's Best Actor: Wen Jiabao)*, (Hong Kong: New Century, 2010). See also Michael Wines, "China Seeks to Halt Book That Faults Its Prime Minister," *New York Times*, July 7, 2010.

24. Yang, "The Internet and the Rise of a Transnational Chinese Cultural Sphere," 471.

25. "Accidental casualties" are not unidirectional. Several interviewees reported being labeled as both the fifty-cent army and "U.S. cents" by netizens. Interview OBJ 2009–05, online communication with a veteran forum user and board manager, January 3, 2009; interview RBJ 2009–11, with a veteran forum user and junior economics faculty member, Beijing, August 23, 2009; interview RBJ 2010–33, with a media student, Beijing, April 23, 2010; interview RBJ 2010–35, with a veteran BBS user and observer, Beijing, May 6, 2010.

26. Zhang Lei, "Invisible Footprints of Online Commentators," *Global Times*, February 5, 2010, http://special.globaltimes.cn/2010-02/503820.html. The report quoted the following article by Zhang Shengjun, who argues that Western media are crucial in spreading the term. And because of this article, Zhang Shengjun was labeled many times as a member of the fifty-cent army. See Zhang Shengjun, "'Wumao Dang' de Maozi Neng Xiazhu Shui?" ("Who Will Be Intimidated by Being Labeled as Fifty-Cent Army?"), *Netease*, January 20, 2010, http://news.163.com/10/0120/16/5TG1UTRM00012GGA.html.

27. As discussed in chapter 4, the nickname often shows an affinity to the Chinese Communist Party because for the voluntary fifty-cent army, it is the Party's yokel (*tu*) nature that lessens the distance between the Party and the people.

28. See "Guanyu 2000 Nian—2005 Nian Renkou Zengzhang de Linglei Jieshi" ("An Alternative Explanation to Population Growth from 2000 to 2005"), *Ccthere*, March 7, 2007, http://www.ccthere.com/article/996699.

29. Andy Yinan Hu, "The Revival of Chinese Leftism Online," *Global Media and Communication* 3, no. 2 (2007): 233–38.

30. The two labels are often intentionally, and sarcastically, misspelled so that they instead mean "elite fly" (精蝇) and "male spider" (公蛛), respectively.

31. These netizens are not necessarily pro-censorship. Even though some of them believe that online expression should be regulated, many simply see the idea of a "free Internet" as utopian. Cynical as it is, the belief is not totally unfounded. Indeed, if the West can justify its control with concerns of terrorism or public security, why can China not censor for the sake of stability or national interest? See Ronald J. Deibert, John Palfrey, Rafal Rohozinski, and Jonathan Zittrain, eds., *Access Controlled: The Shaping of Power, Rights, and Rule in Cyberspace* (Cambridge, MA: MIT Press, 2010), 4–5.

32. The post states, "I remember after the Wenchuan quake, many jumped up shouting that the China Earthquake Administration was incompetent and China was incompetent for failing to forecast the earthquake! They claimed countries like Japan have advanced technologies to forecast earthquakes with high success! They . . . attacked anyone daring enough to say that earthquakes cannot be forecasted! Then what about this earthquake in Japan? . . . I am waiting for their explanations!" See "Dangnian Wenchuan Dizhen Shi Naxie Yubao Dang Ne?? Wo Jintian Lai Dalian le" ("Where Are Those Earthquake Forecasters After the Wenchuan Earthquake? I am Going to Face-Slap Today"), *Cjdby*, March 12, 2011, http://lt.cjdby.net/thread-1090661-1-1.html; see also "Qiguai, Riben de Dizhen Xuejia Zenme Ye Yubao Buliao Dizheng Ah" ("Is It Strange That Japanese Seismologists Could Not Forecast an Earthquake Either?"), *Tianya*, March 11, 2011, http://www.tianya.cn/publicforum/content/free/1/2114334.shtml.

33. "Nanfang Riwu Zhoukan Pinming wei Riben Dizhen Biaoxian Xidi" ("*Southern People Weekly* Is Trying Its Best to Justify Japan's Behaviors After the Earthquake"), *jinbushe.org*, March 31, 2011, http://xinu.jinbushe.org/index.php?doc-view-4740.html; "Nanfang Zhoumo: Di Luan Le, Xin Que Bu Luan, Zai Da Zhenzhai Li Du Riben" (*Southern Weekend*: "The Earth Is a Mess, The Heart Isn't: Read About Japan's Disastrous Earthquake"), *NewSmth*, March 17, 2011, www.newsmth.net/bbstcon.php?board=MilitaryJoke&gid=139829; "Chaoxiao Guizi Dizhen de, Dou Yinggai Qukan Zuixin de Nanfang Renwu Zhoukan" ("All Those Laughing at the Japanese Earthquake Should Read the Latest Issue of *Southern People Weekly*"), *NewSmth*, March 26, 2011, www.newsmth.net/bbstcon.php?board=MilitaryJoke&gid=141451.

34. A star destroyer is a nonexistent powerful space weaponry platform depicted in science fiction. See "Ah, Buyao Piaofu de Haishang Guanchai, Women Yao Jianxing Jian" ("Ah, No Floating Coffin on the Sea, We Want a Star Destroyer"), *Ccthere*, August 9, 2011, http://www.ccthere.com/article/3528859.

35. Calling the Chinese aircraft carrier a coffin was not rare. For instance, see "Meiguo Zhuanjia: Dalu Hangmu Shige 'Tie Guanchai', Taiwan Wuxu Danxin" ("American Experts: Mainland's Aircraft Carrier Is an Iron Coffin, Taiwan Should Not Worry"), *Global Times Online*, October 19, 2011, http://taiwan .huanqiu.com/taiwan_military/2011-10/2096184.html.

36. The slogan, frequently used by Falun Gong media outlets, hinges on the traditional political belief that natural disasters are indicators of heaven's outrage toward an illegitimate or incompetent ruler.

37. Many netizens (and dissidents) attribute the 2008 Sichuan earthquake to the Three Gorges Dam project. See Li Ping, "Sanxia Gongcheng Hui Shengtai, Yuanshi: Daba Jiancheng Dizhen Duo" ("Three Gorges Project Damages the Ecology, Chinese Academy of Sciences Academic: More Earthquakes to Come After Dam Constructed"), *Epoch Times*, June 9, 2011, www.epochtimes.com /gb/11/6/9/n3280858.htm; "1992 Nian Sanxia Shuiku Kaijian shi Fanduipai de Beitan, Rujin Sanxia Zhishang Zhende Yingyan le" ("Sigh of Someone Who Opposed Three Gorges Project in 1992, and Now Worries Are Becoming Real"), *Tianya*, May 21, 2011, www.tianya.cn/publicforum/content/free /1/2169063.shtml.

38. See "Niuyue Dazhen, Tianmie Zhonggong" ("New York Shakes and Heaven Condemns the Chinese Communist Party"), *Mitbbs*, August 23, 2011, www. mitbbs.com/article_t/Joke/31999563.html. Aside from the title, the post has only one line: "It is all caused by the Three Gorges."

39. The term "Kuomintang fans" derides netizens who support the Kuomintang, the nationalist party that ruled China prior to 1949. The "truth discovery party" refers to netizens those who claim to have found historical truths concealed by the Chinese Communist Party. Both groups share the goal of delegitimizing the Party.

40. "Muhaogu," "Liuyan de Cuihuawu: Diaoyu yu Zhengwei" ("Catalyst for Rumor: Fishing and Falsification"), *Jianghuai Chenbao* (*Jianghuai Morning Post*), January 7, 2011.

41. The title of the post is "Gaotie: Qiaoqiao Kaiqi Qunfaxing Dizhi Zhaihai de Mohe" ("High-Speed Rail: Quietly Opening a Pandora's Box of Geological Disasters"). The original post has been deleted. For reference, see "[Taolun] Gaotie: Qiaoqiao Kaiqi Qunfaxing Dizhi Zhaihai de Mohe" ("[Discussion] High-Speed Rail: Quietly Opening a Pandora's Box of Geological Disasters"), *Songshuhui Sciences Forum*, September 12, 2010, http://songshuhui.net/forum /viewthread.php?tid=14993. Even the name of the figure, "Zhang Shimai," is a straightforward parody. *Shimai*, meaning "ten miles," corresponds to *Wanli*; that is, "ten thousand *li*." "*Li*" is a Chinese distance unit of a half-kilometer.

42. "Chuan Zhongguo Dizhi Bushihe Jian Gaotie, Zhongkeyuan Cheng Xi Yaoyan" ("Rumors Say China's Geological Conditions Not Suitable for High-Speed Rail, Chinese Academy of Sciences Refutes Claim as Groundless"), *Netease*, October 31, 2011, http://news.163.com/10/1031/11/6KAR20VS0001124J.html.

43. Zhang Lihua and Zhang Li, "Gaotie 'Zizhu Chuangxin' Zhimi" ("The Myth of the 'Self-Reliant Innovation' of High-Speed Rail"), *Diyi Caijing (China Business Network)*, July 29, 2011, www.yicai.com/news/2011/07/970535.html. The quotation from "Professor Zhang Shimai" was removed from the link after netizens criticized the report. But as of April 20, 2017, the original article with the quotation was still available at http://finance.qq.com/a/20110729/000413.htm.

44. See Xinhuashe Wen Jing's microblog, http://weibo.com/1461830555/xivWBzQ9Z. Upon criticism, the blogger deleted the entry and claimed that the deletion was for "reasons she could not share." Netizens saw the claim as an excuse to cover up her ignorance by depicting herself as a victim of state censorship. For more, see "Jiao Nimen Ya de Hai Diaoyu" ("You Guys Fishing Again!"), *NewSmth*, August 13, 2011, http://www.newsmth.net/bbstcon.php?board=RailWay&gid=719820.

45. It is both interesting and ironic to note that many voluntary fifty-cent army members are not actually in favor of state propaganda. They often join their opponents to criticize CCTV, the *People's Daily*, and other official media outlets, as well as the propaganda system as a whole. In their eyes, propaganda officials are either China's new compradors or completely incompetent, as they have been defeated technically and ideologically by the West and cannot communicate effectively with the people.

46. See "Xiaobaitu de Guangrong Wangshi" ("The Glorious Past of the Little White Bunny"), *Cjdby*, February 24, 2011, http://lt.cjdby.net/thread-1066806-1-1.html.

47. See "Jingli guo Haiwan, Yinhe, Taihai, 58, Zhuangji, Gunzi, Jingli guo BKC Mantianfei de Toushinian de Xiongdi tou TMD Jinlai ya" ("Come in! Brothers Lived Through the Gulf War, Yinhe Incident, Strait Crisis, May 8th Incident, Air Collision, J-10, and the Ten Years When the Sky Was Full of BKC!"), *Cjdby*, January 11, 2011, http://lt.cjdby.net/thread-1048839-5-1.html. The thread title invokes memories of a series of historical events, all of which, except J-10, are considered to be humiliating by nationalist netizens. The Gulf War shocked Chinese by demonstrating the technological gap between China and the United States. The Yinhe Incident was a 1993 Sino–U.S. confrontation in which the U.S. Navy forced the Chinese container ship Yinhe to stop in international waters for three weeks for allegedly carrying chemical weapons to Iran. The United States refused to apologize even after the allegation was proved false following a joint Saudi–U.S. search. The "Strait Crisis" refers to

the 1995–1996 Taiwan Strait Crisis in which U.S. intervention was viewed as violent interference with Chinese sovereignty. The "May 8th Incident" refers to the bombing of the Chinese embassy in Belgrade in 1999 by the U.S. air force. The "air collision" refers to the 2001 collision of a U.S. EP3-E intelligence aircraft and a Chinese J-8II fighter, which resulted in the death of the Chinese pilot. The J-10 is China's domestically made third-generation fighter and symbolizes the nation's achievements in catching up with the latest military technology. "BKC," meaning "white underpants," refers to surrender, because "white underpants" resemble white flags. Conversely, "HKC," meaning "red underpants," refers to self-confidence and pride.

48. One reason netizens liked the lyrics was that they understood all the inside references. Methodologically, this is one instance in which long-term online ethnographic work paid off.

49. See "The Surrounding Gaze," *China Media Project*, January 4, 2011, http://cmp.hku.hk/2011/01/04/9399/; "Zhongguo Hulianwang 16 Nian: Weiguan Gaibian Zhongguo" ("Sixteen Years of China's Internet: Onlooking Changes China"), *Xin Zhoukan (New Weekly)*, no. 22 (November 2010); and Wang Xiuning, "Weibo Zhili Shidai Shida Shijian: Weiguan Gaibian Zhongguo" ("Top Ten Big Events in the Era of Microblog Governance: Onlooking Changes China"), *Shidai Zhoubao (Time Weekly)*, November 29, 2010.

50. For instance, see replies to the post, "Mao Huijian Riben Shehui Dang Weiyuanzhang Zuozuomu Gengshan" ("Mao Meeting Japan Socialist Party Chairman Sasaki Kouzou"), *Ccthere*, April 5, 2009, http://www.ccthere.com/article/2118383.

51. See "[Wenzhai Jizhang] BBC: Yizhang Zhaopian Yong Banian, Yushijujin Hao Bangyang" ("[Account-Keeping Digest]: BBC Uses the Same Photo for Eight Years, Good Example for Keeping Pace with the Times"), *Ccthere*, August 1, 2008, www.ccthere.com/article/1717029.

52. This does not mean that voluntary fifty-cent army members are truly more factually correct or rational than their opponents. But they emphasize facts and rationality in their rhetoric. For an interesting study on how the state and its critics struggle over "facts" in content control, see Li Shao, "The Continuing Authoritarian Resilience Under Internet Development in China: An Observation of Sina Micro-Blog" (master's thesis, University of California, Berkeley, 2012), 1–51, http://oskicat.berkeley.edu/record=b21909970~S1.

53. For an excellent example, see "[Heji] Zhe Neng Diao Shang Shayu Bu?" ("[Compilation] Can This Hook Some Foolish Fish?"), *NewSmth*, September 12, 2011, http://www.newsmth.net/bbstcon.php?board=MilitaryJoke&gid=165373.

54. Sometimes they may ask the original author for permission to post the bait on other forums; other times, they simply do it. Once it becomes popular, it starts to disseminate just as rumors do.

55. "Yige Meiyou Renquan de Guojia, Zao Hangmu You Shenme Yong?" ("For a Country Without Human Rights, What's the Point of Building Aircraft Carriers?"), *Mitbbs*, August 15, 2011, http://www.mitbbs.com/article_t /Military/36266465.html; "Mou Zheng Jianzao Hangmu de Daguo, Ni Minzhu le Ma?" ("The Power That Is Building an Aircraft Carrier, Are You Democratized?"), *Ccthere*, August 15, 2011, http://www.ccthere.com/article/3535578.

56. Members of the voluntary fifty-cent army recognize the dilemma. See "[Heji] Xinzhu Yihou Cai Zhidao, Gen Kandaha de Wanggong Bi, Zhongguo de Gugong Zhishi ge Nongzhuang" ("[Compilation] Didn't Know Until I Believed in God: The Forbidden City Is Only a Farm Compared to Kandahar's Palaces"), *NewSmth*, June 11, 2012, http://www.newsmth.net/bbstcon.php?board=Milit aryJoke&gid=166906.

57. Technically, both Mitbbs and NewSmth are no longer based on any university campus. But both have inherited a huge influence among college students (overseas and domestically, respectively) from their predecessors.

58. For a discussion on the attention economy, see Thomas H. Davenport and John C. Beck, *The Attention Economy: Understanding the New Currency of Business* (Cambridge, MA: Harvard Business School Press, 2001).

59. From 2008 onward, Mitbbs records show that the "Military" board regularly had more than two thousand users online simultaneously during peak hours, whereas "ChinaNews" typically has fewer than two hundred.

60. Both QQ and WeChat are popular social media platforms provided by China's IT giant, Tencent.

61. Cass R. Sunstein, *Republic.com* (Princeton, NJ: Princeton University Press, 2002), 59–60.

62. It is not just the voluntary fifty-cent army communities that form cross-site links. Other groups do so as well. For instance, users on NewSmth's "Reader" board are close to certain groups on douban.com.

63. "Weishenme Yao Zhichi Wuyou Zhixiang?" ("Why We Should Support WYZX?"), *Ccthere*, August 14, 2011, www.ccthere.com/article/3534277. Most Ccthere users do not identify themselves with users of WYZX, as they perceive them as ultra-left.

64. For a brief history of April Media, see "Siyue Licheng" ("The Journey of April Media"), *Siyue Wang (The April Net)*, http://www.m4.cn/about/#m4history. Guancha.cn is an online news and comment aggregator. Its editor in chief and several columnists used to be active on platforms such as Sonicbbs, the predecessor of Sbanzu, and Ccthere, where members of the voluntary fifty-cent army concentrate.

65. For instance, see "Diba Chuzheng Yiyi Zhihou Ziganwu Shengshi Yuanchao JY" ("After the Battle of the Diba Expedition, the Voluntary Fifty-Cent Army Overwhelms the Elites"), *Tianya*, January 22, 2016, http://bbs.tianya.cn/post -worldlook-1619685-1.shtml.

66. Ning Hui and David Wertime, "Is This the New Face of China's Silent Major-ity?" *Foreign Policy*, October 22, 2014; "Sheping: Weigong Zhou Xiaoping Bushi Wangluo Da V de Guangrong" ("Editorial: It Is Not Glorious for Big Vs to Attack Zhou Xiaoping"), *Global Times*, October 17, 2014; Xin Lin, "Liang 'Ziganwu' Zuojia Huo Xi Jinping Dianming Biaoyang Yin Zhengyi" ("Contro-versies Arise from Two 'Voluntary Fifty-Cent' Writers Praised by Xi Jinping"), *Radio Free Asia*, October 17, 2014, www.rfa.org/mandarin/yataibaodao/meiti /xl1-10172014093716.html.

67. Xin, "Liang 'Ziganwu' Zuojia Huo Xi Jinping Dianming Biaoyang Yin Zhengyi."

68. Adam Kramer, Jamie E. Guillory, and Jeffrey T. Hancock, "Experimental Evidence of Massive-Scale Emotional Contagion Through Social Networks," *Proceedings of the National Academy of Sciences* 111, no. 24 (2014): 8788–90.

69. See J. Xie, S. Sreenivasan, G. Korniss, W. Zhang, C. Lim, and B. K. Szymanski, "Social Consensus Through the Influence of Committed Minorities," *Physical Review E* 84, no. 1 (2011): 1–9.

70. See "Xianhua 67: Zidai Ganliang de Wumao" ("Casual Talk Serial 67: The Fifty-Cent Army Carries Its Own Rations"), *Ccthere*, March 1, 2011, www.ccthere.com/article/3304108.

71. Edward Wong, "Pushing China's Limits on Web, if Not on Paper," *New York Times*, November 7, 2011.

72. Eric Harwit and Duncan Clark, "Shaping the Internet in China: Evolution of Political Control Over Network Infrastructure and Content," *Asian Survey* 41, no. 3 (2001): 377–408; Lagerkvist, *After the Internet*; Guobin Yang, "The Internet and Civil Society in China: A Preliminary Assessment," *Journal of Contemporary China* 12, no. 36 (2003): 453–75; Yang, "The Co-evolution of the Internet and Civil Society in China"; Yang, "How Do Chinese Civic Associations Respond to the Internet?"; Yang, *The Power of the Internet in China*; Ashley Esarey and Qiang Xiao, "Political Expression in the Chinese Blogosphere," *Asian Survey* 48, no. 5 (2008): 752–72; Ronald Deibert, John Palfrey, Rafal Rohozinski, and Jonathan Zittrain, eds., *Access Denied: The Practice and Policy of Global Internet Filtering* (Cambridge, MA: MIT Press, 2008); Deibert, Palfrey, Rohozinski, and Zittrain, *Access Controlled*; Ronald Deibert, John Palfrey, Rafal Rohozinski, and Jonathan Zittrain, eds., *Access Contested: Security, Identity, and Resistance in Asian Cyberspace* (Cambridge, MA: MIT Press, 2011); Gary King, Jennifer Pan, and Margaret E. Roberts, "How Censorship in China Allows Government Criticism but Silences Collective Expression," *American Political Science Review* 107, no. 2 (2013): 1–18.

73. For instance, see Eva Bellin, "The Robustness of Authoritarianism in the Middle East: Exceptionalism in Comparative Perspective," *Comparative Politics* 36, no. 2 (2004): 139–57; Yanhua Deng and Kevin J. O'Brien, "Rela-tional Repression in China: Using Social Ties to Demobilize Protesters," *The China Quarterly*, no. 215 (2013): 533–52; Kevin J. O'Brien and Yanhua Deng,

"The Reach of the State: Work Units, Family Ties and 'Harmonious Demo-lition,'" *The China Journal*, no. 74 (2015): 1–17; Ching Kwan Lee and Yong-hong Zhang, "The Power of Instability: Unraveling the Microfoundations of Bargained Authoritarianism in China," *American Journal of Sociology* 118, no. 6 (2013): 1475–1508; Julia Chuang, "China's Rural Land Politics: Bureau-cratic Absorption and the Muting of Rightful Resistance," *The China Quarterly*, no. 219 (2014): 649–69; Rachel E. Stern and Jonathan Hassid, "Amplifying Silence: Uncertainty and Control Parables in Contemporary China," *Compara-tive Political Studies* 45, no. 10 (2012): 1230–54; Andrew Nathan, "Authoritarian Resilience," *Journal of Democracy* 14, no. 1 (2003): 6–17; David L. Shambaugh, *China's Communist Party: Atrophy and Adaptation* (Berkeley: University of California Press, 2008); Suzanne E. Scoggins, "Policing China: Struggles of Law, Order, and Organization for Ground-Level Officers" (Ph.D. dissertation, University of California, Berkeley, 2016).

8. AUTHORITARIAN RESILIENCE ONLINE

1. The topic has attracted the interest of first-rate scholars who have produced several exceptional monographs. See Daniela Stockmann, *Media Commercial-ization and Authoritarian Rule in China* (New York: Cambridge University Press, 2013); Guobin Yang, *The Power of the Internet in China: Citizen Activism Online* (New York: Columbia University Press, 2009); Yongnian Zheng, *Technological Empowerment: The Internet, State, and Society in China* (Stanford, CA: Stanford University Press, 2008); Johan Lagerkvist, *After the Internet, Before Democracy: Competing Norms in Chinese Media and Society* (Bern, Switzerland: Peter Lang, 2010); Haiqing Yu, *Media and Cultural Transformation in China* (Abingdon, Oxon: Routledge, 2009); Paola Voci, *China on Video: Smaller-Screen Realities* (Abingdon, Oxon: Routledge, 2010); Eric Harwit, *China's Telecommunications Revolution* (New York: Oxford University Press, 2008); Jack Linchuan Qiu, *Working-Class Network Society: Communication Technology and the Information Have-Less in Urban China* (Cambridge, MA: MIT Press, 2009).

2. Carolina Vendil Pallin, "Internet Control Through Ownership: The Case of Russia," *Post-Soviet Affairs* 33, no. 1 (2017): 16–33.

3. Zheng, *Technological Empowerment*.

4. Gary King, Jennifer Pan, and Margaret E. Roberts, "How Censorship in China Allows Government Criticism but Silences Collective Expression," *American Political Science Review* 107, no. 2 (2013): 1–18; Peter Lorentzen, "China's Stra-tegic Censorship," *American Journal of Political Science* 58, no. 2 (2014): 402–14.

5. Philip N. Howard and Muzammil M. Hussain, *Democracy's Fourth Wave? Digital Media and the Arab Spring* (Oxford: Oxford University Press, 2013); Philip N. Howard, *The Digital Origins of Dictatorship and Democracy: Information Technology and Political Islam* (New York: Oxford University Press, 2010).

6. Andrew Nathan, "Authoritarian Resilience," *Journal of Democracy* 14, no. 1 (2003): 6–17; David L. Shambaugh, *China's Communist Party: Atrophy and Adaptation* (Berkeley: University of California Press, 2008).

7. Barry Naughton, *The Chinese Economy: Transitions and Growth* (Cambridge, MA: MIT Press, 2007); Gabriella Montinola, Yingyi Qian, and Barry R. Weingast, "Federalism, Chinese Style: The Political Basis for Economic Success in China," *World Politics* 48, no.1 (1995): 50–81; Barry Naughton, *Growing Out of the Plan: Chinese Economic Reform, 1978-1993* (Cambridge: Cambridge University Press, 1996).

8. Dingxin Zhao, "The Mandate of Heaven and Performance Legitimation in Historical and Contemporary China," *American Behavioral Scientist* 53, no. 3 (2009): 416–33; Bruce Gilley and Heike Holbig, "In Search of Legitimacy in Post-Revolutionary China: Bringing Ideology and Governance Back," *GIGA Working Paper*, GIGA Research Programme: Legitimacy and Efficiency of Political Systems, March 8, 2010.

9. Lowell Dittmer and Guoli Liu, *China's Deep Reform: Domestic Politics in Transition* (Lanham, MD: Rowman & Littlefield, 2006); Nathan, "Authoritarian Resilience"; Shambaugh, *China's Communist Party*.

10. Gang Lin, "Leadership Transition, Intra-Party Democracy, and Institution Building in China," *Asian Survey* 44, no. 2 (2004): 255–75; Cheng Li, "Intra-Party Democracy in China: Should We Take It Seriously?" *China Leadership Monitor* 30, no. 3 (2009): 1–14; Neil Jeffrey Diamant, Stanley B. Lubman, and Kevin J. O'Brien, eds., *Engaging the Law in China: State, Society, and Possibilities for Justice* (Stanford, CA: Stanford University Press, 2005); Randall Peerenboom, "A Government of Laws: Democracy, Rule of Law and Administrative Law Reform in the PRC," *Journal of Contemporary China* 34, no. 12 (2003): 45–67; Kevin J. O'Brien and Rongbin Han, "Path to Democracy? Assessing Village Elections in China," *Journal of Contemporary China* 18, no. 60 (2009): 359–78; Kevin J. O'Brien and Lianjiang Li, "Accommodating 'Democracy' in a One-Party State: Introducing Village Elections in China," *The China Quarterly*, no. 162 (2009): 465–89; Kevin J. O'Brien, "Villagers, Elections, and Citizenship in Contemporary China," *Modern China* 27, no. 4 (2001): 407–35; Thomas Heberer and Gunter Schubert, eds., *Regime Legitimacy in Contemporary China: Institutional Change and Stability* (Abingdon, Oxon: Routledge, 2008); Dittmer and Liu, *China's Deep Reform*.

11. Yanhua Deng and Kevin J. O'Brien, "Relational Repression in China: Using Social Ties to Demobilize Protesters," *The China Quarterly*, no. 215 (2013): 533–52; Kevin J. O'Brien and Yanhua Deng, "The Reach of the State: Work Units, Family Ties and 'Harmonious Demolition,'" *The China Journal*, no. 74 (2015): 1–17; Ching Kwan Lee and Yonghong Zhang, "The Power of Instability: Unraveling the Microfoundations of Bargained Authoritarianism in China," *American Journal of Sociology* 118, no. 6 (2013): 1475–1508; Rachel E. Stern and Jonathan Hassid, "Amplifying Silence: Uncertainty and Control Parables in Contemporary China," *Comparative Political Studies* 45, no. 10 (February 23, 2012): 1230–54.

12. Susan II. Whiting and Hua Shao, "Courts and Political Stability: Mediating Rural Land Disputes," in *Resolving Land Disputes in East Asia: Exploring the Limits of Law*, ed. Hualing Fu and John Gillespie (Cambridge: Cambridge University Press, 2014), 222–47; Sarah Biddulph, *The Stability Imperative: Human Rights and Law in China* (Vancouver: UBC Press, 2015); Yue Xie and Wei Shan, "China Struggles to Maintain Stability: Strengthening Its Public Security Apparatus," in *China: Development and Governance*, ed. Gungwu Wang and Yongnian Zheng (Singapore: World Scientific, 2012), 55–62.

13. Yang Su and Xin He, "Street as Courtroom: State Accommodation of Labor Protest in South China," *Law and Society Review* 44, no. 1 (2010): 157–84; Robert P. Weller, "Responsive Authoritarianism and Blind-Eye Governance in China," in *Socialism Vanquished, Socialism Challenged: Eastern Europe and China, 1989-2009*, ed. Nina Bandelj and Dorothy J. Solinger (New York: Oxford University Press, 2012), 83–102; Yongshun Cai, *State and Agents in China: Disciplining Government Officials* (Standford, CA: Stanford University Press, 2014); Kevin J. O'Brien and Lianjiang Li, "Suing the Local State: Administrative Litigation in Rural China," *The China Journal*, no. 51 (2004): 75–96.

14. Kevin J. O'Brien and Lianjiang Li, *Rightful Resistance in Rural China* (New York: Cambridge University Press, 2006); Peter Lorentzen, "Regularizing Rioting: Permitting Public Protest in an Authoritarian Regime," *Quarterly Journal of Political Science* 8, no. 2 (2013): 127–58.

15. Lily L. Tsai, "Constructive Noncompliance," *Comparative Politics* 47, no. 3 (2015): 253–79.

16. Bruce Gilley, "The Limits of Authoritarian Resilience," *Journal of Democracy* 14, no. 1 (2003): 18–26; Minxin Pei, *China's Trapped Transition: The Limits of Developmental Autocracy* (Cambridge, MA: Harvard University Press, 2009).

17. Andrew J. Nathan, "Authoritarian Impermanence," *Journal of Democracy* 20, no. 3 (2009): 37–40.

18. David Shambaugh, "The Coming Chinese Crackup," *Wall Street Journal—Eastern Edition*, March 7, 2015, www.wsj.com/articles/the-coming-chinese-crack-up-1425659198.

19. Cheng Li, "The End of the CCP's Resilient Authoritarianism? A Tripartite Assessment of Shifting Power in China," *The China Quarterly*, no. 211 (2012): 595–623; see also Susan Shirk, *China: Fragile Superpower* (New York: Oxford University Press, 2007).

20. Eric X. Li, "The Life of the Party: The Post-Democratic Future Begins in China," *Foreign Affairs*, December 3, 2012, www.foreignaffairs.com/articles/china/2012-12-03/life-party.

21. Yasheng Huang, "Democratize or Die: Why China's Communists Face Reform or Revolution," *Foreign Affairs*, December 3, 2013, www.foreignaffairs.com/articles/china/2012-12-03/democratize-or-die.

22. King, Pan, and Roberts, "How Censorship in China Allows Government Criticism but Silences Collective Expression."

23. Timothy Brook, *Quelling the People: The Military Suppression of the Beijing Democracy Movement* (Stanford, CA: Stanford University Press, 1998); Sara Meg Davis and Hai Lin, "Demolished: Forced Evictions and the Tenants' Rights Movement in China," *Human Rights Watch* 16, no. 4 (2004); Human Rights Watch, *"Walking on Thin Ice": Control, Intimidation, and Harassment of Lawyers in China* (New York: Human Rights Watch, 2008); Jean-Philippe Béja, "The Massacre's Long Shadow," *Journal of Democracy* 20, no. 3 (2009): 5–16; Dingxin Zhao, *The Power of Tiananmen: State-Society Relations and the 1989 Beijing Student Movement* (Chicago: University of Chicago Press, 2001); Deng and O'Brien, "Relational Repression in China"; O'Brien and Deng, "The Reach of the State"; Stern and Hassid, "Amplifying Silence"; Lee and Zhang, "The Power of Instability"; Julia Chuang, "China's Rural Land Politics: Bureaucratic Absorption and the Muting of Rightful Resistance," *The China Quarterly*, no. 219 (2014): 649–69.

24. Similarly, scholars find that media commercialization may benefit authoritarian rule by allowing the state to increase its responsiveness. See Stockmann, *Media Commercialization and Authoritarian Rule in China*.

25. Lagerkvist, *After the Internet*.

26. Clay Shirky, "The Political Power of Social Media," *Foreign Affairs* 90, no 1 (2011): 28–41.

27. Leon Aron, "Everything You Think You Know About the Collapse of the Soviet Union Is Wrong," *Foreign Policy*, no. 187 (July/August 2011): 64–70.

28. Chinese Communist Youth League Central Committee, *Wangluo Xuanchuanyuan Duiwu Jianshe Tongzhi (Circular on Establishing an Internet Propaganda Troop)*, March 19, 2014; Chinese Communist Youth League Central Committee, *Gongqingtuan Zhongyang Guanyu Guangfan Zujian Qingnian Wangluo Wenming Zhiyuanzhe Duiwu, Shenru Tuijin Qingnian Wangluo Wenming Zhiyuan Xingdong de Tongzhi (Chinese Communist Youth League Central Committee Circular on Widely Establishing a Youth Internet Civilized Volunteers Troop and Heavily Promoting Youth Internet Civilized Action)*, February 16, 2015.

29. Gary King, Jennifer Pan, and Margaret E. Roberts, "How the Chinese Government Fabricates Social Media Posts for Strategic Distraction, not Engaged Argument," *American Political Science Review* 111, no. 3 (2017): 484–501.

30. For a discussion on displays of political loyalty in China, see Victor Shih, " 'Nauseating' Displays of Loyalty: Monitoring the Factional Bargain Through Ideological Campaigns in China," *The Journal of Politics* 70, no. 4 (2008): 1177–92.

31. An Chen, "Capitalist Development, Entrepreneurial Class, and Democratization in China," *Political Science Quarterly* 117, no. 3 (September 15, 2002): 401–22;

Jie Chen and Bruce J. Dickson, *Allies of the State: China's Private Entrepreneurs and Democratic Change* (Cambridge, MA: Harvard University Press, 2010); see also Jie Chen and Chunlong Lu, "Democratization and the Middle Class in China: The Middle Class's Attitudes Toward Democracy," *Political Research Quarterly* 64, no. 3 (September 1, 2011): 705–19.

32. O'Brien and Li, *Rightful Resistance in Rural China*; Daniel Kelliher, "The Chinese Debate Over Village Self-Government," *China Journal* 37 (1997): 63–86; O'Brien and Li, "Accommodating 'Democracy' in a One-Party State."

33. Jonathan Hassid, "Safety Valve or Pressure Cooker? Blogs in Chinese Political Life," *Journal of Communication* 62, no. 2 (2012): 212–30.

34. Lorentzen, "China's Strategic Censorship."

35. See Li Gao and James Stanyer, "Hunting Corrupt Officials Online: The Human Flesh Search Engine and the Search for Justice in China," *Information, Communication & Society* 17, no. 7 (2014): 814–29.

36. Local authorities are often reluctant to respond to the online disclosure of corruption cases unless there is sufficient popular pressure. See Malcolm Moore, "Chinese Internet Vigilantes Bring Down Another Official," *Telegraph*, December 30, 2008, www.telegraph.co.uk/news/worldnews/asia/china/4026624/Chinese-internet-vigilantes-bring-down-another-official.html; Tom Phillips, "Chinese Civil Servant Sacked Over Luxury Wardrobe," *Telegraph*, September 21, 2009, www.telegraph.co.uk/news/worldnews/asia/china/9558179/Chinese-civil-servant-sacked-over-luxury-wardrobe.html.

37. Chinese citizens trust the central government more than local authorities. They also distinguish between the central government's intent and its capacity to make local officials enforce its policies. See Lianjiang Li, "Political Trust and Petitioning in the Chinese Countryside," *Comparative Politics* 40, no. 2 (2008): 209–26; Lianjiang Li, "Political Trust in Rural China," *Modern China* 30, no. 2 (2004): 228–58.

38. Taylor C. Boas, "Weaving the Authoritarian Web: The Control of Internet Use in Nondemocratic Regimes," in *How Revolutionary Was the Digital Revolution? National Responses, Market Transitions, and Global Technology*, ed. John Zysman and Abraham Newman (Stanford, CA: Stanford Business Books, 2006), 361–78.

39. Lagerkvist, *After the Internet*.

40. Zheng, *Technological Empowerment*.

41. Markus Prior, "News vs. Entertainment: How Increasing Media Choice Widens Gaps in Political Knowledge and Turnout," *American Journal of Political Science* 49, no. 3 (2005): 577–92.

42. James Leibold, "Blogging Alone: China, the Internet, and the Democratic Illusion?" *The Journal of Asian Studies* 70, no. 4 (2011): 1027.

43. Jens Damm, "The Internet and the Fragmentation of Chinese Society," *Critical Asian Studies* 39, no. 2 (2007): 290.

44. Guobin Yang, "The Internet and the Rise of a Transnational Chinese Cultural Sphere," *Media, Culture & Society* 24, no. 4 (2003): 469–90; Johan Lagerkvist, *The Internet in China: Unlocking and Containing the Public Sphere* (Lund, Sweden: Lund University Publications, 2007).

45. Wael Ghonim, *Revolution 2.0: The Power of the People Is Greater Than the People in Power: A Memoir* (New York: Houghton Mifflin Harcourt, 2012).

46. Both Johan Lagerkvist and Yong Hu see the Internet as an unfinished "public sphere" with the repressive state being the main obstacle. The findings in this book suggest that independence from the state will not automatically lead to public deliberation. See Lagerkvist, *The Internet in China*; Yong Hu, *Zhongsheng Xuanhua: Wangluo Shidai de Geren Biaoda Yu Gonggong Taolun (The Rising Cacophony: Personal Expression and Public Discussion in the Internet Age)* (Nanning: Guangxi Normal University Press, 2008).

47. Lagerkvist, *After the Internet.*

48. Wenfang Tang, *Populist Authoritarianism: Chinese Political Culture and Regime Sustainability* (New York: Oxford University Press, 2016); Tianjian Shi, "China: Democratic Values Supporting an Authoritarian System," in *How East Asians View Democracy*, ed. Larry Diamond, Andrew J. Nathan, and Doh Chull Shin (New York: Columbia University Press, 2008), 209–37; Tianjian Shi, "Cultural Values and Political Trust: A Comparison of the People's Republic of China and Taiwan," *Comparative Politics* 33, no. 4 (2001): 401–19; Melanie Manion, "Democracy, Community, Trust: The Impact of Elections in Rural China," *Comparative Political Studies* 39, no. 3 (2006): 301–24; Jie Chen, *Popular Political Support in Urban China* (Stanford, CA: Stanford University Press, 2004); Li, "Political Trust in Rural China."

49. See Lagerkvist, *The Internet in China*, 31–33.

50. Jessica Chen Weiss, *Powerful Patriots: Nationalist Protest in China's Foreign Relations* (New York: Oxford University Press, 2014), 229.

51. The anti-establishment trend is nothing new and certainly not unique to China. See John Kenneth Galbraith, *The New Industrial State* (Boston: Houghton Mifflin, 1967), 323–24; William Manchester, *The Glory and the Dream: A Narrative History of America, 1932-1972* (Boston: Little, Brown, 1973), 1083.

52. Jean-Philippe Béja, "The Massacre's Long Shadow," 9.

53. Yanqi Tong and Shaohua Lei, "War of Position and Microblogging in China," *Journal of Contemporary China* 22, no. 80 (2013): 292–311.

54. Lagerkvist, *After the Internet, Before Democracy.*

55. However, the evolution of ideologies and values is twisted, as revealed in the following joke: "In 1949 only socialism could save China; in 1979 only capitalism could save China; in 1989 only China could save socialism; in 2009 only China could save capitalism." See Jonathan Watts, "The World's Most Important Story," *China Dialogue*, April 17, 2012, https://www.chinadialogue.net/article/show/single/en/4876--The-world-s-most-important-story-.

56. Patricia M. Thornton, "Crisis and Governance: SARS and the Resilience of the Chinese Body Politic," *The China Journal*, no. 61 (2009): 23–48.

57. Ching Kwan Lee and Eli Friedman, "China Since Tiananmen: The Labor Movement," *Journal of Democracy* 20, no. 3 (2009): 21. Similarly, O'Brien finds "cooperation across class lines" to be "rare" in rural protest. See Kevin J. O'Brien, "China Since Tiananmen: Rural Protest," *Journal of Democracy* 20, no. 3 (2009): 27.

58. Ian Johnson, "Blogging the Slow-Motion Revolution: An Interview with China's Huang Qi," *New York Review of Books*, February 9, 2013, www.nybooks. com/daily/2013/02/09/blogging-slow-revolution-interview-huang-qi/. The site initially focused on human trafficking and abuse of workers. But then it started to cover Falun Gong and victims of the 1989 democratic movement. Subsequently, the state blocked the site and jailed Huang for "subversion."

59. This partially explains why cases such as the fall of Bo Xilai or other top officials have caused little social turmoil at the grassroots level. After all, fights at the top, no matter whether a result of ideological conflicts or conflicts of interest, are remote to the average person.

60. Ye Bing, "Sima Nan Tan VOA Dianshi Bianlun, Huiying Wangshang Pingyi" ("Sima Nan Talks About Debate at VOA and Responds to Online Comments"), *VOA Chinese*, November 15, 2012, www.voachinese.com/content/sima-nan -voa-debate-remarks-20121115/1546487.html.

61. Shambaugh, *China's Communist Party*, 161.

62. Li, "The End of the CCP's Resilient Authoritarianism?"

63. Lian Yuming and Wu Jianzhong, eds., *Wangluo Xinzheng (New Politics of the Internet)* (Beijing: Zhongguo Shidai Jingji Chubanshe, 2009).

64. Jesper Schlæger, *E-Government in China: Technology, Power and Local Government Reform* (Abingdon, Oxon: Routledge, 2013); Xiang Zhou, "E-Government in China: A Content Analysis of National and Provincial Web Sites," *Journal of Computer-Mediated Communication* 9, no. 4 (June 23, 2006): 0; Jesper Schlæger and Min Jiang, "Official Microblogging and Social Management by Local Governments in China," *China Information* 28, no. 2 (2014): 189–213; Ashley Esarey, "Winning Hearts and Minds? Cadres as Microbloggers in China," *Journal of Current Chinese Affairs* 44, no. 2 (2015): 69–103; Jens Damm, "China's E-Policy: Examples of Local E-Government in Guangdong and Fujian," in *Chinese Cyberspaces: Technological Changes and Political Effects*, ed. Jens Damm and Simona Thomas (London: Routledge, 2006).

65. "Premier Calls for Accelerating Political Reform," *People's Daily Online*, August 23, 2010, http://english.peopledaily.com.cn/90001/90776/90785/7113368.html.

66. Ronald Deibert, John Palfrey, Rafal Rohozinski, and Jonathan Zittrain, eds., *Access Denied: The Practice and Policy of Global Internet Filtering* (Cambridge, MA: MIT Press, 2008); Ronald J. Deibert, John Palfrey, Rafal Rohozinski, and Jonathan Zittrain, eds., *Access Controlled: The Shaping of Power, Rights, and Rule*

in Cyberspace (Cambridge, MA: MIT Press, 2010); Ronald Deibert, John Palfrey, Rafal Rohozinski, and Jonathan Zittrain, eds., *Access Contested: Security, Identity, and Resistance in Asian Cyberspace* (Cambridge, MA: MIT Press, 2011).

67. Ron Deibert, "Cyberspace Under Siege," *Journal of Democracy* 26, no. 3 (2015): 64–78.

68. Katie Davis, "Revealed: Confessions of a Kremlin Troll," *Moscow Times*, April 18, 2017, https://themoscowtimes.com/articles/revealed-confessions -of-a-kremlin-troll-57754.

69. Richard Rose, William Mishler, and Neil Munro, *Popular Support for an Undemocratic Regime: The Changing Views of Russians* (Cambridge: Cambridge University Press, 2011).

70. Deibert, "Cyberspace Under Siege." The *Journal of Democracy* published a special issue on the authoritarian resurgence in April 2015.

71. Robert D. Putnam, *Making Democracy Work: Civic Traditions in Modern Italy* (Princeton, NJ: Princeton University Press, 1993) Robert D. Putnam, *Bowling Alone: The Collapse and Revival of American Community* (New York: Simon and Schuster, 2001); Alexis de Tocqueville, *Democracy in America*, vol. 2 (New York: Vintage, 1840), 98–99.

72. Juan J. Linz and Alfred Stepan, *Problems of Democratic Transition and Consolidation: Southern Europe, South America, and Post-Communist Europe* (Baltimore, MD: Johns Hopkins University Press, 1996); Andreas Schedler, "What Is Democratic Consolidation?" *Journal of Democracy* 9, no. 2 (1998): 91–107; Larry Diamond and Leonardo Morlino, "Assessing the Quality of Democracy" (Baltimore, MD: Johns Hopkins University Press, 2005).

BIBLIOGRAPHY

"Ai Weiwei China Tax Bill Paid by Supporters." *BBC*, November 7, 2011. www.bbc
.co.uk/news/world-asia-pacific-15616576.

Almond, Gabriel A., and Sidney Verba. *The Civic Culture: Political Attitudes and Democracy in Five Nations*. Princeton, NJ: Princeton University Press, 1963.

Amies, Nick. "Europe Praises, China Condemns Liu Xiaobo Choice for Nobel
Peace Prize." *Deutsche Welle*, October 8, 2010. www.dw-world.de/dw/article
/0,,6093118,00.html.

Anceschi, Luca. "The Persistence of Media Control under Consolidated Authoritarianism: Containing Kazakhstan's Digital Media." *Demokratizatsiya* 23, no. 3
(2015): 277–95.

Anderson, Lisa. "Demystifying the Arab Spring." *Foreign Affairs* 90, no. 3 (2011): 2–7.

Aron, Leon. "Everything You Think You Know About the Collapse of the Soviet
Union Is Wrong." *Foreign Policy*, (July/August 2011): 64–70.

Bandurski, David. "China's Guerrilla War for the Web." *Far Eastern Economic Review*
171, no. 6 (2008): 41–44.

Bandurski, David, and Martin Hala, eds. *Investigative Journalism in China: Eight Cases
in Chinese Watchdog Journalism*. Hong Kong: Hong Kong University Press, 2010.

Bao, Qian. "Shanghai Shizhengfu Jieru Diaoyu Zhifa Shijian, Lüshi Shenqing Xinxi
Gongkai" ("Shanghai Municipal Government Steps in in Illegal Cab Entrapment
Case, and Lawyer Asks for Information Disclosure"). *Legal Daily (Fazhi Ribao)*,
October 19, 2009.

Bao, Ying. "Xin Diannao Xuzhuang Guolü Shangwang Ruanjian" ("Filtering Software to Be Installed on New Computers"). *Xin Jingbao (Beijing News)*, June 10,
2009.

Barboza, David. "Billions in Hidden Riches for Family of Chinese Leader." *New York
Times*, October 26, 2012.

———. "China Leader Encourages Criticism of Government." *New York Times*, January 27, 2011.

Barmé, Geremie R. "A View on Ai Weiwei's Exit." *China Heritage Quarterly*, no. 26 (2011). www.chinaheritagequarterly.org/articles.php?searchterm=026_aiweiwei .inc&issue=026.

Béja, Jean-Philippe. "The Massacre's Long Shadow." *Journal of Democracy* 20, no. 3 (2009): 5–16.

Bellin, Eva. "The Robustness of Authoritarianism in the Middle East: Exceptionalism in Comparative Perspective." *Comparative Politics* 36, no. 2 (2004): 139–57.

Bennett, W. Lance, and Alexandra Segerberg. *The Logic of Connective Action: Digital Media and the Personalization of Contentious Politics.* New York: Cambridge University Press, 2013.

Berman, Sheri. "Civil Society and the Collapse of the Weimar Republic." *World Politics* 49, no. 3 (1997): 401–29.

Bernstein, Thomas. P, and Xiaobo Lü. *Taxation Without Representation in Rural China.* New York: Cambridge University Press, 2003.

Biddulph, Sarah. *The Stability Imperative: Human Rights and Law in China.* Vancouver: UBC Press, 2015.

Bimber, Bruce. "Information and Political Engagement in America: The Search for Effects of Information Technology at the Individual Level." *Political Research Quarterly* 54, no. 1 (2001): 53–67.

Blecher, Marc, and Vivienne Shue. "Into Leather: State-Led Development and the Private Sector in Xinji." *The China Quarterly*, no. 166 (2001): 368–93.

Boas, Taylor C. "Weaving the Authoritarian Web: The Control of Internet Use in Nondemocratic Regimes." In *How Revolutionary Was the Digital Revolution? National Responses, Market Transitions, and Global Technology*, edited by John Zysman and Abraham Newman, 361–78. Stanford, CA: Stanford Business Books, 2006.

"Boke Shimingzhi Anran Tuichang, Wangluo Guanzhi Yiyou Fansi" ("Real-Name Registration of Blog Services Abandoned, We Need Reflections on Internet Control"). *Nanfang Dushibao (Southern Metropolis Daily)*, May 25, 2007.

Brady, Anne-Marie. *Marketing Dictatorship: Propaganda and Thought Work in Contemporary China.* Lanham, MD: Rowman & Littlefield, 2008.

Branigan, Tania. "China's Jasmine Revolution: Police but No Protesters Line Streets of Beijing." *Guardian*, February 27, 2011.

Bremmer, Ian. "Why China's Leaders Fear the Teletubbies." *Foreign Policy*, June 13, 2012. http://eurasia.foreignpolicy.com/posts/2012/06/13/why_china_s_leaders _fear_the_teletubbies.

Brook, Timothy. *Quelling the People: The Military Suppression of the Beijing Democracy Movement.* Stanford, CA: Stanford University Press, 1998.

Buckley, Chris. "China Demotes Editor After Obama Interview: Sources." *Reuters*, December 13, 2009. www.reuters.com/article/2009/12/13/us-obama-china -censorship-idUSTRE5BC0BM20091213.

Buckley, Chris. "Crackdown on Bloggers Is Mounted by China." *New York Times*, September 11, 2013.

Cahill, Tom. "Pro-Clinton Super PAC Spending $1 Million Hiring Online Trolls." *U.S. Uncut*, April 21, 2016. http://usuncut.com/politics/clinton-super-pac-busted/.

Cai, Xiaoquan. "Suqian 26 Wangpingyuan Jin Shanggang" ("Twenty-six Internet Commentators in Position Today"). *Yangzi Wanbao (Yangtse Evening Post)*, April 29, 2005.

Cai, Yongshun. *Collective Resistance in China: Why Popular Protests Succeed or Fail.* Stanford, CA: Stanford University Press, 2010.

——. "Disruptive Collective Action in the Reform Era." In *Popular Protest in China*, edited by Kevin J. O'Brien, 163–78. Cambridge, MA: Harvard University Press, 2008.

——. *State and Agents in China: Disciplining Government Officials.* Stanford, CA: Stanford University Press, 2014.

"Can't We All Just Get It On?" *Economist* 404, no. 8803 (2012): 54.

Cao, Guoxing. "Guanzhong Kuibao: Zhanggongqu Wangxinban Xinxiang Baoguang Wumao Yunzuo Jizhi" ("Zhanggong District Cyberspace Administration Email Leak Reveals How the 'Fifty-Cent Army' Operates"). *Radio France Internationale*, May 12, 2014. www.chinese.rfi.fr/中国/20141205-管中窥豹：章贡区网信办信箱曝光五毛运作机制.

Castells, Manuel. "A Network Theory of Power." *International Journal of Communication* 5, no. 1 (2011): 773–87.

——. *Communication Power.* Oxford: Oxford University Press, 2009.

Central Propaganda Department, Ministry of Information Industry, State Council Information Office, Ministry of Education, Ministry of Culture, Ministry of Health, Ministry of Public Security, Ministry of State Security, Ministry of Commerce, State Administration of Radio, Film, and Television, General Administration of Press and Publication, State Secrets Bureau, State Administration for Industry and Commerce, China Food and Drug Administration, Chinese Academy of Sciences, and General Staff Department Communication Department. *Hulian Wangzhan Guanli Xietiao Gongzuo Fangan (Work Program for the Coordination of Internet Website Management)*. February 17, 2006.

Chang, Meng. "Xi's Cartoon Depiction Breaks Taboo." *Global Times*, February 20, 2014. www.globaltimes.cn/content/843632.shtml.

Chase, Michael S., and James C. Mulvenon. *You've Got Dissent.* Santa Monica, CA: RAND, 2002.

Chen, An. "Capitalist Development, Entrepreneurial Class, and Democratization in China." *Political Science Quarterly* 117, no. 3 (2002): 401–22.

Chen, Hanci. "Xinwen Chunban Zongshu Zaici Qiangdiao Wangluo Youxi Shenpiquan Guishu" ("The General Administration of Press and Publication Reasserts Its Authority of Online Gaming Approval"). *Diyi Caijing Ribao (China Business News)*, October 12, 2009.

Chen, Jie. *Popular Political Support in Urban China*. Stanford, CA: Stanford University Press, 2004.

Chen, Jie, and Bruce J. Dickson. *Allies of the State: China's Private Entrepreneurs and Democratic Change*. Cambridge, MA: Harvard University Press, 2010.

Chen, Jie, and Chunlong Lu. "Democratization and the Middle Class in China: The Middle Class's Attitudes Toward Democracy." *Political Research Quarterly* 64, no. 3 (September 1, 2011): 705–19.

Chen, Liangqiu. "Guifan Yindao Liucheng, Zhuangda Wangping Duiwu" ("Standardize Opinion Guidance Procedures and Strengthen the Internet Commentating Troop"). *Zhongguo Xinwen Chuban Bao (China Press and Publishing Journal)*, June 24, 2008.

Cheng, Shuwen. "Woguo Wangluo Fanfu Chuxian 'Duanyashi Jiangwen'" ("Online Anti-corruption Cools Down Dramatically"). *Nanfang Dushibao (Southern Metropolis Daily)*, December 26, 2014.

Chen, Xuedong. "Liang Buwei Boyi Hulianwang Dianshi" ("The Struggle Between the State Administration of Radio, Film, and Television and the Ministry of Industry and Information Technology Over Internet TV). *Xin Kuaibao (New Express News)*, August 27, 2009.

Chen, Xueyi, and Tianjian Shi. "Media Effects on Political Confidence and Trust in the People's Republic of China in the Post-Tiananmen Period." *East Asia* 19, no. 3 (2001): 84–118.

China Internet Network Information Center. *Di 39 Ci Zhongguo Hulian Wangluo Fazhan Zhuangkuang Tongji Baogao (The 39th Statistical Report on Internet Development in China)*. January 22, 2017.

China Media Project. "The Surrounding Gaze." Accessed November 14, 2011. http://cmp.hku.hk/2011/01/04/9399/.

Chinese Communist Party Hefei Municipal Committee Propaganda Department. *Guanyu Nanchang, Changsha, Zhengzhou Xuanchuan Wenhua Gongzuo de Kaocha Baogao (Research Report on the Propaganda and Cultural Work of Nanchang, Changshang, and Zhengzhou)*. CCP Hefei Municipal Committee Propaganda Department, May 24, 2006. http://swxcb.hefei.gov.cn/ContentDir/20065/24124915293.shtml.

Chinese Communist Party Hubei Provincial Commission for Discipline Inspection. "Zhongyang Jiwei Gaodu Zhongshi Wangluo Pinglun Gongzuo" ("Central Commission for Discipline Inspection Attaches Much Importance to Online Commentary Work"). *CCP Hubei Provincial Commission for Discipline Inspection*, January 1, 2005. www.hbjwjc.gov.cn/wzlm/info/18944.htm.

Chinese Communist Party Zhengding County Committee Propaganda Department. "Guanyu Zhaopin Hulianwang Wangluo Xuanchuan Pinglunyuan de Tongzhi" ("Circular on Recruiting Internet Commentators"). June 18, 2009. www.zd.gov.cn/ReadNews.asp?NewsID=12226&BigClassName=%B9%AB%B8%E6%C0%B8&SmallClassName=%B9%AB%B8%E6%C0%B8&SpecialID=0.

Chinese Communist Youth League Central Committee. "Gongqingtuan Zhongyang Guanyu Guangfan Zujian Qingnian Wangluo Wenming Zhiyuanzhe Duiwu, Shenru Tuijin Qingnian Wangluo Wenming Zhiyuan Xingdong de Tongzhi" ("Chinese Communist Youth League Central Committee Circular on Widely Establishing a Youth Internet Civilized Volunteers Troop and Heavily Promoting Youth Internet Civilized Action"). February 16, 2015.

Chinese Communist Youth League Central Committee Office. "Wangluo Xuanchuanyuan Duiwu Jianshe Tongzhi" ("Circular on Establishing an Internet Propaganda Troop"). March 19, 2014.

Christensen, Henrik Serup. "Political Activities on the Internet: Slacktivism or Political Participation by Other Means?" *First Monday* 16, no. 2 (2011). http://firstmonday.org/article/view/3336/2767.

"Chuan Zhongguo Dizhi Bushihe Jian Gaotie, Zhongkeyuan Cheng Xi Yaoyan" ("Rumors Say China's Geological Conditions Not Suitable for High-Speed Rail, Chinese Academy of Sciences Refutes as Groundless"). *Netease*, October 31, 2011. http://news.163.com/10/1031/11/6KAR20VS0001124J.html.

Chuang, Julia. "China's Rural Land Politics: Bureaucratic Absorption and the Muting of Rightful Resistance." *The China Quarterly*, no. 219 (2014): 649–69.

Clinton, Hillary Rodham. "Remarks on Internet Freedom." *U.S. Department of State*, January 21, 2010. https://2009-2017.state.gov/secretary/20092013clinton/rm/2010/01/135519.htm.

Cohen, Michael D., James G. March, and Johan P. Olsen. "A Garbage Can Model of Organizational Choice." *Administrative Science Quarterly* 17, no. 1 (1972): 1–25.

"Comment on False Web Postings Regarding RAND Work on China." *RAND Corporation*, October 4, 2010 (revised January 20, 2012). www.rand.org/news/announcements/2012/01/20.html.

Crandall, Jedidiah R., Masashi Crete-Nishihata, Jeffrey Knockel, Sarah McKune, Adam Senft, Diana Tseng, and Greg Wiseman. "Chat Program Censorship and Surveillance in China: Tracking TOM-Skype and Sina UC." *First Monday* 18, no. 7 (2013). http://firstmonday.org/ojs/index.php/fm/article/view/4628/3727.

Cui, Qingxin. "Woguo Yi Chubu Jianli Hulianwang Jichu Guanli Zhidu" ("Our Country Has Established a Basic Internet Regulation System"). *Xinhua Net*, May 2, 2010. http://news.xinhuanet.com/fortune/2010-05/02/c_1269514.htm.

Cyberspace Administration of China, and Ministry of Industry and Information Technology. *Hulianwang Xinxi Fuwu Guanli Banfa (Xiuding Caoan Zhengqiu Yijian Gao) (Administrative Measures on Internet Information Services: Revised Version for Public Comment)*. June 7, 2012.

Dahlberg, Lincoln. "Computer-Mediated Communication and the Public Sphere: A Critical Analysis." *Journal of Computer-Mediated Communication* 7, no. 1 (2001): 0.

——. "The Internet and Democratic Discourse: Exploring the Prospects of Online Deliberative Forums Extending the Public Sphere." *Information, Communication & Society* 4, no. 4 (2001): 615–33.

——. "Rethinking the Fragmentation of the Cyberpublic: From Consensus to Contestation." *New Media & Society* 9, no. 5 (2007): 827–47.

"Dali Jiaqiang Woguo Hulianwang Meiti Jianshe" ("Strengthen the Construction of Our Internet Media"). *People's Daily*, August 9, 2000.

Damm, Jens. "China's E-Policy: Examples of Local E-Government in Guangdong and Fujian." In *Chinese Cyberspaces: Technological Changes and Political Effects*, edited by Jens Damm and Simona Thomas. Abingdon, Oxon: Routledge, 2006.

——. "The Internet and the Fragmentation of Chinese Society." *Critical Asian Studies* 39, no. 2 (2007): 273–94.

"'Dangxiao Zhendi' Wangpingyuan Guanli Banfa" ("Regulations on the Internet Commentator Management of the 'Party School Front'"). *Hengyang Party Building Net*, January 8, 2010. http://dx.hydjnet.gov.cn/News_View.asp?NewsID=28290

Dann, Gary Elijah, and Neil Haddow. "Just Doing Business or Doing Just Business: Google, Microsoft, Yahoo! and the Business of Censoring China's Internet." *Journal of Business Ethics* 79, no. 3 (2008): 219–34.

Davenport, Thomas H., and John C. Beck. *The Attention Economy: Understanding the New Currency of Business*. Cambridge, MA: Harvard Business School Press, 2001.

Davis, Katie. "Revealed: Confessions of a Kremlin Troll." *Moscow Times*, April 18, 2017. https://themoscowtimes.com/articles/revealed-confessions-of-a-kremlin-troll-57754.

Davis, Sara Meg, and Hai Lin. "Demolished: Forced Evictions and the Tenants' Rights Movement in China." *Human Rights Watch* 16, no. 4 (2004).

Dawkins, Richard. *The Selfish Gene*. Oxford: Oxford University Press, 1989.

Deibert, Ron. "Cyberspace Under Siege." *Journal of Democracy* 26, no. 3 (2015): 64–78.

Deibert, Ronald, John Palfrey, Rafal Rohozinski, and Jonathan Zittrain. *Access Contested: Security, Identity, and Resistance in Asian Cyberspace*. Cambridge, MA: MIT Press, 2011.

——. *Access Controlled: The Shaping of Power, Rights, and Rule in Cyberspace*. Cambridge, MA: MIT Press, 2010.

——. *Access Denied: The Practice and Policy of Global Internet Filtering*. Cambridge, MA: MIT Press, 2008.

Delli Carpini, Michael X. "The Political Effects of Entertainment Media." In *The Oxford Handbook of Political Communication*, edited by Kate Kenski and Kathleen Hall Jamieson. New York: Oxford University Press, 2014.

Demick, Barbara. "Protests in China Over Local Grievances Surge, and Get a Hearing." *Los Angeles Times*, October 8, 2011.

Deng, Yanhua, and Kevin J. O'Brien. "Relational Repression in China: Using Social Ties to Demobilize Protesters." *The China Quarterly*, no. 215 (2013): 533–52.

Diamant, Neil Jeffrey, Stanley B. Lubman, and Kevin J. O'Brien, eds. *Engaging the Law in China: State, Society, and Possibilities for Justice*. Stanford, CA: Stanford University Press, 2005.

Diamond, Larry, and Leonardo Morlino. "Assessing the Quality of Democracy." Baltimore, MD: Johns Hopkins University Press, 2005.

Dickson, Bruce J. *The Dictator's Dilemma: The Chinese Communist Party's Strategy for Survival.* New York: Oxford University Press, 2016.

——. *Red Capitalists in China: The Party, Private Entrepreneurs, and Prospects for Political Change.* Cambridge: Cambridge University Press, 2003.

Ding, Li, and Zheng Lingyu. "Diaoyudao Qingtian Bairi Qi, Zhongguo Meiti Nanti, Zaojiazhe Aipi Daoqian" ("The Flag of the Republic of China Over Diaoyu Islands Poses a Dilemma for Chinese Media, and Forgers Apologize After Being Criticized"). *VOA Chinese,* August 20, 2012. www.voachinese.com/content/hk _newspaper_20120820/1491305.html.

Dingtao No. 1 Middle School. "Guanyu Zujian Dingtao Yizhong Wangluo Pinglu-nyuan Duiwu de Yijian" ("Opinions on Establishing an Internet Commentator Troop at Dingtao No. 1 Middle School"). December 21, 2009. www.sddtyz.cn /web/pro/detail.php?tid=1450

Dittmer, Lowell, and Guoli Liu. *China's Deep Reform: Domestic Politics in Transition.* Lanham, MD: Rowman & Littlefield, 2006.

Durkheim, Emile. "The Cultural Logic of Collective Representations." In *Social Theory: The Multicultural, Global, and Classic Readings,* edited by Charles Lemert, 98–108. Westview Press, 1993.

Edin, Maria. "Remaking the Communist Party-State: The Cadre Responsibility System at the Local Level in China." *China: An International Journal* 1, no. 1 (2003): 1–15.

——. "State Capacity and Local Agent Control in China: CCP Cadre Management from a Township Perspective." *The China Quarterly,* no. 173 (2003): 35–52.

Eltantawy, Nahed, and Julie B. Wiest. "Social Media in the Egyptian Revolution: Reconsidering Resource Mobilization Theory." *International Journal of Communication* 5 (2011): 1207–24.

Enstad, Nan. *Ladies of Labor, Girls of Adventure: Working Women, Popular Culture, and Labor Politics at the Turn of the Twentieth Century.* New York: Columbia University Press, 1999.

Epstein, Gady. "A Revolution Is Not a Tweetup: Jasmine Revolution and the Limits of China's Internet." *Forbes,* February 22, 2011.

Epstein, Gady, and Lin Yang. "Sina Weibo." *Forbes Asia* 7, no. 3 (March 2011): 56–60.

Erikson, Andrew S., and Andrew R. Wilson. "China's Aircraft Carrier Dilemma." *Naval War College Review* 59, no. 4 (2006): 13–45.

Esarey, Ashley. "Cornering the Market: State Strategies for Controlling China's Commercial Media." *Asian Perspective* 29, no. 4 (2005):37–83.

——. "Winning Hearts and Minds? Cadres as Microbloggers in China." *Journal of Current Chinese Affairs* 44, no. 2 (2015): 69–103.

Esarey, Ashley, and Qiang Xiao. "Political Expression in the Chinese Blogosphere." *Asian Survey* 48, no. 5 (2008): 752–72.

Faison, Seth. "E-Mail to U.S. Lands Chinese Internet Entrepreneur in Jail." *New York Times*, January 21, 1999.

Fallows, James. "Arab Spring, Chinese Winter." *Atlantic*, September 2011.

Florini, Ann, Hairong Lai, and Yeling Tan. *China Experiments: From Local Innovations to National Reform*. Washington, DC: Brookings Institution, 2012.

Franklin, Bob. *Packaging Politics: Political Communications in Britain's Media Democracy*. 2nd ed. London: Bloomsbury Academic, 2004.

"Freedom on the Net: A Global Assessment of Internet and Digital Media." *Freedom House*, April 1, 2009. https://freedomhouse.org/sites/default/files/Freedom %20OnThe%20Net_Full%20Report.pdf.

Fu, King Wa, Chung Hong Chan, and Michael Chau. "Assessing Censorship on Microblogs in China: Discriminatory Keyword Analysis and the Real-Name Registration Policy." *IEEE Internet Computing* 17, no. 3 (2013): 42–50.

Fuyang Public Health Bureau. "Woshi Weishengju Jianzhi Wangpingyuan Shang-gang" ("Part-Time Internet Commentators at the Public Health Bureau in Position"). *Fuyang Public Health Bureau Website*, September 7, 2009. http://wsj .fuyang.gov.cn/zwdt_8848/20090907226641.shtml.

Galbraith, John Kenneth. *The New Industrial State*. Boston: Houghton Mifflin, 1967.

"Gansu Jiang Jian 650 Ren Wangping Duiwu Tixi" ("Gansu Province to Set Up an Internet Commentator Troop with Six Hundred Members"). *Nanfang Dushi Bao (Southern Metropolis Daily)*, January 20, 2010.

Gao, Jie. "Political Rationality vs. Technical Rationality in China's Target-Based Performance Measurement System: The Case of Social Stability Maintenance." *Policy and Society* 34, no. 1 (2015): 37–48.

Gao, Li, and James Stanyer. "Hunting Corrupt Officials Online: The Human Flesh Search Engine and the Search for Justice in China." *Information, Communication & Society* 17, no. 7 (2014): 814–29.

Geddes, Barbara, and John Zaller. "Sources of Popular Support for Authoritarian Regimes." *American Journal of Political Science* 33, no. 2 (1989): 319–47.

General Administration of Press and Publication, and Ministry of Information Industry. *Hulianwang Chuban Guanli Zanxing Guiding (Provisional Regulations on Administration of Internet Publications)*. June 27, 2002.

Ghonim, Wael. *Revolution 2.0: The Power of the People Is Greater Than the People in Power: A Memoir*. New York: Houghton Mifflin Harcourt, 2012.

Gilley, Bruce. "The Limits of Authoritarian Resilience." *Journal of Democracy* 14, no. 1 (2003): 18–26.

Gilley, Bruce, and Heike Holbig. "In Search of Legitimacy in Post-Revolutionary China: Bringing Ideology and Governance Back." *GIGA Working Paper*. GIGA Research Programme: Legitimacy and Efficiency of Political Systems. March 8, 2010.

Gitlin, Todd. *How the Torrent of Images and Sounds Overwhelms Our Lives*. New York: Henry Holt, 2007.

——. "Public Sphere or Public Sphericules?" In *Media, Ritual and Identity*, edited by Tamar Liebes and James Curran, 168–174. London: Routledge, 1998.

Goldsmith, Jack, and Tim Wu. *Who Controls the Internet? Illusions of a Borderless World*. New York: Oxford University Press, 2006.

Gong, Jian. "Jianchi Sanjiehe, Zujian Wangluo Pinglunyuan Duiwu" ("Stick to the Three-in-One Combination and Establish a Troop of Online Commentators"). In *Changsha Yearbook 2006*, edited by Changsha Municipal Office of Local Chronicles, 55–56. Beijing: Fangzhi Chubanshe, 2006.

"Gongxin Buzhang Fouren Fengsha Geren Wangzhan, Cheng Zhili Yao Jiada Lidu" ("Ministry of Industry and Information Technology Minister Denied Banning Personal Websites, Asserts that Rectification Will Be Strengthened"). *Netease*, March 9, 2010. http://news.163.com/10/0309/09/61ASVNQK000146BD.html.

Gries, Peter. "Chinese Nationalism: Challenging the State?" *Current History* 104, no. 683 (2005): 251–56.

Guo, Shaohua. "Ruled by Attention: A Case Study of Professional Digital Attention Agents at Sina.com and the Chinese Blogosphere." *International Journal of Cultural Studies* 19, no. 4 (2016): 407–23.

"Guojia Hulianwang Xinxi Bangongshi Sheli" ("The Cyberspace Administration of China Is Set Up"). *Xinhua Net*, May 5, 2011. http://news.xinhuanet.com/it/2011-05/04/c_121376056.htm.

"Guoxinban Fuzeren: Liyong Hulianwang Zaoyao Chuanyao shi Weifa Xingwei" ("Cyberspace Administration of China Officials: Using the Internet to Fabricate and Spread Rumors Is Against the Law"). *Xinhua Net*, April 12, 2012. http://news.xinhuanet.com/politics/2012-04/12/c_111772774.htm.

Hail, Henry Chiui. "Patriotism Abroad: Overseas Chinese Students' Encounters with Criticisms of China." *Journal of Studies in International Education* 19, no. 4 (January 12, 2015): 311–26.

Hall, Stuart. "Cultural Studies: Two Paradigms." *Media, Culture & Society* 2, no. 1 (1980): 57–72.

Han, Rongbin. "Defending the Authoritarian Regime Online: China's 'Voluntary Fifty-Cent Army.'" *The China Quarterly*, no. 224 (2015): 1006–25.

——. "Manufacturing Consent in Cyberspace: China's 'Fifty-Cent Army.'" *Journal of Current Chinese Affairs* 44, no. 2 (2015): 105–34.

——. "Withering Gongzhi: Cyber Criticism of Chinese Public Intellectuals." *International Journal of Communication*, forthcoming.

Hartford, Kathleen. "Dear Mayor: Online Communications with Local Governments in Hangzhou and Nanjing." *China Information* 19, no. 2 (2005): 217–60.

Harwit, Eric. *China's Telecommunications Revolution*. New York: Oxford University Press, 2008.

Harwit, Eric, and Duncan Clark. "Shaping the Internet in China: Evolution of Political Control Over Network Infrastructure and Content." *Asian Survey* 41, no. 3 (2001): 377–408.

Hassid, Jonathan. *China's Unruly Journalists: How Committed Professionals Are Changing the People's Republic*. New York: Routledge, 2015.

——. "Safety Valve or Pressure Cooker? Blogs in Chinese Political Life." *Journal of Communication* 62, no. 2 (2012): 212–30.

Hassid, Jonathan, and Wanning Sun. "Stability Maintenance and Chinese Media: Beyond Political Communication?" *Journal of Current Chinese Affairs* 44, no. 2 (2015): 3–15.

Hauben, Ronda, Jay Hauben, Werner Zorn, Kilnam Chon, and Anders Ekeland. "The Origin and Early Development of the Internet and of the Netizen: Their Impact on Science and Society." In *Past, Present and Future of Research in the Information Society*, edited by Wesley Shrum, Keith R. Benson, Wiebe E. Bijker, and Klaus Brunnstein, 47–62. Boston: Springer, 2007.

He, Qinglian. *The Fog of Censorship: Media Control in China*. New York: Human Rights in China, 2008.

——. " 'Renmin Luntan' Diaocha Cuihuile Beijing de Zhidu Zixin" ("People's Forum Survey Defeats Beijing's Confidence in System"). *VOA Chinese*, April 15, 2013. www.voachinese.com/content/public-opinion-survey-20130415/1641814.html.

Heberer, Thomas, and Gunter Schubert, eds. *Regime Legitimacy in Contemporary China: Institutional Change and Stability*. Abingdon, Oxon: Routledge, 2008.

Herold, David Kurt, and Peter Marolt. "Online Society in China: Creating, Celebrating, and Instrumentalising the Online Carnival." *Media, Culture and Social Change in Asia*. New York: Routledge, 2011.

Heydemann, Steven, and Reinoud Leenders. "Authoritarian Learning and Authoritarian Resilience: Regime Responses to the 'Arab Awakening.' " *Globalizations* 8, no. 5 (2011): 647–53.

Hill, Kevin A., and John E. Hughes. *Cyberpolitics: Citizen Activism in the Age of the Internet*. Lanham, MD: Rowman & Littlefield, 1998.

Hindman, Matthew. *The Myth of Digital Democracy*. Princeton, NJ: Princeton University Press, 2009.

Hirschman, Albert O. *Exit, Voice, and Loyalty: Responses to Decline in Firms, Organizations, and States*. Cambridge, MA: Harvard University Press, 1970.

Hong, Sha. "Liu Xiaobo 'Ruanjin' Bairi yu Qizi Dierci Jianmian" ("After One-Hundred-Day House Arrest, Liu Xiaobo Sees His Wife Again"). *Sina North America*, March 20, 2009. http://news.sina.com/ch/dwworld/102-000-101-105/2009-03-20/04163726082.html.

Hong, Yanqing. "Woqu Shouci Zuzhi Wangpingyuan Peixun" ("Our District Organizes Its First Internet Commentator Training"). *Jinri Jiangdong (Jiangdong Today)*, October 27, 2009.

Horkheimer, Max, and Theodor W. Adorno. *Dialectic of Enlightenment: Philosophical Fragments*. Edited by Gunzelin Schmid Noeri. Stanford, CA: Stanford University Press, 2002.

Hou, Lei. "Poor Construction Blamed for Shanghai Building Collapse." *China Daily*, June 30, 2009. www.chinadaily.com.cn/china/2009-06/30/content_8338226 .htm.

Hou, Zhenwei. "Geren Weihe Bei Jin Zhuce '.cn'" ("Why Individuals Are Forbidden to Register for .cn Domains"). *Beijing Wanbao (Beijing Evening News)*, December 24, 2009.

Howard, Philip N. *The Digital Origins of Dictatorship and Democracy: Information Technology and Political Islam*. New York: Oxford University Press, 2010.

Howard, Philip N., Aiden Duffy, Deen Freelon, Muzammil Hussain, Will Mari, and Marwa Mazaid. "Opening Closed Regimes: What Was the Role of Social Media During the Arab Spring?" Project on Information Technology and Political Islam. Seattle, 2011.

Howard, Philip N., and Muzammil M. Hussain. *Democracy's Fourth Wave? Digital Media and the Arab Spring*. New York: Oxford University Press, 2013.

Hu, Andy Yinan. "The Revival of Chinese Leftism Online." *Global Media and Communication* 3, no. 2 (2007). 233–38.

Hu, Yong. *Zhongsheng Xuanhua: Wangluo Shidai de Geren Biaoda Yu Gonggong Taolun (The Rising Cacophony: Personal Expression and Public Discussion in the Internet Age)*. Nanning: Guangxi Normal University Press, 2008.

Hu, Zhongbin. "Huarui Fengdian Ziben Chuanqi Xintianyu Sannian Huibao 145 Bei" ("Legendary Capital Operations of Sinovel New Horizon Capital Earned 145-Times Return in Three Years"). *Jingji Guanchabao (Economic Observer)*, January 10, 2011.

Huang, Haifeng. "International Knowledge and Domestic Evaluations in a Changing Society: The Case of China." *American Political Science Review* 109, no. 3 (2015): 613–34.

——. "Propaganda as Signaling." *Comparative Politics* 47, no. 4 (July 2015): 419 37.

Huang, Haifeng, and Yao-Yuan Yeh. "Information from Abroad: Foreign Media, Selective Exposure and Political Support in China." *British Journal of Political Science* (2007): 1–26. https://doi.org/10.1017/S0007123416000739.

Huang, Yasheng. "Democratize or Die: Why China's Communists Face Reform or Revolution." *Foreign Affairs*, December 3, 2012. www.foreignaffairs.com/articles /china/2012-12-03/democratize-or-die.

Hui, Ning, and David Wertime. "Is This the New Face of China's Silent Majority?" *Foreign Policy*, October 22, 2014.

Human Rights Watch. *"Walking on Thin Ice": Control, Intimidation, and Harassment of Lawyers in China*. New York: Human Rights Watch, 2008.

Hung, Chin-fu. "China's Propaganda in the Information Age: Internet Commentators and the Weng'an Incident." *Issues & Studies* 46, no. 4 (2010): 149–81.

——. "Citizen Journalism and Cyberactivism in China's Anti-PX Plant in Xiamen, 2007–2009." *China: An International Journal* 11, no. 1 (2013): 40–54.

——. "The Politics of Cyber Participation in the PRC: The Implications of Contingency for the Awareness of Citizens' Rights." *Issues and Studies* 42, no. 4 (2006): 137–73.

Huntington, Samuel P. *Political Order in Changing Societies.* New Haven, CT: Yale University Press, 1968.

Inglehart, Ronald. *Culture Shift in Advanced Industrial Society.* Princeton, NJ: Princeton University Press, 1990.

"Internet Filtering in China in 2004–2005: A Country Study." OpenNet Intiative, 2005.

Jacobs, Andrew. "China Requires Censorship Software on New PCs." *New York Times,* June 8, 2009.

——. "Lawyer for Released Chinese Artist Seeks Review on Taxes." *New York Times,* June 29, 2011. www.nytimes.com/2011/06/30/world/asia/30artist.html.

Ji, Tianqin, and Tang Ailin. "BBS Wangshi" ("The Legend of BBS"). *Nandu Zhoukan (Southern Metropolis Weekly),* no. 20 (May 28, 2012): 56–63.

Jiang, Min. "Authoritarian Informationalism: China's Approach to Internet Sovereignty." *SAIS Review of International Affairs* 30, no. 2 (2010): 71–89.

——. "The Coevolution of the Internet, (Un)Civil Society, and Authoritarianism in China." In *The Internet, Social Media, and a Changing China,* edited by Jacques DeLisle, Avery Goldstein, and Guobin Yang, 28–48. Philadelphia: University of Pennsylvania Press, 2016.

Jiao, Likun. "Shouji Shimingzhi Zuiwan Xiayue Tuichu, Zhongguo Yi Fengsha Wanbu Shouji" ("Real-Name Registration of Cellphones Will Be Implemented Next Month Onward, China Has Banned More Than Ten Thousand Cellphones"). *China News,* December 22, 2005. www.chinanews.com/news/2005/2005-12-22 /8/668715.shtml.

Jin, Yi. "Zhongguo Dangdai Yishujia Aiweiwei Zuopin 'Tonghua' Bei Zhi Chaoxi" ("Chinese Contemporary Artist Ai Weiwei's Work 'Fairy Tale' Charged with Plagiarism"). *Xinhua Net,* June 21, 2007. http://news.xinhuanet.com/shuhua /2007-06/21/content_6272614.htm.

Jing, Xiaolei. "The Business of Manipulation." *Beijing Review* 54, no. 2 (January 2011): 18–19.

Johnson, Ian. "Activists Call for a 'Jasmine Revolution' in China." *New York Times,* February 24, 2011.

——. "Blogging the Slow-Motion Revolution: An Interview with China's Huang Qi." *New York Review of Books,* February 9, 2013. www.nybooks.com/daily/2013/02/09 /blogging-slow-revolution-interview-huang-qi/.

Kalathil, Shanthi. "China's New Media Sector: Keeping the State In." *The Pacific Review* 16, no. 4 (2003): 489–501.

Kang, Cecilia. "Secretary Clinton Dines with High-Tech Titans to Talk Diplomacy." *Washington Post,* January 11, 2010. http://voices.washingtonpost.com/posttech /2010/01/sec_clinton_dines_high-tech_ti.html.

Kelliher, Daniel. "The Chinese Debate Over Village Self-Government." *China Journal* 37 (1997): 63–86.

Kennedy, John James. "Maintaining Popular Support for the Chinese Communist Party: The Influence of Education and the State-Controlled Media." *Political Studies* 57, no. 3 (2009): 517–36.

Khazan, Olga. "Russia's Online-Comment Propaganda Army." *Atlantic*, October 9, 2013. www.theatlantic.com/international/archive/2013/10/russias-online -comment-propaganda-army/280432/.

King, Gary, Jennifer Pan, and Margaret E. Roberts. "How Censorship in China Allows Government Criticism but Silences Collective Expression." *American Political Science Review* 107, no. 2 (2013): 1–18.

——. "How the Chinese Government Fabricates Social Media Posts for Strategic Distraction, Not Engaged Argument," *American Political Science Review* 111, no.3 (2017): 484–501.

——. "Reverse-Engineering Censorship in China: Randomized Experimentation and Participant Observation." *Science* 345, no. 6199 (2014): 1–10.

Koesel, Karrie J., and Valerie J. Bunce. "Diffusion-Proofing: Russian and Chinese Responses to Waves of Popular Mobilizations Against Authoritarian Rulers." *Perspectives on Politics* 11, no. 3 (2013): 753–68.

Kong, Pu. "Jiemi Wangluo Weiji Gongguan" ("Deciphering Online Crisis Management"). *Xin Shiji Zhoukan (Century Weekly)* 340, no. 28 (October 2008): 62–63.

Kramer, Adam, Jamie E. Guillory, and Jeffrey T. Hancock. "Experimental Evidence of Massive-Scale Emotional Contagion Through Social Networks." *Proceedings of the National Academy of Sciences* 111, no. 24 (2014): 8788–90.

Laffont, Jean-Jacques, and David Martimort. *The Theory of Incentives: The Principal-Agent Model.* Princeton, NJ: Princeton University Press, 2009.

Lagerkvist, Johan. *After the Internet, Before Democracy: Competing Norms in Chinese Media and Society.* Bern, Switzerland: Peter Lang, 2010.

——. "Internet Ideotainment in the PRC: National Responses to Cultural Globalization." *Journal of Contemporary China* 17, no. 54 (2008): 121–40.

——. *The Internet in China: Unlocking and Containing the Public Sphere.* Lund, Sweden: Lund University Publications, 2007.

——. "Principal-Agent Dilemma in China's Social Media Sector? The Party-State and Industry Real-Name Registration Waltz." *International Journal of Communication* 6 (2012): 2628–46.

Lam, Oiwan. "China: Censoring the Red and Bo Xilai's Supporters." *Global Voices*, March 16, 2012. http://advocacy.globalvoicesonline.org/2012/03/16/china -censoring-the-red-and-bo-xilais-supporters/.

Larmer, Brook. "In China, an Internet Joke Is Not Always Just a Joke. It's a Form of Defiance—and the Government Is Not Amused." *New York Times Sunday Magazine*, October 30, 2011.

Le, Yuan, and Boxu Yang. "Online Political Discussion and Left–Right Ideological Debate: A Comparative Study of Two Major Chinese BBS Forums." Paper presented at the 7th Annual Chinese Internet Research Conference, University of Pennsylvania, Philadelphia, PA, May 27–29, 2009.

Lee, Ching Kwan, and Eli Friedman. "China Since Tiananmen: The Labor Movement." *Journal of Democracy* 20, no. 3 (2009): 21–24.

Lee, Ching Kwan, and Yonghong Zhang. "The Power of Instability: Unraveling the Microfoundations of Bargained Authoritarianism in China." *American Journal of Sociology* 118, no. 6 (2013): 1475–1508.

Leibold, James. "Blogging Alone: China, the Internet, and the Democratic Illusion?" *The Journal of Asian Studies* 70, no. 4 (2011): 1023–41.

——. "More Than a Category: Han Supremacism on the Chinese Internet." *The China Quarterly*, no. 203 (2010): 539–59.

Lessig, Lawrence. *Code and Other Laws of Cyberspace.* New York: Basic Books, 1999.

"Li Joins Xi in Viral Cartoon Celebrity." *Global Times*, February 28, 2014. www .globaltimes.cn/content/845260.shtml.

Li, Bin. "Wangyou Chuangzao 'Shida Shenshou'" ("Netizens Create Top Ten Holy Animals"). *Xinxi Shibao (Information Times)*, January 6, 2009.

Li, Cheng. "The End of the CCP's Resilient Authoritarianism? A Tripartite Assessment of Shifting Power in China." *The China Quarterly*, no. 211 (2012): 595–623.

——. "Intra-Party Democracy in China: Should We Take It Seriously?" *China Leadership Monitor* 30, no. 3 (2009): 1–14.

Li, Eric X. "The Life of the Party: The Post-Democratic Future Begins in China." *Foreign Affairs*, December 3, 2012. www.foreignaffairs.com/articles/china/2012-12-03 /life-party.

Li, Guang. "'Siyue Qingnian': Wangluo Minzu Zhuyi Xin Shili" ("'April Youth': The New Force of Cyber Nationalism"). *Fenghuang Zhoukan (Phoenix Weekly)*, 434, no. 13 (May 2012): 24–31.

Li, Jun. "Cisheng Wukui 'Zhongguo Hangmu Zhifu', Zhi Han Weineng Qinjian Zhongguo Hangmu Xiashui" ("He is Worth of Being Considered the 'Father of China's Aircraft Carrier,' His Only Regret Is Not Seeing China's Aircraft Carrier in Service"). *Yangzi Wanbao (Yangtse Evening News)*, January 15, 2011.

Li, Liang, and Yu Li. "14 Buwei Lianhe Jinghua Hulianwang" ("Fourteen Ministries and Commissions Jointly Cleanse the Internet"). *Nanfang Zhoumo (Southern Weekend)*, August 18, 2005.

Li, Lianjiang. "The Magnitude and Resilience of Trust in the Center: Evidence from Interviews with Petitioners in Beijing and a Local Survey in Rural China." *Modern China* 39, no. 1 (2013): 3–36.

——. "Political Trust and Petitioning in the Chinese Countryside." *Comparative Politics* 40, no. 2 (2008): 209–26.

——. "Political Trust in Rural China." *Modern China* 30, no. 2 (2004): 228–58.

———. "Rights Consciousness and Rules Consciousness in Contemporary China." *The China Journal*, no. 64 (2010): 47–68.

Li, Ping. "Sanxia Gongcheng Hui Shengtai, Yuanshi: Daba Jiancheng Dizhen Duo" ("Three Gorges Project Damages the Ecology, Chinese Academy of Sciences Academic: More Earthquakes to Come After Dam Constructed"). *Epoch Times*, June 9, 2011. www.epochtimes.com/gb/11/6/9/n3280858.htm.

Li, Yonggang. *Women de Fanghuoqiang: Wangluo Shidai de Biaoda Yu Jianguan (Our Great Firewall: Expression and Governance in the Era of the Internet)*. Nanning: Guangxi Normal University Press, 2009.

Lian, Yuming, and Wu Jianzhong, eds. *Wangluo Xinzheng (New Politics of the Internet)*. Beijing: Zhongguo Shidai Jingji Chubanshe, 2009.

Liang, Wendao. "Zai Fanhua Langchao yu Kuangre Minzu Zhuyi Zhijian" ("Between China-Bashing and Frenetic Nationalism"). *University Students Online*, April 27, 2008. www.univs.cn/newweb/univs/hust/2008-04-27/837018.html.

Liao, Jingwen, and Yao Wenjun. "Guangdong Jiang Zaijian Wanren Wangluo Yuqing Yindaoyuan Tuandui" ("Guangdong to Establish Another Ten-Thousand-Member Public Opinion Guidance Troop"). *Netease*, February 21, 2012. http://news.163.com/12/0221/05/7QOTQNCA0001124J.html.

Lieberthal, Kenneth, and David M. Lampton, eds. *Bureaucracy, Politics, and Decision Making in Post-Mao China*. Berkeley: University of California Press, 1992.

Lieberthal, Kenneth, and Michel Oksenberg. *Policy Making in China: Leaders, Structures, and Processes*. Princeton, NJ: Princeton University Press, 1988.

Lin, Gang. "Leadership Transition, Intra-Party Democracy, and Institution Building in China." *Asian Survey* 44, no. 2 (2004): 255–75.

Linz, Juan J., and Alfred Stepan. *Problems of Democratic Transition and Consolidation: Southern Europe, South America, and Post-Communist Europe*. Baltimore, MD: Johns Hopkins University Press, 1996.

"Liu Xiaobo Bei Kong Shandong Dianfu Guojia Zhengquan Zui" ("Liu Xiaobo Accused of Inciting Subversion of State Authority"). *BBC Chinese*, June 24, 2009. http://news.bbc.co.uk/chinese/trad/hi/newsid_8110000/newsid_8116000/8116019.stm.

Liu, Qing. "Ai Weiwei Wangluo Xingwei Yishu Biaoda Yuanfen" ("Ai Weiwei Expresses Resentment Through Online Performance"). *Radio Free Asia*, July 7, 2009. www.rfa.org/mandarin/pinglun/teyuepinglun-07072009112454.html.

Liu, Yawei. "A Long Term View of China's Microblog Politics." Paper presented at the 10th Annual Chinese Internet Research Conference, University of Southern California, Annenberg, Los Angeles, CA, May 21–22, 2012.

Liu, Yiheng. "Ai Weiwei Zhen Mianmu: Wu Wan Yishu Jia—Wudu Juquan" ("Ai Weiwei's True Colors: An Five-Play Artist—Full of Evil"). *Wenweipo*, April 15, 2011.

Lollar, Xia Li. "Assessing China's E-Government: Information, Service, Transparency and Citizen Outreach of Government Websites." *Journal of Contemporary China* 15, no. 46 (2006): 31–41.

Lorentzen, Peter. "China's Strategic Censorship." *American Journal of Political Science* 58, no. 2 (2014): 402–14.

——. "Regularizing Rioting: Permitting Public Protest in an Authoritarian Regime." *Quarterly Journal of Political Science* 8, no. 2 (2013): 127–58.

Lotan, Gilad, Erhardt Graeff, Mike Ananny, Devin Gaffney, Ian Pearce, and Danah Boyd. "The Revolutions Were Tweeted: Information Flows During the 2011 Tunisian and Egyptian Revolutions." *International Journal of Communication* 5 (2011): 1375–1405.

Lu, Yang. "Ai Weiwei Hexie Yan Zhuizong Baodao" ("Follow-Up Reports on Ai Weiwei's River Crab Feast"). *VOA Chinese*, November 7, 2010. www.voachinese .com/content/article-20101107-ai-weiwei-106847008/772266.html.

Lyons, Dave. "China's Golden Shield Project: Myths, Realities and Context." Paper presented at the 7th Chinese Internet Research Conference, University of Pennsylvania, Philadelphia, PA, May 27–29, 2009.

Lyotard, Jean-François. *The Postmodern Condition: A Report on Knowledge, Theory and History of Literature*, vol. 10. Minneapolis: University of Minnesota Press, 1984.

Ma, Liang. "The Diffusion of Government Microblogging." *Public Management Review* 15, no. 2 (February 28, 2013): 288–309.

MacKinnon, Rebecca. "China's Censorship 2.0: How Companies Censor Bloggers." *First Monday* 14, no. 2 (2009). http://firstmonday.org/article/view/2378/2089.

——. "China's 'Networked Authoritarianism.'" *Journal of Democracy* 22, no. 2 (2011): 32–46.

——. "Flatter World and Thicker Walls? Blogs, Censorship and Civic Discourse in China." *Public Choice* 134, no. 1–2 (2008): 31–46.

——. "The Green Dam Phenomenon: Governments Everywhere Are Treading on Web Freedoms." *Wall Street Journal*, June 18, 2009. http://online.wsj.com /article/SB124525992051023961.html.

——. "Shi Tao, Yahoo!, and the Lessons for Corporate Social Responsibility." *RConversation Blog*, December 30, 2007. http://rconversation.blogs.com /YahooShiTaoLessons.pdf.

MacLeod, Calum. "Media Controls Leave Most Chinese Unaware of Activist Chen." *USA Today*, May 5, 2012. https://usatoday30.usatoday.com/news/world /story/2012-05-04/China-media-blackout/54773020/1.

Manchester, William. *The Glory and the Dream: A Narrative History of America, 1932–1972*. Boston: Little, Brown, 1973.

Manion, Melanie. "Democracy, Community, Trust: The Impact of Elections in Rural China." *Comparative Political Studies* 39, no. 3 (2006): 301–24.

Mao, Tse-Tung. "On Protracted War." In *Selected Works of Mao Tse-Tung*, vol. 2:113–94. Peking: Foreign Languages Press, 1965.

"Meiguo Zhuanjia: Dalu Hangmu Shige 'Tie Guanchai', Taiwan Wuxu Danxin" ("American Experts: Mainland's Aircraft Carrier Is an Iron Coffin, Taiwan Should Not Worry"). *Global Times Online*, October 19, 2011. http://taiwan.huanqiu.com /taiwan_military/2011-10/2096184.html.

Meng, Bingchun. "From Steamed Bun to Grass Mud Horse: E Gao as Alternative Political Discourse on the Chinese Internet." *Global Media and Communication* 7, no. 1 (April 21, 2011): 33–51.

——. "Mediated Citizenship or Mediatized Politics? Political Discourse on Chinese Internet." Paper presented at the 10th Annual Chinese Internet Research Conference, University of Southern California, Annenberg, Los Angeles, CA, May 21–22, 2012.

——. "Moving Beyond Democratization: A Thought Piece on the China Internet Research Agenda." *International Journal of Communication* 4 (2010): 501–8.

Mertha, Andrew. " 'Fragmented Authoritarianism 2.0': Political Pluralization in the Chinese Policy Process." *The China Quarterly*, no. 200 (2009): 995–1012.

Michelson, Ethan. "Lawyers, Political Embeddedness, and Institutional Continuity in China's Transition from Socialism." *American Journal of Sociology* 113, no. 2 (2007): 352–414.

Miller, Blake Andrew Phillip. "Automatic Detection of Comment Propaganda in Chinese Media." *SSRN Electronic Journal*, 2016, 1–38. doi:10.2139/ssrn.2738325.

Miller, Joshua Rhett. "Microsoft to Continue Censorship in China as Google Opens Up." *Fox News*, March 16, 2010. www.foxnews.com/scitech/2010/03/16/google-reportedly-ends-censorship-china/.

Ministry of Culture. *Hulianwang Wenhua Guanli Zanxing Guiding (Provisional Regulations on Internet Culture Management)*. May 10, 2003.

Ministry of Information Industry. *Fei Jingyingxing Hulianwang Xinxi Fuwu Beian Guanli Banfa (Administrative Measures of the Registration of Noncommercial Internet Information Services)*. January 28, 2005.

——. *Hulianwang Dianzi Gonggao Fuwu Guanli Guiding (Regulation on Internet News and Bulletin Boards)*. October 27, 2000.

Montinola, Gabriella, Yingyi Qian, and Barry R. Weingast. "Federalism, Chinese Style: The Political Basis for Economic Success in China." *World Politics* 48, no.1 (1995), 50–81.

Moore, Malcolm. "Chinese Internet Vigilantes Bring Down Another Official." *Telegraph*, December 30, 2008. www.telegraph.co.uk/news/worldnews/asia/china/4026624/Chinese-internet-vigilantes-bring-down-another-official.html.

Moore, Matthew. "CNN Apologises to Chinese Over Host's 'Goons and Thugs' Outburst." *Telegraph*, April 16, 2008. www.telegraph.co.uk/news/worldnews/1895792/CNN-apologises-to-Chinese-over-hosts-goons-and-thugs-outburst.html.

Morozov, Evgeny. "The Brave New World of Slacktivism." *Foreign Policy*, May 19, 2009.

——. *The Net Delusion: How Not to Liberate the World*. London: Penguin, 2011.

Muhaogu. "Liuyan de Cuihuawu: Diaoyu yu Zhengwei" ("Catalyst for Rumor: Fishing and Falsification"). *Jianghuai Chenbao (Jianghuai Morning Post)*, January 7, 2011.

Nathan, Andrew J. "Authoritarian Impermanence." *Journal of Democracy* 20, no. 3 (2009): 37–40.

——. "Authoritarian Resilience." *Journal of Democracy* 14, no. 1 (2003): 6–17.

Naughton, Barry. *The Chinese Economy: Transitions and Growth.* Cambridge, MA: MIT Press, 2007.

——. *Growing Out of the Plan: Chinese Economic Reform, 1978–1993.* Cambridge: Cambridge University Press, 1996.

Noesselt, Nele. "Microblogs and the Adaptation of the Chinese Party-State's Governance Strategy." *Governance* 27, no. 3 (2014): 449–68.

O'Brien, Kevin J. "China Since Tiananmen: Rural Protest." *Journal of Democracy* 20, no. 3 (2009): 25–28.

——. "Neither Transgressive nor Contained: Boundary-Spanning Contention in China." *Mobilization* 8, no. 1 (2003): 51–64.

——, ed. *Popular Protest in China.* Cambridge, MA: Harvard University Press, 2008.

——. "Villagers, Elections, and Citizenship in Contemporary China." *Modern China* 27, no. 4 (2001): 407–35.

O'Brien, Kevin J., and Yanhua Deng. "The Reach of the State: Work Units, Family Ties and 'Harmonious Demolition.'" *The China Journal*, no. 74 (2015): 1–17.

O'Brien, Kevin J., and Rongbin Han. "Path to Democracy? Assessing Village Elections in China." *Journal of Contemporary China* 18, no. 60 (2009): 359–78.

O'Brien, Kevin J., and Lianjiang Li. "Accommodating 'Democracy' in a One-Party State: Introducing Village Elections in China." *The China Quarterly*, no. 162 (2009): 465–89.

——. *Rightful Resistance in Rural China.* New York: Cambridge University Press, 2006.

——. "Suing the Local State: Administrative Litigation in Rural China." *The China Journal*, no. 51 (2004): 75–96.

O'Donnell, Guillermo, and Philippe C. Schmitter. *Transitions from Authoritarian Rule.* Baltimore, MD: Johns Hopkins University Press, 1986.

Oi, Jean. *Rural China Takes Off: Institutional Foundations of Economic Reform.* Berkeley: University of California Press, 1999.

Osnos, Evan. "Angry Youth: The New Generation's Neocon Nationalists." *New Yorker*, July 28, 2008. www.newyorker.com/reporting/2008/07/28/080728fa_fact_osnos.

Page, Jeremy. "Call for Protests Unnerves Beijing." *Wall Street Journal*, February 21, 2011.

——. "What's He Doing Here? Ambassador's Unusual Protest Cameo." *Wall Street Journal*, February 23, 2011. http://on.wsj.com/17d6nlq.

Pang, Cuiming. "Self-Censorship and the Rise of Cyber Collectives: An Anthropological Study of a Chinese Online Community." *Intercultural Communication Studies* VXII, no. 3 (2008): 57–76.

Parker, Emily. *Now I Know Who My Comrades Are: Voices from the Internet Underground.* New York: Farrar, Straus and Giroux, 2014.

Peerenboom, Randall. "A Government of Laws: Democracy, Rule of Law and Administrative Law Reform in the PRC." *Journal of Contemporary China* 34, no. 12 (2003): 45–67.

Pei, Minxin. *China's Trapped Transition: The Limits of Developmental Autocracy*. Cambridge, MA: Harvard University Press, 2009.

Perry, Elizabeth J. "Chinese Conceptions of Rights: From Mencius to Mao—and Now." *Perspectives on Politics* 6, no. 1 (2008): 37–50.

Phillips, Tom. "Chinese Civil Servant Sacked Over Luxury Wardrobe." *Telegraph*, September 21, 2009. www.telegraph.co.uk/news/worldnews/asia/china/9558179 /Chinese-civil-servant-sacked-over-luxury-wardrobe.html.

Pierson, David. "Protesters Gather at CNN." *Los Angeles Times*, April 20, 2008. http:// articles.latimes.com/print/2008/apr/20/local/me-cnn20.

"Premier Calls for Accelerating Political Reform." *People's Daily Online*, August 23, 2010. http://english.peopledaily.com.cn/90001/90776/90785/7113368.html.

Prior, Markus. "News vs. Entertainment: How Increasing Media Choice Widens Gaps in Political Knowledge and Turnout." *American Journal of Political Science* 49, no. 3 (2005): 577–92.

Putnam, Robert D. *Bowling Alone: The Collapse and Revival of American Community*. New York: Simon and Schuster, 2001.

——. *Making Democracy Work: Civic Traditions in Modern Italy*. Princeton, NJ: Princeton University Press, 1993.

Qian, Yanfeng. "Shanghai Residents Fight Forced Demolitions." *China Daily*, February 26, 2010. www.chinadaily.com.cn/china/2010-02/26/content_9506528 .htm.

Qiao, Long. "Heike Baoguang Wumao Shujuku Dangju Jiankong Yuqing Fenbu Zhuangkuang" ("Hacker Exposes Database of the 'Fifty-Cent Army' and How Authorities Monitor Public Opinion"). *Radio Free Asia*, May 20, 2015. www.rfa .org/mandarin/yataibaodao/renquanfazhi/ql1-05202015101938.html.

Qin, Wang. "Zhuli Zhe de Xin Jianghu" ("New Rivers and Lakes for Profit-Seekers"). *Nandu Zhoukan (Southern Metropolis Weekly)*, no. 3 (2010): 34–37.

Qiu, Jack Linchuan. "Virtual Censorship in China: Keeping the Gate Between the Cyberspaces." *International Journal of Communications Law and Policy*, no. 4 (2000): 1–25.

——. *Working-Class Network Society: Communication Technology and the Information Have-Less in Urban China*. Cambridge, MA: MIT Press, 2009.

Ramzy, Austin. "China's Alarming Spate of School Knifings." *Time*, April 30, 2010. http://content.time.com/time/world/article/0,8599,1985834,00.html.

——. "China's Domain-Name Limits: Web Censorship?" *Time*, December 18, 2009. www.time.com/time/world/article/0,8599,1948283,00.html.

——. "State Stamps Out Small 'Jasmine' Protests in China." *Time*, February 21, 2011. http://content.time.com/time/world/article/0,8599,2052860,00.html.

Rauchfleisch, Adrian, and Mike S. Schäfer. "Multiple Public Spheres of Weibo: A Typology of Forms and Potentials of Online Public Spheres in China." *Information, Communication & Society* 18, no. 2 (2015): 139–55.

Rea, Christopher G. "Spoofing (E'gao) Culture on the Chinese Internet." In *Humour in Chinese Life and Culture*, edited by Jessica Milner Davis and Jocelyn Chey, 149–72. Hong Kong: Hong Kong University Press, 2013.

Repnikova, Maria. *Media Politics in China: Improvising Power Under Authoritarianism.* Cambridge: Cambridge University Press, 2017.

——. "Thought Work Contested: Ideology and Journalism Education in China." *The China Quarterly* (2017): 1–21. https://doi.org/10.1017/S0305741017000583.

Repnikova, Maria, and Kecheng Fang. "China's New Media: Pushing Political Boundaries Without Being Political." *Foreign Affairs*, October 12, 2016. www.foreignaffairs.com/articles/china/2016-10-12/chinas-new-media.

Richburg, Keith B. "China's 'Netizens' Holding Officials Accountable." *Washington Post*, November 9, 2009. www.washingtonpost.com/wp-dyn/content/article/2009/11/08/AR2009110818166_pf.html.

Roberts, Dexter. "Inside the War Against China's Blogs." *BusinessWeek*, June 12, 2008.

Rose, Richard, William Mishler, and Neil Munro. *Popular Support for an Undemocratic Regime: The Changing Views of Russians.* New York: Cambridge University Press, 2011.

Rosenthal, Rob, and Richard Flacks. *Playing for Change: Music and Musicians in the Service of Social Movements.* Abingdon, Oxon: Routledge, 2016.

Said, Edward W. *Culture and Imperialism.* New York: Vintage, 1993.

Schedler, Andreas. "What Is Democratic Consolidation?" *Journal of Democracy* 9, no. 2 (1998): 91–107.

Scheufele, Dietram A., and Matthew C. Nisbet. "Being a Citizen Online: New Opportunities and Dead Ends." *Harvard International Journal of Press/Politics* 7, no. 3 (2002): 55–75.

Schlæger, Jesper. *E-Government in China: Technology, Power and Local Government Reform.* Abingdon, Oxon: Routledge, 2013.

Schlæger, Jesper, and Min Jiang. "Official Microblogging and Social Management by Local Governments in China." *China Information* 28, no. 2 (2014): 189–213.

Scoggins, Suzanne E. "Policing China: Struggles of Law, Order, and Organization for Ground-Level Officers." PhD diss., University of California, Berkeley, 2016.

Scott, James C. *Seeing Like a State: How Certain Schemes to Improve the Human Condition Have Failed.* New Haven, CT: Yale University Press, 1998.

——. *Weapons of the Weak: Everyday Forms of Peasant Resistance.* New Haven, CT: Yale University Press, 1985.

Shambaugh, David. "China's Propaganda System: Institutions, Processes and Efficacy." *China Journal*, no. 57 (2007): 25–58.

——. "The Coming Chinese Crackup." *Wall Street Journal—Eastern Edition*, March 7, 2015.

Shambaugh, David L. *China's Communist Party: Atrophy and Adaptation*. Berkeley: University of California Press, 2008.

Shandong University of Traditional Chinese Medicine. "Guanyu Jianli Shandong Zhongyiyao Daxue Wangluo Pinglunyuan Duiwu de Tongzhi" ("Circular on Establishing an Internet Commentator Troop at the Shandong University of Traditional Chinese Medicine"). November 27, 2008. http://xcb.web.sdutcm.edu.cn/htm/tz/646.html;

"Shanxisheng Shoupi Wangluo Bianji he Wangluo Pinglunyuan Peixunban Xueyuan Zhengshi Zai Bing Jieye" ("Commencement of the First Training Class of Internet Editors and Commentators of Shanxi Province"). *Jincheng News*, December 20, 2006. www.jcnews.com.cn/Html/guondongtai/2006-12/20/120854983.html.

Shao, Li. "The Continuing Authoritarian Resilience Under Internet Development in China—An Observation of Sina Micro-Blog." MA thesis, University of California, Berkeley, 2012.

Shen, Simon, and Shaun Breslin, eds. *Online Chinese Nationalism and China's Bilateral Relations*. Lanham, MD: Lexington, 2010.

"Sheping: Weigong Zhou Xiaoping Bushi Wangluo Da V de Guangrong" ("Editorial: It Is Not Glorious for Big Vs to Attack Zhou Xiaoping"). *Global Times*, October 17, 2014.

Shi, Tianjian. "China: Democratic Values Supporting an Authoritarian System." In *How East Asians View Democracy*, edited by Larry Diamond, Andrew J. Nathan, and Doh Chull Shin, 209–37. New York: Columbia University Press, 2008.

——. "Cultural Values and Political Trust: A Comparison of the People's Republic of China and Taiwan." *Comparative Politics* 33, no. 4 (2001): 401–19.

Shie, Tamara Renee. "The Tangled Web: Does the Internet Offer Promise or Peril for the Chinese Communist Party?" *Journal of Contemporary China* 13, no. 40 (2004): 523–40.

Shih, Victor. "'Nauseating' Displays of Loyalty: Monitoring the Factional Bargain Through Ideological Campaigns in China." *The Journal of Politics* 70, no. 4 (2008): 1177–92.

Shirk, Susan. *China: Fragile Superpower*. New York: Oxford University Press, 2007.

——, ed. *Changing Media, Changing China*. New York: Oxford University Press, 2011.

Shirky, Clay. "The Political Power of Social Media." *Foreign Affairs* 90, no.1 (2011): 28–41.

Shue, Vivienne. *The Reach of the State: Sketches of the Chinese Body Politic*. Stanford, CA: Stanford University Press, 1988.

"Social Media Dominates Asia Pacific Internet Usage." *Nielsen*, July 9, 2010. http://blog.nielsen.com/nielsenwire/global/social-media-dominates-asia-pacific-internet-usage/.

Soghoian, Christopher. "The Spies We Trust: Third Party Service Providers and Law Enforcement Surveillance." PhD diss., Indiana University, 2012.

Sohu. "Tencent QQ Jiang Shixing Wangluo Shimingzhi, QQ Qun Chuangjianzhe Xu Shiming Dengji" ("Tecent QQ Intends to Introduce Real-Name Registration, QQ Group Owners Must Register with Real Names"). *Sohu*, July 21, 2005. http://it.sohu.com/20050721/n240175776.shtml.

State Administration of Radio, Film, and Television. "Guanyu Jiaqiang Tongguo Xinxi Wangluo Xiang Gongzhong Chuanbo Guangbo Dianying Dianshi Jiemu Guanli de Tonggao" ("Circular on Strengthening the Management of Broadcasting Radio, Film and TV Programs via the Internet"). October 1999.

——. *Hulianwang Deng Xinxi Chuanbo Shiting Jiemu Guanli Banfa (Regulations on Broadcasting Video and Audio Programs Through the Internet)*. January 7, 2003.

State Administration of Radio, Film, and Television, and Ministry of Information Industry. *Hulianwang Shiting Jiemu Fuwu Guanli Guiding (Administrative Provisions on Internet Audiovisual Program Services)*. December 29, 2007.

State Council Information Office. *Hulianwang Shangwang Fuwu Yingye Changsuo Guanli Tiaoli (Regulations on the Administration of Business Sites of Internet Access Services)*. September 29, 2002.

——. *Hulianwang Xinxi Fuwu Guanli Banfa (Administrative Measures on Internet Information Services)*. September 25, 2000.

——. *Zhonghua Renmin Gongheguo Dianxin Tiaoli (Telecommunications Regulations of the People's Republic of China)*. September 20, 2000.

——. *Zhonghua Renmin Gongheguo Jisuanji Xinxi Xitong Anquan Baohu Tiaoli (Regulations on the Safety and Protection of Computer Systems of the People's Republic of China)*. February 18, 1994.

State Council Information Office, and Ministry of Information Industry. *Hulian Wangzhan Congshi Dengzai Xinwen Yewu Guanli Zanxing Guiding (Interim Provisions for the Administration of News Publication by Internet Sites)*. November 6, 2000.

——. *Hulianwang Xinwen Xinxi Fuwu Guanli Guiding (Administrative Provisions of Internet News Information Services)*. September 25, 2005.

Steinbruner, John. *The Cybernetic Theory of Decision: New Dimensions of Political Analysis*. Princeton, NJ: Princeton University Press, 2002.

Steinhardt, H. Christoph. "From Blind Spot to Media Spotlight: Propaganda Policy, Media Activism and the Emergence of Protest Events in the Chinese Public Sphere." *Asian Studies Review* 39, no. 1 (2015): 119–37.

Stern, Rachel E., and Jonathan Hassid. "Amplifying Silence: Uncertainty and Control Parables in Contemporary China." *Comparative Political Studies* 45, no. 10 (2012): 1230–54.

Stern, Rachel E., and Kevin J. O'Brien. "Politics at the Boundary: Mixed Signals and the Chinese State." *Modern China* 38, no. 2 (2011): 174–98.

Stirland, Sarah Lai. "Cisco Leak: 'Great Firewall' of China Was a Chance to Sell More Routers." *Wired*, May 20, 2008. www.wired.com/threatlevel/2008/05/leaked-cisco-do/.

Stockmann, Daniela. *Media Commercialization and Authoritarian Rule in China*. New York: Cambridge University Press, 2013.

Stockmann, Daniela, and Mary E. Gallagher. "Remote Control: How the Media Sustain Authoritarian Rule in China." *Comparative Political Studies* 44, no. 4 (2011): 436–67.

Streitfeld, David. "The Best Reviews Money Can Buy." *New York Times*, August 26, 2015.

Su, Yang, and Xin He. "Street as Courtroom: State Accommodation of Labor Protest in South China." *Law and Society Review* 44, no. 1 (2010): 157–84.

Su, Yongtong. "Guoxinban 'Kuobian,' Wangluo Guanli Jusi Yi Bian Er" ("State Council Information Office Expansion: One Internet Administration Bureau Becomes Two"). *Nanfang Zhoumo (Southern Weekend)*, May 20, 2010.

Sullivan, John. "China's Weibo: Is Faster Different?" *New Media & Society* 16, no. 1 (2014): 24–37.

Sun, Helen. *Internet Policy in China: A Field Study of Internet Cafés*. Lanham, MD: Lexington, 2010.

Sunstein, Cass R. *Infotopia: How Many Minds Produce Knowledge*. New York: Oxford University Press, 2006.

——. *On Rumors: How Falsehoods Spread, Why We Believe Them, What Can Be Done*. New York: Farrar, Straus and Giroux, 2009.

——. *Republic.com*. Princeton, NJ: Princeton University Press, 2002.

Szablewicz, Marcella. "The 'Losers' of China's Internet: Memes as 'Structures of Feeling' for Disillusioned Young Netizens." *China Information* 28, no. 2 (July 15, 2014): 259–75.

Tai, Zixue. *The Internet in China: Cyberspace and Civil Society*. London: Routledge, 2006.

Tang, Fang. "Zhengzhi Wangmin de Shehui Jingji Diwei yu Zhengzhi Qingxiang: Jiyu Qiangguo he Maoyan de Tansuoxing Fenxi" ("Political Netizens' Socioeconomic Status and Political Orientations: Exploratory Research on the Qiang Guo and Mao Yan Forums"). *China Media Report* 8, no. 3 (2009): 96–107.

Tang, Lijun, and Helen Sampson. "The Interaction Between Mass Media and the Internet in Non-democratic States: The Case of China." *Media, Culture & Society* 34, no. 4 (2012): 457–71.

Tang, Wenfang. *Populist Authoritarianism: Chinese Political Culture and Regime Sustainability*. New York: Oxford University Press, 2016.

Tang, Xujun, Wu Xinxun, Huang Chuxin, and Liu Ruisheng, eds. *Zhongguo Xinmeiti Fazhan Baogao No. 5 (Annual Report on the Development of New Media in China, 2014)*. Beijing: Social Science Academic Press, 2014.

Mr. Tao [pseud]. *China: Journey to the Heart of Internet Censorship*. Paris: Reporters Without Borders, 2007.

Tao, Xizhe. "Jiekai Zhongguo Wangluo Jiankong Jizhi de Neimu" ("Uncovering the Inside Stories of China's Internet Censorship Regime"). *Reporters Without Borders*, October 10, 2007. http://archives.rsf.org/IMG/pdf/China_Internet _Report_in_Chinese.pdf

Tarrow, Sidney. *Power in Movement: Social Movements and Contentious Politics*. New York: Cambridge University Press, 1998.

Thompson, Clive. "Google's China Problem (and China's Google Problem)." *New York Times*, April 23, 2006.

Thornton, Patricia. "Manufacturing Dissent in Transnational China: Boomerang, Backfire or Spectacle?" In *Popular Protest in China*, edited by Kevin J. O'Brien, 179–204. Cambridge, MA: Harvard University Press, 2008.

Thornton, Patricia M. "Crisis and Governance: SARS and the Resilience of the Chinese Body Politic." *The China Journal*, no. 61 (2009): 23–48.

Tiananmen: The Gate of Heavenly Peace. Directed by Richard Gordon and Carma Hinton. Boston: Long Bow, 1995.

Tocqueville, Alexis de. *Democracy in America*, vol. 2. New York: Vintage, 1840.

Toepfl, Florian. "Blogging for the Sake of the President: The Online-Diaries of Russian Governors." *Europe-Asia Studies* 64, no. 8 (2012): 1435–59.

——. "Managing Public Outrage: Power, Scandal, and New Media in Contemporary Russia." *New Media & Society* 13, no. 8 (2011): 1301–19.

Tong, Yanqi, and Shaohua Lei. "War of Position and Microblogging in China." *Journal of Contemporary China* 22, no. 80 (2013): 292–311.

"The Trial of Xu Zhiyong: A New Citizen." *Economist*, no. 8871 (2014): 52.

Tsai, Kellee S. *Capitalism Without Democracy: The Private Sector in Contemporary China*. Ithaca, NY: Cornell University Press, 2007.

Tsai, Lily L. "Constructive Noncompliance." *Comparative Politics* 47, no. 3 (2015): 253–79.

Tsui, Lokman. "An Inadequate Metaphor: The Great Firewall and Chinese Internet Censorship." *Global Dialogue* 9, no. 1/2 (2007): 60–68.

Tufekci, Zeynep. "Social Movements and Governments in the Digital Age: Evaluating a Complex Landscape." *Journal of International Affairs* 68, no. 1 (2014): 1–18.

Tufekci, Zeynep, and Deen Freelon. "Introduction to the Special Issue on New Media and Social Unrest." *American Behavioral Scientist* 57, no. 7 (2013): 843–47.

Tufekci, Zeynep, and Christopher Wilson. "Social Media and the Decision to Participate in Political Protest: Observations from Tahrir Square." *Journal of Communication* 62, no. 2 (April 2012): 363–79.

Vendil Pallin, Carolina. "Internet Control Through Ownership: The Case of Russia." *Post-Soviet Affairs* 33, no. 1 (2017): 16–33.

Voci, Paola. *China on Video: Smaller-Screen Realities*. Abingdon, Oxon: Routledge, 2010.

Walton, Greg. "China's Golden Shield: Corporations and the Development of Surveillance Technology in the People's Republic of China." International Centre for Human Rights and Democratic Development, 2001. http://www.dd-rd.ca/site/_PDF/publications/globalization/CGS_ENG.PDF.

"Wang Shuai Yihuo Guojia Peichang, Gong'an Juzhang Dengmen Daoqian" ("Wang Shuai Receives State Compensation, Police Chief Visits His House and

Apologizes"). *Fuzhou Ribao—Xin Dushi (Fuzhou Daily—New Metropolitan)*, April 20, 2009.

Wang, Hao. "Beijingshi Hulianwang Xuanchuan Guanli Lingdao Xiaozu Huiyi Zhaokai" ("Beijing Municipal Internet Propaganda Administration Leadership Group Conference Convened"). *Beijing Ribao (Beijing Daily)*, July 13, 2007.

Wang, Jiajun. "Cong Caogen dao Jingying–Dalun Wangluo Minzu Zhuyi Liubian" ("From Grassroots to Elitism: The Transformation of Mainland Cyber-Nationalism"). *Fenghuang Zhoukan (Phoenix Weekly)* 434, no. 13 (May 2012): 36–38.

Wang, Junxiu. "Yipian Tiezi Huanlai Bei Qiu Bari" ("One Online Posting Results in Eight Days in Detention"). *Zhongguo Qingnian Bao (China Youth Daily)*, April 8, 2009.

Wang, Qihua. "'Lüba' Huangong" ("'Green Dam' Implementation Postponed"). *Caijing Magazine*, no. 14 (July 6, 2009).

Wang, Xin. "Xinlang Tengxun Weibo Zanting Pinglun 3 Tian" ("Sina and Tencent Suspend Comment Function of Microblog Services for Three Days"). *Chengdu Ribao (Chengdu Daily)*, April 1, 2012.

Wang, Xing. "Zhongshihua Beibao Zuizhi Renyuan zai Wangshang Xuanchuan Zhangjia Heli" ("Sinopec Exposed for Organizing Personnel to Justify Price Increase Online"). *Nanfang Dushi Bao (Southern Metropolis Daily)*, February 13, 2011.

Wang, Xiuning. "Weibo Zhili Shidai Shida Shijian: Weiguan Gaibian Zhongguo" ("Top Ten Big Events in the Era of Microblog Governance: Onlooking Changes China"). *Shidai Zhoubao (Time Weekly)*, November 29, 2010.

Wang, Yuhua, and Carl Minzner. "The Rise of the Chinese Security State." *The China Quarterly*, no. 222 (2015): 339–59.

Wang, Yunhui. "Gongye he Xinxihua Bu: Shouji Saohuang 'Shenhoushi'" (The Ministry of Industry and Information Technology: The Aftermath of the Mobile Phone Anti-Pornography Campaign"). *Nanfang Zhoumo (Southern Weekend)*, January 21, 2010.

"Wangbao Shaanxi Ankang Huanyun 7 Yue Yunfu Qiangzhi Yinchan" ("Internet Discloses Seven-Month Pregnant Women Forced to Abort in Ankang, Shaanxi"). *Netease*, June 12, 2012. http://news.163.com/12/0612/18/83QP5TAI00011229.html.

"Wangpingyuan Jishu Fudao Tigang" ("Technical Training Outline for Internet Commentators"). *Hengyang Party Building Net*, January 8, 2010. http://dx.hydjnet.gov.cn/News_View.asp?NewsID=28291.

Wasserstrom, Jeffrey N., and Elizabeth J. Perry, eds. *Popular Protest and Political Culture in Modern China*. Boulder, CO: Westview, 1994.

Watts, Jonathan. "The World's Most Important Story." *China Dialogue*, April 17, 2012. www.chinadialogue.net/article/show/single/en/4876--The-world-s-most-important-story-.

Weber, Max. *The Protestant Ethic and the Spirit of Capitalism*, vol. 1. New York: Penguin, 2002.

Wei, Cheng. "Shui shi Xizang Saoluan Zhong de Shujia?" ("Who Loses in the Tibet Riots?"). *Financial Times Chinese*, March 31, 2008. www.ftchinese.com/story/001018283.

Weiss, Jessica Chen. *Powerful Patriots: Nationalist Protest in China's Foreign Relations.* New York: Oxford University Press, 2014.

Weller, Robert P. "Responsive Authoritarianism and Blind-Eye Governance in China." In *Socialism Vanquished, Socialism Challenged: Eastern Europe and China, 1989–2009*, edited by Nina Bandelj and Dorothy J. Solinger, 83–102. New York: Oxford University Press, 2012.

Wellman, Barry, and Milena Gulia. "Net-Surfers Don't Ride Alone: Virtual Communities as Communities." In *Networks in the Global Village: Life in Contemporary Communities*, edited by Barry Wellman, 331–66. Boulder, CO: Westview, 1999.

Wen, Jiabao. "Yangwang Xingkong" ("Looking Up to the Starry Sky"). *Renmin Ribao (People's Daily)*, September 4, 2007.

Wen, Yunchao. "Shouquan Fabu: Dalu Wangluo Pinglunyuan Jianru Gongzhong Shiye" ("Authorized Release: China's Internet Commentators Gradually Gaining Public Sight"). *Zuiren Yiyu Blog*, July 17, 2007. https://wenyc1230.wordpress.com/2008/07/17/授权发布：大陆网络评论员渐入公众视野/.

"What Do You Really Want from Us?" *Washington Post*, May 18, 2008.

Whiting, Susan H., and Hua Shao. "Courts and Political Stability: Mediating Rural Land Disputes." In *Resolving Land Disputes in East Asia: Exploring the Limits of Law*, edited by Hualing Fu and John Gillespie, 222–47. Cambridge: Cambridge University Press, 2014.

Wilhelm, Anthony G. "Virtual Sounding Boards: How Deliberative Is Online Political Discussion?" *Information, Communication & Society* 1, no. 3 (1998): 313–38.

Wines, Michael. "China Creates New Agency for Patrolling the Internet." *New York Times*, May 4, 2012.

——. "China Seeks to Halt Book that Faults Its Prime Minister." *New York Times*, July 7, 2010.

——. "China's Censors Misfire in Abuse-of-Power Case." *New York Times*, November 17, 2010.

——. "A Dirty Pun Tweaks China's Online Censors," *New York Times*, March 12, 2009.

Wong, Edward. "Pushing China's Limits on Web, if Not on Paper." *New York Times*, November 7, 2011.

——. "Xinjiang, Tense Chinese Region, Adopts Strict Internet Controls." *New York Times*, December 11, 2016.

Wright, Teresa. *Accepting Authoritarianism: State-Society Relations in China's Reform Era.* Stanford, CA: Stanford University Press, 2010.

Wu, Xu. *Chinese Cyber Nationalism: Evolution, Characteristics, and Implications.* Lanham, MD: Lexington, 2007.

Xi, Jinping. "Zai Quanguo Dangxiao Gongzuo Huiyi Shangde Jianghua" ("Talk at the National Party School Work Meeting"), *Qiushi*, April 30, 2016. www.qstheory.cn/dukan/qs/2016-04/30/c_1118772415.htm.

Xi, Yihao, and Zhang Wei. "Wangjing Huilu Wangjing: Ti Lingdao Shantie" ("Internet Police Bribe Internet Police: Delete Posts for Local Leaders"). *Nanfang Zhoumo (Southern Weekend)*, April 17, 2014.

Xiao, Qiang. "1984bbs Wangzhan Guanbi you Chongkai Shuoming le Shenme?" ("What Can We Learn from the Shutdown and Resurrection of 1984bbs?"). *Radio Free Asia*, October 26, 2010, www.rfa.org/mandarin/pinglun/xiaoqiang /xq-10262010171852.html.

——."The Battle for the Chinese Internet." *Journal of Democracy* 22, no. 2 (2011): 47–61.

Xie, J., S. Sreenivasan, G. Korniss, W. Zhang, C. Lim, and B. K. Szymanski. "Social Consensus Through the Influence of Committed Minorities." *Physical Review E* 84, no. 1 (2011): 1–9.

Xie, Yue. "Rising Central Spending on Public Security and the Dilemma Facing Grassroots Officials in China." *Journal of Current Chinese Affairs* 42, no. 2 (2013): 79–109.

Xie, Yue, and Wei Shan. "China Struggles to Maintain Stability: Strengthening Its Public Security Apparatus." In *China: Development and Governance*, edited by Gungwu Wang and Yongnian Zheng, 55–62. Singapore: World Scientific, 2012.

"Xifang Zongxiang Gei Zhongguo Fayuan 'Pi Tiaozi'" ("The West Always Wants to Issue Directives to the Chinese Court"). *Global Times*, June 24, 2011.

Xin, Lin. "Liang 'Ziganwu' Zuojia Huo Xi Jinping Dianming Biaoyang Yin Zhengyi" ("Controversies Arise from Two 'Voluntary Fifty-Cent' Writers Praised by Xi Jinping"). *Radio Free Asia*, October 17, 2014. www.rfa.org/mandarin/yataibaodao /meiti/xl1-10172014093716.html.

Xing, Jun, Chen Wei, Ji Yu, and Zhang Gaofeng. ".cn Geren Yuming Shenqing Bei Jiaoting, Wangyou Zhiyi Tuixie Jianguan Zeren" ("Individuals' Applications to .cn Domain Name Suspended, Netizens Criticize It as Shirking Regulating Responsibility"). *Netease*, December 15, 2009. http://news.163.com/09/1215/08 /5QIHRTVE0001124J.html.

"Xinxi Chanye Bu Jiang Zhengdun Yumin Zhuce" ("The Ministry of Industry and Information Technology to Start Rectifying Domain Name Registration"). *Xinhua Net*, November 2006. http://news.xinhuanet.com/politics/2006-11/06 /content_5297176.htm.

Xiong, Li. "Ma Huateng deng Si Gaoguan Baoyuan Hulianwang Jianguan Yidaoqie" ("Four Senior Internet Executives Including Ma Huateng Complain About One-Size-Fits-All Internet Censorship"). *Netease*, March 28, 2010. http://tech.163 .com/10/0328/01/62R0RT6B000947HQ.html.

Yadley, Jim. "Detained AIDS Doctor Allowed to Visit U.S. Later, China Says." *New York Times*, February 17, 2007.

Yalkin, Çağri, Finola Kerrigan, and Dirk vom Lehn. "(Il)Legitimisation of the Role of the Nation State: Understanding of and Reactions to Internet Censorship in Turkey." *New Media & Society* 16, no. 2 (2013): 271–89.

Yan, Xiaojun. "Engineering Stability: Authoritarian Political Control Over University Students in Post-Deng China." *The China Quarterly*, no. 218 (2014): 493–513.

Yang, Guobin. "China Since Tiananmen: Online Activism." *Journal of Democracy* 20, no. 3 (2009): 33–36.

——, ed. *China's Contested Internet*. Copenhagen: Nordic Institute of Asian Studies, 2015.

——. "The Co-Evolution of the Internet and Civil Society in China." *Asian Survey* 43, no. 3 (2003): 124–41.

——. "How Do Chinese Civic Associations Respond to the Internet? Findings from a Survey." *The China Quarterly*, no.189 (2007): 122–43.

——. "The Internet and Civil Society in China: A Preliminary Assessment." *Journal of Contemporary China* 12, no. 36 (2003): 453–75.

——. "The Internet and the Rise of a Transnational Chinese Cultural Sphere." *Media, Culture & Society* 24, no. 4 (2003): 469–90.

——. *The Power of the Internet in China: Citizen Activism Online*. New York: Columbia University Press, 2009.

——. "Technology and Its Contents: Issues in the Study of the Chinese Internet." *The Journal of Asian Studies* 70, no. 4 (2011): 1043–50.

Yang, Guobin, and Craig Calhoun. "Media, Civil Society, and the Rise of a Green Public Sphere in China." *China Information* 21, no. 2 (2007): 211–36.

Yang, Guobin, and Min Jiang. "The Networked Practice of Online Political Satire in China: Between Ritual and Resistance." *International Communication Gazette* 77, no. 3 (2015): 215–31.

Yang, Tingting. "Ningcaishen: Aiji Nashier Huisi Wo le!" ("Ningcaishen: That Egypt Thing Really Ruined Me!"). *Economic Observer*, February 17, 2011. www.eeo.com.cn/Business_lifes/wenhua/2011/02/17/193600.shtml.

Yao, Yuan, and Rongbin Han. 2016. "Challenging, but Not Trouble-Making: Cultural Elites in China's Urban Heritage Preservation." *Journal of Contemporary China* 25, no. 98: 292–306.

Ye, Bing. "Sima Nan Tan VOA Dianshi Bianlun, Huiying Wangshang Pingyi" ("Sima Nan Talks About His TV Debate at VOA and Responds to Online Comments"). *VOA Chinese*, November 15, 2012. www.voachinese.com/content/sima-nan-voa-debate-remarks-20121115/1546487.html.

"Yi Li Xiaolu Seqingpian Cang Liu Si Guanggao Wangshang Fengchuan" ("June 4 Ads Found in Suspected Li Xiaolu Sex Videos and Go Viral Online"). *DW News*, May 11, 2014. http://china.dwnews.com/news/2014-05-11/59470725.html.

Ying, Ni. "'Wangyou Shimingzhi' Jin Qi Shixing, Xinzheng Zaoyu Zhixingnan" ("Real-Name Registration of Online Gaming Effective Today, the New Policy Encounters Difficulty in Enforcement"). *China News*, August 1, 2010. www.chinanews.com/it/2010/08-01/2438659.shtml.

Yu, Haiqing. *Media and Cultural Transformation in China*. Abingdon, Oxon: Routledge, 2009.

Yu, Jianrong. *Kangzhengxing Zhengzhi: Zhongguo Zhengzhi Shehuixue Jiben Wenti (Contentious Politics: Basic Questions of Chinese Political Sociology)*. Beijing: People's Publishing House, 2010.

Yu, Jie, *Zhongguo Yingdi Wen Jiabao (China's Best Actor: Wen Jiabao)*. Hong Kong: New Century, 2010.

Yue, Sheng. "Ruhe Rang Quanli zai Yangguang Xia Yunxing" ("How to 'Exercise Power Under the Sun'"). *BBC Chinese*, March 8, 2010. www.bbc.co.uk/zhongwen /simp/china/2010/03/100308_china_media_liu.shtml.

Yuezhi Zhao. "Toward a Propaganda/Commercial Model of Journalism in China? The Case of the *Beijing Youth News*." *International Communication Gazette* 58, no. 3 (1997): 143–57.

Zakaria, Fareed. "Interview with Wen Jiabao." *CNN Global Public Square*, October 3, 2010. http://transcripts.cnn.com/TRANSCRIPTS/1010/03/fzgps.01.html.

Zayani, Mohamed. *Networked Publics and Digital Contention: The Politics of Everyday Life in Tunisia*. Oxford: Oxford University Press, 2015.

Zhang, Dongfeng. "Tatie 'Feibang' Bei Panxing Shijian Wangshang Taolun Relie" ("Hot Discussions Arise Among Netizens on the Incident of Being Jailed for Online 'Libel'"). *Nanfang Dushi Bao (Southern Metropolis Daily)*, April 21, 2009.

Zhang, Lei. "Invisible Footprints of Online Commentators," *Global Times*, February 5, 2010. http://special.globaltimes.cn/2010-02/503820.html.

—— "Wang Jingguan, Wo Xiang Bao Nin Yixia" ("Officer Wang, I Want to Hug You"). *Fazhi Wanbao (Legal Evening News)*, February 23, 2012.

Zhang, Lena L. "Behind the 'Great Firewall': Decoding China's Internet Media Policies from the Inside." *Convergence: The International Journal of Research Into New Media Technologies* 12, no. 3 (2006): 271–91.

Zhang, Lihua, and Zhang Li. "Gaotie 'Zizhu Chuangxin' Zhimi" ("The Myth of the 'Self-Reliant Innovation' of High-Speed Rail"). *Diyi Caijing (China Business Network)*, July 29, 2011. www.yicai.com/news/2011/07/970535.html.

Zhang, Shengjun. "'Wumao Dang' de Maozi Neng Xiazhu Shui?" ("Who Will Be Intimidated by the 'Fifty-Cent Army' Hat?"). *Netease*, January 20, 2010. http:// news.163.com/10/0120/16/5TG1UTRM00012GGA.html.

Zhang, Shunhe. "Wangluo Tuishou Jiemi Chaozuo Neimu: Yige Fengjie Ke Fu Yige Tuandui" ("Internet Spin Doctor Discloses Inside Story of Spinning: A Sister Phoenix Can Make a Whole Group Rich"). *Sina*, April 15, 2010. http://tech.sina .com.cn/i/2010-04-15/11484061901.shtml.

Zhang, Wu. "Lingdaoren Manhua Youxue Yourou, Baozhi Shichang Chuxian" ("Vivid Cartoon Images of Top Leaders Often Appear in Newspapers). *Xinwen Chenbao (Shanghai Morning Post)*, February 20, 2014.

Zhang, Yi. "Zhuce CN Yumin Jin Qi Ju Geren" ("CN Domain-Name Registration Closed for Individuals from Today Onward"). *Xin Jingbao (Beijing News)*, December 14, 2009.

Zhao, Dingxin. "The Mandate of Heaven and Performance Legitimation in Historical and Contemporary China." *American Behavioral Scientist* 53, no. 3 (2009): 416–33.

——. *The Power of Tiananmen: State-Society Relations and the 1989 Beijing Student Movement.* Chicago: University of Chicago Press, 2001.

Zheng, Yongnian. *Technological Empowerment: The Internet, State, and Society in China.* Stanford, CA: Stanford University Press, 2008.

Zheng, Yongnian, and Guoguang Wu. "Information Technology, Public Space, and Collective Action in China." *Comparative Political Studies* 38, no. 5 (2005): 507–36.

"Zhongguo Gansu Chengren Zujian Wumao Dang, Beipi Niuqu Minyi" ("China's Gansu Province Admits Establishing Fifty-Cent Army and Is Criticized for Distorting Public Opinion"). *VOA Chinese*, January 24, 2010. www.voachinese .com/a/china-20100124-82548812/460017.html.

"Zhongguo Hulianwang 16 Nian: Weiguan Gaibian Zhongguo" ("Sixteen Years of China's Internet: Onlooking Changes China"). *Xin Zhoukan (New Weekly)*, no. 22 (November 2010).

Zhongguo Xin Tongxin. "Zhuceliang Die Zhi Disi, CN Yuming Ruhe Shoufu Shidi?" ("Registration Rate Falls to Number 4, How Would CN Domain Name Reclaim the Loss?"). *Zhongguo Xin Tongxin (China New Telecommunications)*, no. 14 (2010): 27–28.

"Zhongyang Waixuanban Yuan Fujuzhuang Gao Jianyun Shouqian Shantie Beicha" ("Former Deputy Bureau Director at Central International Communication Office Gao Jianyun Under Investigation for Taking Bribes to Delete Online Postings"). *Xinhua Net*, January 21, 2015. http://news.xinhuanet.com/legal/2015 -01/21/c_1114076120.htm.

Zhou, Chunlin. "Jiekai Wangluo Tuishou Zhizao 'Zuimei Nüjiaoshi' Beihou Neimu" ("Uncovering How Internet Spin Doctors Crafted the 'Most Beautiful Female Teacher'"). *Xinhua Net*, July 28, 2007. http://news.xinhuanet.com/2007-07/28 /content_6441463.htm

Zhou, Kai. "Shanghai Putuoqu Chengguan Guren Baoli Zhifa Shijian Diaocha" ("Investigation of Violent Law Enforcement by Agents Hired by Putuo District Urban Management in Shanghai"). *China Youth Online*, July 3, 2009. http://zqb .cyol.com/content/2009-07/03/content_2739631.htm.

Zhou, Nan. "Zhou Nan Koushu: Xu Jiatun Pantao" ("Zhou Nan's Account: Defection of Xu Jiatun"). *Lingdao Wencui (Leadership Digest)*, no. 16 (2010): 109–112.

Zhou, Peng. "Zhongxiao Wangzhan Handong 'Duanwang'" ("Small and Medium-Size Websites 'Down' in Freezing Winter"). *Nandu Zhoukan (Southern Metropolis Weekly)*, no. 3 (January 2010): 26–30.

Zhou, Xiang. "E-Government in China: A Content Analysis of National and Provincial Web Sites." *Journal of Computer-Mediated Communication* 9, no. 4 (2006): 0.

Zhou, Yongming. *Historicizing Online Politics: Telegraphy, the Internet, and Political Participation in China.* Stanford, CA: Stanford University Press, 2005.

Zhu, Jiangnan, Jie Lu, and Tianjian Shi. "When Grapevine News Meets Mass Media: Different Information Sources and Popular Perceptions of Government Corruption in Mainland China." *Comparative Political Studies* 46, no. 8 (2012): 920–46.

Zhu, Xiaokun. "Baozhengshu de Shijie" ("In the World of Affidavits"). *Diyi Caijing Zhoukan (CBN Weekly)*, no. 134 (November 22, 2010): 56–64.

Zittrain, Jonathan, and Benjamin Edelman. "Internet Filtering in China." *IEEE Internet Computing*, (2003): 70–77.

Zoonen, Liesbet van. *Entertaining the Citizen: When Politics and Popular Culture Converge*. Lanham, MD: Rowman & Littlefield, 2005.

Zorn, Werner. "How China Was Connected to the International Computer Networks." *The Amateur Computerist Newsletter* 15, no. 2 (2007): 72–98.

Zuckerman, Ethan. "Cute Cats to the Rescue? Participatory Media and Political Expression." In *From Voice to Influence: Understanding Citizenship in a Digital Age*, edited by Danielle Allen and Jennifer S. Light, 131–54. Chicago: University of Chicago Press, 2015.

——. "The First Twitter Revolution?" *Foreign Policy*, January 15, 2011.

——. "Intermediary Censorship." In *Access Controlled: The Shaping of Power, Rights and Rule in Cyberspace*, edited by Ronald J. Deibert, John G. Palfrey, Rafal Rohozinski, and Jonathan Zittrain, 71–85. Cambridge, MA: MIT Press, 2010.

INDEX

access, 25; as anonymous, 61, 67; to
    pornography, 91
activism: for netizens, 26; online and
    offline, 1–2; as pop, 78; pop activism
    as, 13; social media and, 10; state
    control versus, 4. *See also* pop
    activism
activism entrepreneurs, 97–99
actors: censorship and, 12–13, 46–47;
    discourse competition for, 96; as
    nonstate, 54; public opinion and,
    129, 132–35; role of, 11. *See also*
    intermediary actors
adherence, 61
*Administration Measures on Internet
    Information Services*, 66
After the Internet, Before Democracy
    (Lagerkvist), 153–54
Ai Weiwei, 48; netizens and, 99;
    responses of, 97–98
alliances, 144, 171
Anderson, Lisa, 1
anonymity, 247n8; access and, 61,
    67; comments and, 117; exchange
    of information and, 45; of online
    expression, 128, 144, 180; poem
    with, 136–37

anti-extermination campaign, *12*
anti-pornography campaign of 2009,
    61, 75
Arab Spring, 140; contrast to, 1–3;
    social media and, 176, 183
astroturfing, 14, 45; for business,
    247n12; for dissidents, 133; Internet
    commentators and, 107–9, 123;
    mobilization through, 241n53;
    propaganda and, 180; technique
    for, 112
asylum, 145, 147
authoritarian regimes, 203n46;
    capacity of, 128; digital
    empowerment and, 3–6;
    fragmentation of, 11, 17–18, 19,
    50–53, 129; images of, 178; Internet
    forums between netizens and,
    59–69; online expression for, 104;
    state adaptation and, 2–3
authoritarian resilience: digital
    empowerment and, 16–22; in digital
    era, 102, 176–87; as online, 175–91
avatars, *146*

backlash: enemies and, 135–43; on
    Mitbbs.com, 99

on QQ.com, 141, 142; samples of,
118; translation of, *119, 121*
Communist Youth League, 111; Central
Committee of, 52, *116*, 245*n*85;
Internet Propaganda Troop quota
for, *124*; Shanghai branch of, 114,
115
community, 154; as discursive, 131;
voluntary fifty-cent army as
identity and, 156–58, 262*n*62
compensation, 112
compliance: noncompliance and, 7;
resistance or, 55–76. *See also specific
forms of compliance*
conferences, 23, 63, 64, 65
conflict: functions and interests in, 50;
ideologies in, 52
Consenz, 72
conspiracy, 141
constructive noncompliance, 182
content: control of, 53, 70, 131;
formality and, 82; governance of
Internet and, 30–40; monitoring
of, 7; pluralization of, 78; as pro-
regime, 15, 180; violence and
erotica as, 73
content providers: screening by, 43;
state as, 131
corruption, 140, 268*n*36
creativity: Ai Weiwei responses as,
98; criticism and, 92; of online
expression, 12, 55, 157, 180
criticism, 179; creativity and, 92; of
regime, 150, 186; substantiation of,
181
cross-talk (*xiangsheng*), 162
culture: online expression as, 79–83,
152; politics and, 78
cyberculture, 85; nationalism and, 95
cyber-narratives, 88–89
cybernetic model of organizational
choice, 47

cyberpolitics: pluralism and, 1–28; pop
activism and netizens in, 77–100,
234*n*108
Cybersecurity Law (2016), 211*n*43
cyberspace: in China, 77, 155; discourse
competition in, 102, 185; fluidity of,
92, 170; fragmentation of, 17 18, 19,
27, 153–56, 173; Lagerkvist on, 130;
state media in, 104
Cyberspace Administration of China, 41
cyber-vocabulary, 86; examples of, *87*;
for military forums, 93

dalian (face-slapping), 161–62
Damm, Jens, 81
data, 112; from history, 24; requests
for, 218*n*29; from research, 22–25;
sources of, 108–9; from users, 62
debates: about ideologies, 71; among
netizens, 52
defamation, 16; ubiquity of, 21
democracy, 3; expectation of, 28;
Internet and, 20–22; Jasmine
Revolution and, 179; nationalism
and, 19
deviant expression, 62
diaosi, 90
Diaoyu (Senkaku) Islands, 94, 204*n*54
digital contention, 80; embedding of,
82; genres of, 228*n*47; pop activism
and, 83–95
digital empowerment: authoritarian
regimes and, 3–6; authoritarian
resilience and, 16–22; threat and,
183–87
digital hidden transcript, 85
disaggregation, 5; of state and Internet,
17–18
discipline, 182
discontented compliance, 13, 26,
55; forum managers and, 60–64;
spectrum of, 69–75

state-capitalist cooperation, 58
state control: acquiescence to, 185;
    activism versus, 4; agencies and,
    11, 208nn21–23; intermediary actors
    and, 176; Internet and, 57; over
    online expression, 13, 28, 29–54;
    studies on, 80
State Council Information Office, 66
state-society interaction, 153
statist model, 56
Stockmann, Daniela, 76
students, 116, 125
studies, 202n35; on astroturfing, 108;
    on digital empowerment, 183; on
    discourse and behavior, 81; on
    Internet politics, 101; by Repnikova,
    105; on stability maintenance,
    215n82; on state control, 80
subcultures, 94, 232nn85–86
Sunstein, Cass, 154
surveys, 159; of citizens, 80

taboo words and topics, 62; discussion
    of, 253n66; list of, 210n29;
    monitoring of, 47; as playful, 89;
    screening for, 63
tactics, 160–69
Tang, Fang, 155
Tarrow, Sidney, 79
Technical and Administrative Control,
    39–40
technical architecture (code), 4, 31
technical barriers, 67
technology: Castells on relevance of,
    17; information and, 30
Tencent, 262n60; QQ.com by, 71–72
Thornton, Patricia, 187
threat, 175–91
Three Gorges Dam Project, 164, 259n37
Tiananmen Square, 130; 1989
    movement in, 48, 49, 98, 139

Tiananmen: The Gate of Heavenly Peace,
    130, 246n1
Tianya, 74, 219n36; Free board on, 132;
    Grassroots Voices board on, 224n77;
    Outlook board on, 172; users on, 89
Tibet, 134, 137–38
tools: pop activism as, 78, 82, 100; of
    state, 26
training, 127
trolling: on Mitbbs, 226n27; for the
    Party-state, 101–29; techniques for,
    132
trust, 183, 186, 268n37
Tsai Ing-wen, 172
Tsinghua University, 61, 68
Tugong, 149, 159
tweets, 139, 140

United Nations (UN), 145
United States, 146, 149
universal elites, 140
universities, 43; campus forum
    relationships with, 73; "fifty-cent
    army reserve" at, 111; mobilization
    at, 115. *See also specific* universities
University of California, Berkeley, 25
users: accounts for, 247n10; avatars
    of, *146*; on BBS, 202n39; data from,
    62; invitations to, 67; party-state
    invisibility to, 59; profit generation
    through, 71; sample profile of, *120*;
    Tianya for, 89

values, 141
violence, 14; as content, 73

wall-climbing, 91
Wall Street Journal, 177
Wang, Dan, 20
Wang Juntao, 139
Wang Zhidong, 60

CPSIA information can be obtained
at www.ICGtesting.com
Printed in the USA
JSHW032202020123
35616JS00008B/11